JESUS OF NAZARETH

MICHAEL HESEMANN

Jesus of Nazareth

Archaeologists
Retracing the Footsteps of Christ

Translated by Frank Nitsche-Robinson
and Michael J. Miller

IGNATIUS PRESS   SAN FRANCISCO

Original German edition:
Jesus von Nazareth: Archäologen auf den Spuren des Erlösers
© 2009, 2013 by Sankt Ulrich Verlag GmbH, Augsburg, Germany
(slightly revised by author)

Cover art:
Christ Pantocrator, a 13th-century icon in the collection of
St. Catherine's Monastery at Mt. Sinai, Egypt
© 2021 by St. Catherine's Monastery at Mt. Sinai

Cover design by Enrique J. Aguilar

ISBN 978-1-62164-307-4 (PB)
ISBN 978-1-64229-155-1 (eBook)
Library of Congress Control Number 2020950995
Printed in the United States of America ∞

Dedicated to His Holiness Pope Emeritus Benedict XVI,
who led us back to Nazareth

CONTENTS

NOTE ON THE SECOND EDITION

Since the publication of the first edition of this book in September 2009, ten years have passed, during which the spades of the archaeologists have not been idle. In their work, they again came upon important evidence from the time of Jesus, each piece of which, like a stone in a mosaic, brings the overall picture into sharper focus by adding new contours and aspects to it.

In order to do justice in the second edition also to the claim of presenting the current state of the research, corrections and additions were necessary. For this purpose, I regularly visited the Holy Land during the last three years and took part in the excavations in Magdala, inspected Cana again, and had the discoveries from Nazareth scientifically dated.

Even though the narrative frame has remained the historical papal visit in 2009, which inspired me to write this book, the descriptions of the archaeological sites have been supplemented by the latest discoveries and research findings and thus brought up to date.

To all who offered their comments and friendly criticism, my heartfelt thanks.

Düsseldorf, November 2019
Michael Hesemann

INTRODUCTION

"All of us need to return to Nazareth"
(Pope Benedict XVI, May 14, 2009)

I cannot sleep tonight. And the same goes for many others, it seems. Again and again feet patter on the stone pavement of the street beneath my window, sometimes at a leisurely pace, other times hurriedly; now a single pair, then a whole group. Only the direction in which they disappear into the night is always the same. The whole city seems to be up and about; expectant suspense is in the air.

Long before sunrise, I realize that my attempt to get a little sleep has failed. I phone Yuliya, who has also stayed awake. We set a time to meet at the reception desk, pay the hotel bill, and get into the car. As the gate of the underground garage slowly opens, the light of the sun that has just risen shines on our faces and blinds our sleep-deprived eyes. A few seconds later, I am wide awake, observing the memorable spectacle.

All Nazareth is empty, as though swept out. Our car is the only automobile on the streets, aside from the police vehicles that are parked in front of various sorts of roadblocks. We, too, are stopped several times, but again and again our press badge gets us safe conduct. Finally we see people. There are so few of them that they seem to be stragglers. Only as we reach the press center in the Golden Crown Hotel does the picture change all of a sudden. Now large gatherings of patiently waiting people are standing at the bus stops; we, too, have to take the shuttle. The slightly curving slope of a mountain, a natural amphitheater, which not long ago was furnished with platforms and benches, is strewn with people. Ten thousand evidently spent the night here. At midnight, we learn, the gates were opened, and after only a few hours the stands were full. The rising sun probably did not wake one single Catholic in this city. All the "Latins" from Nazareth, and with them thousands of Christians from all parts of the Holy Land, have gathered here to greet one of the most beautiful days of their lives.

Waiting for us is not pious devotion but, rather, a World Youth Day mood, except that in this case all generations are celebrating likewise. Flags from all over God's good earth are waving in the stands; even the Free State of Bavaria is represented with its white and blue diamonds. A ship's mast towers over the altar stage; its hoisted sail forms a baldachin. The activity onstage is like the warm-up before a rock concert. An Italian priest waves a gigantic Vatican flag and bellows into the microphone: "*Benedetto—Benvenuto—a Nazareth.*" "Benedict—Welcome—to Nazareth" reechoes ten thousandfold from the stands. Then Christian pop music is heard again from the loudspeakers. A half dozen local teenagers with long hair, elegantly dressed in black slacks and white shirts, stand in the first row, their arms and hips rotating in tempo. When the pope's helicopter finally appears in the sky and lands shortly afterward, when at last the popemobile passes the blockades and keeps making its way through the crowd, the high spirits become an ecstasy. Who would have ever dreamed that Benedict XVI, the scholar-pope, the shy intellectual, would be acclaimed in the cradle of Christianity like a pop star? I aim my telescopic lens at him, see how he is smiling, how relaxed he seems at the end of his difficult and strenuous trip to the Holy Land. I am happy for him and with him. And I catch myself making a comparison that is perhaps irreverent, although not entirely false: we were both on the way for a long time and now have finally come to our destination, on this May 14, 2009. The theologian Joseph Ratzinger, whose book *Jesus of Nazareth* is one of the most profound and spiritually rewarding works of contemporary literature, and somewhere, too, the historian Michael Hesemann, who from an altogether different perspective is tracking down the mystery by which God became man and who with the present book claims to make perhaps a small contribution to our understanding of the historical Jesus of Nazareth and of the world in which he worked.

"In the name of the Father, and of the Son, and of the Holy Spirit." As soon as the pope recites the opening words of this Eucharistic Celebration in his unmistakably German-tinged English, the mood changes all of a sudden. The cheerful ecstasy gives way to a solemn seriousness. The morning mist has long since lifted, making room for a warm May day drenched in sunlight. I look around and only now realize where I am. And yet, simultaneously, time and space blur.

The natural semicircle on which the benches of the forty thousand Mass-goers stand is one of the turning points of salvation history. The slope is called "The Mount of Precipice". Jesus had revealed himself in his hometown. He had gone to the synagogue on the Sabbath, as he had always done. It is part of the Jewish worship service that one of the grown men over age thirty presents and interprets a passage from Scripture. So this time Jesus went to the front and took the scroll with the Book of the Prophet Isaiah that the synagogue leader handed to him.

We can imagine the scene very vividly, because just such a scroll of Isaiah from the time of Jesus has been preserved. It was discovered sometime before 1947 by Bedouins in a cave above Qumran on the Dead Sea. The Bedouins sold it to Kando, a Christian antique dealer in Bethlehem, who offered it to his archbishop, Athanasius Samuel, whose headquarters was the Syrian Saint Mark Monastery in the Armenian quarter of Jerusalem. The archbishop, who was both highly educated and crafty, recognized the enormous potential of the discovery, but his attempt to find a buyer in the United States failed at first. Not until seven years later, in 1954, did the Israeli archaeologist Yigael Yadin purchase the four scrolls for $250,000 via American middlemen and bring them back to Jerusalem. There his colleague Eliezer Sukenik had just bought three additional scrolls directly from Kando. He was fascinated by the legend (which meanwhile has been disproved) that the discovery had been made in 1947. The rediscovery of Sacred Scriptures almost simultaneously with the founding of the State of Israel seemed like the fulfillment of an ancient prophecy and became the myth associated with the birth of the Jewish state. This made the seven Qumran texts almost documents of the Providence standing behind it all. Today the two-thousand-year-old scrolls made of goat- and sheepskin are kept in a snow-white tabernacle, the "Shrine of the Book", within view of the Knesset, the Israeli Parliament. It is reminiscent of the cover of one of the jars in which the Sacred Scriptures survived the two millennia of the Jewish diaspora. In the center of it, the longest, best-preserved of the Qumran scrolls is spread out, precisely the prophetic Book of Isaiah, from which Jesus, too, at that

time presented the announcement of the Kingdom of God and the
promise of the Messiah:

> The Spirit of the Lord GOD is upon me,
>   because the LORD has anointed me
> to bring good tidings to the afflicted;
>   he has sent me to bind up the brokenhearted,
> to proclaim liberty to the captives,
>   and the opening of the prison to those who are bound;
> to proclaim the year of the LORD's favor. (Is 61:1–2)

At that place Jesus stopped. He interrupted the text right before
the prophet proclaimed a "day of vengeance of our God" and promised a new beginning, which later the founders of the State of Israel
referred to their era:

> They shall build up the ancient ruins,
>   they shall raise up the former devastations;
> they shall repair the ruined cities,
>   the devastations of many generations. . . .
> Instead of your shame you shall have a double portion,
>   instead of dishonor you shall rejoice in your lot;
> therefore in your land you shall possess a double portion;
>   yours shall be everlasting joy. (Is 61:4–7)

Instead of reading further, he rolled up the book again and handed
the scroll to the attendant of the synagogue. All eyes were fixed on
him. People had heard a lot about him, about miracles, healings, his
powerful sermons in the synagogues of Galilee. With great clarity,
in words that touched their hearts, he was proclaiming to them that
the words of Scripture were fulfilled. The hour had now come about
which Isaiah the prophet had spoken. Yet along with their astonishment about his sermon came the first doubts. If he was right, then
that could only mean that he, Jesus, was the Lord's Anointed, the
promised Messiah, who proclaims the Good News (Greek: *evangelion*) to the poor. But that was too much for the Nazarenes. Jesus, the
son of Joseph, whom they had seen just a few years before with his
stepfather at work, was supposed to be the redeemer sent by God?
He, Mary's son, who not so long ago romped through their streets

with his cousins Jacob, Joses, Judas, and Simon and also his female cousins? How dare he make himself out now to be sent by God, as though he had just descended from heaven?

Well, he sure could speak, but was that all? What about the miracles that he reportedly had worked in Capernaum and the other cities and villages down by the lake? Please, Jesus, if you want to be the Messiah, then show us what you can do!

Yet Jesus refused to work miracles as a method of self-promotion. Nor was he willing to slip into the role of the political messiah, the liberator from the unpopular Roman rule, for whom so many had hoped. He had deliberately ended his citation from the Book of Isaiah before the "day of vengeance" was announced. He had come, not to fulfill expectations, but rather to redeem mankind.

The Nazarenes were indignant. That was not what they had counted on, what they had hoped for. People had been waiting for a freedom fighter with supernatural powers, and the one who had arrived was the meek-mannered man from their midst. Jesus, the Messiah? That seemed to them sheer blasphemy. Luke relates (4:29–30): "And they rose up and put him out of the city, and led him to the brow of the hill on which their city was built, that they might throw him down headlong. But passing through the midst of them he went away."

In fact, Nazareth is built on high ground that towers high above the plain of Jezreel, between two mountain ridges, one of which forms a steep cliff. The plain is also named after its oldest city, Megiddo (in Hebrew, *Har-Mageddon*: Mount Megiddo). If we are to believe the Revelation of Saint John, here one day the eschatological battle between the forces of good and the armies of evil is supposed to take place. I am sitting right on the slope that leads up to the aforementioned cliff, together with forty thousand Nazarenes, who are devoutly listening to the papal Mass. Today, as I mentioned, it is called "The Mount of Precipice".

Over the centuries, it became the object of pious legends and fanciful interpretations. Since Johannes von Würzburg (1165), it has also been called *Saltus Domini*, "the Lord's Leap". People believed that Jesus escaped his pursuers by jumping to a nearby slope. "You see the outlines of his body and his clothes imprinted there", Burchard von Schwanden, Grand Master of the Teutonic Knights, thought in the year 1283. After that, he allegedly hid in a cave, in which liturgies were still celebrated as late as the twentieth century. Mary, his mother, supposedly ran after the bloodthirsty mob until she broke down in tears; to this day, a chapel on one ridge is dedicated to her fear.

And the synagogue? A pilgrim from Piacenza in Northern Italy, who visited Nazareth in the year 570, claims to have seen it together with its relics. Among them were "the book in which the Lord wrote his ABC" and "the bench on which he sat with the other children".[1] There is no doubt that the synagogue served as a Torah school for Jewish boys and that Jesus learned to read and write there; Judaism was at that time the only religion that made it possible for youths of all social strata to have access to its sacred writings. Later pilgrims from the times of the Crusades report that it had been transformed into a church. Nowadays, tour guides like to show pilgrims to Nazareth the Maronite (Greek-Catholic) Synagogue Church, which the Arabs call *Madrasat al-maih*, "Messiah's school". But the vault dates back to the Arabian era and served the Turks initially as a cattle stall, until a wily Turkish silk weaver declared it a Jewish school in 1740 and started charging admission. It does not fulfill the precepts of the Jewish Talmud, according to which a synagogue is always supposed to stand at the highest point of the city. Thus Clemens Kopp, a Catholic priest and one of the most eminent experts on the Holy Land and its traditions, suspected as early as 1959 that it had stood on the tract that is now a Moslem cemetery north of Saint Joseph's Church. Four gray granite pillars were found there; the Franciscans acquired two of them, and the Greeks—the other two. This may have been the scene of Jesus' self-revelation in his hometown.

The Nazarenes' attempt on his life shows all too clearly what they thought of him. They wanted to stone him, because they accused him of blasphemy. "He who blasphemes the name of the LORD shall be put to death; all the congregation shall stone him" (Lev 24:16), it says in the Law of Moses. According to the description in the Talmud, the delinquent was pushed backward off an elevation "twice the height of a man" by the first witness. "If he dies of it, he has satisfied his duty; if not, he takes the stone and drops it on his heart." Then the people threw their stones, if necessary. Whether this in

---

[1] The Piacenza Pilgrim, *Travels from Piacenza*, in John Wilkinson, *Jerusalem Pilgrims Before the Crusades* (Jerusalem: Ariel, 1977), p. 79.

fact was supposed to happen on the "Mount of the Abyss"—it is, after all, 1.24 miles distant from the center of Nazareth—is doubtful, but it makes no difference, either. For at the very least the Mount of Precipice remains a powerful symbol for the rejection of Jesus in Nazareth: Mark records his disappointment: "A prophet is not without honor, except in his own country, and among his own kin, and in his own house" (6:4).

Now, though, two thousand years later, Nazareth cheers the Vicar of Christ on earth and listens devoutly to the Gospel, this time without false expectations, without the fury of disappointment. And this is happening at the very spot where the Nazarenes once gave Jesus the ultimate brush-off, where they almost anticipated his execution. I see something coming full circle after two thousand years. I look down onto the plain of Megiddo and worry about what may perhaps still come in this turbulent time that has turned the Near East into the world's powder keg. Then I turn around again. Behind me looms a gray cupola pointed into the sky, shaped like the inverted calyx of a lily. It is the Church of the Annunciation, built over a cave in which, as it all began, a Virgin gave her consent for the mightiest event in world history. Her *fiat* made God's redemptive work possible in the first place: "I am the handmaid of the Lord; let it be to me according to your word" (Lk 1:38).

"What happened here in Nazareth, far from the gaze of the world, was a singular act of God, a powerful intervention in history, through which a child was conceived who was to bring salvation to the whole world", Pope Benedict will declare that same day, in that very calyx in which God's work was accomplished: "The wonder of the Incarnation continues to challenge us to open up our understanding to the limitless possibilities of God's transforming power, of his love for us, his desire to be united with us. Here the eternally begotten Son of God became man, and so made it possible for us, his brothers and sisters, to share in his divine sonship."

He will then add: "When we reflect on this joyful mystery, it gives us hope, the sure hope that God will continue to reach into our history, to act with creative power so as to achieve goals which by human reckoning seem impossible."[2]

---

[2] Pope Benedict XVI, Homily, Celebration of Vespers, Nazareth, May 14, 2009.

The purpose of my journey to the Holy Land, the twelfth in my life, was to get to the bottom of this mystery. It was a turbulent trip, as hazardous as pilgrimages have been ever since antiquity. In Caesarea Maritima, our car was broken into while we were sightseeing at the Praetorium and looking at the only extant inscription of Pontius Pilate. The thieves stole all our suitcases, our clothing and papers, my travel guide and reference books, my notebook computer. Our plan to travel ahead to meet Pope Benedict in Jordan was thus ruined. Instead, we looked for the nearest shopping center so as to supply ourselves with at least the most necessary things. I understood: anyone who follows Jesus of Nazareth, anyone who wants to trace his footsteps, must first leave everything behind, free himself, and be open to what is new. So we visited the sites of his public life in new clothing, fresh and clean as baptismal garments, until we returned a week later to where it had all begun.

Here in Nazareth, God became man through the supernatural act of begetting by the Holy Spirit. The light shone in the darkness, even though it took the darkness a long time to comprehend this. As the Council of Chalcedon (a suburb of Constantinople, modern-day Istanbul) defined in the year 451, this Jesus of Nazareth was "truly God and the same truly man". I am not a theologian; it is not my field or my job to fathom the divine mysteries. But if God became "true man", then he entered history and, thus, the field in which the historian works. Historical personages leave traces behind. That is true quite particularly about Jesus of Nazareth. For someone who follows the traces that he left behind, which were often brought to light only in recent years and decades by archaeologists in the Holy Land, there can be no more doubt: our faith is not based on pretty legends and pious fantasies, such as the fabulous story about the "Lord's leap". No, it is based on historical events, which were handed down by eyewitnesses and written down by chroniclers. When we, with the archaeologist's spade, unearth the scenes that they describe, it shows how exact their reports are. The one who makes his way layer by layer down to the native soil of salvation history will find him, the historical Jesus of Nazareth. This is why I set out on the search for him.

I

Good Things from Nazareth

The Secret of the Holy House

Quite often coincidence is an archaeologist's best friend. At any rate, Elias Shama only wanted to renovate his souvenir shop right next to Mary's Well in Nazareth, when he chanced upon an archaeological sensation. He knew the area pretty well, too. He had grown up in Jesus' hometown, played on the square before the fountain as a child, refreshed himself with its water on hot summer days. Then, like many Christian Palestinians, he went to Jerusalem and finally emigrated to Belgium, where he married. But his home never really let him go. As soon as he had earned enough money, he returned with his wife, Martina, first to Jerusalem, then to Nazareth. With their savings, the young couple wanted to open a souvenir shop, where Martina, a trained jewelry designer, could exhibit her most beautiful pieces. When they learned that one of the shops right next to Mary's Well had been for sale for years, they jumped at the chance. The location was ideal. Buses with hundreds of pilgrims from Greece and Russia, for whom Mary's Well is the actual site of the Annunciation, stop here. Since the elevation, at the foot of which the well springs forth, is called Cactus Hill in Arabic, they had soon found a name for their business: Cactus Gallery.

But the shop was in a catastrophic condition when the Shamas took it over in 1993. The previous owners had simply thrown their rubble down the cellar steps, and Elias had to struggle to clear the debris away. When in the process he chanced upon an obviously ancient vault, he immediately had the idea of starting a rustic cafe there, too. This would require extensive renovations, but the sturdy man from Nazareth was not afraid of hard labor. Then he discovered that the brick vault was only part of a large underground installation, which turned out to be a *hypocaustum*, a floor heating system. The room above must have been a *caldarium*, the Greco-Roman version of a sauna. Elias came upon precious marble tiles and clay pipes, whose concourses were covered with clay tiles adorned with the image of a palm tree.

Astonished and irritated, he informed the Israel Antiquities Authority (IAA) of his find, but they just put him off. They knew about the installation, an employee explained to him. It was a Turkish bathhouse from around the year 1870, which of course was of little interest to them. He could do with the ruins whatever he wanted, even demolish them if necessary.

But Elias Shama was not content with that. He knew enough about the Turks not to accept that explanation. In the nineteenth century, Palestine had been only a remote province of the Ottoman Empire, Nazareth not much more than a dusty hamlet, its inhabitants mostly Arab Christians, Greek monks, and Franciscans from Italy. For whom, then, did the Turks supposedly build such a luxurious *hamam* furnished with white marble?

More and more, he got the sense of being on the trail of something important. And so he spent the next two years systematically uncovering these allegedly "insignificant" ruins. The results of his work proved him right. When in preparation for the Holy Year 2000 the municipal administration of Nazareth had the square in front of Mary's Well remodeled and in the process archaeologically examined by experts from the IAA, the excavators came upon the remains of an ancient water line, which supplied the bathhouse from the Marian wellspring. In addition, they managed to uncover the entrance through which the laborers or slaves entered the thermal bath. Remains of a Roman road, a Corinthian capital—clearly part of a portico—and clay shards dating back to the Hellenistic period were also discovered. Encouraged by the finds, right on time for the jubilee, Elias Shama opened the ruins of "his" bathhouse to the public. Only the outbreak of the Second Intifada in September 2000 put an abrupt end to the anticipated stream of visitors.

But in the nine months during which the Cactus Gallery was a meeting place for guests from all over the world, its proud owner made important initial contacts and received valuable advice as to the time from which his find might originate. A visitor from Bath in England, for instance, noticed right away the similarities to the Roman thermal baths in her hometown. Another visitor was interested in the clay pipes, which resembled those used in Pompeii and on Cyprus. The *frigidarium*, or cool-down room typical of Roman baths, as well as a *praefurnia*, the heating chamber, could be identified. It was time for experts to attend to the installation. Finally, Elias Shama invited archaeologists to take a look at the brick vaults under the Cactus Gallery.

The first to accept this invitation was Professor Richard Freund, director of the Maurice Greenberg Center for Jewish Studies at Hartford University in Connecticut. The American had caused a stir among experts when he examined a cave by the Dead Sea, which during the Jewish resistance served as a hiding place for bronze implements from the Temple in Jerusalem and in which half a century later letters from the rebel leader Simon Bar Kochba were hidden. Furthermore, together with Rami Arav, he coordinated the American-Israeli excavations in Bethsaida on the northern coast of Lake Gennesaret, the birthplace of several apostles. When Freund, a faithful Jew himself, left the Cactus Gallery, he was convinced: "What we are dealing with here is a bathhouse from the time of Jesus—and the consequences of that for archaeology and our knowledge of the life of Jesus are enormous."

Other archaeologists followed—and arrived at different conclusions. Tzvi Shacham from the Museum of Antiquities in Tel Aviv, for instance, is convinced that Shama's bathhouse was not built until the time of the Crusades. Three charcoal fragments, which in 2003 were examined by means of the radiocarbon method (C14), were from the fourteenth century. At that, Shacham seemed to have forgotten that the Crusaders may have used existing bathhouses but did not build a single one.

Freund in fact even found a medieval pilgrim's account that mentions the installation. It comes from Rabbi Moshe Bassola (1480–1560), a highly educated Jew from Ancona, Italy, who in his old age visited the Holy Land. "I spent the night in a village called Nasira [Nazareth], the place of Jesus the Christian, which is a parasang from Kafre Kanna", he wrote in his travel journal from 1542, "They say that there is a bathhouse with hot water where his mother immersed

herself."[1] He was therefore not talking about a *mikveh*, a Jewish purification bath, where the water would never be heated, but rather
about a *caldarium* like the one Elias Shama had discovered.

Then again, the account of the traveling rabbi is rather unique. Not
one of the Christian pilgrims who visited Nazareth from the fourth
century up to the time of the Crusades mentions an ancient bathhouse. Even if it already existed at that point in time, it was plainly
of no interest to them. Finally, it is almost impossible that Mary as a
faithful Jewish woman would have frequented a thermal bath. Like
many of her rather conservative contemporaries, she would have
considered the Greco-Roman bath culture obscene. Even if Shama's
vault had originated from the first century, it was quite certainly not
"Mary's Bathhouse" or the "Thermae Christi". But the possibility
remained that it had been built for Roman legionnaires.

This would mean, however, that everything we thought we knew
about Nazareth until now was wrong. The seemingly remote mountain village, consequently, was anything but a poor hillbilly settlement in a remote province at the outskirts of the empire, a backward
idyll, far from the turmoil of its times. With a Roman bathhouse of
this size, it must have been the site of a garrison, a camp perhaps,
whose remains are still waiting to be discovered somewhere under the
modern Arab city. That would mean that Jesus grew up shoulder to
shoulder with the occupying power, an experience that no doubt
must have been reflected in his teaching, too.

But the last word about the bathhouse under the Cactus Gallery
had not yet been spoken. In order to determine the extent of the
installation, a team of American scientists, at Freund's suggestion,
conducted high-definition ground-penetrating radar (GPR) tests in
the winter of 2004/2005. In the course of these, anomalies in the
subsurface—for instance, the remains of buildings—were measured
through the reflection of electromagnetic radiation. The result com-
plicated the riddle: "The reflections measured under the current
floor of the Cactus House could indicate that the upper bathhouse
was constructed on the remains of an earlier bathhouse, which was

---

[1] Joses Basolla, *In Zion and Jerusalem: The Itinerary of Rabbi Moses Basola (1521–1523)* (Jerusalem: C. G. Foundation Jerusalem Project Publications of the Martin (Szusz) Department of
Land of Israel Studies of Bar-Ilan University, 1999), p. 70.

even more closely aligned with the water system that was located and excavated in the neighboring Marian well."

But when was the present-day bathhouse built? In archaeology, there are three methods of determining the age of a find. The first, by the stratum and possible pottery or even coins remaining in it, was inapplicable in this case; on top of the bathhouse stood a modern residence, and Elias Shama assured me that he had not come upon either coins or shards during its excavation. The second method searches for organic material, which could be dated using the radiocarbon method; through the use of this method, as noted earlier, it was established that the bathhouse must have already existed in the fourteenth century. But this, too, says relatively little about the time of its construction. I noticed, however, that unfinished natural stones were not used as building material, as was common in Nazareth at the time of Jesus, but bricks. The water pipes, too, as was common in antiquity, were made of fired clay. Pottery can now be dated using a third procedure, the so-called thermo-luminescence method (TL-dating).

Developed theoretically in 1952 by Daniel, Boyd, and Saunders, as early as 1957/1958 scientists from the University of Bern demonstrated the practical application of this procedure for dating archaeological finds. It is based on the principle that solid bodies, when heated, give off energy previously stored in the crystal lattice in the form of light. When pottery, which contains feldspar and quartz, is fired, this energy is almost completely discharged. Only in the following decades and centuries is it continuously recharged with radiation. In TL-dating, the sample is heated again. Its age is equivalent to the amount of energy it radiates, which can be measured precisely. This of course is such a complex process that worldwide only a few experts in specialized laboratories can conduct it. One of the most renowned institutions worldwide that have specialized in TL-dating is located in Germany. The Curt-Engelhorn-Center for Archaeometry headquartered in Mannheim, directed by Professor Dr. Ernst Pernicka, is affiliated with the University of Tübingen. For his outstanding achievements, Pernicka was honored in 2013 with the "Advanced Grant" by the European Research Council, the most highly endowed research fund of the European Union.

Shama quickly agreed to my plan to have samples of the tiles and pipes in the bathhouse secured under documented circumstances and dated in Mannheim. And so in December 2010, I traveled to Nazareth again to meet with him and his wife, Martina, on December 8 in the Cactus Gallery. One tile we broke from one of the supporting walls of the hypocaustum, one hand-sized fragment from one of the water pipes running on current ground level. After we had photographed and certified them with our signatures, I flew back to Germany with the fragments in my luggage. I arranged for a meeting with Professor Pernicka on February 7, 2011, in which Martina Shama also participated; she had traveled here for just that purpose. Labeled with laboratory number MA-111839 (clay pipe) and MA-111840 (tile), samples from both pieces were at first subjected to a neutron activation analysis, so as then to be dated by means of thermally stimulated luminescence. The result, as Professor Pernicka communicated it to me on April 28, 2011, was rather interesting:

> MA-111839   clay pipe   1650 +/- 740 years
>   (mean date of origin: ca. A.D. 360)
> MA-111840   tile   1330 +/- 680 years
>   (mean date of origin: ca. A.D. 680)

What is convincing about the two datings is the fact that the mean dates seem quite plausible in a historical context. Toward the end of the fourth century, the traffic of Christian pilgrims started in Nazareth. Since Helena, the mother of the Roman emperor, had made a pilgrimage to the Holy Land in autumn/winter 325/326, it became an obligatory duty for pious women from the imperial family to emulate her. Around 392/393, Poimenia, a relative of Emperor Theodosius, traveled to the Holy Land in lavish pomp; in 438, Eudocia, the wife of Theodosius II, followed suit with no less opulence. The inscription on a marble tile, which she had installed in a spa that was popular with pilgrims in Hammath Gader overlooking Lake Gennesaret, attests to her predilection for *thermae* and *balneae*. Nothing makes more sense than to date the construction of the bathhouse in Nazareth to around the time when the infrastructure for the pilgrimage business in Jesus' home village emerged. The need for baths must have been great, since even the relatively little-frequented Kursi on the eastern shore of the Sea of Galilee got one in the late fourth century, although furnished much more modestly than the find in Nazareth.

When the Persians raided the Holy Land in the year 614, not only churches and monasteries, but also pilgrims' inns and bathhouses were plundered, pillaged, and destroyed. Only in the course of the seventh century was much of it rebuilt, so that the second dating also seems sensible. Had the supporting walls been torn down back then, they naturally must have been rebuilt with new, intact tiles, if the pilgrims' bath was to be used again from then on. Since the pilgrimage business continued without restriction even in the first decades of the Islamic rule, the need must indeed have existed.

Therefore, it seems certain that the Cactus bathhouse in its current form stems from the Byzantine era. Nevertheless, as the GPR dates indicate, it could well have had a precursor that is yet to be dated.

Unfortunately, until now only isolated excavations have taken place in Nazareth. With seventy thousand inhabitants, the city is too densely populated. For a time some researchers denied that a place by this name existed at all in Jesus' time. In fact, the mountain village is mentioned in none of the first-century Jewish sources or in the writings of the Jewish historian Flavius Josephus, who, after all, as military commander during the Jewish uprising against the Romans, coordinated the defense of Galilee from A.D. 66 on. But the nonexistence of proofs is not automatically proof of nonexistence. After all, Josephus writes there were 204 cities and villages in Galilee, but he mentions only forty-five of them by name. Today, then, after excavations in the areas of the Church of the Annunciation in the center of the city, Nazareth Village in the east, as well as on open-air grounds in the west of the city, there is no doubt that already in the first century B.C. Nazareth was a village inhabited solely by Jews (which, of course, does not rule out a Roman camp nearby). That the Evangelists nevertheless call it a "city" (Greek: *polis*) was not due to a desire to enhance the reputation of the Redeemer's hometown. The reason was, rather, that in Hebrew there was only one term for an autonomous community, namely, *'ir*, regardless of how big or how small it was. Thus the Septuagint, the first Greek Bible translation from the third century B.C., already generally used the term *polis* wherever *'ir* was written in the original text. Although Nazareth was an insignificant hamlet, it was certainly autonomous, so that its designation as a "city" was accurate to the Jewish way of thinking.

When the Jews conquered the land in the fifteenth century B.C., Galilee was already densely populated and ruled by multiple Canaanite city states. Here the tribes of Naphtali and Zebulon settled, surrounded by Issachar, Asher, and Dan. King Solomon, the Book of Kings tells us, divided the land into four administrative provinces. At the time of the kingdom's division, it belonged to the northern kingdom of Israel, which in 732 B.C. was conquered by the Assyrians under King Tiglath-Pileser III. Most of the Israelites were deported to Assur; Galilee, with Megiddo as its capital, was declared an Assyrian province. Later on the Persians reestablished the southern kingdom of Judah as an autonomous state and allowed the Jews to rebuild their Temple, yet Galilee remained under their rule.

The land must have been almost completely depopulated, so rare are the findings of Assyrian and Persian pottery from this period. Even the fertile region around Lake Gennesaret was then only sparsely populated, the few remaining Jews being a minority there, also. The prophet Isaiah had good reason, then, to speak of the "Galilee of the nations [= Gentiles]" (Is 9:1). This changed only when Alexander the Great conquered the Persian Empire and all of the Middle East came under Greek influence. When the empire was divided among the generals whom he had declared his heirs, Galilee at first went to General Ptolemaeus, who ruled from Egypt. Under the rule of his successors, the Greek-influenced cities of Gadara and Hippos emerged at the eastern shore of Lake Gennesaret; in the south, Scythopolis (Beth She'an) blossomed again. A good century later, the descendants of General Seleucus, to whom Syria had been assigned, conquered the land up to the border of Egypt. The Greek-friendly Jew Menelaus offered a great amount of money to the Seleucid king Antiochus IV (175–163 B.C.) if he would appoint him high priest of the Temple in Jerusalem. The king accepted the offer, but the Jews refused to accept the newly rich parvenu as their spiritual leader. Antiochus IV in turn took this as open rebellion. He had his troops march against Jerusalem, raze the city walls, and confiscate the Temple treasure. In order to humiliate the Jews completely, he dedicated the Temple of Yahweh to the Greek father of the gods, Zeus, and sacrificed a pig there, which according to Jewish belief was an *unclean* animal.

But with this blasphemous provocation he had gone too far. The Jews were enraged over the "abomination of desolation" of their sanctuary, and they revolted. The leader of the rebellion was the aged priest Mattathias from the tribe of the Hasmoneans, followed by his sons, headed by Judas, whose fighting name was Maccabeus, "the hammer". Hard as a hammer, the Maccabees conducted an outright guerilla war against the Seleucid occupants and were victorious through their clever attrition tactics. On the 25th of Kislev in 164 B.C., it was possible to rededicate the Temple, an event that is still commemorated today in the annual feast of Chanukah. But the Hasmoneans were still not content with this. For twenty-two more years, they continued the fighting and played the successors of Antiochus off against each other so cleverly that in 142 B.C. Judaea finally gained national autonomy, also. The head of the tribe then, Simon, subsequently declared himself both "head of civil administration" and high priest. His sons were even supposed to wear the king's crown and bequeath the office of high priest to their descendants. This, however, went too far for many conservative Jews. After all, it was a clear violation of tradition whereby the high priest had to be a descendant of Zadok, the first high priest in Solomon's Temple. As much as they had welcomed the insurrection of the Maccabees and the restoration of the Jewish kingship, here they had to part ways decisively with the new dynasty.

In the years 104–103 B.C., the Hasmoneans Hyrcanus and Alexander Jannaeus also conquered Galilee and started a radical re-Judaification of the new province. Its inhabitants were presented with the choice either to convert to Judaism by circumcision or to leave the land. In addition, Jewish families from the south and returnees from Persian exile were settled in the new territories.

In those days, new cities and villages emerged everywhere in the mountains of Galilee and around Lake Gennesaret, often inhabited by only a single but of course widely ramified family clan. At this time, the resettling of the village of Nazara = Nazareth also took place. Its name is derived from the word "sprout" (Hebrew, *nezer*). This says little about its location, but a lot about its inhabitants. When Matthew wrote about the choice of Nazareth as the dwelling place of Jesus, he stated: "That what was spoken by the prophets might be fulfilled. 'He shall be called a Nazarene'" (Mt 2:23). Generations of exegetes have wondered to which Scripture passage the quote could refer, since in the form recorded by the Evangelist it is not found in any book of the

Prophets. But in Isaiah, just as he announces the Messiah, it actually states: "There shall come forth a shoot from the stump of Jesse, and a branch shall grow out of his roots" (Is 11:1). Since Jesse was the father of King David, the prophecy can only be interpreted in the sense that the Messiah, too, would be a "shoot" or "sprout" (that is, in Hebrew, a *nezer*) from the house of David. Also in the scrolls found near Qumran by the Dead Sea, the Messiah is called "Sprout of the divine planting" (thus in 1QS 6:15; 8:6, 13). The term *nezer* originally referred to all offspring from the family of David's descendants. Did the village name Nazara = "Shootstown" consequently indicate that a Davidic clan lived here? Did some of the founders of Nazareth perhaps belong to the Jewish aristocrats, who had been deported to Babylon by King Nebuchadnezzar in the sixth century B.C. and who had just now, in the late second century B.C., returned to their homeland? Perhaps the Maccabees had deliberately settled members of the rivaling dynasty far from Jerusalem in order to keep them away from the daily political business.

That Jesus "was descended from David according to the flesh" is the most ancient Christian tradition; even Paul in his Letter to the Romans (1:3), composed in A.D. 57 at the latest, recalls that. The family tree of Saint Joseph, his foster father, is known. We find it in two variations in the Gospels of Matthew and Luke, which the author of the first history of the Church, Eusebius of Caesarea (260–340), already explains by saying that Joseph, after the premature death of his father, Jacob, was adopted by a relative named Eli. We can with a clear conscience identify him with Eliachim (Greek: Joachim), the father of Mary, even though there was another reason for the adoption: if parents had no son, their daughter was considered an "heiress" by the Jews. Since according to Jewish Law, daughters were not entitled to inherit by themselves, the father had to find a son-in-law from the same family and formally adopt him.[2] Thereby Joseph legally received a second family tree, just as Jesus, too, became the "son of Joseph" only in the legal sense (Lk 3:23: "being the son [as was supposed] of Joseph"). Concerning Mary, the usually well-informed Patriarch Eutychius of Alexandria (tenth century), citing

---

[2] See Michael Hesemann, *Mary of Nazareth: History, Archaeology, Legends*, trans. Michael J. Miller (San Francisco: Ignatius Press, 2016).

older sources, stated: "Her father was Joachim, the son of Binthir of the sons of David (i.e., from the house of David), the tribe of the king, and her mother was Anna of the daughters of Aaron from the tribe of Levi, the tribe of the priesthood." Jesus, too, who likewise lamented his rejection in Nazareth "in his own country, and among his own kin, and in his own house" (Mk 6:4), seems to have equated country, kin, and house.

In fact, the early Christian author Julius Africanus (170–240), who himself was from Palestine, tells us that in his time the blood relations of Jesus were still living in the neighboring villages of Kochaba and Nazareth and had proudly preserved their Davidic genealogical tables and family trees. Twice indeed, under the emperors Domitian (81–96) and Trajan (98–117), these *relatives of the Lord* had to answer to the Romans. It was feared that they could assert a claim to the Jewish royal throne and lead a new rebellion against the occupants. Two of them swore they were only cultivating their small piece of farmland (thirty-nine acres), and for evidence they presented the calluses on their hands; they were released again. The third, the Jewish-Christian bishop Symeon, one of Jesus' cousins, was crucified in the year 107 on account of his descent from King David. He was seen as a potential contender for the throne. Apparently the tradition of the Lord's relatives (Greek *desposynoi*) continued even into the third century, when a certain Conon or Konon was executed during the persecution of Christians under Emperor Decius in the year 250. During his trial, he had declared: "I come from the city of Nazareth in Galilee, and I am a relative of Christ, whom I serve as my forefathers did."

In the early first century, therefore, the more recent history of Nazareth began. Its first inhabitants were kinsmen of the Davidic royal house, but they were poor. For centuries they had lived in exile, had mourned the lost Zion by the streams of Babylon. The news that a Jewish kingdom was rising again had lured them back to their old homeland. There they shared the fate of almost all late repatriates: lack of property. But the Maccabees' Judaification program for Galilee offered them an opportunity. The land was still sparsely populated, and its parcels were distributed among the new settlers of Jewish faith. Now at least they could again live according to the laws of the Torah without hindrance, and the object of their longing, Jerusalem with its Temple, was only a three days' journey away.

Three times a year, for the major feasts of *Pessach*, *Shavuot* (Feast of Weeks), and *Sukkot* (Feast of Tabernacles), usually in April, May, and September, they made the pilgrimage to their holy city.

Archaeological finds in Nazareth confirm that after a centuries-long vacancy the high plateau was settled anew in the first century B.C. The oldest oil lamp fragments that were excavated came from elongated lamps of the Hellenistic type that was in use before King Herod the Great thoroughly modernized the country half a century later. Moreover, ancient Nazareth was surrounded by twenty-three Jewish stone tombs, the earliest of which were from the first century B.C. Eighteen of the burial caves showed so-called *kokhim*, long, narrow shafts radiating from a central chamber that served for secondary burials. This burial custom was common in the first post-Christian century. At first, a dead person, wrapped in cloths and linen bandages, was laid on a burial bench or in a trough grave in the main chamber of the tomb. When the corpse had decomposed, the relatives put the bundle with the mortal remains into a so-called ossuary (bone chest): a rectangular bone urn made from stone, which was pushed into the *kokhim*-shaft. Four of the tomb chambers of Nazareth were closed off with rolling stones of the kind that can be authenticated in Jerusalem from the time of King Herod. Since tombs, according to Jewish custom, were placed at least eighty-two feet from a settlement, their location can tell us something about the size of the ancient village, which extended only to today's Church of the Annunciation. It could have been at most 765.5 yards in length and 240.5 yards in width, with large empty spaces between the houses for the keeping of animals, horticulture, and production. Probably not more than three hundred to four hundred people were living in Jesus' village.

The houses they inhabited were undecorated. The excavators found neither roof shingles nor stone floors, neither mosaics nor frescoes from the time around Christ's birth. As in the other Galilean villages, so also here the buildings consisted largely of unworked field stones, which were simply stacked and covered with clay or mud. The floor was made of hard-packed dirt, wooden crossbeams bearing thick layers of straw served as roofs. Often enough the houses were built in front of one of the many natural caves in the slopes of Nazareth, which served as nicely climate-controlled living space. They stayed cool even in the hot summer, and they were dry and warming in the dank winter months. Next to the houses, deep holes were hewn into the soft limestone, which served as cisterns and granaries. Additionally, the archaeologists discovered stone winepresses and olive presses. The location of the village facilitated the cultivation of grain, olives, and grapes. In order to enlarge the cultivation area, artificial terraces and irrigation systems were constructed on the slopes. Pigeons were raised in tower-shaped columbaries.

There is a way to travel back to this time. On the slope before the hospital of Nazareth, American Christians, coordinated by the University of the Holy Land, have erected Nazareth Village, a museum village, in which life at the time of Jesus is simulated. It would not do it justice to talk about a "Christian Disneyland", since the project has nothing to do with kitsch and entertainment. On the contrary: under the direction of competent archaeologists and historians, a first-century Jewish village was reconstructed in loving detail and with the greatest possible authenticity. Well-instructed actors— mostly locals—wear garments from that time and demonstrate the everyday life of Jewish farmers and craftsmen. Their houses and tools have been reconstructed according to antique manufacturing methods, based on archaeological evidence. A visit to Nazareth Village thus provides a good insight into the world in which Jesus once grew up and to which he first turned with his message.

However, before construction of Nazareth Village began in 1998, the project's funding association had the construction site archaeologically examined. In the process, it became apparent that the terraced slope had been used for agriculture as early as New Testament times. Wine was grown here, as a sophisticated irrigation system and an early Roman winepress revealed. Yet the most spectacular find proved to be the remains of three watchtowers. Late Hellenistic and early Roman shards made it possible to date them to the time of Jesus. In his parable of the wicked vintners, the Nazarene referred to a well-fortified and guarded vineyard: "A man planted a vineyard, and set a hedge around it, and dug a pit for the wine press, and built a tower, and leased it to tenants, and went into another country" (Mk 12:1).

The excavations showed for the first time that in this parable Jesus referred back to images from his own hometown and environment.

In the meantime, two dwellings of his home village were also unearthed and identified. In 1881, the French Sisters of Nazareth purchased a property west of the Basilica of the Annunciation, about which it was reported that a "great church" had once stood above the "Tomb of the Righteous". In 1884, in the course of construction work, they indeed came upon a rectangular cellar room, which was surmounted by a mighty cruciform vault—evidently the crypt of a church from the Byzantine period. Today the Sisters willingly and not without a certain sense of pride show the excavations to visitors. We pass two mighty arches and come to a niche that at one point led down to a well. A winch must have stood here; the limestone today still shows the deep grooves that were once scraped by the ropes. Is this what was described by the Gallic bishop Arculf, who visited the Holy Land in 670 and later on reported:

> Nazareth ... has large stone buildings, including two very large churches. One, which is in the centre of the city, and stands on two vaults, is on the site where once the house stood in which our Lord and Saviour was brought up. This church, supported, as we have said, on two vaults with arches between them, contains between the vaults a very clear spring. All the population goes there to draw water, and from this spring the water is drawn up into the church above by a winch. The other church has been built on the site of the house in which the archangel Gabriel came to Blessed Mary, and spoke to her there, finding her alone.[3]

We descend into the crypt via a staircase and find masonry from all different periods of time, from unworked stacked natural stones up to carefully chiseled squared stones. Our path leads us even deeper into a rock tomb, which was once sealed by a massive rolling stone; *kokhim*, i.e., shafts for ossuaries, reveal that this impressive gravesite must be from the first century, the time of Jesus. Was it the "Tomb of the Righteous" of which people in Nazareth spoke when the Sisters purchased the property?

For a long time, the carefully preserved remains of masonry were ignored and the discoveries of the Sisters were dismissed as "irrelevant", simply because they were unearthed, not in the course of a controlled archaeological excavation, but, rather, like Elias' bathhouse, in

[3] Adomnan, *The Holy Place*, in John Wilkinson, *Jerusalem Pilgrims Before the Crusades* (Jerusalem: Ariel, 1977), p. 109.

a "do-it-yourself" procedure. After all, Arculf spoke of a spring with clear water, not of a cistern, the excuse soon went. But the actual well of Nazareth (we will discuss this later) was at another site. And yet, the existing traces unequivocally indicate that in Byzantine times water was plainly drawn here quite intensively.

Not until 2006, when in the course of the Nazareth Archaeological Project they attempted an inventory, did British archaeologists become aware of the excavations below the convent of the Sisters of Nazareth. Dr. Ken Dark from the University of Reading, who had earned his doctorate degree in Cambridge and had taught there as well as in Oxford, spent the next few years conducting a thorough examination and reevaluation of the finds. His report "The Early Roman Nazareth and the Convent of the Sisters of Nazareth", published in September 2012 in the *Antiquaries Journal*, was nevertheless consistently ignored by the experts.

For Dark, there is no doubt that one part of the walls, which we too were able to inspect in the cellar of the convent, is from the time of Jesus. They are the remains of a typical Jewish house, partially hewn into the rock, which had been built around a patio. Shards of "Herodian" cooking pots and a spindle suggest that at least one woman must have also lived here. This house must have been abandoned as early as the beginning or the middle of the first century, when the rock tomb was installed below it; the reverse order of events is unthinkable, since faithful Jews would have never built on top of a tomb. Even at that time, the property was apparently located within the village, near the edge.

The Englishman's research leaves no doubt that Arculf's account referred to this very site and the Byzantine church erected over it. In the process, Dark also determined that it was not, as earlier researchers believed, merely a cistern that supplied the well; rather, it was very likely a spring, exactly as the Gallic bishop had reported. But should this mean that the Jewish house from the time of Jesus was indeed the one "in which our Lord and Saviour was brought up"? And was Saint Joseph perhaps really laid to rest in the burial site, as the local legend of the "Tomb of the Righteous" seems to indicate? These are questions that only faith can answer. It is quite possible that after his return from Egypt the *tekton* built a bigger house for his family than the one in which he had previously lived alone and in which the angel appeared to Mary. That was subsequently abandoned when Joseph died and Jesus' public ministry began, while Mary at first lived with relatives, only to follow him then to Capernaum and finally to Jerusalem.

Dark's interpretation is quite plausible, as is already shown by the fact that right on the neighboring property another house from the time of Jesus was excavated, which resembles the find below the convent almost like a twin.[4] Only this time its excavation was conducted under archaeologically controlled conditions.

In November 2009, when the Mary of Nazareth International Center of the French community *Chemin Neuf* (New Way) was supposed to be built right across from the Basilica of the Annunciation, the construction workers happened upon ancient walls here as well. Right away, as the law of the State of Israel demands, the find was reported to the IAA. An archaeologist, Yardenna Alexandre, was commissioned to inspect it. At her orders, construction work was suspended for a month, the time necessary to excavate and examine the antique structure. During a press conference on December 14, 2009, in the presence of the IAA district archaeologist Barshod Dror, an expert from the neighboring Franciscans, and the bishop of Nazareth, she finally announced the results of her excavation. Unlike Dark's report, they were to cause a worldwide sensation.

For again—not "for the first time", as the reports stated—remains of a house from the time of Jesus had been discovered in Nazareth. It was small and modest, consisting merely of two rooms, which were laid out in an L-shape around a small patio. Its walls consisted of slightly worked and stacked limestone, once plastered with mud. Fragments of "Herodian" cooking pots and Jewish stone vessels make it possible to date it to the first century. In the center of the patio, a silo had been hewn into the rocky ground, next to an escape tunnel, which was likely constructed in A.D. 67, when Roman troops were marching into Galilee to subdue the rebellion of the Jews. But

---

[4] The construction method and atrium form were identical. Unlike the house under the convent, it was free-standing and, thus, not built into the rock. The additional escape tunnel suggests at least rather long use; it seems all the more certain that the "convent house" had already been abandoned by the mid-first century.

apparently Nazareth was spared at that time. In any case, the house survived the four-year "Jewish war" unscathed and was still inhabited in the second century as well, as pottery fragments from this time prove. Today its ruins can be viewed on the premises of the Mary of Nazareth Center, which was ceremoniously opened in 2012.

If through these finds the southwest end of ancient Nazareth had been determined, one could also tell rather precisely how far north it reached. Most certainly it extended to what is today its most important well in front of the Marian Spring, which is still bubbling inexhaustibly. While Mary's Well of Nazareth was moved forward at a later time and is now located in the middle of the village square, the Greeks erected their Saint Gabriel Church above the original ancient well right by the wellspring. For them it is the place of the first appearance of the angel, the Annunciation to Mary.

This tradition goes back to a mysterious book that probably originated in the second century A.D. It was called *The Birth of Mary— Revelation of Jacobus*, but today it is generally known under the title *Protoevangelium of James*. Its author, so it says, was the Lord's brother by the same name, which gave the writing a high degree of authority, at least with the Eastern Churches. After all, Western feasts like the conception of Mary and the nativity of Mary, as well as the veneration of Mary's parents, Joachim and Anna, go back to this "Pre-Gospel", which contains a lot of information that is missing in Luke. Although it was at first dismissed by the critical research of the nineteenth and twentieth century, the pendulum now swings back again in its favor. While at that time some of the customs and practices it describes were considered "completely non-Jewish" and "a clear indication of an author unfamiliar with Judaism", the analysis of the Dead Sea Scrolls has shown that this was not the case. Thus, one of the foremost experts in Christian archaeology, the late Benedictine Father Bargil Pixner (1921–2002), finally determined it "was not impossible that some of its content was indeed based on the traditions of the Jesus family".

Mary, so it says there, had been designated for Temple service by her parents and had completely consecrated herself to God from the time she was a little girl. Her uncle Zacharias, a Temple priest, had entrusted her to the widower Joseph, who betrothed himself to her. While he had to travel in order to pursue his profession, literally "to

build my buildings", he left her behind in his house, where by commission of the high priest she wove a curtain for the Holy of Holies in
the Temple. They wanted to postpone the marriage until it was winter
and the building projects were suspended. One day the girl, just thirteen years old, took "the pitcher and went out to fill it with water".
She arrived at the well of Nazareth,

> And, behold, a voice saying: Hail, thou who hast received grace; the
> Lord is with thee; blessed art thou among women! And she looked
> round, on the right hand and on the left, to see whence this voice
> came. And she went away, trembling, to her house, and put down the
> pitcher; and taking the purple, she sat down on her seat, and drew it
> out [i.e., spun thread]. And, behold, an angel of the Lord stood before
> her, saying: Fear not, Mary; for thou hast found grace before the Lord
> of all, and thou shalt conceive, according to His word.[5]

But even without the *Protoevangelium*, the well of Nazareth would be
a holy place. There is no doubt that Mary fetched water here daily,
that the village youth gathered here and the children played—among
them Jesus, too—and that here, when his public ministry was well
underway, the latest stories of his miracles were told.

In any event, the well church was soon in direct competition with
the church above the Grotto of the Annunciation, which confes-
sional rivalries—one belongs to the Orthodox Greeks, the other to
the Catholic Franciscans—made even more obvious; for a time, both
houses of God called themselves "Church of the Annunciation" and
competed for the favor of the pilgrims like two feuding brothers,
when in truth the well and the house simply belong together. Both
are authentic sites of the miracle of Nazareth, the conception by a
virgin, who unconditionally said Yes to the Incarnation of God.

We descend into the ancient vault, past female pilgrims from Russia, who now journey to the Holy Land in droves and ardently venerate the icons that have been set up. Like them, we fill a bottle with
the water from Mary's Well, light a candle. Our way to the outside is
the same path Mary once walked, confused, amazed, overwhelmed,
and filled with anguish. We leave the car parked and walk this stretch

---

[5] "The Protoevangelium of James", 9, 11, in *Ante-Nicene Fathers*, ed. Alexander Roberts
and James Donaldson, vol. 8 (1886; Peabody, Mass.: Hendrickson, 1995), p. 363.

on foot: past the contemporary Mary's Well, diagonally across the square, into the narrow Al-Bishara street. We cannot miss our destination; it is unmistakable.

The Roman Catholic Church of the Annunciation today is the landmark of Nazareth, simply because it towers over the entire old city. It was built between 1960 and 1969 according to plans by the Milanese architect Giovanni Muzio, and it symbolizes the inverted calyx of a lily—the flower that from time immemorial stands for purity and virginity. It was supposed to replace a smaller baroque church from the seventeenth century that had become dilapidated. But before they began the construction work, the Franciscans had the premises thoroughly examined archaeologically. The excavations were directed by the erudite Franciscan archaeologist Father Bellarmine Bagatti, who carefully documented and subsequently published the results of them internationally.

At first Bagatti and his helpers discovered impressive evidence of antique agriculture. The area between the Church of Saint Joseph and the Basilica of the Annunciation was honeycombed by a network of subterranean storage rooms. Additionally, they unearthed three silos, a cistern, an oil press, a winepress, and an oven, as well as the foundations of several residences. Findings of shards attest to utilization as early as Herodian times, i.e., between 37 B.C. and A.D. 44. That they did not come upon recognizable traces of an ancient carpenter's workshop need not come as a surprise. After all, in the Gospels, Saint Joseph is referred to as a *tekton*, which can mean both "carpenter" and "builder". The architect derives the name of his profession from this Greek word; he is the "chief builder". As a *tekton*, Joseph certainly would have made agricultural implements, for instance, plows and yokes, but he primarily built houses. This does not preclude the possibility that he did a little farming on the side, as the archaeological finding indicates. Much more interesting, on the other hand, is the baptismal font that was unearthed in its midst. It has its exact counterpart below the Church of the Annunciation. The shape of the two square pits and the stairs that lead down to them indicate that originally they served as *mikvehs* or *mikvaoth*, as ritual purification baths for devout Jews. Perhaps in the second century, but at the latest in the early third century, they were subsequently remodeled. In both cases, steps were added until there were seven that led down into the basin. Additionally, they were freshly plastered, and signs were carved into the still-wet plaster—a cross with three dots, small boats, a fishing net, a plant. They seemed to have been symbols of a very special group of early Christians, namely, the Jewish Christians.

The seven steps had a very special meaning for them. According to the Church Father Irenaeus of Lyon (135–202), the Jewish Christians believed that the Word of God would descend from the seventh heaven and the soul would ascend to God into the seventh heaven. Bishop Cyril of Jerusalem (315–386) quotes their baptismal formula: "Bravely you will stride then over the Jordan and through the seven heavens ascend into the Promised Land. After you have tasted of its milk and honey, you shall receive the anointing of spiritual baptism." Was there then on the premises of today's Church of the Annunciation a Jewish-Christian sanctuary, which was perhaps even maintained by direct successors of Jesus?

As is so often the case, here, too, archaeology has to rely on contemporary sources in order to interpret its findings. What is striking about Nazareth is the fact that in the earliest accounts of Christian pilgrims to the Holy Land, it is treated rather perfunctorily. When Saint Paula came to Galilee as a pilgrim in 386, "she went quickly on through Nazareth, the nurse of the Lord; through Cana and Capernaum", as it says in her biography.[6] Why the haste? Saint Jerome who accompanied her, gives us the answer. He wrote that "the Nazarenes were neither Jews nor Christians", since "with the former they had in common their lifestyle customs, with us—the faith."

We read something similar in an account written in 360 by the Bishop of Salamis on Cyprus, Epiphanius, who had been born in Palestine. In it he tells the story of Joseph of Tiberias (286–356), the descendant of a Jewish family of priests, who converted to Christianity. When the Roman Emperor Constantine the Great appointed him a count, he asked for permission to erect churches in Galilee. The privilege was granted to him, and Joseph, who apparently had substantial financial means at his disposal, went to work. So far, he had unfortunately observed, "no one had ever been able to found churches [there yet], since there are no Greeks, Samaritans or Christians among the population. This [rule] of having no gentiles among

---

[6] Jerome, *Letter 108 to Eustochium—Extracts*, in Wilkinson, *Jerusalem Pilgrims*, p. 52.

them is observed especially in Tiberias, Diocaesarea, Sepphoris, Nazareth and Capernaum."[7] "Them" of course referred to the Galileans, who considered themselves Jews, while "Christians" plainly meant Gentile Christians. Only after 400 did the pilgrims of late antiquity stream to Nazareth, also: inns for them were springing up and, as we believe, the aforementioned bathhouse, as well.

Two centuries later, around 570, a pilgrim from Piacenza in Northern Italy was visiting the hometown of Jesus and reported something astonishing: "We travelled on to the city of Nazareth, where many miracles take place.... The Jewesses of the city are better-looking than any other Jewesses in the whole country. They declare that this is Saint Mary's gift to them, for they also say that she was a relation of theirs. Though there is no love lost between Jews and Christians these women are full of kindness."[8]

Thus, as before, relatives of the Lord were still living in Nazareth, who by their "love for the Christians" and their special veneration of the Mother of God were clearly distinguished from the Jewish men and women in other parts of the country. Their "love for the Christians" and their veneration of the Mother of God reveal that they were Jewish Christians. They thereby belonged to the oldest church in Christianity, the Church of the Circumcision, from which the Church of the Gentiles split off at one point. The first step in that direction was the decision by the Apostolic Council in A.D. 48 that henceforth Gentiles could profess Christ even without the "detour" via Judaism. It opened the door to the worldwide missionary effort; the Gospel was even more attractive without the tedious rules and prescripts of the Torah, especially without painful circumcision, which—in times of inadequate hygiene—was often risky. So Paul of Tarsus, who was assigned to lead the mission to the Gentiles, during the next fifteen years founded communities in some of the most important cities of the Roman Empire, in Troas and Philippi, Thessaloniki and Corinth, Ephesus and Rome. On the other hand, the proto-community in Jerusalem under the leadership of the brother of the Lord, Jesus' cousin James, remained deeply rooted in Judaism.

---

[7] Epiphanius, *The Panarion of Epiphanius of Salamis, Book I (Sects. 1–46)*, trans. Frank Williams, 2nd ed., rev. and enlarged (Leiden and Boston: Brill, 2009), sec. 2, no. 12, p. 140.

[8] The Piacenza Pilgrim, *Travels from Piacenza*, in Wilkinson, *Jerusalem Pilgrims*, pp. 80–81.

It did however permanently cut ties with the Jewish establishment when James was stoned in 63 and Peter fled to Rome. Instead of participating in the Jewish rebellion against the Romans, the proto-community under the leadership of their new bishop, Simeon, another cousin of Jesus, went to Pella in the Decapolis. After the destruction of Jerusalem by Titus, they settled on Mount Zion and erected a Judeo-Christian synagogue in the midst of the ruins, the foundations of which are still standing today. The contact with the Gentile Christians, who now had Rome as their new center, broke off at this point. In the capital, they were proud of the heritage of Peter, the Prince of the Apostles, and there was little interest in the refugee community in the troubled province. Besides, the recognition of the new religion was at stake. In times when the empire was waging war against the Jews, it was imprudent to profess the Mosaic faith. The result was a gradual alienation, followed by continuously growing distrust. Only a century later, the Church Father Irenaeus of Lyon listed a group of Jewish Christians—he called them Ebionites (from Hebrew, *ebyonim*, the poor)—in his index of early Christian heretics. Another Church Father, Tertullian, referred to the Jewish Christians as Nazoreans, which points toward a strong relation to the home village of Jesus. From early on, the Christians were called *Nozrim* among the Jews, named after *Yeshua ha-Nozri*, Jesus of Nazareth. But traditional Jews, too, lived in the mountain village. The Midrash *Kerevoth* (hymns), a Jewish manuscript from the third century, mentions it as the home of the priestly family of the Hofzaz or Happizzez (1 Chron 24:15). Also, in an inscription found in 1962 in the course of excavations in the provincial capital of Caesarea Maritima, which likely dates back to the third or early fourth century, Nazareth (Nazara) is named as the residence of this clan of priests. After the suppression of the Bar-Kochba rebellion in A.D. 135, the twenty-four traditional priestly families (or "classes of priests", Hebrew, *Mishmarot*) had settled in Galilee, and this was one of them. That presupposes the existence not only of a Jewish-Christian but also of a strictly Mosaic synagogue in Nazareth. Perhaps the different communities stayed out of each other's way; perhaps a nearly harmonious coexistence was even possible at this time. In any event, the history of the Jewish and Jewish-Christian Nazareth ended only when the Jews made a crucial mistake. During the incursion of the Persians in the year 614, they supported the invaders, in the hope of being freed by them from the rule and the tax burden of the Byzantines. Together with the Persians, they destroyed churches and monasteries and killed countless Christians. But the Persian rule lasted only a short time. It ended in 628, when the Byzantine Emperor Heraclius defeated the Persian King Khosrau II in front of his capital city of Ctesiphon. When the emperor came to the Holy Land a year later, he was celebrated euphorically by the Christians. The Jews, however, suffered a cruel revenge. The ones who were not killed were driven from the land. This applied to Nazareth, too. Eleven years later, the Muslim Arabs took over the vacant synagogue of Nazareth and remodeled it into a mosque. What about the Jewish Christians? They henceforth vanished from history. We can assume that under the pressure from the Byzantines, they converted to Orthodoxy.

Up to that point—in Nazareth, at least—Jewish-Christian relatives of the Lord guaranteed a continuity of tradition. I first understand how strong this is during my visit to the Basilica of the Annunciation. We quickly leave the modern superstructure with its gigantic mosaics and colorful stained-glass windows and descend a staircase into the crypt. Here, below a modern concrete framework, illuminated by twelve lamps that are reminiscent of the Virgin's crown of stars in John's Revelation, are the remains of holy places from two thousand years of history.

In its center, under a wooden baldachin, radiant yet mysterious, the Grotto of the Annunciation opens like a window into the beginnings of salvation history. Walls and columns reveal that this was not the first time it had been enclosed by a shrine. When the archaeologists under the guidance of Father Bagatti applied their spades here, they discovered age-old foundations. In front of a second cave to the left of the Grotto of the Annunciation, which is thought to be the grave of the martyr Conon, a relative of the Lord, they chanced upon an age-old mosaic, adorned with crosses. It must have been made before the year 427, when an imperial edict prohibited the depiction of the Cross on floor mosaics; the symbol of salvation was not to be trampled underfoot! A Greek inscription reveals that it had been donated by a certain "Conon, Deacon of Jerusalem", in honor of his namesake. It was likely part of the floor of a Byzantine basilica from the late fourth or early fifth century whose semicircular apse was discovered during the excavations. Likewise, part of the Byzantine construction was a mosaic of similar style outside the church premises, which probably adorned an adjacent Byzantine monastery. When the archaeologists carefully lifted off the mosaic in order to be able to dig deeper, they made a spectacular discovery. The floor beneath was filled up with columns, capitals, and ornaments typical of Galilean synagogues of the second and third century. They counted eighty different elements of architecture. They must have originated from a predecessor building that was replaced by the Byzantine church. This can only have been a Jewish–Christian synagogue, to which the two baptismal *mikvehs* as well as a transverse wall plainly belonged also. These fragments were covered completely with graffiti that reveal who was venerated here: "Under the holy site of M." read one carved inscription in Greek, another one "XE MARIA", which the archaeologists interpreted as *Chaire Maria*, "Hail Mary". It is dated back to the third century and would thus be the oldest invocation of the Blessed Virgin ever. Similar to the graffiti on the side wall of Peter's tomb in Rome,[9] it confirms that Mary was already venerated before the Council of Ephesus in 431 officially conferred on her the title of Theotokos, the "God-Bearer" or Mother of God. Even relics of her could have been preserved and venerated here in Nazareth, as the pilgrim from Piacenza (around 570) relates: "The house of Saint Mary is now a basilica, and her clothes are the cause of frequent miracles."[10]

The house itself, however, which the pilgrim mentions and above which the first church was apparently built at this spot, has disappeared. The Grotto of the Annunciation in itself, though, is far too wide open to have served as the sole residence. It can have served some purpose only if (as is the case with all grotto homes) there was also a house standing before its entrance. Indeed, pilgrims, like Bishop Arculf around 670, relate that the chapel "has been built on the site of the house in which the archangel Gabriel came to Blessed Mary".[11] John Phokas, a Greek monk from the island of Patmos,

[9] See Michael Hesemann, *Der Erste Papst: Archäologen auf der Spur des historischen Petrus* (Munich: Pattloch, 2003).

[10] Piacenza Pilgrim, *Travels*, in Wilkinson, *Jerusalem Pilgrims*, p. 79.

[11] Adomnan, *Holy Place*, in Wilkinson, *Jerusalem Pilgrims*, p. 109.

who visited the Church of the Annunciation between 1177 and 1185, even described it very exactly. On the left side of the medieval church nave, he writes, approximately by the altar, "whereof is a cave, opening into the bowels of the earth, but upon the surface.... Entering, then, within the mouth of the cave, you descend a few steps, and then you behold the ancient house of Joseph, wherein ... the Archangel announced the good tidings to the Virgin."[12] But this house of Joseph and Mary, although described again and again from the days of Antoninus up to the pilgrimage of Saint Francis of Assisi in 1219 (the founder of the order had come to Nazareth for the sole purpose "of venerating the house in which the Word was made flesh") is gone today. Thus, an inexplicable gap yawns in front of the Grotto of the Annunciation; there are not even any mosaics to adorn the holy ground.

The answer to this riddle can perhaps be found 1386 miles northwest of Nazareth, on a hill overgrown with laurel trees in the Italian region of Le Marche. As the traveler approaches it from a distance, for example on the highway from Ancona to Pescara, he can already recognize on its ridge a dome, towering high into the sky. It is part of a church, mighty as a cathedral, which seems somewhat out of place here. For it stands, not in the center of a city, but in the middle of nowhere. A few houses have gathered around it, whose inhabitants apparently live off the pilgrimage business; otherwise, the hill is surrounded by fields and meadows. The nearest major city, Ancona, after all, is 15.5 miles away from this hamlet that calls itself Loreto, after its laurel trees.

The reason why, nevertheless, the most important Marian pilgrimage site of medieval and early modern Europe emerged here was an alleged miracle. Three years after the Muslims had expelled the Crusaders from the Holy Land in 1291, legend has it that angels brought Mary's house from Nazareth to Loreto. At the time, it supposedly also made a stop in Croatia along the way. Since its arrival in Italy, people believed that the Holy House and the Black Madonna that was found therein worked miracles. So they built the church with the mighty marble dome as the largest reliquary in the world. The

---

[12] As quoted in Denys Pringle, *The Churches of the Crusader Kingdom of Jerusalem: A Corpus*, vol. 2, L–Z (Cambridge: Cambridge University Press, 1993), p. 120.

Holy House itself was surrounded by a marble shrine by no less an architect than Bramante.

Since then fifty-five popes, most recently Benedict XVI in October 2012 [and Francis in March 2019], have paid reverence to the Holy House. "Among all the temples dedicated to the Mother of God and the Immaculate Virgin there is one that takes the first place and shines in an incomparable splendor. The ... house of Loreto, consecrated by the divine mysteries, glorified by countless miracles ... is rightfully the object of veneration of all peoples and generations", Blessed Pius IX wrote in August 1852. Eight years later, he commissioned the Roman prelate and scholar Bartolini to investigate it. Bartolini obtained stones and mortar samples from the Holy House and from the Grotto of the Annunciation in Nazareth, in front of which there was still a foundation. Then he had both samples analyzed by the geologist Professor Ratti. The result: mortar and stones from Loreto and Nazareth were identical.

The Holy House is indeed a phenomenon. Archaeological examinations from the 1960s prove that it has no foundation but stands in the middle of a medieval road. Between the stones, five cloth crosses were found, the kind the participants of the Crusades attached to their garments. Once they had safely reached their destination, they used to leave them behind as votive offerings at one of the holy sites. Between the bricks, stones are cemented into the walls that are undoubtedly not of Italian origin. Some are unhewn, others show traces of superficial working, as was customary among the Arabian Nabataeans, who found imitators also in the Holy Land.

From such stones the houses in the villages of Galilee were also made. Graffiti have been carved on many of them, which have their counterpart in the Grotto of the Annunciation in Nazareth. One of these scrawled inscriptions—it reads "O Jesus Christ, Son of God"—consists of Greek and two Hebrew letters (a *lamed* and a *waw*). It still seems to come from a later Jewish Christian. A renewed geological examination, whose results were published by the author Giorgio Nicolini in April 2006 in his book *The Historical Truth behind the Miraculous Transportation of the Holy House from Nazareth to Loreto*, removed all doubts. The stones from the Grotto of the Annunciation in Nazareth showed the same geological structure as the stones in the altar area of the Holy House. Thus it originated at least in part

Grotto

The three walls
brought to Loreto

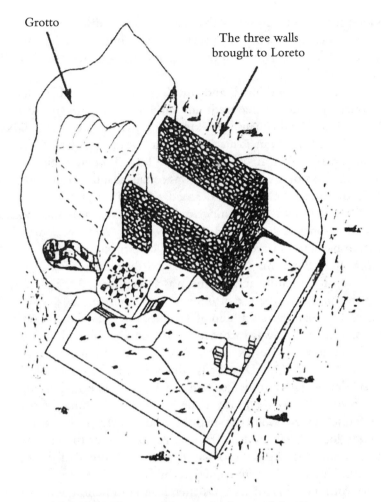

The Holy House of Loreto in front of the Grotto
of the Annunciation in Nazareth

in Nazareth—which is hard to doubt anyway, since it fits perfectly
into the gap in front of the Annunciation grotto.

The pretty legend that the Holy House had been brought to Italy
by angels by air, so to speak, proved to be only a historical misunderstanding. As early as 1900, the papal archivist Giuseppe Lapponi had
found the answer to the riddle in the secret archive of the Vatican.

And yet it was not until 1985 that the document discovered by him was published in a scholarly journal. According to it, not angels, but members of the family of the Angeloi salvaged the stones of the Holy House.

In 1263, the bloodthirsty and utterly unscrupulous Mamluk Sultan Baibars had raided Nazareth and completely destroyed the Crusader Basilica. All Christians were killed or carried off into slavery. Not until 1260 did the Franciscans once again ensure a lasting Christian presence in Nazareth. In 1291, when the last Christian bastion fell in Akkon, the port of the Crusaders, it was certain that the Holy Land was lost. In that year, the Angeloi, descendants of the Byzantine imperial line of the Komneni, in a manner unknown to us, came into possession of the stones of the Holy House. Maybe they sent a well-disguised salvaging party to Nazareth; maybe they commissioned Muslim traders to acquire them; maybe they leveraged their diplomatic relations. The head of the family at the time was Nikephoros Angelos, despot of Epirus on the west coast of Greece. In September 1294, when his daughter Thamar married Philip of Taranto, son of the king of Naples, her generous dowry was recorded in the aforementioned document. Included in it, as it states explicitly, were "the holy stones, transported from the house of Our Dear Lady, the Virgin and Mother of God". In fact, during excavations beneath the Holy House in Loreto, two coins from Philip's vassal, Guy II de la Roche, the duke of Athens, were found as well. Guy II owned the land on which the sanctuary is presently located. His mother, Helena Angelina, was the daughter of Johannes Angelos, the duke of Neopatras and brother of the despot of Epirus. The relics thus remained in the family.

The Annunciation of Mary is therefore commemorated in three churches, at the Well and in the Grotto of Nazareth as well as on the green hills of Italy, in the Adriatic Galilee. The words of the angel may have been a faint whisper, but Mary's *fiat* resounded throughout the world!

II

On the Other Side of Bethlehem

A Tomb for the King of the Jews

Ehud Netzer had a dream. For thirty-five years, he did not lose sight of it, defying all resistance, until he finally reached his goal. Then the day of his greatest triumph also became his most bitter disappointment. And yet he had accomplished something that assures him a permanent place in the annals of archaeology: he had discovered the tomb of one of the greatest villains in world history.

Yet Ehud Netzer (1934–2010) was anything but an adventurer or treasure hunter, even though the hat he used to wear in the burning sun of the Judaean desert was somewhat reminiscent of that of Indiana Jones. On the contrary: in Israel, the college-educated architect with a doctorate in archaeology and a professorship at the Hebrew University in Jerusalem was considered one of the world's leading experts on Hasmonean and Herodian palace buildings. As architect, he had collaborated influentially in the renovation of the Jewish Quarter in the old city of Jerusalem; as archaeologist, he had taken part in the excavations of the legendary Yigael Yadin—considered one of the fathers of Israeli archaeology—in Hathor and Masada. There, on the Jewish people's Mountain of Fate, which today is a kind of national shrine, he had an encounter in 1963 at the age of twenty-nine that would change his life.

The man who unsuspectingly assigned to him the task of his life was an Italian monk. Padre Virgilio Corbo was one of the great Franciscan archaeologists, who, commissioned by the Custodia Terra Santa and the Studium Biblicum Franciscanum, examined the sites of the New Testament. The friar had come to Masada to get an idea of the work of his Israeli colleagues, but he found no one who could truly help him. None of the Israelis in the excavation team spoke

Italian, and Padre Corbo unfortunately spoke no foreign languages. Netzer, however, had picked up at least a few fragments of the language on various trips to Italy and so declared that he was willing to guide the inquisitive Franciscan through the excavation, hoping to make himself intelligible to him in broken Italian, using hands and feet if need be. This worked pretty well, and while the two men were strolling across the rock plateau of the Herodian fortress, Padre Corbo began to tell about his own excavation project. He had applied the spade in the vicinity of Bethlehem, where, on an artificially raised hill, stood the most monumental of all the Biblical villain's strongholds, the Herodium.

When he heard the name of the Herod-fortress, Ehud Netzer again felt that deep inner longing which had accompanied him all his life. Yet at this point in time, its goal was still in the unattainable distance, no closer than the moon or the legendary Atlantis. Often enough the young Ehud had driven to Ramat Rahel south of Jerusalem to see the Herodium at least through a telescope, and even at that distance the ruin was still breathtakingly beautiful. But for him as an Israeli, there was no way simply to drive there. Bethlehem at the time was in Jordanian territory, and the states were enemies. Eagerly, therefore, he absorbed every word from the mouth of the friar, filled with the sad certainty of never being able to see with his own eyes what was being described.

The Six-Day War of 1967 changed that abruptly. As soon as the border fortifications were gone, Ehud Netzer got into his car, drove over dusty desert roads, climbed up the steep hill—and was overwhelmed by the grandeur of the ancient structure. Then he ran into the Franciscan archaeologists, who were just packing up their gear. Their excavation permit, granted by the Jordanian Antiquities Authority, was now no longer valid. It would take five years until Israeli colleagues finally continued their work. Their excavation director would be Ehud Netzer.

Yigael Yadin, his teacher, was the one who sent him to the Herodium and recommended that he make the fortress the topic of his dissertation. During the following months, Netzer thoroughly studied the excavation reports of his predecessors and all available ancient and medieval sources on the history of the fortress; then in 1972, he himself picked up the spade.

The most important ancient source that relates the history of this structure is the writing of the Jewish historian Flavius Josephus. From him we learn how the place became the Biblical villain's mountain of fate.

The story of King Herod began with yet another changeover of power in the Holy Land. After the death of Alexander Jannaeus, the Hasmonean king, who was responsible for the Judaification of Galilee, his sons Aristobulus and Hyrcanus feuded over the throne for almost two decades. Then they both made the fatal mistake of asking the Roman general Pompey to arbitrate. He used the situation to bring the entire kingdom under his control. Without further ado, he put Hyrcanus, who was weak and submissive to Rome, on the throne, invaded the country, and marched on Jerusalem. In 63 B.C., after a three-month siege, he stormed the Temple, in which Aristobulus and his followers had barricaded themselves. It came to a blood bath: twelve thousand Jews were killed, and the Hasmonean was captured. But what unnerved the Jews even more was that Pompey forced his way into the Holy of Holies of the Temple. In their eyes, by doing so he committed a sacrilege that cried out to heaven; only the high priest, and certainly no Gentile, was allowed to enter the earthly dwelling place of God.

What started under such omens had to end badly. Judaea had lost its autonomy and was henceforth tributary to the Romans. Hyrcanus was no longer allowed to call himself king; instead, he was now high priest and ethnarch, while his Idumaean governor Antipater, commissioned by Rome, managed his former kingdom. Antipater cleverly used his new position of power to build up his own dynasty. He divided the land into five provinces and appointed his sons Phasael and Herod as governors. But his thirst for power and his close ties to Rome displeased many Jews, who simply considered him a potential usurper, although outwardly he acted loyal to Hyrcanus. Eventually, Antipater fell victim to a conspiracy; in 43 B.C., he was poisoned during a banquet in Jerusalem. The energetic Herod now strove for his father's position. When he married the Hasmonean princess Mariamne a year later, the power seemed within reach. But he had not reckoned on Antigonus, the son of Aristobulus. He had allied himself with the Parthians in order to free the Jewish empire from the hands of his uncle and the Romans. Supported by the

Persian army, he conquered Jerusalem in a surprise attack in 40 B.C.,
killed Hyrcanus and Phasael, and crowned himself without further
ado. Only Herod managed to escape in the dead of night with his
small private army, his mother Cyprus, his wife, and his servants.
When just outside of Bethlehem his mother's carriage was pulled
down a slope by a mule that had lost its footing, he thought all was
lost already. He was just about to fall on his sword when his mother
regained consciousness. At that moment, he regained his courage
and was ready to face his persecutors and annihilate them. Thus
he arrived safely first in Egypt and then in Rome, where the Senate
bestowed on him the title King of the Jews and put him in charge
of an army that was to reconquer the renegade vassal state. He had,
however, noted the spot that had become the turning point of his
life; later on, when he was king, he built his safest and therefore
favorite residence here, the Herodium.

The palace-fortress was erected on a natural hill, which, according
to Josephus, "was of the shape of a woman's breast".[1] On it the king
placed a crown of two concentric circles of walls and four towers.
The tower to the east surmounted all the others. In its basement was a
cistern, while the king lived in the very top. A cooling wind was
always blowing here, even in the middle of the desert, and from here
the view reached across the impressive landscape, all the way to the
green hills of Jerusalem in one direction, to the emerald blue of
the Dead Sea and the pale violet of the mountains of Moab in the
other. When the fortress was built, Herod had the hill artificially
raised until the ground reached the fifth story. Now it looked like
a volcano, from the crater of which a fortress projected. The steep
slope that now surrounded its walls made it practically impregnable.
The only entrance to the structure was by way of a steep staircase 560
feet in length, the last 230 feet of which led through a tunnel.

At the foot of the fortress-hill, however, a small city of opulent
luxury developed like an oasis in the middle of the desert. Here Ehud
Netzer started digging first. The architect among the archaeologists
was in the process of unearthing the masterpiece of the greatest architect among the kings of antiquity.

---

[1] Flavius Josephus, *The Jewish War*, bk. 1, chap. 21, no. 10, in *The New Complete Works of
Josephus*, trans. William Whiston (Grand Rapids, Mich.: Kregel, 1999), p. 704.

In the center of the structure, he discovered the remains of a swimming pool 230 feet long, 148 feet wide, and at one point ten feet deep. Herod was known as an untiring and passionate swimmer. In the center of the pool was a small island with a pavilion on it, which could be reached only by swimming or by boat. The entire pool was surrounded by a parklike garden with lush vegetation. Its water was channeled from the spring of Artas three miles away, via an aqueduct built specifically for this purpose. For centuries, the Arabs used to call the ruins of the Herodium *Jebel el Fureidis*, "mountain of the little paradise", which was not in the least an exaggeration. Here at the edge of the desert, the king had created for himself a garden paradise that was supposed to show everyone how his power and wealth defied nature.

In order to be closer to his swimming pool, Herod immediately built a second and of course much larger and more magnificent palace at the foot of the fortress-mountain. At its foot lay a track 1,148 feet long and 98 feet wide, which was reminiscent of the Circus Maximus in Rome, but it was too narrow for a chariot racetrack. For a long time, Netzer puzzled as to what its purpose could have been. The entire structure that he was able to uncover extended over an area of 590,551 square feet. There were only two ancient rulers' residences that surpassed the Herodium in size, namely, the Golden House of Nero in Rome and the Villa Adriana of Hadrian near Tivoli. One was built eighty, the other 150 years later. Their builders were Roman emperors and, thus, the most powerful rulers of the ancient world. Among the contemporary residences, regardless of whether in Rome or Ctesiphon, none could compare with the palace-fortress of Herod.

But it was not enough for him. After his victory over his adversaries, he covered the entire country with a network of monumental buildings, which were supposed to show his subjects and the world that he was more than an illegitimate marionette king who ruled by Rome's favor. He wanted to go down in history as the greatest of all Jewish kings, eclipsing even Solomon in his splendor.

First of all, he saw to it that he could reside fittingly according to his standards. So he erected a whole series of palace structures that were as opulent as they were heavily fortified, not only near Bethlehem, but also on the terrace of Masada, in Jericho, and in Jerusalem. They are the key to the soul of the tyrant, who was both megalomaniac and paranoid, "encompassing the whole nation with guards, that they might by no means get from under his power, nor fall into disturbances...; and that if they did make any commotions, he might ... be able to know what they were attempting, and to prevent it", Flavius Josephus relates.[2]

He then founded two cities, both of which he named after the Emperor Augustus, to demonstrate his loyalty to Rome, namely, Caesarea at the Mediterranean and Sebaste in the heart of Samaria (Sebastos was the Greek translation of Augustus, "the exalted one"). Caesarea was his gate to the world, which at the time meant the same as to Rome. Since the city did not have its own water supply, he simply commissioned a mighty aqueduct that channeled water to it from the slopes of Mount Carmel six miles distant. Then he created the first artificial port of the ancient world, with jetties that extended 1640 feet into the open sea; it became one of the largest in the Mediterranean area. Over its wharf, on an artificial platform, towered the ninety-eight-foot-tall Temple of Augustus and Roma, which dominated the skyline of Caesarea. It was Herod's manifest-in-stone guarantee of his irrevocable loyalty to the emperor. The city became a microcosm of the Roman lifestyle. Arranged strictly according to the rules of Roman city planning, with a north-south axis, the *cardo*, and an east-west axis, the *decumanus*, it was the first in the country to have an amphitheater and a 514-yard-long chariot racetrack, which ended right in front of Herod's palace. This in turn was located spectacularly, like all the king's buildings, on a rocky promontory, lashed about by the waves of the sea. Its exquisite finishing touch consisted in a rectangular pool, in which Herod, surrounded by the sea on three sides, could swim in fresh water. Since the 1960s, each summer Israeli, Italian, or American teams of archaeologists come to Caesarea to research one of the most successful city foundings in antiquity. But not until the late 1990s did they uncover Herod's opulent palace with its magnificent mosaic floors. Today the ruins of the ancient metropolis are one of Israel's most important tourist attractions. It has to be enjoyed with caution, for its parking lots are not guarded. We were not the

---

[2] Flavius Josephus, *Jewish Antiquities*, bk. 15, chap. 8, no. 5, in *New Complete Works of Josephus*, p. 514.

first visitors whose cars were broken into and robbed while we were visiting the excavation site.

Jerusalem, however, Herod's capitol, became his masterpiece. Right after his victory over Antigonus, here too, he had constructed a fortress, in which he felt safer than in the palace of the Hasmoneans. Bira or Baris was the name of the old fortress, which was built on a rock plateau north of the Temple Mount. It was rectangular, and from it projected, as from the Herodium, three smaller towers and a larger one. When he had finished building it, he renamed it Antonia, after his friend Marc Antony. Subsequently, Herod had the old city wall reinforced. The northern part of the city, which until then had been unfortified, was surrounded by a second wall. But in the west, where Jerusalem was the most vulnerable, a bulwark rose up with three mighty towers, the tallest of which reached the dimensions of a fourteen-story building. In the shadow of this fortress, on the highest point of the city, he built his new palace.

When describing this most luxurious of all of Herod's residences, Flavius Josephus, too, goes into raptures: "The king had a palace ... which exceeds all my ability to describe it", he wrote in his book about *The Jewish War*,

> ... adorned ... with large bed-chambers, that would contain beds for a hundred guests apiece, in which the variety of the stones is not to be expressed; for a large quantity of those that were rare of that kind was collected together. Their roofs were also wonderful, both for the length of the beams, and the splendor of their ornaments. The number of the rooms was also very great, and the variety of the figures that were about them was great; their furniture was complete, and the greatest part of the vessels that were put in them was of silver and gold. There were besides many porticoes, one beyond another, around, and in each of those porticoes curious pillars; yet were all the courts that were exposed to the air everywhere green. There were, moreover, several groves of trees, and long walks through them, with deep canals, and cisterns, that in several parts were filled with brazen statues, through which the water ran out. There were also many dove-courts of tame pigeons about the canals. But indeed it is not possible to give a complete description of these palaces.[3]

[3] Flavius Josephus, *The Jewish War*, bk. 5, chap. 4, in *New Complete Works of Josephus*, p. 853.

It is all the more tragic that, other than the foundations of its walls and the palace gate, nothing of this marvel of Herodian architecture survived. Yet, having been able to study the palaces of Jericho and the Herodium, Ehud Netzer knew that Flavius Josephus had not exaggerated here, either.

Only one question remained unanswered for the archaeologist for decades—the question of the king's tomb. This much Ehud Netzer knew: it must have been located somewhere near the Herodium, Herod's mountain of fate, where, as he determined in his will, he wanted to await his Eternal Judge. Again and again the Israeli read through *Jewish Antiquities* by Josephus, who described Herod's funeral service as vividly as if he himself had been present as an eyewitness:

> The body was carried upon a golden bier, embroidered with very precious stones of great variety, and it was covered over with purple, as well as the body itself; he had a diadem upon his head, and above it a crown of gold: he also had a scepter in his right hand. About the bier were his sons and his numerous relations; next to these was the soldiers, distinguished according to their several countries and ranks; and they were put into the following order: First of all went his guards, then the band of Thracians, and after them the Germans; and next the band of Galatians, every one in their full war attire; and behind these marched the whole army in the same manner as they used to go out to war, and as they used to be put in array by the masters of the roll call and centurions; these were followed by five hundred of his servants carrying spices. So they went eight furlongs to Herodium; for there, by his own command, he was to be buried.[4]

As pompous as Josephus described the funeral procession, as opulent as Herod's lifestyle had been, so also must his tomb have been. But where was it? In the course of the thirty-five years during which Ehud Netzer, interrupted time and again by other projects, researched the Herodium, this tomb gradually became a fixation for him, his lifelong dream, the goal of his yearning and striving. For decades he was firmly convinced that it must have been located somewhere at the foot of the fortress, on the expansive grounds of the palace. Was the long narrow track at its foot perhaps the path that the funeral procession

---

[4] Flavius Josephus, *Jewish Antiquities*, bk. 17, chap. 8, no. 3; pp. 570–71.

once took? His conjecture, in fact, seemed to be confirmed when in 1978 he chanced upon the façade of a monument at the end of the track. But no matter how thoroughly he searched, no matter how deep he dug, he found no tomb there. In 1999, he eventually published a standard work about *The Palaces of the Hasmoneans and Herod the Great*, which was actually supposed to be his scholarly legacy. He was now sixty-five and ready for retirement. Resignedly he tried to defend the theory that the monumental structure simply must be the tomb, since he had found nothing better. Colleagues who suspected that the tomb was located on the fortress mount instead met with his flat denial. This was completely out of question, he countered, since a Jew would never have allowed himself to be buried so close to an inhabited structure.

But in August 2006, Netzer finally let his colleagues Yaakov Kalman and Roi Porath persuade him to dig on the east side of the fortress hill, at the foot of the mighty eastern tower. As early as 1983, American geophysicists using ground radar had located a cavity there; a discovery that until now had been rejected by Netzer as "irrelevant" and "in need of interpretation". He soon had to admit that his judgment at the time had been premature. First, his team came upon the remains of a gigantic theater that Herod had installed on the slope of his fortress when in 15 B.C. he received his Roman friend Marcus Agrippa here. Next to it, toward the staircase, was a platform. Netzer gradually realized that the Biblical king's mausoleum must have stood on it. For all these years, he had simply searched at the wrong end of the procession's path. The monument was not its end but its starting point. The path of the funeral procession then led across the 1148-foot-long promenade, directly to the monumental staircase, the ascent to the Herodium. Halfway up, it branched off to the left toward the mausoleum, which thus still maintained the eighty-two-foot distance from the mountain-palace that was demanded by the Torah.

Rather out of curiosity, Porath one day uncovered the entrance to a cistern, which was blocked by retaining walls. Immediately behind it he came upon a fragment of reddish sandstone, which was decorated with ornaments of the finest masonry. When he brought it to Netzer, the eyes of the elderly archaeologist began to sparkle and his hands began to tremble. The Nestor of Herod research knew right away that this could only be a fragment from the sarcophagus of the

Jewish king. The similarity to other stone coffins found in Jerusalem was unmistakable. Only this piece was, according to Netzer, "more beautiful and bigger than everything we have hitherto known from that period".

The farther they dug, the more parts of the king's sarcophagus came to light. Soon they had enough to reconstruct its appearance on the computer. Seven feet ten inches in length, crowned with a richly decorated gable roof, adorned with five rosettes on each side, it was indeed worthy of Herod.

At a press conference on May 7, 2007, Netzer announced the find of his life to the world public—and at the same time had to admit defeat: after thirty-five years of searching, he had found no treasure, not even an inscription. Only a few admittedly rather decorative stone fragments provided a hint as to how transient, indeed, the glamour of the world is.

The fragments, in fact, testify less to the pompous image of himself that the tyrant had presented to the world than to his unpopularity among the people. For his mausoleum had been plundered, not by grave-robbers, but by Jews who in this way took revenge on him. "We could genuinely feel the rage of those who rebelled against Herod", Roi Porath declared at the press conference, "we saw the traces of the hammer blows under which the magnificent tomb was maliciously smashed to bits."

There were plenty of reasons for this rage. For even Flavius Josephus made no secret of the trail of blood that ran through Herod's life. He had ten wives and at least ten sons, but he trusted no one, least of all the members of his family. At the behest of his second wife, the Hasmonean Mariamne, he appointed her sixteen-year-old brother-in-law Aristobulus high priest. But no sooner had the youth made his first public appearance during the Feast of Tabernacles in 35 B.C. than he was drowned in the swimming pool by the king's Gallic servants. Mariamne followed him into death seven years later. In 7 B.C., her sons were accused of high treason and executed, along with three hundred officers who were accused of being accomplices. Henceforth everyone who had come in contact with them was also suspected. "Was [Herod] so hard-hearted, and so very tender in the desire of government ... that he would take no one into a partnership with him, that so whatsoever he would have done himself might continue immovable[?]"[5] Flavius Josephus asks and then answers in his *Antiquities of the Jews*:

> And what more can be said, but that those who before were the most intimate friends, were become wild beasts to one another, as if a certain madness had fallen upon them, while there was no room for defense or refutation, in order to the discovery of the truth, but all were at random doomed to destruction; ... Herod's own life also was entirely disturbed; and because he could trust nobody, he was sorely punished by the expectation of further misery; for he often fancied in his imagination that his son had fallen upon him, or stood by him with a sword in his hand; and thus was his mind night and day intent upon this thing, and revolved it over and over, no otherwise than if he were under a distraction. And this was the sad condition Herod was now in.[6]

Just four days before his own death, he had his oldest son, Antipater, killed. "It is better to be Herod's pig than his son", the disgusted Roman Emperor Augustus commented on the brutality of his vassal. For the Jewish king would never have harmed a pig.

Yet, not only the court but also the people were affected by the madness to which the once equally admired and feared ruler gradually succumbed. His last three years became a nightmare for the Jews.

When sometime between 7 and 5 B.C. an oath of loyalty to the emperor and the king was demanded of the entire people, six thousand Pharisees refused to take it. They believed in the prophecy that "Herod and his offspring ... by God's design would lose the reign" and hoped for the birth of a liberator, the Messiah. At once, the king had the leaders of the Pharisee-rebellion executed, as well as everyone in the court who had believed in the prophecy. Young Pharisees avenged themselves by storming the main gate of the Temple, above which Herod had mounted a golden eagle, the sign of Rome's rule. The eagle was torn down and smashed to bits. Herod had the rioters apprehended and burned alive.

Even on his deathbed, marked by grave illness, he set an example of his "murderous mind, and such as was not easily moved from that

[5] Ibid., bk. 16, chap. 11, no. 8; pp. 551–52.
[6] Ibid., chap. 8, no. 5; p. 543.

which is evil",[7] as Josephus comments, not without bitterness. When he learned that the people believed God had inflicted his suffering upon him as a punishment "for his evilness", he devised a downright monstrous plan. "I know that the Jews will celebrate my death as a joyous occasion", his biographer quotes him as saying, but he wanted the entire people to mourn him. He thus ordered the nobles from all of Israel to gather on the chariot racetrack of his palace in Jericho. Those who opposed the order were executed at once. All who had come—a tremendous crowd of people—he had locked in by his soldiers, mostly Gallic and German mercenaries. Archers received the order to murder the Jewish patricians in a shower of arrows as soon as the king breathed his last. Only in this way could he ensure that "the whole nation should be put into mourning, and indeed made desolate of their dearest family, when he gave order that one out of every family should be killed",[8] as Josephus describes the perfidious plan. Fortunately, it never came to this massacre; Herod's family was not willing to have his last order carried out. The pompous funeral, on the other hand, was granted to him as planned.

Thus Herod lay facing Jerusalem in his 33-by-33-foot mausoleum on the northern slope of his fortress, until the people, who had grown to hate him, attacked his tomb and took bitter revenge. He did go down in history; but not, as he had hoped, as the greatest king of the Jews, but rather as the most terrible monster of all time, at least until a postcard painter from Austria laid claim to that title also. But the reason for his condemnation by posterity was to be found neither on the Herodium nor in Jerusalem. Through one event that occurred somewhere in between the two, yet still along the mausoleum's line of sight, Herod remained forever engraved on the memory of mankind: the infanticide of Bethlehem.

[7] Ibid., bk. 16, chap. 11, no. 8; p. 552.
[8] Ibid., bk. 17, chap. 6, no. 6; p. 566.

III

Where the Word Became History

A Grotto Filled with Mysteries

It is a short distance from Jerusalem to Bethlehem. Starting at the Jaffa Gate, it took us about fifteen minutes by car. But that was nine years ago.

Today, a hideous concrete wall divides the land. You can already see it from Mount Zion. Like a gray serpent, it creeps over the Biblical hills, separating what always belonged together. The age of terrorism—the outbreak of the Second Intifada in September 2000 as well as 9/11 one year later—has drastically altered the face of the Holy Land. In March 2011, I accompanied Pope John Paul II to Israel; today we are on the road with Benedict XVI, and it makes me sad when I compare the mood throughout the country then with the feeling now. Then there was hope in the air; now there is fear. The visit of the messenger of peace from Rome does little to change this, if not the contrary. The Israelis' understandable need for security becomes paranoid at times. We journalists experience this all too clearly. Not much remains of the former nonchalance of the young state, the charm of its female soldiers, who, even with an Uzi under their arm, looked like models. The tone has become harsher; the nonchalance has given way to collective distrust. The bus with the journalists is scheduled to leave the press center at 4:00 in the morning. Anyone who is late will have no chance to pass the checkpoint because at that time, they tell us, Israel closes the wall.

We save ourselves the trouble and observe the visit from the press center. Then in the early afternoon, when security has eased up a little, we head for Jesus' birthplace by car. Inevitably we make various detours, past roadblocks, while the words Benedict XVI spoke on

May 13, 2009, on the site of the manger in Bethlehem, are echoing in our heads:

> Everywhere, Bethlehem is associated with this joyful message of rebirth, renewal, light and freedom. Yet here, in our midst, how far this magnificent promise seems from being realized! How distant seems that Kingdom of wide dominion and peace, security, justice and integrity which the Prophet Isaiah heralded in the first reading (cf. Is 9:6), and which we proclaim as definitively established in the coming of Jesus Christ, Messiah and King!

Today it seems as though no place in the world was more urgently in need of the peace that the angels announced here more than two thousand years ago than the city of David. In order to inspect the newly discovered tomb of Herod, we decide to drive to the Herodium first. Like an eagle's nest, it clings to the steep mountain face at a lofty height, facing a breathtaking panorama. A balmy wind dries the beads of my perspiration and makes me inhale deeply. I let my gaze wander over the mountains and valleys of Judah, over pastures and flocks of sheep and olive tree plantations, scattered houses and entire villages, the minarets of mosques and satellite dishes, and eventually I recognize on the horizon, veiled by the dusty haze of the desert, the golden gleam of the cupola of the Dome of the Rock where the Temple of Jerusalem once stood. It is far in the distance, separated by a wall that cuts the country in two, a cut that reaches deep into the hearts of its people. But in front of it, on the slope of a hill and exactly in the line of sight of the dead king, is Bethlehem. Still in his lifetime, not in the splendor of a palace but in the semi-darkness of a stable-cave, the true King of the Jews, the promised Messiah, the Redeemer of mankind, was born there. His tomb, too, was shattered, but it is still venerated today as a holy place by two billion people. It, too, is empty, but for a different reason. He who lay in it has risen; his kingdom will have no end. It is only because of him that the tyrant of Judaea, too, is forever stuck in the peoples' (worst) memory.

The era of Herod is in fact the first historical benchmark in the biography of Jesus of Nazareth. The mention of him in two of the four Gospels shows that in the case of Jesus we are not dealing with a mythical son of a deity who was perhaps born sometime and somewhere in the deliberately vague "once upon a time" of a fairy tale. On the contrary: the Evangelist Matthew explicitly declares that "Jesus was born in Bethlehem of Judea in the days of Herod ..." (Mt 2:1), and his colleague Luke also places the date for the events he describes "in the days of Herod, king of Judea ..." (Lk 1:5). The King of the Jews who was loyal to Rome ruled from 37 to 4 B.C. At the time of his death, as we read in Matthew, Jesus was still a child. His birth therefore falls in the last years of Herod, which, as we learn from Flavius Josephus, were also his cruelest. Our calendar, which reckons *ab incarnatione Domini*, that is, "since the birth of Christ", therefore, cannot be accurate. Obviously, the Ukrainian-born monk Dionysius Exiguus, who introduced the new reckoning of years in A.D. 437 on behalf of the pope, miscalculated considerably. There never has been a year zero, anyway, since the zero was still unknown in late antiquity; the year 1 B.C. was followed immediately by A.D. 1. Jesus' birthday, Christmas, was moved to December 25 as late as the fourth century, while many Eastern Churches celebrate it on January 6; some even, as Clement of Alexandria relates, on March 9/10 or on April 9, and August 15 was also debated for a while. Only with a revision of the dates does a consistent picture emerge.

From 7 B.C. on, Herod suffered increasingly from paranoia, and the once promising and certainly not incompetent ruler became a bloodthirsty tyrant who suspected conspirators and rivals in every nook and cranny. Meanwhile, in the *Antiquities of the Jews*, we read about an oath of loyalty of "all the people of the Jews" to "Caesar (Augustus) and to the king's government", which six thousand Pharisees openly refused to take.[1] The account places the oath almost immediately after the murder of Herod's sons; therefore it must have been taken between 7 and 5 B.C. This oath is of interest in that it could offer a solution for one of the major problems of research into the life of Jesus, namely, the question of which "census" Luke was referring to when right in the beginning of his Christmas account he wrote: "In those days a decree went out from Caesar Augustus that all the world should be enrolled. This was the first enrollment, when

---

[1] Flavius Josephus, *Jewish Antiquities*, bk. 17, chap. 2, no. 4, in *The New Complete Works of Josephus*, trans. William Whiston (Grand Rapids, Mich.: Kregel, 1999), p. 556.

Quirinius was governor of Syria. And all went to be enrolled, each to his own city" (Lk 2:1–3). We all know these words from the Mass of the Nativity on Christmas Eve, and yet, despite all the familiarity, they are somewhat problematic. At first glance, we encounter an anachronism that could shake the entire historical anchoring of Jesus' birth and perhaps even cause it to collapse completely.

Certainly, Flavius Josephus, too, knows of such a census, and Publius Sulpicius Quirinius is also historically verified as governor of Syria, but for the year A.D. 6. At that time, however, Herod had already been dead for ten years. There is also another date in the Gospel of Luke with which A.D. 6 cannot be reconciled. After all, in the next chapter we read that "in the fifteenth year of the reign of Tiberius Caesar ... Jesus ... was about thirty years of age" (Lk 3:1, 23). Tiberius, the stepson and successor of Augustus, was declared equal co-regent by Augustus in A.D. 13 and confirmed by the Senate after Augustus' death in September of A.D. 14. Thus, the Evangelist is referring to A.D. 27 or 28. "About thirty years of age" can mean at most a range from twenty-seven to thirty-four years, which makes a birth date between 7 B.C. and A.D. 1 possible but definitely rules out A.D. 6. Luke, therefore, cannot have been referring to the census of A.D. 6 under Quirinius.

A clue for solving the riddle can be found in Ankara, of all places, the ancient Ancyra, now the capital of Turkey, then of the province of Galatia. There, as early as 1555, an Austrian delegation discovered a Latin inscription on the walls of an ancient building. The building turned out to be a temple for Augustus and Roma; the inscription was an excerpt from the *Res gestae*, Augustus' account of his accomplishments, which was kept in the temple of Vesta in Rome. It starts with the words: "The deeds of Augustus, by which he subjected the whole wide earth to the rule of the Roman people ...", which is reminiscent of Luke 2:1, at least in choice of words. Part of these deeds, according to the inscription, were three censuses that the emperor ordered in 28 B.C., 8 B.C., and A.D. 14. Over four million Roman citizens were counted in the empire, with numbers rising. The Roman historian Tacitus also mentions censuses in the provinces and vassal states. According to him, Augustus kept a thorough account "... of the resources of the State, of the number of citizens and allies under arms, of the fleets, subject kingdoms, provinces, taxes, direct and indirect...."[2] The historian Dio Cassius, too, reports that Augustus kept "an account of ... the revenues, and of the public expenditures, the amount of money in the treasuries".[3] His interest also in the vassal kingdoms ("allies") makes it almost certain that there was an assessment of assets in Judaea already before the country was officially added to the Roman Empire as a province. After the census in the empire in 8 B.C. at the latest, Augustus likely requested numbers from Judaea, too, and Herod had no choice but to furnish them. The reasons that such a first census, before the one by Quirinius—and this is exactly what Luke could have meant in the original text before later copyists "corrected" him—is not mentioned by Josephus may have been propagandistic in nature. At this point in time, Herod could not have afforded to order the people to enter themselves into Roman tax lists. It would have become too obvious that behind the entire pretentious façade he was, after all, only a marionette, a stooge of Rome. Thus he probably officially demanded the oath of loyalty from all inhabitants of his kingdom, together with the royal tax collectors' usual questions regarding ancestry and possessions. The Roman lawyer and Christian Tertullian (around A.D. 200), who according to his own testimony conducted research in the Roman state archive, also confirms: "There is historical proof that at this very time a *census* had been taken in Judaea by Sentius Saturninus."[4] From 7 until 5 B.C., when he was relieved by Publius Quinctilius Varus, Gaius Sentius Saturninus was indeed *Legatus Augusti pro praetore* in Syria and, thus, responsible also for Judaea. Some historians are even convinced that Quirinius at the time, as *Orienti praepositus*, was the direct superior of governor Saturninus and, thus, the one truly responsible for the census confirmed by Tertullian. An inscription, discovered in 1765 near Tibur, which the renowned German historian Theodor Mommsen identified as Quirinius' tomb inscription as early as 1883, indeed confirms that he

[2] Tacitus, *Annals*, bk. 1, chap. 11, in *The Complete Works of Tacitus*, trans. Alfred John Church and William Jackson Brodribb (New York: Random House, 1942), p. 11.

[3] Cassius Dio, *Roman History, Books LVI–LX*, trans. Earnest Cary and Herbert Baldwin Foster (Cambridge, Mass., and London: Harvard University Press, 1924), vol. 7, bk. 56, chap. 33, no. 2.

[4] Tertullian, *Against Marcion*, trans. Peter Holmes, bk. 4, chap. 19, in *Ante-Nicene Fathers*, ed. Alexander Roberts and James Donaldson, vol. 3 (1885; Peabody, Mass.: Hendrickson, 1995), p. 378.

was "for the second time the delegate of the divine Augustus, with pro-praetorian authority in Syria and Phoenicia". It was not until 1997 that Geza Alföldi confirmed that the inscription indeed referred to the very Quirinius whom Luke mentions.

How much Herod as *rex socius* was dependent on Rome became evident when in 8 B.C. he fell into disgrace with Augustus. Without asking the emperor's permission, he had waged a small lightning campaign against the neighboring Nabataeans. When the emperor heard of this, he reprimanded the King of the Jews, saying that "until now he regarded him as a friend, but henceforth he would treat him as a mere subject." Even in family matters, Herod had to accept the emperor's decision, and once he even had to appear as defendant in Aquileia near Rome. After his death, Augustus immediately sent Sabinus, the procurator of imperial assets in Syria, to Judaea "in order to supervise the possessions of Herod". The emperor could even alter the vassal king's will at his own discretion. The fact that from this time on, as Josephus reports, he waived part of the Samaritans' taxes indicates that Augustus must have had tax data available as early as 4 B.C. This is further evidenced by the fact that also in the neighboring kingdom of Nabataea, a further "ally" of Rome, a certain Fabatus, began his work around 6 B.C.; Josephus explicitly calls him *dioiketes*, a Roman tax official. It would therefore be strange if the kingdom of Herod had been spared from Roman tax assessments. Papyrus finds from Egypt prove that a census was customary in the Roman provinces every fourteen years on average. In the case of Judaea, the second assessment was conducted as early as A.D. 6 because at that time the country was added to the empire as a new province.

In Roman times, there were two taxes, a head tax and a property tax. From the province of Syria we know that men had to pay the head tax from age fourteen to sixty-five and women already from age twelve to sixty-five. For this reason alone, it was mandatory for every family member to appear before the census official, so that he could ascertain who was, in fact, obliged to pay the head tax. The place of taxation was always the place where the property was so that the property tax could be assessed at the same time.

A more recent example of this practice, though from one and a half centuries later, was found in 1961 in the so-called Cave of Letters in Wadi Hahal Hever, west of the Dead Sea. The archaeologists found the private archive of a Jewish woman named Babatha carefully wrapped in linen, stowed in a leather pouch, and then untouched for 1800 years. One of the papyri she had so carefully stored was a certified copy of her tax declaration. It is dated December 2 to 4, 127, since even back then tax officers were not the fastest and needed two days to copy the document. In this year there was indeed a census by Emperor Hadrian, in the province of Arabia, where Babatha's property was located. From her account, we learn that the woman had walked twenty-files miles from her home in Maoza to Rabbath-Moab, because that was the place of the tax office with jurisdiction over her. Right away the historians who evaluated the document noticed the parallels to the account of the "first census" in the Gospel of Luke. Henrike Zilling, a historian from Berlin who is a specialist in ancient history, lists the following:

> 1. Babatha's declaration and Luke name the emperor who ordered the census. 2. They give a date, although Luke only has to mention that it was the first census.... 3. They denote the responsible imperial governor. 4. They mention the fact of the written declaration (Lk 2:3: *apographetai*). 5. They reference the journey necessitated by the census from their home to the place where the tax declaration is made, and in this context the name of the father or the family name, respectively, as well as the inherited "household on her own property" (Babatha) or in loftier terms the "house" of David. 6. They document the necessity for spouses to appear at the census together.

From all this Zilling concludes: "The agreement in details and structure makes it likely that Luke knew the form that was customary for a census." Furthermore, we can assume "that Luke was well informed not only about the messianic expectations of the Jews in the time of Jesus, but also about the much more profane migrations of the populace as necessitated by the census."[5]

Going to Bethlehem, however, presupposes one thing: that Mary or Joseph—in Babatha's case, too, the husband had to act as guardian or "tutor"—must have inherited property in Bethlehem. Since both were from the clan of David, whose hometown

[5] Henrike Zilling, "Überlegungen zum Zensus des Quirinius", *H-Soz-u-Kult*, December 22, 2006, online at: https://www.hsozkult.de/debate/id/diskussionen-853.

was Bethlehem, this is by no means impossible. The *Protoevangelium of James*, at least, even describes Mary's father, Joachim, as a wealthy stock-breeder. Perhaps, then, the pasture on which the Grotto of Jesus' Nativity was located and which was usually leased to shepherds was part of her inheritance. In any event, despite her pregnancy, it was absolutely necessary for her to come to Bethlehem, too. With her, the mystery of God's Incarnation walked from Nazareth to Bethlehem, the old city of David, which now lay in the shadow of the Herodium, and confronted the tyrant with the true "King of the Jews". He was not born in the pompous apartments of a Herodian palace, but—the contrast could not have been starker—in a cave that served as a cattle shed. Humble though the accommodation was, it would never be forgotten.

From the outside, the Church of the Nativity is a bulky, windowless structure that is more reminiscent of a bulwark or a medieval fortress than of the peace and joy of the first Christmas. It has only one entrance that, furthermore, has been made smaller several times and is now only 3 feet, 11 inches tall. Whoever wishes to partake in the greatest miracle in history, the Incarnation of God, must automatically bow first and humble himself as the Creator of the universe did when he became a crying baby in the manger. The entrance is also called "Door of Humility", but the reason for all the partitioning is a different one. Often enough, Christians had to barricade themselves in this holy place, whether during the incursions of the Persians or Muslims, toward the end of the Crusades, or during the Turkish rule. But also during the Second Intifada, the church got caught in the middle when armed Palestinian militia entrenched themselves here in 2002 and the site of Jesus' birth was besieged by the Israeli army for thirty-nine days.

Whoever enters here is overwhelmed by the archaic solemnity of this ancient church, the origins of which date back to the pilgrimage of Saint Helena in the year 325. The emperor's mother had unlimited funds at her disposal. Her son, Constantine the Great, before his battle over Rome, had seen a vision of the Cross of Christ, and subsequently he had the sign of salvation painted on his soldiers' shields. When he was victorious, as if by a miracle, he declared the as-yet persecuted faith the *religio licita*, the legal religion, donated the Lateran Basilica to the pope, and had memorial churches built on the tombs of the apostles Peter and Paul. He then also subdued the eastern part of the empire and moved his seat of government first to Nicomedia and later to Byzantium, which he had renamed Constantinople. He sent his mother to the Holy Land with the commission to found three churches there—on the sites of the Nativity, the empty tomb, and the cave on the slope of Mount Olive, which was venerated as the site of the Ascension. He was not baptized until he was on his deathbed, but by then he had done more for the Church than any ruler in history.

The Constantinian Basilica had five naves and was practically square, eighty-nine feet long on each side. A roughly equal-sized and also practically square atrium, a portico, was placed in front of it. Toward the east, it opened onto an octagonal choir, in the center of which, below a magnificent baldachin, was the entrance to the grotto where Christ was born. Pilgrims' accounts describe this church as being extravagantly splendid: "All you can see is gold and jewels and silk", Egeria the nun reports on her pilgrimage in 383. "The hangings are entirely of silk with gold stripes, the curtains the same.... They are beyond description, and so is the magnificent building itself. It was built by Constantine, and under the supervision of his mother, it was decorated with gold, mosaic, and precious marble, as much as his empire could provide."[6]

Only fragments of the richly ornamented mosaic floor have remained of this splendor and could be uncovered during excavations in 1934. Everything else was destroyed by fire when the Samaritans rose up in 529 and went through the country pillaging and targeting churches in particular. Emperor Justinian had the ruins torn down and a new church built.

This was the Church of the Nativity, still in use today, supported by forty mighty Corinthian columns made from reddish limestone. It was a work built to last. This place of worship withstood even the onslaught of the Persians in 614 unscathed. The Sassanid king Khosrau, the "scourge of Christendom", was just about to have it plundered and its clergy killed when he froze in front of a fresco by the entrance. It depicted three *magi*, members of his own people's caste of priests in Persian garb, adoring the newborn child Jesus. At

---

[6] *Egeria's Travels*, trans. John Wilkinson (London: S.P.C.K., 1971), p. 127.

once he ordered the Church of the Nativity to be spared. Since then it has been expanded with towers, additions, and fortifications, but it is essentially the same as it was almost 1,500 years ago.

To this day the church, always shrouded in a mystical semi-darkness, seems gigantic and awe-inspiring. It is dominated by ancient icons and frescoes, but most of all by its lamps: perpetual lights made of silver, hanging from the crossbeams of the ceiling by yard-long chains, and widely overhanging crystal chandeliers, which suit the taste of the Greeks who are in charge of the basilica. It is a place of quiet and reverence every day of the year except Christmas.

Whoever enters the Church of the Nativity on the evening of January 6, the Holy Night of the Orthodox Christmas feast (the Eastern Churches reckon according to the Julian calendar!), is greeted with a confusion of languages reminiscent of the Tower of Babel. Throaty chants alternate with murmured prayers, the ringing of bells with the clanking of vigorously swung censers, while thick, sweet clouds of incense hang over everything like a light fog. The bright light of a thousand candles, light bulbs, and spotlights refracts in the fog, turning it into a soft twilight. The church bursts at the seams with people from the different confessions of the Eastern Rite. Each community has secured its corner where priests in seemingly archaic garments celebrate in oriental languages, here the Armenians, there the Syrians, on the other side the Ethiopian and Egyptian Copts, in the center the Greeks, next to them the Russians. They all simultaneously recite their liturgy, wearing heavy colorful brocade garments or simple black cowls and moving through the ancient building in solemn processions, their patriarch or archbishop always in the center. If one ventures too provocatively into the other's territory, a fistfight can easily erupt. And sometimes it seems as though violence is the best guarantor for tolerance.

At some point the Greek patriarch rises from his thronelike seat and, accompanied by his archpriests, descends into the Grotto of the Nativity to pray where God became man. For that he kneels in front of a marble-lined niche in the floor of which a silver-colored star is embedded with the Latin inscription: *Hic de Virgine Maria Jesus Christus natus est*—"Here Jesus Christ was born of the Virgin Mary." Then he turns around and descends three steps, hewn into the rock, into a second room of this cave, likewise floored with marble and draped with embroidered brocade. In front of a feeding trough in the rock, like so many others in the Holy Land, he kneels again and recites the words of the angel: "For to you is born this day in the city of David a Savior, who is Christ the Lord. And this will be a sign for you: you will find a baby wrapped in swaddling cloths and lying in a manger" (Lk 2:11–12). Not in any manger, but in *this* stone manger he lay, according to tradition. For the cave was once a stable. Only we Europeans have imagined the stable in Bethlehem as a wooden shed and elaborately recreated it as a manger scene in a thousand variations. In Palestine, however, where wood is scarce, caves have always served as stables for the animals, and often enough they were also part of the houses, as we can still see today in the ruins near Beit Sahour between Bethlehem and the Herodium; here, too, houses were simply placed in front of a rock face that was honeycombed with caves.

The fact that Mary gave birth to her child in a stable-cave was certainly not a matter of inadequate hotel infrastructure in Bethlehem in the first century B.C. Naturally there was a caravanserai, but it offered only community rooms. Joseph would never have dreamed of letting Mary give birth there. And, consequently, Luke also does not use the Greek word for such an inn, *pandocheion*; according to him, Joseph is looking for a *katalyma*, i.e., a room, mostly on the second floor, which a host places at the disposal of his guests. Mary and Joseph certainly had relatives in the village who lived together under one roof as an oriental extended family. However, there would not have been any separate guest rooms here, either; visitors would sleep in one big room with the hosts. The stable-cave, on the other hand, probably even located on their own property, offered them protection and privacy for a while.

For Orientals in the ancient world, spending the night in a cave was nothing unusual. Today we know that the caves of Qumran, where the Dead Sea Scrolls were discovered, served as living quarters for the religious Essene community. The stone building in the front, on the other hand, was strictly a sort of community center where one would eat, pray, and work, but not spend the night. The first Christian monasteries in Palestine, too, were caves—most of them artificial, i.e., hewn into the soft rock.

The cave below the Church of the Nativity has been venerated since the earliest years, which suggests that it is authentically the site of

Christ's birth. It is mentioned as early as the second century in the
Protoevangelium. Around A.D. 135, Justin Martyr, who was from
Neapolis (now Nablus) in Samaria and thus very familiar with local
tradition, wrote in his *Dialogue with Trypho*: "But, when the Child
was born in Bethlehem, since Joseph could not find a lodging in that
village he took up his quarters in a certain cave near the village."[7]
We owe it to the pagan Roman Emperor Hadrian, of all people,
that this site was preserved throughout the turmoil of the following
centuries. After he had quelled the uprising of the Jewish rebel Simon
Bar Kochba in 135, as a preventive measure he took action against all
messianic movements in Judaism. Not only did he drive the Jews out
of Jerusalem and the vicinity, he also had the most important Jewish
and Jewish-Christian sanctuaries paganized, i.e., converted into heathen places of worship. This happened in Jerusalem on the Temple
Mount, with the Pool of Bethesda, and the rock of Golgotha and,
furthermore, on the Samaritan Mount Garizim and in Bethlehem.
Here he commissioned a cultic grove to be designed over the Grotto
of Jesus' Nativity, in honor of the Syrian Tammuz (Greek: Adonis).
Tammuz was a shepherd god who annually in winter, when life dies,
descended into the underworld, only to reemerge from it in spring,
bringing new life.

This pagan repurposing apparently did not keep the Christians
from venerating the site. Around 220, Origen reports: "In Bethlehem the grotto was shown where, according to the Gospels, Jesus
was born, as well as the manger in which, wrapped in swaddling
clothes, he was laid. What was shown to me is familiar to everyone
in the area. The heathens themselves tell everyone who is willing
to listen that in the said grotto there a certain Jesus was born whom
the Christians revered."[8] Around 315, that is, ten years prior to the
visit of Saint Helena, the Church historian Eusebius confirms: "Up
till the present day the local population [of Bethlehem] bears witness
to the ancestral tradition and proceeds to show visitors the grotto
in which the Virgin gave birth to the Child."[9] As late as 385, Saint

[7] Justin Martyr, *Dialogue with Trypho*, chap. 78, in *Ante-Nicene Fathers*, 1:237.
[8] Origen, *Contra Celsum*, bk. 1, chap. 51, quoted in Bargil Pixner, *Paths of the Messiah and
Sites of the Early Church from Galilee to Jerusalem: Jesus and Jewish Christianity in Light of Archaeological Discoveries* (San Francisco: Ignatius Press, 1020), p. 12.
[9] Eusebius of Caesarea, *Demonstratio Evangelica*, bk. 7, chap. 2, no. 15, quoted in Pixner,
p. 12.

Jerome, who lived in Bethlehem for thirty-four years and translated the Bible into Latin in a cave adjacent to the Grotto of the Nativity, reminded us of this in a letter to his friend Paulinus of Nola: "From the time of Hadrian to the reign of Constantine—a period of about one hundred eighty years—... Bethlehem was overshadowed by a grove of Tammuz, that is, of Adonis; and in the very cave where the infant Christ had uttered His earliest cry lamentation was made for the paramour of Venus."[10] Not until Helena, the emperor's mother, did someone have the power to replace the heathen sanctuary with a Christian one. But the Church Father was no fan of the new splendor. Jerome lamented, for example, the silver lining on the manger that had once been covered with dried mud: "Now, as an honor to Christ, we have taken away the manger that is made of clay and have replaced it with a crib of silver, but more precious to me is the one that has been removed. Silver and gold are proper to heathendom; Christian faith is worthy of the manger that is made of clay.... But I wonder at the Lord, the Creator of the universe, who is born, not surrounded by silver, but by mud and clay."[11]

Today the Church of the Nativity is in the center of Bethlehem; the Biblical village, however, started directly east of the cave. The shepherds, therefore, did not have much trouble finding it when after the appearance of the angel they decided: "Let us go over to Bethlehem ..." (Lk 2:15).

But where were the shepherds camped when the birth of Christ was announced to them? Two properties claim to be the authentic site of the proclamation of "Peace on earth". Both are located in Beit Sahour, a good half a mile east of Bethlehem, a village whose name actually locates a different aspect of the Christmas story—after all, it means "House of the Magi". There, on the plain, the road forks. To the left, it leads north to the Latin Shepherds' Field of the Franciscans, farther to the right is the Greek Shepherds' Field of the Orthodox. In both sanctuaries, the curators are firmly convinced that they are in possession of the only authentic site. A few years ago, a friendly Franciscan who spoke English passably, with a charming Italian accent,

[10] Jerome, Letter LVIII, no. 3, in *Nicene and Post-Nicene Fathers*, ed. Philip Schaff and Henry Wace, 2nd series (1893; Peabody, Mass.: Hendrickson, 1995), 6:120.

[11] Jerome, "Homily on the Nativity of the Lord", in *The Homilies of St. Jerome*, trans. Sr. Marie Liguori Ewald, L.H.M., vol. 2, The Fathers of the Church (1966; Washington, D.C.: University of America Press, 2005), p. 222.

explained to me that three tombs had been discovered on the Latin Shepherds' Field in the nineteenth century, which the pilgrim to the Holy Land Bishop Arculf claimed to have visited and venerated as the "tombs of the shepherds" as early as 680. This prompted the Franciscan archaeologist Father Virgilio Corbo to dig here in 1951/1952. In the course of excavations, he came upon the ruins of a monastery that had been built around 400 and abandoned around 800. Next to it were caves, which, as pottery fragments indicated, were used for habitation purposes in Herodian times.

A somewhat sullen Greek countered that "his" shepherds' field was examined by the archaeologist Vassilios Tzaferis in 1972. During the excavations, he came upon the ruins of as many as five sacred buildings that were used between the fourth and tenth century. The oldest sanctuary proved to be a cave that had been floored with marble around A.D. 350.

The two fields are only 1640 feet apart. I was confused when I left the holy places at the time, and I am still undecided today. Since the Franciscans' shepherds' field is closed today on account of the papal visit, I look around the area and spot a newly opened restaurant immediately to the left of it. Right in the front yard I discover an open limestone cave; soot marks on the ceiling tell me that people used to make camp here. Today there is a cement mixer along with a few sacks of cement, plainly left over from the construction of the restaurant. Inside the cave is a second grotto that was integrated into the new building, equipped with shepherd figures, like a life-size manger scene. From the patio of the grotto restaurant I enjoy the view across the mountains, valleys, and olive tree plantations of Beit Sahour, unfortunately surrounded by ugly new buildings. I joke with the owners that their lovingly furnished restaurant for day-trippers has the potential to become a new destination for pilgrims. For indeed, their caves are probably just as authentic as those on the "shepherds' fields" of the Greeks and Franciscans: all around the area shepherds would have camped near their flocks, just like the Ta'amireh Bedouins of Bethlehem until only a few decades ago.

The Gospel of Matthew, however, ignores the shepherds and focuses, instead, on the more prominent visit to the manger of Christ, that of the *magi* or *magoi*. His account leads to one of the most popular misunderstandings of the Bible—and to the fact that the biggest church in Germany is in the city of Cologne. In Spain, they make children's eyes shine when they drive through the cities on floats, for on their feast day (just as in Italy) the children get their presents. In Germany, children in oriental garments go from house to house as *Sternsinger* (star carolers) in order to collect donations for the Third World. They adorn countless paintings; they are an integral part of every manger scene, even though their figures are usually only put in place on January 6: Christmas is inconceivable without the Three Wise Men.

Saint Helena, so the story goes, brought their remains home from the Orient and bestowed them on Bishop Eustorgius of Milan. When Emperor Frederic I Barbarossa had the Lombardic metropolis plundered in 1164, he donated the relics to his chancellor, Archbishop Rainald von Dassel of Cologne. Their veneration on the Rhine triggered such a flood of pilgrims that soon the city commissioned the building of a mighty cathedral for this purpose, the Cologne Cathedral. To this day, every year on January 6, their shrine is opened and their three-crowned skulls emerge.

There is only one blemish in the triumph of the sainted Three Kings. In the Gospel of Matthew, there is neither mention of them being kings nor mention that there were three of them. Instead, they are referred to as *Magoi apo anatolon*, "magi" or "Wise Men from the East". Liberal theology tries to declare Matthew's Christmas story a myth that was based on Psalm 72 ("May the kings of Tarshish and of the isles render him tribute, may the kings of Sheba and Seba bring gifts! May all kings fall down before him, all nations serve him!"), but the attempt fails. If this had been his intention, the Evangelist, too, would have spoken of kings and not of *magi*, about whom there was plainly no suitable Old Testament prophecy. The Church Fathers were the first to try stubbornly to connect this episode to the words of the psalm, starting with Tertullian, who in the early third century claimed that the *magi* "had the appearance of kings". Origen (185–253) was the first to fix their number at three; their names "Caspar, Melchior, and Balthasar" are recorded as of the sixth century. In ancient Roman catacomb paintings, their number fluctuates between two and four, yet one feature is an integral part of their early Christian iconography: they always wear so-called "Phrygian caps", the classic headgear of Medes and Persians.

The term *magi*, in fact, also tells us where their home was. Since the fifth century B.C., more precisely since the writings of Herodotus, the *Magi* are known in the West as a tribe of Medes that—similar to the Levites in ancient Israel—formed the priestly caste of this western Iranian people. Its capital was Ecbatana, modern-day Hamedan. According to Herodotus, the city mountain of Ecbatana was surrounded by seven rings of wall; in the innermost one were the king's palace and the treasuries. Each one of these rings was apparently painted in a different color. They corresponded to the sun, the moon, and the five planets known at the time.

This alone shows the great importance of astronomy and star worship for the culture of the Medes. Even the erudite Jew Philo of Alexandria, a contemporary of Jesus, said about the "Persian Magi" that they "silently make research into the facts of nature to gain knowledge of the truth."[12] According to the Neoplatonist philosopher Iamblichus (around 300), the great Greek mathematician Pythagoras studied with them. When he was deported to Babylon after his apprenticeship in Egypt, he "gladly associated with the Magi, was instructed by them in their venerable knowledge, and learnt from them the most perfect worship of the Gods. Through their assistance likewise, he arrived at the summit of arithmetic, music, and other disciplines."[13]

At this time, around 600 B.C., a prophet came to the court of the Bactrian King Vishtaspa, who called himself Zoroaster or Zarathustra. Two Magi were ordered to test him and found that his wisdom was far beyond theirs. At their advice, the king adopted the new faith. Zarathustra taught that the earth, though created by God, was the battleground for the eternal battle between good and evil, light and darkness. But in the end, good would prevail, Saoshyant would be born, the savior who destroys evil and brings about a new everlasting world. Then, as it says in the writings of Zarathustra, the dead would rise, too. A majority of the Magi apparently followed him; at any rate, their name soon became the synonym for the priesthood of the new teaching.

---

[12] Philo of Alexandria, *Quod omnis liber probus sit*, 74, quoted in *Philo of Alexandria: A Thinker in the Jewish Diaspora*, ed. Mireille Hadas-Lebel (Leiden: Brill, 2012), p. 172.

[13] Iamblichus, *Life of Pythagoras, or Pythagoric Life* ..., trans. Thomas Taylor (London: Watkins, 1818), p. 9.

Early on, the followers of Zoroastrianism came in touch with Judaism. After all, the Assyrians had already settled the deported inhabitants of the northern kingdom of Israel "in the cities of the Medes" among others (2 Kings 17:6). When Darius the Mede took over the kingship from the Babylonians in 539 B.C., he resided in Ecbatana during the summer; the Biblical prophet Daniel, too, was a member of his court. The wife of Ahasuerus (485–465 B.C.), Queen Esther, even founded a Jewish colony in Ecbatana. To this day, her tomb is venerated in Hamedan. Henceforth the Jewish community enjoyed great renown among the Medes. The Acts of the Apostles (Acts 2:9) likewise report that "Parthians and Medes and Elamites" went to Jerusalem for the Feast of Weeks and witnessed the miracle of Pentecost.

How well versed the Magi were in astronomy and astrology is evidenced in the oldest and at the same time most monumental horoscope in antiquity. The *Hierothesion* of King Antiochus I of Commagene (69–36 B.C.) in southern Turkey, now known as Nemrut Dagi (Mount Nimrod), is located on the summit of the highest mountain in the area. It consists of a giant pyramidal burial mound 164 feet high, and at its feet is an assembly of colossal statues that, facing east, greet the rising sun in the morning and the stars at night. Over the course of time, their heads became separated from their bodies on account of heavy earthquakes, but that does not in the least diminish the monumentality of the structure. The statues testify to the faith of Antiochus, which can be characterized as a "Hellenized form of Zoroastrianism": Greek gods were equated with Persian-oriental counterparts. The central figure was Zeus, the godfather of the Greek pantheon, who was identified with Ahura Mazda (lit.: Oromasdes), the light god of Zoroastrianism. Next to him stood the statue of the goddess of destiny Tyche/Ashi; behind her, the effigy of Apollo as Mithras the Persian, with Phrygian cap. At the right hand of Zeus, however, sat the youthful Antiochus himself, alongside Heracles in the guise of Verethragna, the Persian god of victory. The row of five statues was accompanied by lions and eagles, the heraldic animals of the Commagenian crown. The monumental sculpture of a lion is covered with stars. As early as 1920, the German astro-archaeologist Otto Neugebauer noticed that this was not a random depiction but a detailed horoscope. The statue itself stands for the Leo constellation, the three "stars" for the planets Jupiter, Mercury, and Mars. Below the lion's head, the sickle of the moon is depicted. Altogether this forms a very specific astronomical constellation: it points to a date on which these three planets and the moon were in the constellation Leo. As Neugebauer calculated, this was the case on July 14 of 109 B.C., the day Antiochus' father, Mithridates, was crowned, the birth of his dynasty. This day had previously been calculated as auspicious by the Magi, whom Antiochus in his dedicatory inscription called "priests in the robes of the Persian race".

But just as the astronomical-astrological knowledge of the Magi helped determine the day of Mithridates' crowning, it can help us solve the riddle of the Star of Bethlehem.

"Where is he who has been born king of the Jews? For we have seen his star in the East, and have come to worship him", the Magi are quoted by Matthew (Mt 2:2). For centuries, exegetes and scholars have wondered what kind of celestial event could have been meant by this. While at first they thought it was a comet, this explanation soon failed. The last noteworthy comet that appeared around the birth of Christ was Halley's Comet. It was visible from October of 12 B.C. to February of 11 B.C.—too early to fit the presumed date of Jesus' birth.

In the twelfth and fifteenth centuries, Jewish scholars interpreted a conjunction of the planets Jupiter and Saturn in the constellation Pisces as a portent of the Messiah's birth. In 1603, the astronomer Johannes Kepler observed such a conjunction himself, followed one year later by a supernova, the explosion of a star. The astronomer believed that there was a connection between the two events and suspected a similar celestial event at the birth of Christ. Indeed, he calculated that in 7 B.C. nothing less than a triple conjunction had occurred between Saturn and Jupiter. Then, too, Kepler concluded, soon afterward a star must have flared up as brightly as the supernova did in his time. Now we know that there is absolutely no connection between conjunctions in the solar system and the explosion of a star that is a thousand light-years away. And yet, the great astronomer brought us onto the right track.

In 1965, the Italian astronomer Konradin Ferrari d'Occhieppo drew on Kepler's calculation when he interpreted the Star of Bethlehem as the triple conjunction of Jupiter and Saturn in the Pisces constellation. Jupiter, as shown in Nemrut Dagi, was equated by the Magi with the heavenly god Ahura Mazda; Saturn was considered the planet of the Jewish people, who particularly honor the day of Saturn, Saturday or Shabbat. Cuneiform tablets found by archaeologists in 1925 in Borsippa in modern-day Iraq actually confirm the observance of this conjunction by Babylonian astronomers as well. "We have seen his star rising", in d'Occhieppo's opinion, referred to the Magi's observing the two planets in the darkening evening sky around September 15 of 7 B.C. At that time, they had departed, reaching Jerusalem eight weeks later, where they were reminded of the words of the prophet Micah:

> But you, O Bethlehem Ephrathah,
> who are little to be among the clans of Judah,
> from you shall come forth for me
> one who is to be ruler in Israel. (Mic 5:2)

On November 12 of 7 B.C., shortly before sunrise, they would have had the two planets right before their eyes, if they had been riding from Jerusalem toward Bethlehem, which is only six miles away. According to the Italian astronomer, this was the observation to which Matthew (2:10) could have been referring: "When they saw the star, they rejoiced exceedingly with great joy." After the beginning of astronomical dusk, the pair of planets would have stood at the top of the zodiacal light cone. This would have given the impression that this light came from the binary star. The axis of the light cone consistently pointed toward the village in front of them, the silhouette of which became apparent before them.

If d'Occhieppo's thesis is correct, Matthew would have described the celestial event with astonishing linguistic precision. And yet it seems insufficient to me. Was a simple conjunction, as it occurs every few decades, really sufficient to indicate to the Magi the birth of their longingly awaited redeemer?

The renowned British astronomer Mark Kidger, who conducts research at the observatory of Tenerife in the Canary Islands, does not believe the Jupiter-Saturn conjunction in itself is the answer to the riddle. In his 1999 study *The Star of Bethlehem*, published by Princeton University Press, he aims to prove that the Magi observed as many as four significant celestial events. Indeed, Kidger says, the triple conjunction of Jupiter and Saturn would have announced to them that a new great king would be born in Judaea. But this would not yet have been a reason to make the long arduous journey to pay homage to a newborn. But a second celestial sign got their attention. One year later, in 6. B.C., there was another triple conjunction, this time of Jupiter, Saturn, and Mars in the Pisces constellation. Mars indicated a significant upheaval; Pisces indicated the new astrological vernal equinox, i.e., a new era. Of course, this conjunction was relevant only in astrological terms; in the sky it hardly seemed spectacular at all. This changed on February 20 of 5 B.C., when the new moon and Jupiter on one side, Saturn and Mars on the other, formed two uneven pairs in the sky. Astrologically speaking, this not only indicated to the Magi that a great king (Jupiter) is born and rises (new moon) to rule over Israel (Saturn), but also that he will fight evil (Mars) and herald a new era (Pisces).

The Jewish messianic expectations must have been familiar to them; after all, there were enough Jews living in their country, and the parallels to their own hope for the coming of the Saoshyant were obvious. The Jews in turn considered Zarathustra a "disciple of the prophet Daniel", so close were Jewish and Zoroastrian thinking, so obvious the mutual influence. It was no coincidence that the Old Testament prophet "in the first year of Darius the Mede ... stood up to confirm and strengthen him" (Dan 11:1), that the Persian Cyrus released the Jews from captivity and even financed the reconstruction of the Temple in Jerusalem. It was no accident that the Hasmonean Antigonus asked the Parthians for help, and as late as the seventh century the Persian Khosrau was feared by Christians as the "Scourge of God" and celebrated by the Jews as liberator. For 1,100 years, friendship and mutual respect united Jews, Medes, and Persians, and the foundation of this relationship was the teaching of Zarathustra. For this very reason, it is possible that the Magi now considered the birth of their messiah Saoshyant in Israel. While in the weeks to come they observed the winter sky even more attentively and eagerly, the unexpected happened. All of a sudden, when the sun was in the constellation Pisces, a new star flared up. From Chinese and Korean records (namely, the Chinese book *Ch'ien-han-shu* and the Korean chronicle *Samguk Sagi*), Kidger gathered that from the middle of March to the end of May in the Aquila constellation, near the star Theta Aquilae, a supernova, a star explosion, was observed for seventy-six days. This matches the description of the "Star of Bethlehem" in the *Protoevangelium*, which quotes the Magi: "We have seen a star of great size shining among these stars, and obscuring their light".[14] In Judaism, too, a flaring star was considered a portent of the Messiah. Stars were depicted on Hasmonean coins; the leader of the second Jewish revolt called himself Bar Kochba, "Son of the Star", after Rabbi Akiva had declared him the Messiah. Likewise was it prophesied in the days of Moses by the seer Balaam: "A star shall come forth out of Jacob, and a scepter shall rise out of Israel" (Num 24:17). The Magi must have departed for Jerusalem immediately after the fourth and final celestial sign. The seventy-six days during which, according to the Asian sources, the supernova was visible should have been sufficient for the journey. But no one knows where the journey began. Borsippa or Babylon are rather unlikely, since the Parthian empire was at enmity with Rome and Herod, and its inhabitants would not have been received well in Jerusalem. Perhaps the Magi were from Commagene, where their religion had been established since the days of King Mithridates, or straight from Media, which at the time was independent of Persia, and Ecbatana, the city of Daniel and Esther. Both states were at the time allied with Armenia, the third major power in the Middle East during the first century B.C. When the Armenian King Tiridates visited Rome during the reign of Nero, he was accompanied by Magi, as Plinius relates; an indication of their important role in ancient Armenia, too.

According to celestial mechanics, a star that is first visible in the east would appear half an hour earlier each week until after two months it would stand exactly in the south. When the Magi at dawn went on their way from Jerusalem to Bethlehem, which is south of the capital, they consequently must have had the star right in front of them.

Kidger's hypothesis would also explain another statement by Matthew. When they inquired after the newborn king in Jerusalem, the Magi also appeared in Herod's palace. When he learned of the strange visitors, he was struck with fear. Merely a few months before that, the paranoid king had had his two sons killed, along with the Hasmonean

---

[14] "The Protoevangelium of James", 21, in *Ante-Nicene Fathers*, 8:366.

princess Mariamne, because he had accused them of conspiracy. Antigonus, the last king of the Hasmonean dynasty, had already allied himself with the Parthians and put Herod to flight. Would a new claimant to the throne, with the aid of the third major power in the East, Armenia, now reach for the crown? Would Herod's destiny repeat itself? Would his life not end in the luxury of his palaces but in exile? Certainly the old, sick king would not again muster the strength to return at the head of an army and reconquer his kingdom. Thus his reaction to the Magi's strange request, for all its brutality, is at least comprehensible. When he grasped that the delegation from the east was not returning to his court to report to him, he gave an order that, although by far not his bloodiest, caused him to go down in history forever as a monster: "He sent and killed all the male children in Bethlehem and in all that region who were two years old or under, according to the time which he had ascertained from the Wise Men" (Mt 2:16).

The time frame that Matthew describes matches the sequence of the celestial events as Kidger reconstructs them. The Magi, for that matter, did not know when the child they had come to see was born. But they could tell exactly when they had observed the first constellation that announced his birth: in the beginning of May of 7 B.C., Jupiter and Saturn had first met in the constellation Pisces; in the beginning of May of 5 B.C., the supernova had led them to Jerusalem. There were exactly two years in between. It becomes even more interesting when we read in the account of the pilgrim nun Egeria from the year 383 that the feast of the Holy Innocents of Bethlehem was originally celebrated on May 18. Under this date, it is also listed in the old Armenian holiday calendar. Could a specific memory be behind this; did Herod, indeed, on May 18 of 5 B.C., give the order to kill all boys in Bethlehem who had been born since the first constellation in May of 7 B.C.—thus "according to the time which he had ascertained from the wise men"?

Of course, it is much more convenient simply to disregard the Biblical text, to declare it a symbolic preaching theme without real background, as historical-critical Bible exegesis often attempts to do. Certainly, the frequent references to Biblical prophecies is typical, especially for Matthew, who specifically addresses Jewish-Christian readers; but does the fulfillment of a prophecy automatically rule out the possibility that an event did indeed occur in this very way? Should it not, on the other hand, make one wonder why modern astronomy can confirm such a precise date—two years—to the exact month?

Admittedly, only Matthew mentions the massacres of the children of Bethlehem. Nevertheless, the results of archaeological excavations in Bethlehem lead to the conclusion that only three hundred to one thousand people were living in the city of David during the time of Jesus. If Herod had indeed killed all "boys who were two years old or under", the number of his victims might perhaps have been ten to twenty, or thirty at the very most. That is terrible, but it would have gone unnoticed in the bloody frenzy that marked the last years of the paranoid tyrant. On the contrary, the deed fits the image that historical sources, first and foremost Flavius Josephus, convey of the last phase in Herod's life. Only one Jewish document from before A.D. 70, the so-called *Assumption of Moses*, seems to allude to the massacre of the children and liken it to the Biblical Pharaoh's order to have all newborn sons killed (Ex 1:22), when it says there: "And an insolent king shall succeed them, who will not be of the race of the priests, a man bold and shameless, . . . He shall slay the old and the young, and he shall not spare. Then the fear of him shall be bitter unto them in their land. And he shall execute judgements on them as the Egyptians executed upon them."[15]

We do not know how old Jesus was at this time. It is certainly appealing to imagine that he was born when the supernova flared up in the beginning of March of 5 B.C., and nothing speaks against this hypothesis. Censuses were always conducted in the winter when the farmers' work was suspended. But since all over Judaea, starting on the fifteenth day of Adar (in that year February 24), the Temple tax was collected from all adult male Jews anyway, it is quite possible that Herod conducted the census simultaneously. The presence of shepherds and flocks of sheep likewise makes a date in the last weeks of winter plausible. "The herds are brought to the pastures in *Nisan* (March) and led back to the stables in *Marcheshvan* (November)", it says in the Talmud; the first day of Nisan in 5 B.C. fell on March 9. As early as the end of February, the grass in Bethlehem sprouts after

[15] "The Assumption of Moses", 6.5–6, in R. H. Charles, ed., *The Apocrypha and Pseudepigrapha of the Old Testament* (1913; Berkeley: Apocryphile Press, 2004), 2:418–19.

the first winter rain. It grows increasingly luxuriant until it dies in the heat of the spring sun. During this time, larger herds of sheep find plenty of nourishment in the hills and meadows between the village and the desert. The nights are still cool, but in the glow of a warming fire, the shepherds can find shelter in the caves in the area. Luke's scenario therefore corresponds well to a birth of Jesus in March. The Lamb of God came into the world when the Paschal lambs were born, too, as innocent and pure as they whose destiny he would one day share. Eight days after his birth (and thus immediately before or after the *Pessach* feast, which in 5 B.C. started on March 22), he was circumcised as a Jewish boy; after forty days he was subjected to the "purification according to the law of Moses" in the Temple and presented to the Lord (Lk 2:22). This, then, would have occurred toward the end of April. The approaching Jewish Feast of Weeks (on May 12–13 of 5 B.C.) perhaps offered an opportunity to delay the strenuous journey home with the infant when suddenly the Magi appeared. In the *Protoevangelium*, we read: "And, behold, Joseph was ready to go into Judaea. And there was a great commotion in Bethlehem of Judaea, for Magi came...."[16] Heeding the advice of the Magi, the Holy Family did not return to Nazareth now but fled to Egypt. They took the same path on which Herod had escaped with his family thirty-five years before, past the fortress-mountain of the Herodium, past the Dead Sea.

Within a year, the old King of the Jews died in terrible torment. The people interpreted this as God's just punishment for his raving, for the innumerable murders. He believed he would find his final rest on the slope of his favorite fortress, his gaze fixed on Jerusalem, the center of his rule, but also on Bethlehem, from whence he saw it challenged. But his rest in death did not last long; the people took terrible revenge on his precious sarcophagus and the corpse. The time of the tyrant was over. But to this day, Bethlehem has not found the peace that had been promised to it.

---

[16] "Protoevangelium of James", 21, p. 366.

IV

His Father's House

Where Jesus Prayed

Today, Jerusalem is one of the few cities whose historic district is still surrounded by a completely intact city wall. Its current wall enclosure comes from the Ottoman era, but its course has remained unchanged since Roman times—more precisely, since A.D. 135, when Emperor Hadrian founded the new city of Aelia Capitolina on the ruins of the old Jerusalem after the defeat of the Bar Kochba rebellion. He named the city after himself (his full name was Publius Aelius Hadrianus) and after the Capitoline Jupiter (Zeus), to whom he erected a sanctuary on the Temple Mount. In contrast, he forbade the Jews to enter the city. His successor, Antoninus Pius, was the first to allow them to come to Jerusalem once a year, on April 9, in order to mourn their defeat, the destruction of the Temple, and their exile. As the site for their memorial, they chose a piece of the Temple's western supporting wall that once was right next to the Holy of Holies. To this day it is known as the Wailing Wall.

The gates of the city wall were locked, the city center hermetically barricaded, when Pope Benedict XVI came to the Jewish quarter of the historic district on May 12, 2009, in order to pray on the Temple Mount and at the Wailing Wall. So it happens that, with the public practically excluded, the pope humbly and nonchalantly overcomes the chasm between the world religions.

It is still early in the morning, under radiant sunshine, when his black limousine drives into the historic district through the Lion's Gate. His first goal is the cupola of the Dome of the Rock, whose gold shines even brighter on this day. "*As salamu alaikum!*" "Peace be with you", Benedict XVI greets the Islamic Grand Mufti, who is already waiting for him there. And then the pope takes off his shoes. For the Dome of the Rock, he means by this, is also for Christians. After all, it is not a mosque but, rather, a memorial construction erected over the rock on which Abraham once intended to sacrifice his son Isaac, on which King Solomon built the first Temple, on which the Ark of the Covenant once stood. Here resided the Holy of Holies, the center of Judaism, which even the high priest himself was allowed to enter only once a year in order to pray there on the Day of Reconciliation. If in Jerusalem, the holy city of three world religions, there is any ground that is holy to all, then this is it.

Now the pope prays on this spot for a reconciliation between the peoples and religions that seems to be so far away. Unlike the other stops along his trip into the Holy Land, this moment is not broadcast on live television. The cameramen of the Israeli State TV, which had procured the broadcasting rights for Benedict's trip to Israel, had been forbidden by the Muslims to set foot on the Temple Mount. Since the Second Intifada, the Jews are as unwanted here as they were at the time of Emperor Hadrian.

Instead, Benedict XVI comes to them afterward. Across a bridge that once led up to the Temple, he drives down to the plaza in front of the Wailing Wall, which is now officially called the Western Wall. There, where otherwise faithful Jews pray, one sees mainly two kinds of people: a couple of authorized journalists and many, many security officers. All of them wear a Jewish *kippa* on their heads out of respect. The pope's head is, as always, covered with a white *pileolus*. The rabbi of the Wailing Wall, Shmuel Rabinovich, greets the guest from Rome and escorts him to a tall lectern. In a loud voice, he recites Psalm 122 in Hebrew, which Pope Benedict XVI repeats in Latin: " 'Let us go to the house of the LORD!' Our feet have been standing within your gates, O Jerusalem!... May they prosper who love you!... For my brethren and companions' sake I will say, 'Peace be within you!' For the sake of the house of the LORD our God, I will seek your good."

It is the same psalm that all pilgrims to Jerusalem since time immemorial have prayed, Jesus and his family, too, when they visited the Temple during the three great feasts of the Jewish year—*Pessach*, the Feast of Weeks (*Shavuot*), and the Feast of Tabernacles (*Sukkot*). But the prayer has remained unanswered until now. Even today Jerusalem hopes in vain for peace. With every passing year, peace seems to move farther away.

Then the pope turns around and walks directly to the wall. Just as the then already seriously ill John Paul II did nine years ago, so too Benedict XVI slides a folded slip of paper with his very personal prayer for peace into one of the cracks between the ashlars. The slender, small man in white remains standing without speaking before the golden brown wall, and it is as if time would stand still with him. A deep silence settles over the plaza, indeed over all Jerusalem, interrupted only by the shouts of excited security officers. A gentle breeze stirs, catching the papal mozetta as if it wanted to carry the visitor from Rome into heaven. A dove descends and settles above him in a caper bush. Even the chirping of two swallows that built their nest high up in the wall is still clearly audible. Only when this minute has disappeared into eternity does the pope turn around, walk back with his hands still folded in prayer, and greet a waiting group of rabbis.

My friend Gary Krupp, who is following the papal trip from New York, is a bit disappointed with this moment. For years he has worked for reconciliation between Jews and Christians with his Pave-the-Way Foundation. He is himself a Jew and Papal Knight of Honor at the same time, as well as a loyal friend of Benedict XVI. When he was visiting me in Düsseldorf three weeks before, he wrote another email to Monsignor Georg Gänswein, the pope's secretary. Would it not be a nice gesture if the pope would speak about the Wailing Wall as the "place in which Jesus, too, prayed"? Benedict XVI declined the proposed formulation, even though his prayer was itself the most profound bow before the holiness of the place. But nonetheless, I cannot dismiss the thought of Gary's formulation. I had to think of it as I viewed the excavations around the Temple Mount one week before the papal visit. There is no holier ground than this and also no more authentic place of encounter with the historical Jesus of Nazareth, who came here throughout his life to pray "in his Father's house". The Temple was the center of Jewish life in the early first century A.D.—and for this reason the center of Jesus' life, too.

The Temple, however, was also the second face of the Janus-headed child-murderer of Bethlehem, Herod's quasi-courtship of his people's heart. He knew that, with this project, he would inspire and propitiate the Jews who followed with increasing skepticism his

Romanization program for Judaea (the construction of chariot tracks, theaters, and magnificent palaces). It would let him, Rome's puppet-king, appear as the "new Solomon" and as the loyal servant of the Jewish God, and thereby legitimate his rule. And it was supposed to silence the Jewish elite, who increasingly turned up their noses at his pedigree, at the fact that he was not a Hasmonean, much less a descendant of David, and not even a proper Jew. His father, Anti-pater, was an Idumean, thus a member of a Canaanite people who were first forcibly converted to Judaism under King John Hyrcanus. Yet his mother was a Gentile Nabataean from the mountain city of Petra in present-day Jordan. "You should not set someone who is not your brother above yourself", teaches the Torah, which was cited again and again by his opponents. Thus, he needed to prove at all costs that he was in fact a good Jew. He did this by building a temple to God such as the ancient world, which certainly did not lack mag-nificent sanctuaries, had never seen before.

He had the work begin during the eighteenth year of his reign, thus around 20/19 B.C., according to Flavius Josephus. The largest building project of the ancient world since the construction of the pyramids was carefully prepared. Herod began his work only after he had acquired one thousand wagons to transport the stones, selected ten thousand experienced craftsmen, purchased new vestments for one thousand priests, and had the priests educated, partly in masonry and partly in carpentry, so that no unworthy man would have to tread on this holy ground.

First of all, he had the square platform on which the Second Tem-ple already stood appropriately enlarged. If before the surface area amounted to 650 by 650 feet, or 420,000 square feet, the new Tem-ple Mount platform became a trapezoid of 1,590 feet long on the western side and 1,030 feet wide on the northern side, hence with a surface area of over 1,640,000 square feet, or thirty-five acres. That corresponds to a Jewish surface measurement of 144 *dunam*, behind which is hidden the square of the number twelve, the number of the tribes of Israel. In this way, Herod built the biggest temple platform in the Mediterranean region. In comparison to it, even the Acropo-lis of Athens, with its surface area of barely seven acres, or the holy district of Olympia, with its surface area of 8.6 acres, must appear to be meager. This gigantic area was surrounded by a fifteen-foot-thick supporting wall made out of massive ashlars that were up to 150 feet tall. The wall was built at a slight angle in order to withstand better the pressure from within. The stones came from a quarry 1.2 miles northwest of the city, where the girls' school of the Jerusalem suburb Ramat Shlomo now stands. It was first discovered in 2007 during the construction of the school. And one of the stones has a very special history, to which Jesus, too, made reference: "Jesus said to them, 'Have you never read in the Scriptures: "The very stone which the builders rejected has become the cornerstone; this was the Lord's doing, and it is marvelous in our eyes"?'" (Mt 21:42).

This cornerstone really exists. It can still be found today at the southwest corner of the Temple in the eighth course of stones above ground, the twenty-eighth above the rocky ground. With a weight of over a hundred tons, it is likely the heaviest stone of the entire outer wall. It plainly served as a stabilizer. Because, at six feet tall, it was much bigger than the other stones of the Temple wall, the row that began with it was continued by two extra layers of ashlar hewn to be smaller. Clearly, the stone masons had miscalculated during its production. In any case, it did not have the desired size when it reached the construction site, and the builders would have discarded it if one of them had not had a bright idea. He simply had slender stones inserted edgewise on both sides to fill the gaps. Thus the stone with the wrong measurements nonetheless still became the cornerstone, and its sheer size still amazes us.

Usually, the limestone ashlars in use were at least one yard high, one and a half to two yards long, and weighed five to six tons. But where the stress load was most intense, i.e., under the Temple itself, the builders laid stones that had a length of up to forty-six feet and a weight of up to 570 tons—a feat that was first outperformed one and a half centuries later during the construction of the temple platform of Baalbek in Lebanon. The interstice between the old platform and the new boundary wall was not simply filled with dirt; it was, rather, stabilized and neutralized by a three-storied archway construction. This was necessary according to the Jewish faith, in the event that old graves were still located in the rock caverns of Mount Moriah. Only the open space that the archways created would neutralize the impurity that came from the graves and prevent any defilement of the Temple.

Herod had the entire Temple Mount platform paved with golden-brown limestone slabs and surrounded by porticoes. This created a giant courtyard that now was called the Court of the Gentiles, since everyone, even a non-Jew, could set foot in it. A marble balustrade within it demarcated the holy area that was reserved exclusively for Jews. Stone tablets warned that the death penalty awaited non-Jewish trespassers.

The actual Temple was found within this holy area, which in its dimensions roughly corresponded to the old Temple platform. The Temple was situated on a terrace with steps leading up to it on all sides and was surrounded by a two-part atrium. The outer atrium was called the Women's Courtyard, since it was open to all believers. Although it had gates on all three sides, its main entrance was the so-called Beautiful Gate to the east. The gate was fashioned from the finest Corinthian brass and was extravagantly decorated. Its door-wings were so heavy that only two strong men together could move them. Inside, the Women's Courtyard was surrounded on three sides by colonnades. In the corners, there were chambers in which firewood, oil, and wine were stored and in which believers could prepare themselves for their sacrifice in the Temple after a special purification or an oath. In front of these chambers stood mighty candleholders that illuminated the courtyard at night during the Feast of Tabernacles. Thirteen chests with trumpet-shaped attachments served as poor-boxes. Here pilgrims deposited the equivalent of the prescribed minimum offering, two turtle doves.

In the west, the Women's Courtyard borders on the marble-wainscoted façade of the inner court, also called the Courtyard of the Israelites, which is reserved exclusively for male Jews who have first undergone a ritual purification. Its only entrance for non-priests was through the richly decorated, gold-adorned Nikanor Gate, which, like the Heavenly Gates, always stood open. Leading up to it was a semicircular staircase with fifteen steps, which ended in a marble-paved vestibule. It was in this vestibule, in front of the open gate, that everything took place that needed to occur "before the face of the Lord": there lepers showed themselves to the priests after their purification, women who were suspected of adultery drank the "water of jealousy", and here the forty-day-old child Jesus was "presented in the Temple".

The Courtyard of the Israelites, 279 by 203 feet in size, was divided in two once again. A low balustrade made from finely worked limestone separated the area of the lay people from that of the priests.

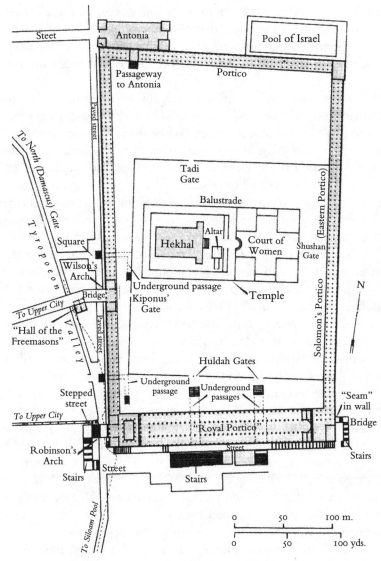

Floor plan of the Temple of Jerusalem at the time of Jesus

In its center stood a square sacrificial altar eighty-two feet wide on which three fires always burned: one for the animal sacrifices, one for incense, and a third from which to reignite the first two. A broad stone ramp led up to it. To the right of the altar, the sacrificial animals were tied up until it was their turn. In one corner of the courtyard stood a huge brass water basin that could be used by twelve priests at once. A perfect supply network ensured that the Temple was always provided with fresh water while sewage and blood could immediately drain off.

Behind the altar, twelve steps once again led up into the Temple, the broad front of which rose majestically above the inner courtyard. Flanked by four columns, its square, white marble façade loomed 164 feet into the air. "Now the outward face of the temple in its front wanted nothing that was likely to surprise either men's minds or their eyes; for it was covered all over with plates of gold of great weight", Flavius Josephus gushed, "and, at the first rising of the sun, reflected back a very fiery splendor, and made those who forced themselves to look upon it to turn their eyes away, just as they would have done at the sun's own rays. But this temple appeared to strangers, when they were coming to it at a distance, like a mountain covered with snow; for as to those parts of it that were not gilt, they were exceeding white."[1]

Behind the façade, the Temple was two-storied; inside it was once again divided in two to form the sanctuary and the Holy of Holies. Its entrance was surrounded by grapevine shoots made of pure gold and man-sized golden grapes. A magnificent curtain concealed the interior of the sanctuary from the eyes of the faithful. The interior was accessible only to the priests on duty. Here stood the seven-branched menorah, the showbread table, and, in the center directly in front of the entrance to the Holy of Holies, the altar of incense. A wooden wall partitioned off the Holy of Holies. Its entrance was covered by a heavy curtain. Its interior was empty; the Ark of the Covenant had already gone missing during the days of the First Temple. Only a bare rock still protruded from the marble floor where the Ark had once stood. The high priest sprinkled it with blood once per year, during Yom Kippur, when he was allowed to appear before God.

But the Temple was neither the sole nor the largest building on the Herodian platform. The Royal Hall, one of the most impressive structures of the Near East, extended diagonally across the platform's south side. It resembled a triple-naved basilica, 607 feet long and 98 feet tall, supported by four times forty columns with

---

[1] Flavius Josephus, *The Jewish War*, bk. 5, chap. 5, no. 6, in *The New Complete Works of Josephus*, trans. William Whiston (Grand Rapids, Mich.: Kregel, 1999), pp. 856–57.

Corinthian capitals, and with a raised central nave that once more rested on two times forty columns. The sight of this splendid hall situated on the platform, which was here over sixty-five feet tall, must have been breathtaking. "This cloister deserves to be mentioned better than any other under the sun", as Josephus described it; "if anyone looked down from the top of the battlements, or down both those altitudes, he would be giddy."[2] The Sanhedrin, or the high council of the Jews over which the high priest presided, met in its apse "forty years before the destruction of the Temple", thus from the year A.D. 30 on. The money changers and animal vendors had their booths in the side naves. This was where the Holy Family purchased the prescribed sacrifice, "a pair of turtledoves or two young doves" for the Presentation of the Child Jesus in the Temple forty days after his birth—in other words, in late April, A.D. 5. That was the minimum offering for the people; for those who could afford, it was better to offer "a lamb a year old for a burnt offering" (Lev 12:6). Archaeologists who dug at the base of the Royal Hall found a stone weight on which the word *corban* (sacrifice) had been engraved in Hebrew along with two doves.

As impressive as the structures on the Temple platform must have been, Herod had designed the staircases that led up to it in just as monumental a fashion. The first of these was the Royal Bridge. It crossed the Tyropaion Valley that separated Mount Moriah, on which the Temple stood, from the new city on the western hill and thereby also from the royal palace. Even today, the beginning of this bridge and its first mighty archway remain intact. It borders the Wailing Wall to the north and is today used by Orthodox rabbis as a school for the Torah and as a place of prayer. It is called Wilson's Arch, named after the British researcher who had first investigated it in 1865. The second monumental staircase crossed Robinson's Arch, named after the American Edward Robinson, who identified it as early as 1838. Its tail end projects even today from out of the southwestern wall of the Temple Mount. From here, a monumental staircase led in two right angles up to a splendidly decorated gate, which was placed in front of the Royal Hall. "Whoever has not seen the Temple of Herod, has never known a truly beautiful building!" as

---

[2] Flavius Josephus, *Jewish Antiquities*, bk. 15, chap. 11, no. 5, in *New Complete Works of Josephus*, p. 524.

one rabbi from Babylon gushed. Even Gentile visitors to Jerusalem could not help agreeing with him. But only archaeology could reveal just how magnificent, how monumental, the construction truly was.

Yet digging on the Temple Mount itself is not allowed. What was once the supreme sanctuary of the Jews is today under the control of the Waqf, the Muslim administration. For them, the place is not holy because Yahweh's Temple once stood here (which the Muslim Palestinians fiercely contest), but rather because they believe that Muhammad visited it one night on a heavenly horse. They even claim to discern the hoofprint of this miraculous animal on the rock beneath the Dome of the Rock. For this reason, they call Temple Mount *Haram Ash-Sharif*, "the sublime sanctuary".

While it is impossible for a historian to understand it, their denial of the sanctuary's Jewish past explains their irresponsible handling of its remains. When in recent years the Waqf built an underground mosque next to the Al Aqsa Mosque on the southern side of the Temple Mount, dirt was shoveled out by the tons using an excavator and indiscriminately dumped in East Jerusalem. Archaeologists were not allowed access during the construction work, allegedly because there was nothing to investigate. Fortunately, the Israeli Antiquities Authority ultimately managed to locate the dump and to save a few fragments that testify to the rich ornamentation of the Royal Hall.

Much better explored, in contrast, is the terrain at the foot of the southwest corner of the Temple Mount, which belongs to the Jewish quarter of Jerusalem's old city. Excavations there began immediately after the conquest of East Jerusalem in the Six Day War. Yet archaeologists had to fight on two fronts at once: on the one side stood the conservative rabbis for whom an archaeological dig was equivalent to a profanation of sacred ground. On the other side, the Waqf, with the support of the Arab world, accused the Israelis of trying to undermine the Al Aqsa Mosque with their excavations. The matter even made it twice, in 1968 and 1974, onto the agenda of the United Nations. This was the first time in history that an archaeological search for clues became a world-class political issue. Luckily, the Israelis ignored the resolution of the UNO and of its culture agency UNESCO, even when they were officially reprimanded in 1974. On the contrary, the political condemnations only led them to work at full speed. Although at first there was talk of finishing the excavations "in our generation", suddenly it took only twelve years. In the process, 79,251,616 gallons of earth were dug up and at least for the most part combed through for potsherds and building fragments. What remained ended up in avalanches of debris that made their way down into the Kidron and Hinnom Valleys. Any pilgrim to Jerusalem who is looking for an authentic antiquity from the time of Jesus can effortlessly (and legally) pull potsherds, handles, and oil lamp fragments from the earth here. The excavation leader, Meir Ben-Dov, occasionally used a bulldozer in order to advance more quickly, a method that fortunately is frowned on by archaeologists elsewhere. Since then, Ben-Dov has been considered a pariah among his colleagues, and his book, *In the Shadow of the Temple Mount*, was not reviewed by any respectable scholarly journal. But no one disputes the fact that he made amazing discoveries, in spite of his controversial and drastic methods.

His most spectacular find was the great Temple staircase on the south side of the platform that was situated in front of the two Hulda Gates, the twofold and the threefold gate. The Hulda Gates were entrances to tunnels that led from under the Royal Hall by an oblique way up into the Temple courtyard. Over three hundred fragments of the rich decoration that once ornamented the walls and ceilings of the passages were also discovered. Although both gates had been walled shut by Muslims, they are still clearly discernible in the masonry. On this staircase, which one can now view in the Archaeological Park all around the southwest corner of the Temple Mount, millions of Jewish pilgrims have entered their greatest holy place—one of them was Jesus of Nazareth. This was also the scene of the only episode from the childhood of Jesus recorded for us by Luke.

The event, which probably occurred on April 20 in A.D. 8 (in that year, Passover took place from April 9–17), is recounted briefly. As they did every year (and the Evangelist expressly emphasizes this; see Lk 2:41), Jesus' parents had made the pilgrimage to Jerusalem in order to celebrate Passover. Participation in the greatest of the Temple celebrations was obligatory for all Jews; thus the whole country rested from work. Entire villages went together on pilgrimage. Half of Galilee crossed through the land of the Samaritans as a single, endless caravan. For the twelve-year-old Jesus, it was the first time that he was allowed to go with them. He was supposed to celebrate his Bar

Mitzvah the next year and was therefore considered to be responsible for practicing his faith, a full-fledged member of the community of believing Jews. From now on, he would be allowed to read from the Torah during worship and to wear the *tefillin* on his hand and head, leather boxes into which verses from the Torah were sewed.

After the conclusion of the eight-day Passover celebration, the pilgrim caravan set off on the return trip. In pilgrim caravans, the women and children usually went ahead while the men and adolescents followed behind. Only in the evenings did everyone come together again in the same tent. So Mary and Joseph first noticed during their first break that Jesus had not come with them. Likely at their wits' end, they therefore returned the next morning to Jerusalem. We can literally hear how Joseph talked to his wife: "Tell me, Mary, where did you last see the boy? Try to remember!" Again and again the answer was: in the Temple. When they finally reached the sanctuary, they did not believe their eyes. The twelve-year-old was sitting there quite calmly, obviously in his element. He seemed to have forgotten everything around him as he discussed the Word of God with the scribes!

There is no child who has not heard his mother say these words a hundred times: "How could you do this to your father and me?" But Jesus did not understand their agitation. After all, he was with his Father, here in the Temple!

I have this scene vividly before my eyes as we stand before the steps to the Hulda Gates. A rabbinical book, the *Tosefta Sanhedrin*, describes how "it happened once with Rabban Gamaliel and the elders that they were sitting on the steps in the Temple Mount."[3] It is quite possible that this was where the young Jesus debated with the scribes. For right next to the staircase to the threefold gate, archaeologists stumbled upon a massive building from the time of Herod. An inscription fragment that lay at its feet bore in Hebrew the words "the elders" (*zequenim*) and could be a reference to the members of the Sanhedrin. If this interpretation is accurate, then it was perhaps the hall in which the High Council of the Jews met, before it moved in A.D. 30 to the apse of the Royal Hall, which had just been completed around that time.

[3] *Tractate Sanhedrin*, trans. Herbert Danby, no. 6 (New York: Macmillan, 1919), p. 32.

We wander through the grounds at the bottom of the ancient Temple staircases. We find *mikvehs* all over (Hebrew: *mikwaot*), Jewish ritual baths that every pilgrim used in order to purify himself ritually before he set foot on the Temple Mount.

Tahara, ritual purity, and *tumah*, ritual impurity, are important concepts in Judaism even today. In particular situations, the Torah demands the restoration of ritual purity. It was prescribed for any visit to the Temple. Everyone was considered impure who had either come into contact with a dead body or had lost bodily substances, such as male seminal fluid or female menstrual blood, but also sickness-related secretions. For people who had become *tameh* (impure), separation from the community and specific purification rituals were required in order to bring them back into a condition of *tahara*. They first needed to clean themselves thoroughly and, then, ultimately to immerse their whole bodies in "living" (running, not standing) water. That could occur in a river, but the only river in Israel that was deep enough for full immersion was the Jordan. For this reason, people built during the time of the Second Temple special basins (*mikveh* = "collection of water") into which a specific amount of "living" (running) water could be fed or that reached all the way down to the groundwater. Steps always led into these water basins. In the case of many *mikvehs*, the steps were divided in two. One side was designated for the entrance, the other for the exit, so that the freshly purified did not come into contact with the old impurities.

When Luke writes that, before the presentation of Jesus in the Temple, the Holy Family performed the "purification according to the law of Moses" (Lk 2:22), then this can only mean they bathed in one of the *mikvehs* around the Temple Mount. As a pious Jew, Jesus would have frequented these *mikvehs* all his life before he went to the Temple in order to be close to his Father.

The Gospels allow no room for doubt that the Temple was for Jesus the center of his teaching activity. "And every day he was teaching in the temple, but at night he went out and lodged on the mount called Olivet. And early in the morning all the people came to him in the temple to hear him", as Luke summarizes his daily routine (Lk 21:37–38). Usually, he would have stayed in Solomon's Portico on the eastern edge of the Temple Mount, which was the meeting place of the original community during the time of the Acts of the Apostles

(Acts 3:11). The hall was considered to be the oldest part of the facility. But he may also have preached in the Women's Courtyard. He saw here how an old widow deposited her "penny", two copper coins, or *lepta*, in one of the offering boxes (Mk 12:41–44; Lk 21:1–4).

John's report concerning Jesus' activity in A.D. 29 during the Feast of Tabernacles, which took place from October 19 to 29 of that year, shows how closely Jesus' public appearances were tied to the Temple celebrations and how much he used the opportunity when all pious Jews gathered on these occasions.

Jesus did not immediately follow his "brothers" but, rather, came to Jerusalem a few days later. When half of the festive week was already over, around October 25, "Jesus went up into the temple and taught" (Jn 7:14), which, as we have seen, is to be understood literally: he likely reached the raised Temple platform by way of the southern staircase and the twofold Hulda Gate.

The Feast of Tabernacles was a Jewish harvest festival. But in the first place, it commemorates the wandering of the Jews in the desert. Therefore, for one week during the festival, all believing Jews lived day and night in huts made out of palm leaves and foliage branches that were constructed on the roof terraces of the city, but also on the open spaces all around the city and on the Mount of Olives. During the festival week, a priest drew water with a golden pitcher from the Pool of Siloam before the morning sacrifice. A second priest, selected by lot, poured this water into a silver bowl on the altar. A third offered wine as a libation. Processions around the altar for burnt offerings followed. Psalms were recited, and during particular verses the participants waved the bundles of palm, willow, and myrtle branches that they had brought with them. It was the only time of year in which all male believers were allowed to pass through the room between the altar and the Temple that was usually reserved for the priests. On the eighth day of the festival, the water offering was omitted. On this day, however, Jesus proclaimed: "If any one thirst, let him come to me and drink. He who believes in me, as the Scripture has said, 'Out of his heart shall flow rivers of living water'" (Jn 7:37–38). No ritual, no ceremonial of the Old Covenant, could satisfy the thirst of the soul. But the Spirit whom all who believe in him receive will refresh all who thirst and make them purer than the "living water" in the *mikveh* or the Pool of Siloam can.

His sermon also made reference to another image of the feast. During the entire festival week, the four high candleholders in the Women's Courtyard cast their bright light over the Temple platform and the whole city. A torch dance, accompanied by music, took place in their radiance at night. At the conclusion of the festival, the lights went out. Jesus, however, proclaimed: "I am the light of the world; he who follows me will not walk in darkness, but will have the light of life" (Jn 8:12). In order that there be no doubt concerning this interpretation, John even mentions the place of this speech, a reference that everyone who then knew the Temple immediately understood: "These words he spoke in the treasury, as he taught in the temple" (Jn 8:20): the trumpet-shaped offertory boxes in the Women's Courtyard are meant here.

The reference to the Temple treasury, however, also contains Jesus' critique of the Temple worship, which too obviously replaced the spiritual with the material. The Temple treasure (*corban*, see Mk 7:11) was legendary, and even the Roman senator and prominent orator Cicero reviled the enormous sums of money that flowed from all over into Jerusalem. When the Roman general Pompey conquered Jerusalem in A.D. 63 and made his way into the Holy of Holies in the Temple, he was amazed not just by the showbread table, the candlesticks, and the Temple cutlery made from pure gold. He counted two thousand gold talents in its treasury (115,000 lbs of gold with a present-day value of 1.2 billion dollars). Nevertheless, and this was to his credit among the Jews, he refrained from taking possession of a single part of the treasure. But where did the Temple fortune come from?

First of all, there were the offerings and the voluntary donations. The daily sale of sacrificial animals, too, produced handsome profits. But by far the greatest income came from the Temple tax of a half shekel, which every male Jew of age had to pay once a year. On the first of Adar, the month before the Feast of Passover, messengers traveled throughout the land and announced the due date of the Temple tax. On the 15th of Adar, money changers' booths were set up everywhere, at which those subject to the tax could exchange the various common coins into the "Temple currency", the Tyrian shekel or *stater* with the value of a tetradrachm. It did indeed bear the image of the heathen god Melkart on the front side, but it was made of the purest silver that was then in circulation. The coin was valued in such a way that the Jews in Jerusalem continued to mint it long after Tyre had had its right to have its own currency revoked by the Romans. Nobody seemed to be bothered by the god's image. Clearly, the first commandment did not apply to good money.

Jesus, too, paid the Temple tax, as, of all sources, the first Gospel attributed to the tax collector Matthew reports: "When they came to Capernaum, the collectors of the half-shekel tax went up to Peter and said, 'Does not your teacher pay the tax?' He said, 'Yes'" (Mt 17:24–25). That was on February 22 of the year 30. Peter knew that Jesus would be threatened by harsh reprisals if he were to refuse. A man who did not pay the Temple tax could even be seized. Nevertheless, it was also a question of principle. As the Son of God, Jesus really did not need to pay any taxes to the servants of God. But so as "not to give offense", he had Peter go to the lake and catch a tilapia, which, being a mouthbreeder, had just happened to pick up a stater from the seafloor: "take that and give it to them for me and for yourself" (Mt 17:27).

After the 25th of Adar, the Temple tax could be paid only in Jerusalem, in the Temple district. Here, in the Royal Hall, the money changers had their booths in order to change the "impure" local currencies into the "pure" Temple currency (which, however, bore the image of an idol). In the process, they were allowed by the law to demand an extra charge of one quarter of a denar for the exchange of each half shekel. A denarius was the daily wage of a worker; four denarii corresponded to a tetradrachm or a shekel. The Temple tax, therefore, amounted to two denarii; the extra charge of the money changers for the exchange alone amounted to a full 12.5 percent. But without the "Temple currency", nothing could be done. The pilgrim could not buy sacrificial animals or even give a donation.

Just how despicable this system was to Jesus, just how much he despised the abuse of genuine Jewish piety for commercial purposes, is shown by the thunderbolt with which he began his mission in Jerusalem. John reports:

> In the temple he found those who were selling oxen and sheep and pigeons, and the money-changers at their business. And making a whip of cords, he drove them all, with the sheep and oxen, out of

the temple; and he poured out the coins of the money-changers and overturned their tables. And he told those who sold the pigeons, "Take these things away; you shall not make my Father's house a house of trade." (Jn 2:14–16)

Only John puts the cleansing of the Temple at the beginning of Jesus' activity, while the Synoptic authors (as Matthew, Mark, and Luke are called on the basis of the many shared features between them) move it to the final week in Jesus' life, probably for dramatic reasons. In their accounts, the cleansing of the Temple provides the occasion for Jesus' arrest a few days later, as Mark, for instance, explains: "And the chief priests and the scribes heard it and sought a way to destroy him; for they feared him, because all the multitude was astonished at his teaching" (Mk 11:18). Jesus' action had struck a vital nerve of the Temple's big business and of its Sadducean management, which from that day on schemed against him. As a matter of fact, they waited yet another two years before they struck with their final retaliation. This emerges unmistakably from the account of John, who not only was acquainted with the presentations of the three Synoptic authors but also selectively corrected and completed them where necessary.

The Jewish scholar David Flusser happened upon an indication that explains even better Jesus' spontaneous outbreak of holy anger. The original Royal Hall constructed by Herod was partially destroyed in A.D. 4 as the Romans put down a rebellion, and it had to be rebuilt. Not until the end of the 20s was its interior restored. Here, as was said, the Sanhedrin met from the beginning of the year 30 on. Its reopening, perhaps shortly before the Passover Feast of the year 28 that Jesus attended, brought a few changes with it. Thus the tables of the money changers, who had previously gone about their business at the foot of the Temple Mount and perhaps also on the Mount of Olives, now stood in the freshly renovated hall. Above all, however, the *hanuth*, the market for sacrificial animals, had been moved here from the Mount of Olives. For many Jews, and also for Jesus, the sight of sheep and cattle in the holy precincts must have been a shock, since their excretions threatened to defile the Temple. Obviously, the commercialization of the Temple cult had thus taken on a new dimension—now nothing was sacred any more; now commerce was more important than the purity of God's house. For Jesus, this was a sacrilege that needed to be denounced with the utmost vehemence.

In all four Gospels, the establishment (that is to say: "the chief priests and the scribes with the elders"; see Lk 20:1) reacted with the question: With what right and with what authority did Jesus teach and act this way? He answered with a counterquestion: Did the baptism of John come from heaven or from man? They did not dare to answer him, for the pious people considered the Baptist a prophet, and so Jesus was silent as well. Matthew adds: "But when they tried to arrest him, they feared the multitudes, because they held him to be a prophet" (Mt 21:46). Only John the Evangelist quotes an answer after all and provides us at the same time with the decisive indication for when this occurred. "The Jews then said to him, 'What sign have you to show us for doing this?' Jesus answered them, 'Destroy this temple, and in three days I will raise it up.' The Jews then said, 'It has taken forty-six years to build this temple, and will you raise it up in three days?' But he spoke of the temple of his body" (Jn 2:18–21).

The indication allows us to make a very precise dating. We know from Flavius Josephus that the construction work was first completed under the Roman governor Albinus (A.D. 62–64). Thus, John cannot have meant the entire construction time but meant, rather, the years that had already passed by this point in time. Since the construction work began in A.D. 19, Jesus' cleansing of the Temple took place shortly before Passover of the year A.D. 28, which means in the week before March 29 of this year. He remained, as it further says, throughout the entire celebration and continued to teach in the Temple. At that time, "many believed in his name" (Jn 2:23).

Jesus' words are still resounding in my ears as we, moving past Robinson's Arch, set foot on a street from the time of Herod that has been uncovered by the archaeologists. It is twenty-eight feet wide; to its right rises the Temple platform, while it is flanked by small stores to the left. In them many copper coins have been found, as well as the remains of stone jugs, stone weights, and typical Herodian ceramics. The paving stones of this street are so well preserved that one assumes they were first set in A.D. 64. At that time, after the end of the work on the Temple, so many builders were out of work in Jerusalem that a drastic renovation program was attempted in order to occupy them in some way. At a depth of five feet below it runs a sewage canal.

Today the street is littered with stone fragments that burst through many of its broad paving stones. They testify to the destruction of the Temple by the Romans in the year 70. One of them carries the Hebrew inscription: "The place, on which the trumpet is blown, to...." We know from Flavius Josephus that a priest blew a trumpet on the pinnacle of the Temple that faced the city whenever the Sabbath started and ended. That happened for the last time on what was perhaps the darkest day of a Jewish history not lacking in dark days, April 9 in the year 3830 after the creation of the world: according to our calendar, on Saturday, August 4, A.D. 70.

Four years earlier, in May 66, the Roman governor Gessius Florus had gone too far with his greed. After he removed seventeen talents of gold from the Temple treasury, there was unrest in the whole province of Judaea. The Roman reacted by raiding and pillaging the wealthy upper city of Jerusalem with his soldiers. To serve as an example, he had 3,600 men, women, and children scourged and crucified on the same day. Then he demanded that two cohorts of Roman soldiers called up from the provincial capital be greeted joyfully nonetheless. The people played along, up to a point, but only to revolt then all the more vehemently. As this unrest was again brutally put down, the people fled to the Temple Mount in order to barricade themselves there.

As Florus of necessity withdrew in order to get reinforcements, a rebellion broke out in the city. While the upper class and the priests continued to work for an agreement with Rome, nationalistic zealots brought the lower city and the Temple district under their control. They laid siege to the Antonia Fortress, the seat of the Roman garrison north of the Temple district, and set part of it on fire. Then they moved against Herod's palace in the upper city, in which the Romans had now taken shelter. After a siege lasting for days, the occupying force asked to make a retreat. This was formally granted to them, but no sooner had they left the protective walls than the rebels slaughtered them from behind. Now the Jews were again the rulers of their city. In the Temple, the offerings for the emperor were halted. But they would presently understand that they had gone too far.

No sooner had the news spread of the cowardly, bloody deed of the nationalistic enthusiasts, or Zealots, than there were assassinations of Jews throughout the Roman Empire. Ultimately, Florus' superior,

Cestius, the governor of Syria, took action and ordered the Twelfth Legion to Judaea. But he had scarcely captured north Jerusalem and begun the siege of the Temple Mount when he suddenly lost his courage. He ordered his troops to retreat, while the rebels celebrated their first victory. Now they prepared to free the entire country from foreign rule.

But Rome, the world power, was not ready to accept defeat. Emperor Nero commissioned his most experienced general, Vespasian, to put down the rebellion. Within a year, all of Galilee was once again firmly in the hands of the occupying force, and an army sixty thousand men strong marched against Jerusalem. There the rebels quarreled over whether they should surrender or resist. The radical faction won out. Nero's death and the confusion over his successor disabled the military campaign. But in the end, Vespasian was called to become the new emperor, and he handed over his command to his son Titus. In the beginning of the year 70, Titus started to besiege the city. After a months-long war of attrition, after five hundred prisoners were crucified daily in the sight of the city walls in order to discourage the rebels, and when for a long time famine held sway over the city, Titus finally succeeded in capturing the Antonia Fortress. After many vain attempts to convince the besieged to surrender, he finally ordered a raid on the Temple. Although the general had explicitly ordered that the sanctuary be spared, it went up in flames during the conflict. While the Jews still carried out a bitter resistance against them, the Roman legionaries now set fire to the other buildings on the Temple Mount out of a sheer rage for destruction. Titus had the smoking ruins razed, if only to prevent them from being used again by the Jews as a bulwark. The treasuries of the Temple were plundered. The gold and silver that was hoarded here sufficed subsequently to build the Colosseum in Rome. But the Temple platform itself was too immense to be torn down. So today it is the sole witness to the former glory of what was considered the "sanctuary that was one of the greatest achievements of human architecture", as even Tacitus, the not very Jewish-friendly Roman historian, had to admit.

Today, Jesus' prophecy concerning the destruction of the Temple is considered by modern Biblical criticism as proof for the late origin of the Gospels. His words fit the actual event too well. So Mark asserts: "And as [Jesus] came out of the temple, one of his disciples said to him, 'Look, Teacher, what wonderful stones and what wonderful buildings!' And Jesus said to him, 'Do you see these great buildings? There will not be left here one stone upon another, that will not be thrown down'" (Mk 13:1–2; see also Mt 24:1–2; Lk 21:5–6).

Whoever today walks along the "Herodian street" in the archaeological park at the southwest corner of the Temple Mount actually finds these words fulfilled. Not a single structure of the sanctuary, neither the Royal Hall nor the Temple itself, escaped destruction. Their stones lie, in part even today, piled up in a heap at the foot of the platform.

Nonetheless, I consider it a rather weak argument to claim that the prophecy was put into Jesus' mouth after the fact, thus as a *vaticinia ex eventu* and therefore a proof that the Gospels were composed after A.D. 70. As a matter of fact, Jesus' prophecy is far too general to refer it to a concrete event and specifically to the Temple conflagration. At the very least, it is no more precise than Psalm 137, which indisputably comes from a pre-Christian time. There the "day of Jerusalem" is announced with the words "Raze it, raze it! Down to its foundations!" How much Jesus liked to cite the Psalms is shown by the fact that his final words on the Cross were taken from Psalm 22. And although the Gospel of John is doubtless the youngest of the four, its author refrains from making any connection to the historical Temple conflagration and instead refers Jesus' words to the destruction of his body, his death, and his Resurrection. Thus the famous theologian from Heidelberg, Klaus Berger, used the same logic as the "late daters" to arrive at the conclusion that the Fourth Gospel must at least have been the first to be composed.

But why should we deny in the first place that the Son of God was able to foresee the destruction of the Temple? The Church historian Eusebius of Caesarea reports that the original Christian community had already left Jerusalem before the outbreak of the Jewish rebellion and had gone to Pella in present-day Jordan pursuant to a prophecy.

Flavius Josephus, who at that time lived in Jerusalem, remembers another "prophet". Four years before the outbreak of the war, in other words in A.D. 62, during the Feast of Tabernacles, an uneducated peasant named Jesus, the Son of Ananias, began suddenly to yell: "Woe, woe, Jerusalem!" While repeating this cry, he wandered around all the streets day and night, to the chagrin of their inhabitants: these cries of impending doom got on their nerves. After he was beaten several times and nonetheless did not keep quiet, he was dragged before the Roman procurator. He had him scourged. But with every blow, insofar as he still had the strength to do so, the unfortunate man uttered his lamentation: "Woe, Jerusalem!" Is this Jesus supposed to have had prophetic abilities that are not to be attributed to Jesus of Nazareth?

Maybe it is time to question preconceived opinions and simply to admit that God acts even in history. Is it then really impossible to predict the future? In the year 1917, three shepherd children in Fatima, a remote village in northern Portugal, claimed that the Mother of God had appeared to them. In one part of a three-part "secret", she allegedly revealed the future to them. Admittedly, two of the three children died within two years (Our Lady had announced this to them, too), but the third, a girl named Lucia, entered the cloister and lived until 2005. Only in the summer of 1941 did the nun write down the prophecy, at the request of her bishop. World War II, which had been foretold to her, was already raging throughout Europe, but the other events were still in the future: for instance, that Russia would spread "its errors" throughout the world, "annihilate" different nations, and harass the Church. That a pope would have much to suffer, and even be the victim of an assassination, before Russia converted. Reasoning after the fact, one would have to conclude from this that the secret of Fatima was first made up after 1991, that is, after the fall of the Soviet Union. But the girl Lucia demonstrably had written it down half a century before the occurrence of these events (and forty years before the prophecy's papal assassination). What now? Must we deny to Jesus, the Incarnate Word of God, something of which shepherd children in the twentieth century were still capable? Or does rationalism perhaps run up against its limits at the point where God is active?

I think that the Gospels were composed at around the same time. They describe in too much detail a Jerusalem that after A.D. 70 was in ruins. They are too exactly acquainted with the customs and localities of the Temple, which had already been forgotten shortly after its destruction. Only slowly, with the help of archaeology and the Dead Sea Scrolls, are we beginning to rediscover the Judaism of the time of Jesus. And suddenly, much that previously was considered legendary appears in an entirely new light.

V

In the Theater in Sepphoris

A Youth Spent in Galilee

Anyone who wants to understand the world in which Jesus grew up must search for it not only in the rural unpretentiousness of Nazareth or in the magnificence and pomp of the capital Jerusalem. For as interesting as the tension between countryside and capital, between the unorthodox village preacher and the powerful Temple establishment may be, it provides only an incomplete picture. Whole generations of exegetes and historians have gone astray. The true Jesus of Nazareth was not a naïve idealist from the conservative, perhaps somewhat backward north, which in its helpless innocence contrasted with the spirit of the modern age, the Greco-Judaic world, and was shattered against its power structures. Instead, he was a child of his time who grew up in a milieu that had long since been swept up in the first wave of globalization in history—and who nevertheless always kept his sights fixed on eternity.

The modern world began for him, not behind the city walls of Jerusalem after a three-day journey; it was only an hour away from him. For as rustic as Nazareth may have been, it nevertheless lay in the hinterland of a city that was numbered among the richest and most splendid in the country. This city fell into oblivion and with it the role that it played for Jesus. Yet it provides us with the key to the "obscure years" in the earthly life of the Son of God, about which all the Evangelists are silent: the time between Jesus' first visit to the Temple and the beginning of his public ministry, in other words between the years A.D. 8 and 27.

There has been much speculation about these nineteen years. Especially imaginative authors maintained even in antiquity that during this time Jesus traveled to Egypt again in order to learn magic; their modern successors send him off to India, where he supposedly encountered the teachings of Buddha. Others claim that he lived then as a monk in the Qumran monastery. With all due respect, that is just nonsense! The solution to the riddle of what he did during this time lies in Sepphoris.

There are two paths to the forgotten city. One goes via Nazareth, which lies only four miles to the south. The other, longer one is much more beautiful, and we take it. Behind Tiberias on the Sea of Galilee, we drive on Highway 77 across a mountain range and pass the Horns of Hattin, the place where the Crusaders suffered their most devastating defeat in 1187. At that time, they lost not only their rule over Jerusalem but also their holiest treasure, the relic of Christ's Cross. All attempts to purchase it later from the Arabs under Salah ad-Din (Saladin) failed; all that they heard from Damascus was that the most sacred wood had disappeared. Finally we come upon the southern side of the fertile Bet Netofa Valley. We detour around Nazareth and its suburbs so as to avoid the traffic and turn off onto Highway 79, which is marked with an exit to Zipori, as Sepphoris is called today. And there it is already ahead of us, like an enchanted island in the middle of the fields, surrounded by mountain ranges as though by the shores of a lake. Visible from afar, it is enthroned on the back of a hill as though it had inspired Jesus to speak the words: "A city set on a hill cannot be hidden" (Mt 5:14). It owes its name to this location. For *zipori* in Hebrew means "like a little bird" that likes to nest on the ridge of a hill.

A Byzantine tradition maintained that Saint Anne, Mary's mother, was from Sepphoris. In her house, a pilgrim from Piacenza around the year 570 claimed to have venerated "the flagon and the bread-basket of Saint Mary" as well as the "chair ... on which she was sitting when the angel came to her".[1] Evidently they had brought relics from Nazareth into the city, maybe because the Holy House was firmly in the hands of the Jewish Christians. Over the ruins of the church that was visited by the pilgrim but was destroyed in 614 by the Persians, the Crusaders later erected an imposing basilica with

---

[1] The Piacenza Pilgrim, *Travels from Piacenza*, in John Wilkinson, *Jerusalem Pilgrims Before the Crusades* (Jerusalem: Ariel, 1977), p. 79.

three naves, which they dedicated to Saint Anne. Its remains were acquired in 1870 by the Franciscans. Today the Sisters of Saint Anne run an orphanage there and preserve the ancient tradition of this forgotten site.

A visit to Sepphoris is worthwhile and should be part of every trip to the Holy Land. We park in the parking lot for visitors and are at first overwhelmed by the beauty of this place. The hill on which ancient Sepphoris was located is wooded today. The deep green of pine trees and shrubs alternates with the bright colors of a thousand flowers and the light beige of old ruins. Lane by lane, we wander through the ancient foundations, walk on its broad *Cardo*, the main street, step over ancient thresholds, and come across mosaics again and again. They are the most beautiful in all Israel. Quite unexpectedly, they display motifs from Greek mythology: Orpheus and the wine-god Dionysius, the drunken Heracles, maenads and satyrs, centaurs and Amazons, but also the enchanting portrait of an unknown woman, whom archaeologists have named "the Mona Lisa of Galilee". The mosaics date back to the third century, when Sepphoris was in its heyday.

We leave the richly adorned lower city and climb up the hill on which the upper city stood. Here archaeologists have been able to unearth the remains of a fortress from the first century. At its highest point stands to this day a completely intact tower, which is made up of elements from three periods. The upper walls are from the Mamluk period; its center is a fortress of the Crusaders. Yet the large, richly ornamented cut stones of its foundation are plainly older; they are part of a building from the time of Jesus. Inside the tower today a little museum is housed with discoveries from the excavations. At its feet lies the most famous and most controversial structure in Sepphoris: its theater. It was also the first evidence for the ancient city that was unearthed when the American Leroy Waterman first wielded a spade here in 1931.

Unfortunately his excavation lasted only one season; then he ran out of money. In the midst of the Great Depression, it was impossible to finance an archaeological project. The aftereffects were accordingly meager. Although the archaeologist published the first detailed descriptions of the theater, the rock tombs, an oil press, a house (that he incorrectly regarded as a Christian basilica), and the impressive cisterns of Sepphoris, his discoveries were consistently ignored. People considered the find as plainly irrelevant. As late as 1949, the German archaeologist Albrecht Alt argued (for many, convincingly) that Jesus could not have visited Sepphoris at all, since rural Jews would have avoided the Hellenic city on principle.

The tide turned only in the mid-1980s. The University of South Florida began a systematic excavation, and the project leader, Richard Batey, published a popular book that emphasized the importance of Sepphoris in Jesus' early life. It is certainly a place where Joseph, the *tekton* [carpenter, builder], found work and was able to train his son, Jesus. Through his impressions of Sepphoris, however, the latter would have gained insights that left their mark on his later life.

As a matter of fact, Jesus' youth coincides with the busiest phase in the history of this city. From the Gospel of Matthew we gather that the Holy Family remained in Egypt until they learned about the death of Herod in March of the year 4 B.C.: "And he rose and took the child and his mother, and went to the land of Israel. But when he heard that Archelaus reigned over Judea in place of his father Herod, he was afraid to go there, and being warned in a dream he withdrew to the district of Galilee. And he went and dwelt in a city called Nazareth" (Mt 2:21–23).

Only five days before his death, the tyrant had ordered in his last will and testament that his son Archelaus was to become his successor. However, his other sons—Antipas and his half-brother Philip—were to govern parts of the kingdom as independent tetrarchies (quarter-kingdoms). The emperor was to have the final say in the matter. Therefore Archelaus, with his baggage containing Herod's signet ring and the documents about the national budget—in other words, the results of the census from the previous year—had to present his case first in Rome.

Even at his departure there was unrest. The people feared, not unjustly, that the son would follow in his father's footsteps. The relatives of the victims of Herod's reign of terror demanded reparations, the dismissal of his favorites, and revenge on the murderers. Jerusalem, where the Feast of Passover was being celebrated and hundreds of thousands of pilgrims had arrived, was seething. When Archelaus sent his soldiers off to arrest the ringleaders of the uprising, the situation escalated; the people openly opposed the soldiers, and during a confrontation in the shadow of the Temple three thousand pious Jews were massacred. The festivities were interrupted, and the pilgrims were forced to go back home.

In Rome, Archelaus met with a second unpleasant surprise: his family had also traveled to the capital and urgently begged the emperor not to grant the throne to the most brutal of Herod's sons. The late king must have already been insane when he drew up his last will. They would have preferred to have a Roman governor, but even Antipas, who had traveled to Rome at the same time with a delegation of his own, seemed to them to be the lesser evil. Nevertheless, with a clever gesture of submissiveness, Archelaus secured for himself the emperor's sympathy, who finally made his decision in a downright Solomonic fashion. The kingdom was divided among the three sons of Herod. Philip became the independent tetrarch (answering only to Rome), of Gaulanitis, Trachonitis, and Batanaea in the northeast part of the land. Awarded to Antipas were Galilee and Peraea, the Jewish region east of the Jordan, which to the south extended as far as Machaerus' fortress on the eastern shore of the Dead Sea. Although Archelaus also had to renounce the crown, he was to rule as ethnarch (national leader) over Judaea, Samaria, and Idumea, whereby the largest inheritance fell to him. At least Antipas and Archelaus made up for the lost title by calling themselves "Herod" from then on, so as to show the world that each of them considered himself the sole legitimate successor of his father. The title King of the Jews, on the other hand, was granted again by Rome only forty-one years later to Herod Agrippa.

Until this decision was announced, the power vacuum had plunged the whole country into chaos. After Archelaus' departure, the governor of Syria, Publius Quinctilius Varus, had marched into Jerusalem with a whole legion (six thousand men in arms) in order to maintain public order. While Varus himself returned to his official seat in Antioch after the situation had quieted down, an imperial official named Sabinus had to reevaluate Herod's wealth, in other words to examine whether the statements made by Archelaus in Rome were accurate, too. His rigorous proceedings infuriated the Jews, who right then were streaming into the city in ever greater numbers for the Feast of Weeks. When the pilgrims set up their tent cities around the camp of the Legion, Sabinus felt surrounded and sounded the trumpet to attack. The Jews fled to the Temple Mount, where they thought they were safe, but the Romans followed them. So the refugees defended their sanctuary by taking up positions at the Royal Basilica and hurling at the legionaries stones that were stored there, probably to be used again at the major construction site of the Temple. Their resistance ended in a hail of burning arrows, fired off by the Roman archers; meanwhile, Herod's magnificent hall went up in flames.

For many who had stayed home, this was the sign to lash out against the unpopular Romans. Troubles broke out now throughout the kingdom of Herod, partly for political motives, partly because bands of robbers took advantage of the hour. In Sepphoris, Judas, the son of the robber chief Ezekias, who had been arrested by Herod, drummed up enough men to storm the royal arsenals. There he found plenty of weapons with which to transform his band into a private army and to terrorize the land from then on.

No sooner had news of the troubles reached Varus than he marched with two legions first into Galilee, so as to make an example of it. It takes Flavius Josephus only one sentence to suggest to us that the commander proceeded with an iron fist against the rebels. "[He] put those that met him to flight, and took the city of Sepphoris, and burned it, and made slaves of its inhabitants."[2] Then he changed course and headed for Jerusalem, where the reports originating from Galilee had caused a panic. The locals blamed the pilgrims, and Varus ordered the crucifixion of two thousand of them, who probably came from Galilee. With that, the "Roman peace" was restored, even before the Ethnarch Archelaus returned to his land. Varus had proved to be an efficient commander; the emperor knew now that he could entrust even difficult missions to him. So the ex-governor of Syria was sent to Germany in A.D. 7 as *legatus Augusti pro praetore* [Augustus' delegate instead of a leader]. There he was supposed to secure the land between the Rhine and the Elbe as a Roman province. Because of the devastating defeat of Varus and his three legions in the Teutoburg Forest in A.D. 9, the Roman plans failed. The Germanic commander-in-chief Arminius sent the general's head to Rome, and Augustus had it laid to rest in his own mausoleum.

---

[2] Flavius Josephus, *The Jewish War*, bk. 2, chap. 5, no. 1, in *The New Complete Works of Josephus*, trans. William Whiston (Grand Rapids, Mich.: Kregel, 1999), p. 733.

If we believe Matthew, then Joseph originally intended to return to Bethlehem. Maybe he wanted to build a little house, like the one he owned in Nazareth, on the piece of land where the Grotto of the Nativity was located. There his wife and his little foster son would have lived, while he continued to pursue his work on the Temple Mount; in any case, the Royal Hall had to be rebuilt after it was destroyed by the Romans. Yet the report that Archelaus now ruled thwarted the plan. Because of his bad reputation, nothing good could be expected; the son resembled his father too much. Therefore Joseph went back with Mary and the exactly one-and-a-half-year-old Child Jesus to his hometown, to Nazareth.

Indeed, the concern was justified. Archelaus proved to be an ill-humored tyrant, who tormented his subjects so much that they complained to the emperor about him nine years later. Augustus promptly ordered him to Rome, dispossessed him, and exiled him to Vienna in Gaul (modern-day Vienne).

Thirty years later, Jesus seemed to allude to him when he told the parable of the money entrusted to the servants. It begins: "A nobleman went into a far country to receive kingly power." Like Archelaus, this man, too, had his opponents: "But his citizens hated him and sent an embassy after him, saying, 'We do not want this man to reign over us'" (Lk 19:12, 14). Nevertheless, the man becomes king and upon his return settles accounts, not only with his stewards, but also with his enemies: "'As for these enemies of mine, who did not want me to reign over them, bring them here and slay them before me'" (Lk 19:27). This is a reaction in which the cruelty of Herod's son is also reflected.

In A.D. 6 (Jesus was just ten years old), Judaea was officially declared a Roman province. Its capital was not Caesarea; only during the three major Temple feasts did the imperial prefect reside in Herod's palace in Jerusalem, in order to guarantee public order and to nip possible disturbances in the bud. The first man who held this post was a certain Coponius. His first task was to carry out a current census together with Quirinius, the new governor of Syria and, thus, his immediate superior.

Resistance was brewing again. A certain Judas from Gamala in Gaulanitis (today's Golan Heights) founded an anti-Roman guerilla movement, the so-called Zealots. They were also called Sicarii (dagger-men), because they crept up on their victims from behind to assassinate them. The agitators of the resistance proclaimed that it was shameful to pay taxes to the Romans and, moreover, to acknowledge mortal men also as lords along with God. For decades they terrorized the land. "One violent war came upon us after another, and we lost our friends which used to alleviate our pains", Flavius Josephus writes about the armed insurgents. "There were also very great robberies and murder of our principal men. This was done in pretense indeed for the public welfare, but in reality for the hopes of gain to themselves; thus arose rebellions and from them murders of men, which sometimes fell on those of their own people (by the madness of these men towards one another, while their desire was that none of the adverse party might be left), and sometimes on their enemies."[3]

In the midst of this insecurity, Jesus grew up. Yet the new era offered opportunities, too. The greatest of them was globalization. Despite all the troubles caused by the Zealots, peace prevailed in foreign affairs—the *pax Romana*—and stability was maintained by a strict hand in internal affairs. Commerce flourished, both imports and exports, and anyone who used his opportunity could profit from it and pile up riches. New goods and commodities as well as new ideas inundated the land. The traditionalists may have seen in everything that was new and foreign a threat, a danger for the Jewish faith and the Jewish identity. Nevertheless, the new era also compelled people to give up their beloved "ghetto existence" screened off from the outside world and to think of what is essential. It was a time of changes and possibilities, of dialogue and exchange.

The fact that the Incarnation of the Son of God took place precisely at this point in time is perhaps no accident but, rather, an indication of a miraculous act of Providence. The time for the proclamation of the Gospel could not have been chosen better. For the first time in human history, so many countries and nations were united in a worldwide empire that, unlike the empire of Alexander, was stable and long-lasting. For the first time, people on three continents spoke the same language and were connected with one another by a network of roads that knew no boundaries from Spain to the Euphrates. Only in this way was it possible that in just one generation after the

---

[3] Flavius Josephus, *Jewish Antiquities*, bk. 18, chap. 1, no. 1, in *New Complete Works of Josephus*, p. 585.

Ascension of Jesus, when the old Judaism of the Temple ceased to exist in a single blow, the tidings of God's New Covenant reached Gaul and Spain in the west, Parthia and India in the east, Scythia in the north, and Ethiopia in the south. Only three hundred years later the Church founded by Jesus dominated the Roman world empire, and from its headquarters in Rome it has outlasted the ages down to the present day.

Jesus' first more intensive contact with the global culture of that time, Greco-Roman civilization, took place in Sepphoris. In the works of Flavius Josephus we read that after the dismissal of Archelaus, Antipas and Philip were confirmed in their office. They thanked Augustus for the favor shown to them in the same way as their father had done, by naming cities after him. Philip expanded the city of Paneas at the fountainhead of the Jordan, named it Caesarea (and to distinguish it from Caesarea on the Mediterranean seacoast: Caesarea Philippi), and made it the capital of his realm. Antipas had Sepphoris rebuilt, named it Autokratoris (after the Greek title for emperor, *autokrator*), and chose it as his capital. Like his father, he wanted to go down in history as a master builder, as the founder of cities. You can tell by looking at Sepphoris that it originated on the drawing board. The residential islands were planned in a checkerboard pattern along the north-south main axis, the *cardo*, and the east-west cross axis, the *decumanus*. On two marketplaces, the "Upper" and the "Lower Market", the farmers from the surrounding villages, among them Cana and Nazareth, offered their produce. On market days, whole caravans of donkeys filed through the city gates, loaded with sacks full of vegetables and grain, while amphorae heavy with oil and wine were transported on carts. In a five-aisled secular basilica, which was reminiscent of the Royal Hall on the Temple Mount but had an area of "only" 1,675 square yards, luxury items were offered: glass vessels and goblets, expensive fabrics and perfumes, balsam and jewelry. Archaeologists estimate that as many as twelve thousand people had settled in Sepphoris. For a construction worker like Joseph, the enlargement of the neighboring city to make it the "security of all Galilee" (thus Josephus)[4] was an absolute windfall. Almost directly in

---

[4] Ibid., bk. 18, chap. 2, no. 1, p. 588. [In other translations of Josephus, this has been rendered "ornament of all Galilee".—Ed.]

front of his own house door, only an hour's walk distant from Nazareth, it offered him work and income for many years.

What was Jesus doing at this time? He "increased in wisdom and in stature, and in favor with God and man", Luke writes rather ambiguously (2:52). Only when the Gospels report on his last visit to Nazareth do they become more precise. At least Mark tells us in this passage that Jesus also learned an altogether specific profession, since the people asked: "Is not this the carpenter ...?" (Mk 6:3). Therefore he practiced the same trade as his foster father. That was no accident. Rather, it was the custom then for the son to be trained in the father's profession or trade. Even a spiritual vocation made no difference in this—just the opposite. In ancient Judaism, priests, rabbis, and even prophets were also obliged to master a trade so as not to become a financial burden to the Temple, their congregation, or the faithful.

"He who teaches his son no trade is a robber", it says in the Talmud, which explains it as follows: "Just as a man is obliged to support his son, so too he must teach him an artisan's trade." When even the great rabbis demanded: "Get yourself an occupation along with your studies", they knew what they were talking about: the great Hillel was a woodcutter, the famous Rabbi Jehuda was a baker, and we know that Paul of Tarsus had learned the tentmaker's craft. The spiritual vocation that Jesus plainly sensed very early (as the episode in the Temple proves) was therefore by no means incompatible with working at a job. "A manual laborer at his work need not be ashamed in the presence of great scholars", it says explicitly in the Midrash. Construction workers and carpenters were even considered particularly educated, because they also mastered mathematics and the mechanics of equilibrium. Thus Jacob Levy in his *Wörterbuch über die Talmudim und Midraschim*[5] quotes a common proverb from this era. When dealing with a particularly difficult theological problem, the rabbis used to ask: "Is there among us a carpenter or the son of a carpenter who can solve this problem for us?"

The fact that Jesus was at home in this profession is demonstrated by his many metaphors concerning wood, construction, and

---

[5] Jacob Levy, *Wörterbuch über die Talmudim und Midraschim* (Dictionary of the Talmudic and Midrashic texts) (Berlin and Darmstadt: Harz/Wissenschaftliche Buchgesellschaft, 1924), p. 338.

buildings: the collapse of the tower of Siloam (Lk 13:4), the construction of a tower in the vineyard (Mk 12:1), the "easy yoke" (Mt
11:30), the "stone which the builders rejected" (Mk 12:10), the three
days to rebuild the Temple (Jn 2:19), the log or beam in your eye and
the speck in your brother's eye (Mt 7:5), and naturally the discourse
about the house that a wise man builds on rock, while a foolish man
builds his house on sand (Mt 7:24–27).

But if Jesus was apprenticed to his foster father and was taken
along to the construction sites, then where if not in Sepphoris, where
there was practically unlimited work for the father-son team? It was
in fact impossible for him to ignore Sepphoris, because the main road
connecting the "security of Galilee" and Jerusalem crossed through
Nazareth. There, Richard Batey wrote in his groundbreaking work,
"Jesus would have experienced first hand life in a new city of elaborate Hellenistic design with its many newcomers, its cosmopolitan
atmosphere, theatre, and royal court. On the streets and in the market places he would have interacted with people who participated in
the economic, political, religious, and cultural life in the capital—a
life distinctly different from that in his own village."

Yet how extensive were these influences? A truly bitter scholarly debate has raged since the publication of Batey's book. Did the
splendid mosaics with the Greek-mythological motifs and the Greek
theater not point to a pagan presence? The reference by Isaiah from
the Assyrian period to the "Galilee of the Gentiles" and a superficial
look at the finds in Sepphoris misled authors like the American New
Testament scholar John Dominic Crossan in the 1990s to formulate
several daring theses. Crossan thought that Jesus, as a societal out-
sider, looked around for alternative lifestyles and in doing so came
in contact with the philosophical schools of the Greeks in Sepphoris.
Thus he became a disciple of one of these schools, a "rural cynic"
who on principle rejected worldly possessions and called societal
norms into question. According to this telling, the Kingdom of God
that he proclaimed had nothing to do with the eschatological notions
of the Jews. Rather, it was a societal utopia in which social barriers
were abolished and outsiders were valued. Crossan's biography of
Jesus became a bestseller, even though his hypothesis, as we now
know, was marred by one little beauty mark. There were no Greek
schools of philosophy in Sepphoris. The evidence of Greek culture,

the wonderful mosaics in the villas of its wealthiest citizens, all come
from the third century—a time in which Judaism became open and
to a certain degree worldly, when there was no longer any Temple
hierarchy and the laws of the Torah and the Halacha were treated
with much greater laxity. Yet while third-century Sepphoris, which
had long since been called Diocaesarea—one can debate whether
"Dio" meant Jupiter or Yahweh—was still just a city with Jewish
character in a Roman province, it is certain today that at the time of
Antipas it must have been completely Jewish. A pagan temple never
stood there.

The purely Jewish settlements in the time of Jesus, we can read
in any textbook, can be recognized by six indicators, the so-called
"Jewish index fossils":

(1) the absence of pig bones (Jews considered pigs unclean animals, and they were strictly forbidden to eat pork, while the pig
was the favorite source of meat among the Gentiles); (2) *mikvehs*
(Hebrew plural: *mikvaoth*) (poorer residential districts or villages
used common *mikvehs*; wealthy Jews had their own purification
baths, always according to the specifications of the Halacha; ritual
purity was one of the most important elements of everyday Judaism); (3) stone vessels, mostly hewn from soft, white limestone, also
served ritual purity (according to the Halacha, stone does not take
on impurity; water that was stored or transported in stone vessels
remained ritually pure; the use of them ended with the destruction
of the Temple, which caused such a strict adherence to the Halacha
to become obsolete); (4) Jewish coins of the Hasmoneans, Herodians, or governors; (5) Hebrew inscriptions; (6) rock-cut tombs with
side shafts (*kokhim*), ossuaries.

On the earliest stratum of Sepphoris, the first-century city, all
these criteria are met. Flavius Josephus, too, speaks about Sepphoris
as a purely Jewish city. Rabbinical traditions even report that priests
from Sepphoris served in the Temple; by reason of their ritual
purity, they were forbidden to stay in a mixed Jewish-Gentile environment. That would mean, though, that for Joseph and Jesus, too,
there would have been no reason at all to make a detour around the
"city on the hill".

In Sepphoris, Jesus could take a look at the world. Did he learn the
international language Greek, at least Koiné, the colloquial speech,

which even the simple folk knew? So far archaeologists have found few inscriptions from the first century in Sepphoris, but an inscribed potsherd (a so-called *ostrakon*, the earthenware "note tablet" in antiquity) and a weight are significant. On the earthenware tablet, red Hebrew letters spell out the Greek word for "treasurer" (*epimeletes*), which shows that he used a Greek official title. The weight is made out of lead and bears a Greek inscription. On one side, the measure of weight itself is indicated, surrounded by a schematic drawing of a colonnade; on the other side, Greek text shows who inspected it: "Under the market supervision of Simon, son of Aianos, son of Justus". Both finds indicate that the commercial language in Sepphoris in Jesus' time was Greek. In fact, the coins minted by Antipas also bear Greek inscriptions. But if Jesus spoke Greek—along with the vernacular Aramaic and the Hebrew of the Sacred Scriptures—then it is possible that the Gospels, which were originally composed in this language, report some of his statements in their original wording. This could apply above all—and this brings us to the most recent controversy about Sepphoris—to one word: *hypokritái*, "hypocrites", which in German is usually translated as *Heuchler* [dissemblers]. The word is used seventeen times in the Gospels, exclusively when Jesus is speaking. Therefore it seems to have become part of his flesh and blood. Yet "dissemblers" is a much too harsh translation for a word that really means nothing but "playactors". Now actors have made it their profession to portray someone who in reality they are not, in other words, to play a set role. And that is precisely what Jesus meant when he said, for instance: "When you fast, do not look dismal, like the hypocrites, for they disfigure their faces that their fasting may be seen by men" (Mt 6:16). They too dissemble, then, and wear a mask in the figurative sense, just like playactors.

Naturally we wonder then: Did Jesus know from his own observation what a playactor is? Did he himself perhaps once attend a Greek drama or a tragedy, possibly—where else then?—in the theater of Sepphoris?

The problem with this hypothesis is that the archaeologists do not agree as to when the theater of Sepphoris, with its four thousand seats and its breathtaking view of the Bet Netofa Valley, was built in the first place. When Leroy Waterman stumbled upon the ruins of this impressive edifice in 1931, it was clear to him:

That the theater was in existence in the reign of Herod Antipas there can scarcely be a doubt. However, there are several considerations that favor his father as the original builder of the theater. Two things emerge as very certain. First, it is scarcely possible under the circumstances to place the theater later than Herod Antipas. Second, it is equally impossible to think of locating it earlier than Herod the Great, since no Hasmonean Jew could be conceived of as a builder of a theater.[6]

His Israeli colleague S. Yeivin agreed with him: "There is no other period in the history of the town when the erection of a similar building was likely, whereas Herod Antipas tried, no doubt, to ape, on his own small-scale, the large program of public buildings initiated by his father."[7]

That was the status of the question until 1983, when the University of South Florida continued the excavations under the direction of J. Strange and R. Batey. Two years later, the joint Israeli–American Sepphoris Project under the direction of E. Netzer and E. M. Meyers went to work on the opposite side of the theater. Strange and Batey dug beneath the seats of the theater and hit on an intact ancient backfill that still contained potsherds. The oldest of them could be dated back to the second century. That meant that the theater had not been built until around that time, more than a century too late to have inspired Jesus, too. That would have tabled the issue had the excavation report by Netzer and Meyers from the year 1985 not said: "During the excavation of one section of the structure beneath the foundation of the theater, potsherds only from the late Hellenistic and early Rome period were identified. Herod Antipas is consequently the probable builder of this theater." Samples taken from beneath the foundation one year later confirmed this finding. In 1987, when the side entrance corridor of the theater was unearthed, the latest potsherds again came from the early Roman period. Since then the contradictory dates keep changing, sometimes even in the publications of the same archaeologists. Finally, the most likely solution of the problem was offered by Batey in 2006. According to his explanation,

---

[6] L. Waterman et al., *Preliminary Report of the University of Michigan Excavations at Sepphoris, Palestine, in 1931* (Ann Arbor: University of Michigan Press, 1937), p. 29.
    [7] Ibid.

the theater was in fact built by Antipas—only to be expanded then in the second century when the city grew again.

Indeed a capital city of Antipas without a theater would be simply unthinkable. His father, Herod, not only equipped Caesarea, Samaria, Jericho, and even Jerusalem with such a theater; he even had his own little private theater installed as an addition to the Herodium. As a young man, Antipas lived in Rome, when Augustus made the theater an instrument of his cultural policy. At that time the Balbus Theater and the still-extant Marcellus Theater were built. The emperor not only promoted the dramatic arts, he also attended performances regularly. He even composed a drama about the Greek hero Ajax. On his deathbed, he summoned his closest friends and advisors and asked whether he had played his role well. When they all told him that he had, he replied: "Now, then, clap your applause, for the comedy has ended." Someone who spent his formative years in such an environment demands drama as entertainment later on, too.

Yet not only the frequent use of the word *hypokritái* reflects Jesus' experience in Sepphoris. Some of his parables, too, appear now in another light. Did Jesus' metaphor about the two men on the way to see the judge, about the officers of the court, the difficult situation of debtors and the threat of imprisonment (Lk 12:58; Mt 5:25) refer to experiences of his fellowmen with the court in the capital? Did he experience how it is when a king gives a banquet and invites guests from all around (Mt 22:1–14; Lk 14:15–24)?

"Herodians" in the Gospels is the term for the minions of Antipas, the "fox", as Jesus calls him. They are generally considered Jesus' opponents. Nevertheless, the Gospel of Luke mentions a "Joanna, the wife of Chuza, Herod's steward" (Lk 8:3), who plainly supported Jesus and the disciples financially. Other translations even call her husband a "trustee", which suggests rank and wealth. Was she originally from Sepphoris? The fact that she is mentioned reveals that Jesus certainly had disciples in the upper class of society, too, even in the household of the tetrarch, whose own relation to Jesus swung back and forth between fear, enmity, and curiosity.

Thus the sheer existence of Sepphoris compels even the theologians to do some rethinking. Proponents of historical-critical exegesis like to distinguish between the "historical" and the "kerygmatic" Jesus—the image of Christ in the Gospels and the Letters of Paul, which they consider unhistorical in several aspects. In the latter they see an initial inculturation, an adaptation of Jesus' teaching to the Hellenistic intellectual world of the mission territory. The "historical Jesus" in their view is merely a Jewish itinerant preacher with a humanitarian message, who wanted to replace worship with morality. Only the apostle Paul declared him the Son of God, reinterpreted his death on the Cross along the lines of the Greek mysteries as a redemptive deed, invented his Resurrection and Ascension into heaven, in short: created a myth that (according to this hypothesis) reached its final development decades later in the Gospels. Thus everything that sounded even halfway like Greek philosophy was interpreted by the proponents of this "historical-critical" exegesis as "not Jesuanic".

Yet this hypothesis fails to recognize the role that Greek civilization played even in Jesus' hometown. First-century Judaea, after all, had long since ceased to be an isolated wilderness kingdom but, rather, was part of a throbbing world with a Hellenistic character. Galilee, indeed, bordered on the flourishing cities of the Decapolis; on its roads merchants from the coastal cities in the east traveled and new ideas spread with great rapidity. The fact that all four Gospels were composed in the Greek language clearly shows, in any case, that the very first "audience" of the proclamation was also part of the Hellenistic "mainstream culture". The genuine "historical Jesus" was therefore anything but a backwoodsman from some remote place in the mountains; he had to walk only four miles to feel the pulse of his time. We can be all the more certain that he was familiar not only with the Greek language but also with Greek thought.

Jesus certainly learned one lesson from the fate of Sepphoris, namely, that it is senseless to resist Rome. The experience from the year 4 B.C. was both the traumatic birth and the creed of the city. Thus nothing in the world could convince the inhabitants of Sepphoris to participate in the Jewish rebellion in the year A.D. 66. They took the resulting hostility of all their Galilean neighbors as part of the bargain. When the Roman general (and later emperor) Vespasian went ashore in Judaea, he was promptly greeted by a delegation from Sepphoris that asked the Romans for help and protection from the resistance fighters. The Roman officer immediately recognized the opportunity and stationed a thousand cavalrymen and six thousand foot soldiers in the vicinity of the city (which prompts us to ask what role Nazareth played then). In order to demonstrate their love of freedom, the Sepphorites even minted coins that bore the inscription "In the time of Vespasian, the city of peace and of Nero (*Eirenopolis Neronias*), Sepphoris". There was no clearer way of signaling to the general and the emperor whose side they took.

And Jesus? He would have been pleased with the attitude of the "city on the hill". Neither tax collectors (see Mt 9:9) nor the Roman system of taxation in general bothered him; he was in favor of giving to Caesar what belongs to Caesar (cf. Mk 12:17). He knew that one can find the Kingdom of God in every political system, that it was a matter of liberating people from within and through love, and not through violence. Experience had also taught him that it was quite possible to be a good Jew in a Roman-Hellenistic environment, that openness to the world is not incompatible with lively faith. In this respect, too, a bit of Sepphoris always remained in him.

VI

The Precursor

Where Did Jesus' Ministry Start?

His heart beat faster and faster while he removed with his finger the last bit of dirt that still covered one detail or another. Shimon Gibson sensed that he had just made a discovery whose scope he slowly began to assess. For the more he angled the flashlight, in order to see better the contours of the drawing that someone one and a half millennia ago had scratched into the long since spotty whitewash on the rock of this cave-wall, the more certain he was that it depicted John the Baptist. The beardless head was surrounded by a sort of turban; the right hand was lifted in a gesture of blessing; the staff in the left hand was crowned by a cross. His loins were girt with a short garment made from rough camel hair, held together by a leather belt, and a lamb at his side seemed to embody the "Lamb of God" whose coming he announced. A hole below the scratched image was apparently once used to preserve a relic. Depictions of crosses, a head, and an arm adorned the rest of the wall.

The archaeologist soon remembered where he had already seen something similar. A comparable image had been discovered near the baptismal font of the old Church of the Annunciation in Nazareth and was dated by the archaeologists back to the "pre-Byzantine" era, i.e., Roman times. Here, too, a beardless John is wearing a turban, the staff that ends in a cross, the skirtlike garment; only, in terms of proportions, the artist worked more realistically. The Franciscans who are responsible for Nazareth described the turban-wearing Baptist as typical of early iconography, still characterized by Jewish-Christian notions: as a faithful Jew, the precursor of Jesus had to keep his head covered. The notion of a bearded John with disheveled hair, on the other hand, was a product of Byzantine art. Although the image in Nazareth was considered until now the earliest known depiction of the Baptist, Gibson's discovery had a very good chance to challenge that claim.

This was the beginning of a first-rate archaeological adventure for the Israeli. Time and again he returned to the damp, narrow cave that he had inspected on that gray November morning in 1999 at the invitation of the local Tzova Kibbutz. Soon he had obtained permission to begin excavations. The scratch-drawing had shown that the cave was a shrine in which John the Baptist was venerated as early as the pre-Byzantine era. The fact that it is located in the hill country of Judah, only three miles west of the Baptist's birthplace in Ain Karem, made the discovery even more significant. Before the founding of the kibbutz, this was no man's land, and in the immediate vicinity, that is, between Ain Karem and Tzova, there was neither a monastery nor a village. Did someone nevertheless have a special reason to venerate the Baptist here specifically? In fact, Adomnan, the biographer of the Gallic bishop and Holy Land pilgrim Arculf, as early as A.D. 670 mentioned a remote shrine of John: "This Arculf saw a small clear spring in the desert, from which people say that Saint John the Baptist used to drink. Its stone roof is covered with lime plaster."[1] Today the hermitage of Saint John the Baptist, two miles west of Ain Karem, on the other side of the Hadassah Clinic, cites this tradition. There, the story goes, the young John supposedly sought solitude, exactly as Luke reports: "The child grew and became strong in spirit, and he was in the wilderness till the day of his manifestation to Israel" (Lk 1:80).

The Greek word *eremos*, which in the American Standard Version is translated as "desert", in fact only means "wilderness" and generally refers to a solitary place in pristine nature. The hermitage is indeed located by a well with excellent water. Seven steps lead into a cave, into the wall of which a stone shelf was hewn, above which an altar was erected. A niche in the rock was likely used for placing an oil lamp. Traces of lime suggest that the rock walls were plastered at some point in time. Over the spring, the chapel of Saint Elizabeth is

---

[1] Adomnan, *The Holy Place*, in John Wilkinson, *Jerusalem Pilgrims Before the Crusades* (Jerusalem: Ariel, 1977), p. 108.

located, built on top of the grave of the Baptist's mother. She is said to have died when John was only seven years old.

But what, then, was the purpose of the grotto in which Gibson found the scratch-drawing? Initial excavations showed that it was in fact used until the Byzantine and early Islamic era. When he applied the spade to one corner of the plastered wall, the archaeologist realized that the plaster reached much deeper than the Byzantine floor level. This meant that the cave had been prepared for worship purposes already at an earlier point in time. Where the whitewash ended, he came upon a new layer of dirt in which shards of vessels from the first century were embedded. Stairs led down a narrow passage to a basin that gave the entire structure the appearance of a large *mikveh*. At the edge of the basin was a circle of rough stones in which a jug had once stood. In front of it, below a niche, was a large oval rock into which the shape of a right foot had been hewn. Above the foot shape an almost circular saucer-shaped basin had been chiseled into the stone, which was connected to the foot shape by a narrow water duct. Remains of small oil jugs were found in the cave that would have fit perfectly into the basin. Gibson concluded from this that in the first century rituals took place here, including a ritual cleansing with water, but also a symbolic anointing of feet. The cave itself had been used as a cistern as early as the Iron Age. Whether it served agricultural or cultic purposes at that time remains a riddle.

There is an old rule for archaeologists, not to be taken too seriously, that says: "If you cannot explain a find, simply declare it a cult object." Critics cited it when Gibson published his discovery in 2004 in the almost four-hundred-page bestseller *The Cave of John the Baptist*. For him, the rock chamber is nothing less than the key to understanding Jesus' precursor, a first concrete proof for his ministry and his cultic practice. The scratched image of the Baptist, below which a relic was once embedded, and the cave's proximity to Ain Karem do in fact allow us to infer that it was at one point associated with his early ministry. Whether he was also involved in the ritual cleansings and anointings that took place during his time is rather questionable.

What the discussion of Gibson's discovery shows, however, is how little we actually know about the man of whom Jesus said: "Truly I say to you, among those born of women there has arisen no one greater than John the Baptist" (Mt 11:11; cf. Lk 7:28). Only that he truly existed is credibly attested. When Antipas suffered a bitter defeat against his father-in-law, the Nabataean King Aretas, in A.D. 33, many Jews saw this as God's punishment for the Baptist's execution four years before. Flavius Josephus thus writes in *The Antiquities of the Jews*:

> ... for Herod slew him, who was a good man, and commanded the Jews to exercise virtue, both as to righteousness towards one another, and piety towards God, and so to come to baptism; for that the washing [with water] would be acceptable to him, if they made use of it, not in order to the putting away [or the remission] of some sins [only], but for the purification of the body; supposing still that the soul was thoroughly purified beforehand by righteousness. Now when [many] others came in crowds about him, for they were very greatly moved [or pleased] by hearing his words, Herod, who feared lest the great influence John had over the people might put it into his power and inclination to raise a rebellion [for they seemed ready to do anything he should advise], thought it best, by putting him to death, to prevent any mischief he might cause.[2]

Mark and John begin their Gospels with an account of the Baptist's ministry; in Luke's Gospel, his appearance is the second important anchoring of Jesus' life in world history. The historian among the Evangelists is able to date it precisely by naming the powerful men of this time:

> In the fifteenth year of the reign of Tiberius Caesar, Pontius Pilate being governor of Judea, and Herod being tetrarch of Galilee, and his brother Philip tetrarch of the region of Ituraea and Trachonitis, and Lysanias tetrarch of Abilene, in the high-priesthood of Annas and Caiaphas, the word of God came to John the son of Zechariah in the wilderness; and he went into all the region about the Jordan, preaching a baptism of repentance for the forgiveness of sins. (Lk 3:1–3)

Tiberius ruled as co-regent from A.D. 13, as sole ruler from 14–37, so that the reference here can only be to the years A.D. 27 or 28.

---

[2] Flavius Josephus, *Jewish Antiquities*, bk. 18, chap. 5, no. 2, in *New Complete Works of Josephus*, trans. William Whiston (Grand Rapids, Mich.: Kregel, 1999), p. 595.

The other data match this. Pontius Pilate was prefect of Judaea from 26/27 to 36/37, Herod Antipas ruled from 4 B.C. to A.D. 39, his half-brother Philip from 4 B.C. to A.D. 33; there are no precise data about Lysanias. Annas was high priest from A.D. 6–15, but was considered the *éminence grise* of a whole dynasty: his five sons, one after another, came to hold the office of high priest; his son-in-law Caiaphas was in office from A.D. 18 to 37. But we can be even more precise. The coins that Pontius Pilate had minted for three consecutive years prove that the rule of Tiberius—at least in Judaea—was reckoned from the year 13 (and not from September 14). The first series bears the date LIF (year 16) and the Greek inscriptions *Tiberiou Kaisaros* and *Ioulia Kaisaros*, which referred to the emperor's mother, Livia, who, when her husband died, was adopted into the Julian clan and declared *Augusta*. Valerius Gratus, the predecessor of Pontius Pilate, had already immortalized her name on the reverse side of his coins. But Julia died in September of the year 29, and thus her name is missing on the second series of coins, which bears the date LIZ (year 17). This can only lead to the conclusion that the year 16 referred to the last year of Julia, i.e., 28/29, and that therefore the fifteenth year was equivalent to 27/28. Unfortunately even authors of numismatic reference books have ignored this fact and misdated Pilate's coins by one year.

Luke's date also corresponds with John's reference that the cleansing of the Temple at the beginning of Jesus' ministry occurred toward the end of March A.D. 28. There is consequently no reason to question what the well-educated physician Luke evidently researched precisely. His next reference to the date also matches: "Jesus was about thirty years old" when this happened. In January of 28, when he probably came to John, he was indeed exactly thirty-one years old. We do not know in which "desert", "wasteland", or "wilderness" the Baptist had stayed before, whether in the hill country of Judah or the desert of Judaea. He must have been a hermit, a recluse, who lived in caves, if it says about him: "John was clothed with camel's hair, and had a leather belt around his waist, and ate locusts and wild honey" (Mk 1:6). Still today, locusts, eaten roasted over the fire or cold with honey, serve as food in parts of Arabia and Africa. Recluses, too, were not a rare occurrence; Flavius Josephus for instance relates that for three years he was the eager pupil of one "whose name was Bannus" who "lived in the desert, and used no other clothing than grew upon trees, and had no other food than what grew of its own accord, and bathed himself in cold water frequently, both by night and by day."[3]

The time into which he came was filled with eschatological speculations, messianic hopes, and conflicts among religious factions. Immediately after the insurrection of the Maccabees, three "factions" or "sects" had emerged that shaped Judaism decisively in Jesus' time, too. The Sadducees (from Hebrew, *saddiq*, "just") had come to a settlement with the powers that be and since the second century B.C. had provided the aristocracy and the priestly nobility in the land. They held the majority in the seventy-person *Sanhedrin*, the "High Council" of the Jews. What mattered to them was not tradition but only the written Law, the Torah; their center of power and religious focus was the Temple with its rituals. In opposition to them were the Pharisees (from Hebrew, *perushim*, "the segregated"). They emerged from the *Chassidim*, the "Pious", who had still fought for the Temple, side by side with the Maccabees. But then they rejected the ruling family and its Sadducee elite as being too opportunistic and eventually charged Herod with selling out Israel to the Romans. Their name indicates that they kept themselves away from everything that could result in ritual impurity. They kept the dietary and purity precepts of the Torah just as painstakingly as the purity and food precepts of the *Halacha*, the "oral Torah", i.e., the tradition that governed all areas of daily life for them. A third group, the Essenes (from Aramaic, *chase*, "pious"), likewise emerged from the Chassidim movement, but their response to the Hasmonean rule was total opposition. For them, a king who was not from the house of David was just as much a usurper as a non-Aaronite high priest. Their founder, who called himself "Teacher of Justice", described the Hasmonean high priest as a "Priest of Sacrilege" and "Man of Lies", and the opportunistic Sadducees as "Seekers of Adulation". The fact that they had control over Jerusalem and the Temple was a sign for him of being in the "last days", when the powers of evil once more gain power before the Messiah defeats them and establishes the Kingdom of God. Besides him, the true King of the Jews, who could only come from the house of David, he also expected a genuine high piest (the *Messiah-Priest*)

---

[3] *The Life of Flavius Josephus*, 2, in *New Complete Works of Josephus*, p. 17.

from the house of Aaron. In order to be able to find them in good time and to support them, the sect maintained close ties with the Davidic and Aaronite families.

Since the discovery of the Dead Sea Scrolls and the monastery of Qumran, it has been considered certain that John came into contact with the Essenes. The geographic proximity to his baptism site on the Jordan, which is only 8.4 miles distant as the crow flies, is not the only indication of this. Both the Essenes and John deliberately chose solitude so that through interior and exterior cleansing they could prepare themselves for a "new annexation of territory", a spiritual conquest of Israel. Thus the pious of Qumran called the area in which their monastery was located "the wilderness" and thereby referred the words of the prophet Isaiah to themselves: "A voice cries: In the wilderness prepare the way of the LORD; make straight in the desert a highway for our God" (Is 40:3). It was the same prophecy that, according to the unanimous testimony of all four Gospels, John saw fulfilled by his mission ("He said, 'I am the voice of one crying in the wilderness, "Make straight the way of the Lord"'" [Jn 1:23; cf. Mt 3:3, Mk 1:2f., Lk 3:4f.]).

Flavius Josephus relates about the Essenes: "[they] choose out other persons' children, while they are pliable, and fit for learning, and esteem them to be as their own family, and form them according to their own manners".[4] Since John had lost his father when he was not even a year old and his mother when he was seven, he grew up as an orphan. Most likely the sect had already monitored his development attentively since he came from the family of the Aaronites with which the Essenes were in contact. So they knew both about the miraculous circumstances of his birth and also about the murder of his father by Herod's men, which the *Protoevangelium* mentions. It probably did not bother them much that he was the son of a Temple priest. They rejected the non-Aaronite high priests and the Sadduceean hierarchy, of course, but not the Temple as an institution. Since they had at least initially supported Herod the Great and under his rule for the first time had taken up quarters in Jerusalem, we can even assume that they were involved in the planning of the new

[4] Flavius Josephus, *The Jewish War*, bk. 2, chap. 8, no. 2, in *New Complete Works of Josephus*, p. 736.

Temple and enjoyed special privileges there. It is therefore quite possible that after the death of his mother, they took the boy under their
wing and educated him.

What also speaks in favor of a connection to the Essenes is the fact
that John's ministry, at least according to the Fourth Gospel, began at
a place named "Bethany beyond the Jordan" (Jn 1:28). As early as the
third century, Origen was troubled by the fact that there was no city
of this name. He thus concluded that the copyists had made a mistake
and that the Evangelist must have meant the village of Bethabara
("House of Crossing") near the mouth of the Jordan by the Dead Sea.
This appeared plausible to him for the simple reason that the actual
baptism site (as we will see) was less than five miles away. On account
of the similar spelling, Origen said, it must have been confused with
the village of Bethany on the eastern slope of the Mount of Olives,
where Jesus brought Lazarus back to life. Today we know that Origen oversimplified things for himself. Even the earliest manuscripts of
the Fourth Gospel from the second century always mention "Bethany", while the alternative spelling of "Bethabara" is only evidenced
from the time after Origen. But Bethabara cannot be meant at all
since from the Jewish perspective it was and is in fact located "on this
side of the Jordan", not "beyond" it. Identification with the area of
Batanaea, as suggested by Padre Bargil Pixner among others, can also
be excluded. Batanaea, after all, was not located on the Jordan River,
in which Jesus was baptized according to the unanimous opinion of
all four Evangelists, but rather east of the Gaulanitis, the modern-
day Golan Heights. It can also be ruled out grammatically since the
reference to the location lacks an article that would have been lin-
guistically necessary to denote an area. Furthermore, Batanaea is also
much too far away for "all the country of Judea, and all the people
of Jerusalem" (Mk 1:5) to have gone there. In the Gospel of John,
we finally find an approximate indication of the distance. When in
March of the year 30 Jesus "went away again across the Jordan to the
place where John at first baptized" (Jn 10:40), it took exactly one
day for the message of his friend Lazarus' death to reach him. Jesus
stayed for another two days, then he traveled the distance in one
more day, so that Lazarus "had already been in the tomb four days"
(Jn 11:17) when Jesus raised him to life. One day's journey equaled
twenty-two to twenty-five miles, much too short, therefore, for the

eighty-seven-mile linear distance to Batanaea, but exactly right to reach the right bank of the Jordan near Jericho (from Bethany at the Mount of Olives a distance of about twenty-two miles).

But could there in fact have been two settlements with the same name, one near Jerusalem, the other on the east bank of the Jordan? And was it a coincidence that Jesus ministered in both? The British New Testament scholar Brian J. Capper of Canterbury Christ Church University offers a stunning answer to this question.

Bethany, according to Capper, was, first of all, not a place but an institution, part of a network of Essene charity houses and settlements that were called *beth anya*, literally, "House of the Poor". Here members of the order, supported by wealthy benefactors, took care of the needy. The network was part of the Essenes' endeavor to found a new, just, and God-fearing societal order that was referred to as the New Covenant. Here, finally, Jesus, who advocated similar values, met with enthusiastic acceptance.

Flavius Josephus in fact also describes the Essene community as a sort of predecessor of later Christian orders: "These men are despisers of riches, and so very communicative as raises our admiration. Nor is there anyone to be found among them who has more than another; for it is a law among them, that those who come to them must let what they have be common to the whole order".[5] There were community houses in every city, he writes, in which an Essene would find everything necessary for living. Simultaneously he emphasizes their care for the needy: "... only these two things are done among them at everyone's own free will, which are to assist those that want it, and to show mercy; for they are permitted of their own accord to afford help to such as deserve it, when they stand in need of it, and to bestow food on those that are in distress."[6]

The Temple Scroll of the Essenes that was found in the caves of Qumran demands: "And you shall make three places to the east of the city, separated one from one another, into which shall come the lepers and the people who have a discharge and the men who have had a nocturnal emission."[7] Here the impure were supposed to

---

[5] Ibid., no. 3, p. 736.

[6] Ibid., no. 6, p. 737.

[7] Yigael Yadin, *The Temple Scroll: The Hidden Law of the Dead Sea Sect* (New York: Random House, 1985), p. 173.

be able to purify themselves and wait until, according to the Jewish purity laws, they were allowed to reenter the City of the Temple. One can rightfully compare them to the medieval pilgrim hospices from which our hospitals emerged. These "three places", we further learn in the Temple Scroll, had to be at least 3,000 cubits (about 4,500 feet) away from the city, and in such a manner that nothing impure could be seen from the Temple.

Three places at the southeastern edge of the Mount of Olives meet all these criteria, namely, En-Shemesh, Bethphage, and Bethany. And they were conveniently located for another reason: the road from Jericho to Jerusalem went past them, the route taken by most pilgrims, who avoided hostile Samaria and preferably traveled via the Jewish territories east of the Jordan so as then to cross the river again near Jericho. Thus we can assume that here the Essenes built their "social service stations" under the banner of the "New Covenant".

Anyone who during the pilgrimage became the victim of a skin disease or suffered from a discharge or a seminal emission was here able to undergo the three- to seven-day purification that was pre-scribed before the Temple could be entered. At the same time, the houses likely served for the care of the needy. They were pilgrim hospices, kitchens for the poor, and hospitals in one, Capper claims.

A whole series of clues supports this thesis. First of all, there are the people who in the four Gospels are named as inhabitants of Bethany by the Mount of Olives. Several things are striking about them. For one thing, there are the three siblings Lazarus, Mary, and Martha. The fact that they lived together plainly unmarried, even though all three of them were adults, was more than unusual among Jews. After all, early marriage and procreation of children were considered a duty before God. The only exceptions were the Essenes, who, as Flavius Josephus emphasizes, "esteem continence, and the conquest over our passions, to be virtue [and] neglect wedlock"[8]—most of them lived in celibacy. Then there was "Simon the Leper", in whose house Jesus was a guest and of whom we do not know whether he indeed once suffered from leprosy and was healed or whether his "leprosy" was in fact only a skin disease, neurodermatitis, for instance.

---

[8] Flavius Josephus, *The Jewish War*, bk. 2, chap. 8, no. 2, in *New Complete Works of Josephus*, p. 736.

For a long time exegetes challenged the idea that actual leprosy (also called Hansen's disease) was widespread at all in Palestine at the time of Jesus. They readily declared all "lepers" in general to be carriers of relatively harmless skin diseases. As of June 2000, we know that this explanation is false. At that time, the archaeologists James Tabor and Shimon Gibson discovered an old rock tomb on the "Field of Blood", *Hakeldama*, on the other side of the Hinnom Valley, across from Jerusalem's Southern Wall. It had been robbed recently; the fragments of ossuaries (bone chests made of stone) and human bones still lay scattered in front of its entrance. The tomb raiders had not been interested in the decomposed remains of a person, now only a skeleton, that lay in one of the shafts (*kokhim*) of the tomb, still wrapped in the remains of an ancient burial cloth. For the archaeologists, this was an unbelievable discovery. Immediately they sent a fragment of the burial cloth to the United States for radiocarbon dating; it was from the first century. Forensic pathologists who subsequently examined the bone fragments came to the conclusion that the dead person suffered from tuberculosis and leprosy. A metatarsal bone exhibited the sort of changes that are typical as a result of Hansen's disease. The finding of the skeleton was therefore the first proof that leprosy was widespread in the Holy Land at the time of Jesus—and that at least some of the "lepers" he encountered could actually have been infected with it.

The fact that this "Simon the Leper" had a house in Bethany seems to support the settlement's character as an Essene colony for the ritually impure. It makes no difference that Simon was apparently a Pharisee (Lk 7:36–44) since the Essenes sympathized with the Pharisees; their common enemies were the Sadducees, the "Temple lobby". The strongest evidence, however, is archaeological in nature. In 1951, the famous Dominican archaeologist and head of the École Biblique in Jerusalem, Father Pierre Benoit, made a sensational discovery in Bethany. In the garden of the convent of the Daughters of Charity of Saint Vincent de Paul, he came upon a structure that he at first thought was a Jewish-Christian baptistery. Following a staircase hewn into the limestone, one descends into a cave that ends in a basin sixteen feet wide and thirteen feet deep. Benoit was surprised to find that through a low wall foundation in the center of the steps the staircase was divided into an ascent and a descent. The whitewashed walls were covered all over with graffiti. Through a duct, the "baptismal cellar" was connected to a cistern that evidently supplied the basin with fresh water.

Now we know that the structure was originally a *mikveh*, supplied with "living water" through the duct. *Mikvehs* of this sort were found in Qumran, on Jerusalem's Mount Zion—where, according to Flavius Josephus, the Essene quarter was found—and in the immediate vicinity of the Temple. It was too big, too elaborate, to serve a private purpose. Everything indicates that it was the cleansing bath for the Essene hospice of Bethany. Jesus and his disciples could have bathed here, too, before they came into city of the Temple.

Apparently a second *beth anya*, a hospice for Jerusalem pilgrims, was located on the east bank of the Jordan opposite Jericho, where the throngs of pilgrims crossed the river. From here it was only a day's walk to Jerusalem. Enough reason to stop one more time on this last leg of the pilgrimage, to be cleansed physically and spiritually, and, if help was needed, to seek the care of the Essenes. For the order this place was significant. Joshua had once crossed the river here to conquer Canaan, and here the Essenes intended to start their new spiritual conquest. Jesus' spiritual connection to Joshua was established at his birth. For Joshua and Jesus are just two variations of the same Biblical name Jehoshua (God is help), which in its short form turned into Joshua, but later, at the time of the Second Temple, into Jeshu, the very name we Latinized into Jesus. The name was not uncommon. Flavius Josephus named twenty-one who bore it, and it ranks fifth on Jewish ossuary inscriptions with eleven documented instances, which is why the Son of God was identified outside of his homeland only through the addition of "from Nazareth" (*ha-Nozri*) or simply as "the Nazarene" (*Nazari*). Yet as common as the name was, it had a deeper meaning; otherwise the angel would not have revealed it both to his mother (cf. Lk 1:31) and to his foster father (cf. Mt 1:21). He was indeed the new Joshua, who would lead the new Israel into the Kingdom of God, and he, too, started on the east bank of the Jordan. It was therefore no coincidence that the public ministry both of John the Baptist and of Jesus began precisely here.

But there is yet another interesting detail. According to the Essene *Community Rule for Israel in the End Times*, which was discovered in the first cave of Qumran, there was a minimum age for each task in the community. At age twenty, a boy became a man and was allowed to join the sect and, if he did not want to live as a celibate, to marry also. At age twenty-five, he could begin his service for the community, but only at age thirty was he considered mature and ready to participate in a debate or to assume a leadership role. John was thirty-one when he began his mission before Yom Kippur in autumn A.D. 27; Jesus was thirty-one when he came to the baptism site in January A.D. 28.

Yet there were two big differences between John and the Essenes. One of them was in their target group. The order was elitist and consciously separated itself from the "world" and the "men of error", while the Baptist addressed his cry to all men. In the Qumran writings, we encounter a Law-centered piety in which they surpassed even the most scrupulous Pharisees. Even if a man fell into a well on the Sabbath, the Essenes were forbidden to rescue him. Out of constant concern about ritual impurity, they subjected themselves to ritual cleansing several times a day. John's baptism was in formal accord with these cleansings—as a river, the Jordan was the *proto-mikveh*, its "living waters" satisfying all prescripts of the Halacha—but he pursued a different purpose with it. For him, it was not about the cleansing of the body but about that of the soul. His baptism with water was only a preparation for the baptism with the Holy Spirit that he foresaw. Regardless, at least some of the Essenes seem to have supported John, whom they considered a prophet, and then also Jesus.

Bethany beyond the Jordan was of interest for John not only because Joshua crossed the Jordan here in order to conquer the Promised Land. The place was also closely linked to an Old Testament prophet to whom he felt a strong connection: Elijah. About him, too, we read (in 2 Kings 2:7–8) that he crossed the Jordan at the ford near Jericho in order to ascend to heaven in a fiery chariot on the other side of the river. Since antiquity, a cave has been venerated there, in which Elijah is said to have lived, along with a hill from which he was taken up into heaven. The prophet would return to announce the Messiah, the Jews said. "And he will go before [the Lord] in the spirit and power of Elijah, to turn the hearts of the fathers to the children, and the disobedient to the wisdom of the just" (Lk 1:17), the angel had declared to his father, Zachariah, before John's birth. How much the Baptist identified with the prophet is already evidenced by his appearance. About Elijah we read: "He wore a garment of haircloth, with a belt of leather about his loins" (2 Kings 1:8); the Gospels report almost verbatim about the Baptist: "John wore a garment of camel's hair, and a leather belt around his waist" (Mt 3:4; cf. Mk 1:6). Jesus, too, explained to his disciples: "'Elijah has already come, and they did not know him, but did to him whatever they pleased'.... Then the disciples understood that he was speaking to them of John the Baptist" (Mt 17:12–13).

The memory of the site of his ministry evidently never died. The very first pilgrimage account from the Holy Land, the *Itinerarium*, written by a pilgrim from Bordeaux in 333, mentions: "From there [the Dead Sea] to the Jordan, where the Lord was baptized by John, [is] five miles. There is a place above the river, a little hill on that shore, where Elijah was seized up into heaven."[9]

Around 530, the archdeacon Theodosius from Jerusalem put it more exactly:

At the place where my Lord was baptized is a marble column, and on top of it has been set an iron cross. There also is the Church of Saint John Baptist, which was constructed by the Emperor Anastasius. It stands on great vaults which are high enough for the times when the Jordan is in flood.... On the far side of the Jordan [is] the "little hill" ... where Saint Elijah was taken up.... It is five miles from the place where my Lord was baptized to the point where the Jordan enters the Dead Sea.[10]

Forty years later, the pilgrim from Piacenza came to the place "where the Lord was baptized. There is an obelisk there surrounded by a screen, and in the water, where the river turned back in its bed, stands a wooden cross. On both banks there are marble steps leading down to the water."[11]

As early as 1899, the Franciscan friar Federlin identified the spot the pilgrims had mentioned on the east bank of the Jordan. He described the ruins of several churches, one of which was indeed built on top

---

[9] *The Bordeaux Pilgrim (c. 333 C.E.)*, trans. Andrew S. Jacobs, at www.andrewjacobs.org/bordeaux.html.

[10] Theodosius, *The Topography of the Holy Land*, in Wilkinson, *Jerusalem Pilgrims*, p. 69.

[11] The Piacenza Pilgrim, *Travels from Piacenza*, in Wilkinson, *Jerusalem Pilgrims*, p. 82.

of a vault, as Theodosius had described it. As late as 1955, the Greek monk M. Kl. Karapiperis claims to have seen a twenty-foot-long marble pillar in the waters of the Jordan, as the Holy Land expert par excellence, Clemens Kopp, learned from him personally. But it still took almost a century for systematic archaeological excavations to take place here.

The reason for this was the state of war between Israel and Jordan. From 1967 on, the Jordan was the boundary between the two enemy nations; the terrain on both banks was mined and declared a military restricted area. Only the peace agreement between the two states in 1994 changed the situation. Now Jordan, otherwise poor in Christian sites, saw its chance to offer a destination for pilgrimages. The country began to advertise with the English slogan "Jordan: The Land and River of the Baptism". King Hussein gave the go-ahead for the founding of a "royal commission for developing a park of the baptism of the Lord and Messiah (Peace be with him) in the Jordan valley". After the last mines had been removed, the excavations at the mouth of the Wadi al-Kharrar began in 1996, under the direction of Mohammed Waheeb, an experienced archaeologist of the Jordan Antiquities Authority. Waheeb, indeed, found the ruins of four Byzantine churches here, one of which once stood on top of an impressive arch construction. The oldest structure was a rectangular prayer hall made of natural stone that was built as early as the third century. A simple white mosaic adorned its floor; its ceiling was likely made of wood. Several paved pools, which were supplied through water channels, seem to have served for mass baptisms in Byzantine times, in case the Jordan was too deep or the current too swift. At another spot, stairs seem to have led directly to where the bank of the Jordan was at that time—these are probably the stairs that the pilgrim from Piacenza mentioned. Today the river runs a full 328 feet west from here and is merely a narrow brook since its water has already been diverted upstream to supply water to the villages and plantations in Israel and Jordan. The river carries about 317 billion gallons of water annually, 264,000 of which are drawn off in equal parts by its two riparian states. What remains and reaches Jericho is rather sparse. Even the Dead Sea is in danger of drying up in the not too distant future. Yet, in the first half of the twentieth century, the Jordan still rose to a width of several hundred yards in the months of spring.

Sixty-two miles east, in the headwater region of the Wadi al-Kharrar, where the Hill of Elijah is located, Waheeb came upon a Byzantine monastery complex. It consisted of three churches and a baptismal font, as well as a sophisticated water-duct system. A church and adorned with a magnificent mosaic floor, stood right on top of a hill on whose western slope a second, presumably older, sanctuary used a cave as its apse. An author by the name of John around the year 600 reports that a hundred years earlier a monk by the same name had had a mystical vision here on his pilgrimage to Sinai. The Baptist himself had appeared to him in a dream and assured him: "This small cave is bigger than Mount Sinai. Our Lord Jesus Christ himself came here to visit me." In the Byzantine era, this monastery settlement was called Ainon (well site) after the nearby well, or Sapsaphas (pasture), two names that we also find on a mosaic map of the Holy Land that was made in the late sixth century in the Church of Saint George in Madaba. As late as 1106 the Russian Abbot Daniel visited the site, when the monastery was long gone, and reported: "Not far away from the river, a distance of two arrow throws, is the place where Prophet Elijah was taken into heaven in a chariot of fire. There is also the grotto of Saint John the Baptist. A beautiful torrent full of water flows over the stones towards the Jordan, the water is very cold and has a very good taste; it is the water that John drank while he lived in the holy grotto."[12]

The traces of human settlement—clay and stone vessels, coins, and inscriptions—that were discovered here by the archaeologists are from two phases of settlement. The first began in the second century B.C., thus coinciding with the founding of the Essene community, and ended in the second century A.D. Of special significance were the remains of some massive stone vessels for ritual cleansing purposes, such as are considered "Jewish index fossils". They indicate the presence of a strictly religious community that was familiar with the rules of the Halacha. This, therefore, could indeed have been the location of an Essene beth-anya camp. The second phase lasted from the fifth until the eighth century, i.e., from the Byzantine to the early Islamic period, when Christian pilgrimage experienced its first heyday.

---

[12] Quoted by Mohammed Waheeb in "A Unique Byzantine Architectural Remains on the Eastern Bank of Jordan River", *American International Journal of Contemporary Research*, vol. 7, no. 4 (December 2017): 96.

No wonder, therefore, that, to the increasing enthusiasm of the Jordanians, churches discovered this spot for themselves. New stairs leading down to the river have already been built at the mouth of the Wadi al-Kharrar, in front of which a Greek-Orthodox church with golden cupolas has been situated. Reason enough for Pope Benedict XVI not only to put the Park of the Lord's Baptismal Site on the program for his visit to Jordan but, in the presence of King Abdullah and Queen Ranja, even to bless the cornerstones of two churches that were to be built here—one each for the Catholics of the Latin and of the Greek rite. Anglicans and Russians, Copts and Armenians are building in the immediate vicinity. A well-marked path connects the monastery complex by the Hill of Elijah, where John's grotto is located, with the church complex on the bank of the Jordan. To date, it is a modest but well-tended and appealing facility, inviting visitors and attracting more and more pilgrims—as many as 280,000 in 2008.

This, of course, was bad news for the Israeli baptismal site that is located directly across from it on the Jordan's west bank. It owes its existence not so much to the fact that Origen confused Bethany with Bethabara as to the safety and convenience of Jerusalem pilgrims. Especially in the last months of winter, when the river (at that time still) rose considerably, it was difficult to cross it. Furthermore, the east bank was considered unsafe; too frequently Bedouin tribes robbed the pilgrims, and later on the area was firmly under Muslim control. In order to be able to celebrate the Feast of the Epiphany by the Jordan in spite of that, a church and a monastery were built on the west bank, on a hill above the Jordan, in the sixth century. Both must have been destroyed during the incursion of the Persians in 614. On their ruins, Emperor Manuel Komnenos (1143–1180) commissioned the building of the Orthodox Prodromos ("Precursor") Monastery, which owes its name to the Baptist's Greek title and for good reason resembles a fortress. Nevertheless, it was abandoned only a century later and was not refurbished and restaffed by the Greek Orthodox Patriarchate until 1882. The Syrian Christians call it Mar Yuhanna (literally: "Lord John"); the Arabs call it Qasr el-Yehud ("Fortress of the Jews") on account of its fortifications. Right next to it the Franciscans built a chapel in 1935; a little farther south, the Russians, the Rumanians, and the Copts. Since all of these are located in the military restricted zone, Israel allowed the denominations access to the Jordan only twice a year, on their respective Feasts of the Epiphany. When Pope John Paul II visited Israel and Jordan in 2000, he very diplomatically visited both baptismal sites. The fact that his successor picked the Jordanian site may have stirred the competitor's envy. In any event, Israel showed generosity, and the Ministry of Tourism allocated 1.75 million dollars to the expansion of the pilgrimage site on the left bank of the Jordan. As of December 2011, it can be visited daily from 9 A.M. to 4 P.M. (in the summer; in the winter from 9 A.M. to 3 P.M., on Fridays only until 2 P.M.). It is certain, however, that Jesus was baptized neither on the Israeli nor on the Jordan side but in the middle of the river, i.e., exactly on the boundary between the two states.

Whenever I visit one of the sites, I get a sense of how lively the Gospel descriptions are. Standing here it becomes evident that they are based on eyewitness accounts. When we read that Jesus asked the crowd about John: "What did you go out into the wilderness to behold? A reed shaken by the wind?" (Mt 11:7 and Lk 7:24), these words become more powerful and impressive when we see with our own eyes how abundant the reeds on the bank of the Jordan are to this day. Or let us take John's speech scolding the Pharisees, whom he called "brood of vipers" (Mt and Lk 3:7); according to the ancient pilgrims' accounts, the Wadi el-Kharrar was literally teeming with snakes. Again and again, people ask the Baptist whether he is Elijah (for instance, Jn 1:21); this question, too, is justified, since he ministered on the site of the ascension of the prophet whom the Jews expected to return for the end times. It is significant when the son of a priest who offered sacrifice, who perhaps himself tended sheep in his youth, calls Jesus the "Lamb of God, who takes away the sin of the world" (Jn 1:29).

As much as the accounts of the three Synoptic Gospels—Matthew, Mark, and Luke—resemble each other, the additions of John are all the more interesting. I say "additions" since the Fourth Gospel was written as a reaction to the first three. In part, it intends to deepen, sometimes even correct (John, for instance, explicitly states that Jesus' public ministry began during John's ministry, not after his arrest, as one might falsely conclude from the Synoptic Gospels; see John 3:24), but often to complete. In this case, the author does not need to repeat what was already known from three Gospels. He took it for granted.

Immediately after his baptism, Jesus at first withdrew into the desert. He wanted to pray and fast in order to prepare for his mission. He most likely did not venture far from the baptism site, which was located, after all, on the edge of the desert. He probably withdrew into the mountains west of Jericho. An ancient tradition even claims to identify the "very high mountain" on which Jesus was tempted by the devil. It is a rock face north of Jericho, 1142 feet tall, towering almost precipitously over the Jordan plain. The mountain is named Quarantana, after the forty-day fast, and on its slope lies a Greek monastery, allegedly built over the cave in which Jesus lived at that time. Indeed, so it would seem, "all the kingdoms of the world and the glory of them" (Mt 4:8) lay at his feet, at least the fertile oasis of Jericho, together with Herod's palace complex, which was as gigantic as it was luxurious. But Jesus resisted the temptation of worldly power and worldly riches.

Then we experience a gap in the Synoptic Gospels. They do not resume the narrative until "after John was arrested" (Mk 1:14–15) and describe Jesus' ministry in Galilee and how he called his disciples, as if he encountered them randomly and for the first time. But John knows that it was not quite like that. And thus he relates everything that happened in the meantime, not without shedding light on the allegedly rather spontaneous calling of the disciples.

The fourth Evangelist starts where the gap in the Synoptic Gospels begins. The Baptist proclaimed that someone greater had come. On the next day, he saw how Jesus returned to the Jordan from the desert. Now he gave witness and proclaimed what he had experienced when he baptized Jesus forty days earlier: "I saw the Spirit descend as a dove from heaven and remain on him.... I have seen and have borne witness that this is the Son of God" (Jn 1:32, 34). On the third day, he explicitly referred two of his disciples to Jesus, who presumably had built himself a hut from reeds or moved into a cave near the *beth anya* camp. The disciples became curious and followed Jesus, who invited them to his place. They listened to him and were fascinated; they stayed until about "the tenth hour" (Jn 1:39), that is, until 4 P.M. One of the Baptist's disciples appears to be John, son of the fisherman Zebedee and the author of the Fourth Gospel; the other was Andrew, also a young fisherman from Bethsaida in Galilee. He told his brother Simon about the encounter, for he was certain: "We have found the Messiah" (Jn 1:41). When Jesus saw the brother of Andrew, it was as if two well-acquainted souls were meeting: "Jesus looked at him, and said, 'So you are Simon the son of John? You shall be called Cephas'" (Jn 1:42). The Aramaic word means "rock", in Greek: *petros*. We know him better by his Latinized name, Petrus, or Peter. But yet another one of the Baptist's disciples was from Bethsaida: Philip. He, too, was summoned by Jesus: "Follow me." (1:43); likewise a fourth Galilean: Nathanael. The six of them left for their home in Galilee. Together they attended a wedding and eventually settled in Capernaum, where Peter lived in the house of his mother-in-law. Naturally they went as a group on the pilgrimage to the Passover feast in Jerusalem in the year 28, where the disciples became witnesses of the cleansing of the Temple. Initially, they appeared to have been somewhat irritated by the vehemence of Jesus' reaction, but then they calmed down. Was it not already written in the Psalms (69:9): "Zeal for your house has consumed me"? However, they also experienced how popular Jesus became and felt his charisma: "Now when he was in Jerusalem at the Passover feast, many believed in his name when they saw the signs which he did" (Jn 2:23).

Later on, the first five disciples of Jesus were with him when their Master received a visit from one of the most prominent Jews of his time. The man's name was Nicodemus, and John tells us in another passage that he was a member of the party of the Pharisees in the Sanhedrin. From Jewish sources we know more, for instance, that his full name was Nakdimon ben Gurion (Nicodemus, son of Gurion). He was one of the three wealthiest patricians of Jerusalem and a benefactor of almost proverbial generosity. He was considered "just" with a downright saintly way of life; John, therefore, is not exaggerating when he calls him "teacher of Israel". Meanwhile, he maintained close ties to the Roman administration. Like Jesus, he was from Galilee (as John 7:52 confirms) and owned a vast amount of land in Ruma. During the Jewish War, fanatic rebels burned down his granaries. Nicodemus presumably died in the course of those events—he must have been in his seventies at the time. Of his daughter it is related that from then on she lived in abject poverty. Flavius Josephus mentions "Gorion, son of Nicodemus" (who was apparently named after his

grandfather), who at the start of the Jewish rebellion was part of a delegation negotiating with the Romans. His son Josephus—the grand-
son of Nicodemus—was later on appointed commander-in-chief of
the city of Jerusalem, together with the high priest Ananus, probably
in an effort to satisfy both parties, Pharisees as well as Sadducees.

Jesus confided in Nicodemus. He even revealed to him his Messiah-
secret, which until then he had kept to himself. He said he was the
one "who descended from heaven: the Son of man":

> "As Moses lifted up the serpent in the wilderness, so must the Son of
> man be lifted up, so that whoever believes in him may have eternal
> life." For God so loved the world that he gave his only-begotten Son,
> that whoever believes in him should not perish but have eternal life.
> For God sent the Son into the world, not to condemn the world, but
> that the world might be saved through him. (Jn 3:13–17)

These are the key sentences of John's Gospel. Nicodemus was apparently deeply impressed by this revelation. In any event, in John's
Gospel we read how later, at the Feast of Tabernacles (*Sukkot*) in
the year 29, Nicodemus defended Jesus before the Sanhedrin. When
Jesus was sentenced to death, Nicodemus, together with Joseph of
Arimathea—another wealthy patrician from the Sanhedrin—ensured
that Jesus received a dignified, in fact, kingly funeral. In the year 28,
probably for the Feast of Weeks (*Shavuot*), Jesus returned with his
disciples to Judaea (Jn 3:22). John had at this time found another
baptism site for himself, namely, "at Aenon near Salim, because there
was much water". The Greek word *ainon* simply means "springs"
(the Madaba map uses the term also for the springs of Bethany
beyond the Jordan), but the name Salim helps us to identify the place.
It was, indeed, never forgotten. Around the year 300, Eusebius of
Caesarea already writes in his *Onomasticon* an index of Biblical place
names: "The site is still shown today, eight miles south of Scythopolis, near Salim and the Jordan". The reason for the change of location,
therefore, was probably political. Bethany by the Jordan belonged
to Peraea, the Jewish East-Jordan land, and thus to the dominion of
Antipas. If John was reprimanding the king, as the Gospels and Flavius Josephus unanimously report, it was smart to choose a politically
neutral area for the purpose—and Salim was in one. Scythopolis,

modern-day Beth She'an, at the time belonged to the Decapolis, a union of free cities with Greek (and thus heathen) influence, which had joined together in the first century B.C. in order to preserve their independence and to elude Herod's grasp. Here the Baptist did not need to fear any reprisals.

When a nun by the name of Egeria visited the site during a pilgrimage in 383, she wrote: "We set off. He led us along a well-kept valley to a very neat apple-orchard, and there in the middle of it he showed us a good clean spring of water which flowed in a single stream. There was a kind of pool in front of the spring at which it appears holy John Baptist administered."[13]

The pilgrim learned that since ancient times the orchard had been called the Orchard of Saint John and had been visited by the faithful. The Madaba map also shows this "Ainon near Salim" near Beth She'an. Indeed, 7.5 miles south of the ruins of ancient Scythopolis, there is an area with numerous springs and a lake that is now used as a fish pond. Below the hill of Tell Shalem, only one mile away, the ancient Salim could have been located. If it was identical with Salem from the Book of Genesis, then this was indeed a holy place. For it was in Salem that the priest-king Melchizedek brought Abraham bread and wine and blessed him before the forefather of the Jews made his eternal covenant with God (Gen 14:18–20). John could have intentionally connected to this covenant, to this blessing of the land. Unfortunately, Tell Shalem has not yet been excavated. In addition, Egeria even claims to have seen the ruins of Melchizedek's palace here. In Israel, however, this is considered an invention by the rival Samaritans, and Jerusalem is identified with Salem.

While John ministered in Salim/Salem, Jesus took over the camp of *bet'anya*. Although he himself did not baptize—his disciples, who had been disciples of the Baptist before, did this, as the Evangelist particularly mentions (Jn 4:2)—he stayed there, taught, and continued the tradition of his precursor. It was apparently important to him to be a presence in a place where perhaps many seekers were rushing because they suspected that John was there. Some of the Baptist's disciples were probably irritated by this, and they indignantly reported: "Rabbi, he who was with you beyond the Jordan, to whom you bore

---

[13] *Egeria's Travels*, trans. John Wilkinson (London: S.P.C.K., 1971), p. 103.

witness, here he is, baptizing, and all are going to him." But their Master reassured them: "He must increase, but I must decrease" (Jn 3:26, 30).

What John only hinted at with these words, we learn from the Synoptic Gospels. No sooner had John departed and entered Peraea, the Jewish East-Jordan land, on his way to the Feast of Weeks, than he was arrested by the men of Antipas. This was probably a preventive measure. Naturally, the king also participated in the Temple festival, and through the arrest of the prominent admonisher he tried to choke off all criticism directed at him. Moreover, there were very concrete moral transgressions in which a king, in his function as a role model, could not indulge. He had repudiated his own wife and taken away his brother's wife in order to marry her. Flavius Josephus' *Antiquities of the Jews* has this account:

> But when [Antipas] was once at Rome, he lodged with Herod, who was his brother indeed, but not by the same mother; ... However, he fell in love with Herodias, this last Herod's wife, who was the daughter of Aristobulus their brother, and the sister of Agrippa the Great. This man ventured to talk to her about a marriage between them; which address, when she admitted, an argument was made for her to change her habitation and come to him as soon as he should return from Rome.[14]

Herodias' condition for the relationship was that Antipas would separate from his current wife, none other than the daughter of Nabataean King Aretas. She, indignant as much as disappointed and humiliated, ran home to her father, who took the actions of his former son-in-law as a personal affront and swore revenge. For five years he waited for the right opportunity, then finally a border conflict provided him with the pretext to strike. At that time, in 33, Antipas suffered the aforementioned heavy defeat. In the eyes of the Jews, the Baptist's criticism had proven right, and now the tetrarch received God's just punishment—not only for his immoral relationship but most of all because he had ignored the accusations of the man of God; he had silenced the "voice of one crying in the wilderness". John's accusation

---

[14] Flavius Josephus, *Jewish Antiquities*, bk. 18, chap. 5, no. 1, in *New Complete Works of Josephus*, p. 594.

was indeed justified. Marrying a woman who was not only his sister-in-law but also his niece was a grave violation of several Jewish laws and was considered both adultery and incest.

The same is written in the Gospels, with one minor difference: Mark (6:17, and thus also Matthew) names Herodias' ex-husband as Philip. Since Josephus does not tell us his real name (he is commonly known as Herodes Boethos), we do not know whether Philip really was his name. It is equally possible that Mark confused him with Philip the Tetrarch, who married Herodias' daughter Salome shortly thereafter. Luke acknowledges the possible mistake and plainly writes: "But Herod the tetrarch, who had been reproved by him for Herodias, his brother's wife, and for all the evil things that Herod had done, added this to them all, that he shut up John in prison" (Lk 3:19–20).

When Jesus learned of the arrest, he sensed that his own freedom was also in jeopardy. He was known as the Baptist's successor; he had taken over some of the latter's disciples; and although he avoided political topics, Antipas could have targeted him also. He knew that the tetrarch was a "fox" (Lk 13:32), he was also warned about him again and again in the days to come, and he was careful to evade him. This time, therefore, he did not return to his homeland via Peraea but, instead, chose the more direct, albeit riskier, path through hostile Samaria. It was still May; Jesus mentioned that the harvest was four months away, and he was referring to the harvest festival *Sukkot*. Everybody knew that he was a Jew who was coming right from the *Shavuot* Feast in the Temple. But even the Samaritans understood that he was more than a prophet; in fact, they realized: "this is indeed the Savior of the world" (Jn 4:42).

At home in Galilee, he first visited the place where only two months earlier he had worked his first miracle: Cana, not far from Nazareth.

VII

A Wedding and Six Jars

The Search for Cana

The road from Sepphoris to Nazareth (the route that Jesus must have traveled so often in his youth) runs through a bustling Arabic village named Kafr Kenna, which means approximately "Village of the Daughter-in-Law". On the left side of the street, a sign points toward Church Road, an area of the town that is completely different from the rest—tranquil and inviting. "Inviting" is meant quite literally: on either side of the narrow street are Christian souvenir shops that serve a heavy, sweet, but delicious wine to tourists and pilgrims in the hopes that they will immediately purchase a few bottles. The label reveals what makes this wine so special. The wine is advertised as "Cana Wedding Wine".

We enjoy the wine tasting but decide against buying any. Instead, we make our way into the Catholic wedding church, which is in the care of the Franciscans. We have no idea that we have arrived on the wrong day. Weddings are celebrated on Saturdays here. A group of Ethiopian Christians march in a dancing procession around the altar, while others sing and drum. We do not want to disturb them; our hardly festive apparel reveals that we are not in the wedding party. So we open a door that leads down to the archaeological excavations. A hefty stone jar is supposed to remind the visitor of Jesus' first miracle, which allegedly took place here. Hundreds of devout pilgrims have written their prayer intentions on small pieces of paper and slid them in between the glass that surrounds the stone jar. I have to smirk, for this stone jar never served as a water jug. Rather, it is an ancient oil mill. Later on, we finally find at least one authentic water jug from Jesus' time in the Greek church situated diagonally across the street. In such stone jars Jesus is said to have transformed water into delicious wine. John the Evangelist (probably one of Jesus' first disciples and as such an eyewitness to the event) reports:

> On the third day there was a marriage at Cana in Galilee, and the mother of Jesus was there; Jesus also was invited to the marriage, with his disciples. When the wine failed, the mother of Jesus said to him, "They have no wine." And Jesus said to her, "O woman, what have you to do with me? My hour has not yet come." His mother said to the servants, "Do whatever he tells you." Now six stone jars were standing there, for the Jewish rites of purification, each holding twenty or thirty gallons. Jesus said to them, "Fill the jars with water." And they filled them up to the brim. He said to them, "Now draw some out, and take it to the steward of the feast." So they took it.... [T]he steward of the feast tasted the water now become wine. (Jn 2:1–9)

Archaeologists have discovered such stone jars throughout Israel. These jars were in use only during a single, short period of Israel's four-thousand-year-long history, namely, during the time of the Second Temple, exactly between 19 B.C. and A.D. 70. Even if we had only this one clue from an old text, it would suffice to date the event with a precision of less than one hundred years. The increasing foreign infiltration of Judaea and the reconstruction of the Temple, which many faithful Jews considered to be a sign for the arrival of the Messiah and the coming Kingdom of God, led to a downright obsession on the part of the faithful with the Halacha and questions of ritual purity. People feared becoming unclean faster, whereas now especially they wanted to be ritually pure, both in order to set themselves apart from foreign influences and in order to prepare for the end times. The Jewish *Tosefta* describes this situation with the words, "Purity erupted in Israel." This situation reappears in the Gospels, for instance, in the Gospel of Mark (7:2–23), where Jesus clearly rejects this concern for purity with the words, "There is nothing outside a man which by going into him can defile him; but the things which come out of a man are what defile him." The role played in the Judaism of this time by the Halacha's purity laws was reflected in the culture surrounding jars and vessels. As previously stated, stone jars function in archaeology virtually like a "Jewish index fossil". If one discovers them in an ancient site, one can be sure that pious Jews lived here in the first century A.D.

It was nearly impossible to avoid becoming impure. All contact with the bodily discharges of birth or menstruation was thought to make a person unclean. Likewise any contact with skin diseases, reptiles, a cadaver, or the pagan cult of idols (including pagan coins). A human corpse was considered to be the "father of the fathers of impurity"; whoever came into contact with a dead body would himself become a "source of impurity", rendering impure everything that he touched. He could purify himself in the *mikveh*, but the Torah also identifies various materials of household objects that can similarly become impure and transfer impurity: metal, wood, leather, bones, and clay. Only stone was naturally kosher, because it was created by God and was thus considered unable to transfer impurities. For this reason, water that had been set aside for the ritual purification of objects could be stored in and drawn from stone vessels only. Archaeologists have discovered thousands of jars made from soft, white limestone that are reminiscent of modern coffee cups but that served as cups for drawing water. Water was drawn either directly from the *mikveh* or from hefty mixing bowls, called *krater* in Greek or *kallal* in Hebrew, especially splendid examples of which have been found in the Jewish quarter of Jerusalem's old city. Archaeologists have dug up additional mixing bowl fragments on the Herodium, in Qumran, Nazareth, Tiberias, and—we will return to this one later— Kafr Kenna. The last three examples show that Galilee was in no way exempted from this practice. It is of course an exaggeration when the *Einheitsübersetzung* [German Unity Translation] of the Bible indicates that the volume of the jars from Cana was "approximately twenty-six gallons". The original text speaks of "two or three firkins". A firkin ("bath") corresponds to exactly 5.77 gallons, so that one can calculate a holding capacity of 11.5–17.4 gallons, which is slightly less than the volume of the *krater* discovered in Jerusalem.

But then it should hardly come as a surprise that a cynic once reproached Saint Jerome since Jesus had transformed seventy-nine gallons of water into the finest wine, even though the wedding party was already somewhat tipsy. Are they supposed to have enjoyed the new wine, too? "No," answered the Church Father, tranquilly and with subtle humor, "we drink from it to this day."

As a matter of fact, the eucharistic symbolism of Jesus' first miracle is unmistakable. For of course Jesus was not concerned with sparing the groom from some embarrassment or with rescuing a cheerful wedding celebration. The "wine miracle" would not have even been that original, since the pagan god Dionysus is supposed to have done something similar. But as is the case with all of Jesus' miracles, a deeper significance is hidden at a meta-level, which is why John speaks explicitly about a "sign". The wine that flowed so generously then through Jesus' influence did not replace ordinary water but, rather, the water in the stone jars that was specially set aside for ritual purifications. The wine became a symbol of the Blood of Christ that truly cleanses from all guilt and sin, that is, blots out all spiritual impurities. With this Blood, the ritual purifications of the Halacha became superfluous. Metaphorically, the water was replaced with the wine that, as Saint Jerome says, suffices for all ages and flows in all eternity. Thus the episode of the wedding feast at Cana becomes one of the most significant events of the New Testament.

Nonetheless, we find this event only in the Gospel of John, since it took place before Jesus began the public ministry with which the Synoptic Gospels initiate their narration. The wedding miracle must have taken place in March of the year A.D. 28, after the baptism in the Jordan, after Jesus' forty-day fast, after his return to John, the calling of Jesus' first five disciples, and his return to Galilee, but still before Passover. Unfortunately, the date indicated by the Evangelist ("on the third day") does not help us much. It may be the third day after Jesus' arrival in Galilee, the third day of the month of Nisan 3788 (i.e., March 18, 28), or an altogether ordinary Tuesday, a weekday on which Jews were wont to get married—we do not know. The location given by the Gospels is all the more concrete by comparison: "in Cana in Galilee". We can easily rule out a Cana in Lebanon (whose Christians claim that the miracle took place in their hometown). The fact that Mary was plainly the more important guest at the wedding speaks for a certain nearness to Nazareth; Jesus and his disciples merely accompanied her—they were "also" invited. Consequently the possibility that Nathanael was the groom (or a brother of the groom) is ruled out, although we know that he came from Cana. This Nathanael, whose name is mentioned only in John's Gospel, seems to be identical with the Bartholomew of the Synoptic Gospels.

That is not surprising, since the name Bar Tholmai (Bartholomew is the Latinized version) means simply "Son of Tholmai", and while it could have been the name he went by, it could not have been his first name. It is unclear if Simon the Canaanite, like Nathanael bar Tholmai, also hailed from Cana. Since Simon was also known as "the eager one" (or "the zealot"), it is more likely that "Canaanite" here is derived from "Canaanean", the Aramaic translation of this title.

The wedding of course did not take place in a private home. Whenever a marriage was celebrated in a village, at least half the local population took part, and the cramped homes did not offer sufficient space for that. Instead, there was the *triclinium*, a rentable dining room often located on the second floor of a home, named for the horseshoe-shaped arrangement of its reclining benches, mats, or cushions. Evidence for the fact that the wedding at Cana took place in such an upper room furnished with cushions (a *katalyma*, such as the one prepared for Jesus' Last Supper) is given by the reference to a man who was "steward for the feast", i.e., the owner of the *triclinium*, who was explicitly not a relative of the groom. This man had already organized many festivities and was for this reason all the more amazed that the wine of poorer quality had been served first (wine that the groom had himself obviously provided—maybe he was a vintner).

But where was Cana? Is it in fact beneath the contemporary locale of Kafr Kenna? There is a second candidate right nearby. Khirbet Qana, "the ruin of Cana", as it is promisingly called. Khirbet Qana lies eight miles directly north of Nazareth. But we cannot take this direct route, because the Bet Netofa plain with its cultivated fields and modern canal stretches in between. So, we take Highway 79 and County Road 784 to Kfar Manda, a backwater town on the northwestern end of the plain with a majority Muslim population. A bumpy dirt road approximately 2.5 miles long leads from there to Khirbet Qana. This road runs along the northern border of the plain, right at the foot of the Har Azmon mountain range. We try to drive around the potholes. I have to get out every couple hundred of yards in order to clear a boulder out of the way. The sun begins to set, and evening approaches. We pray that our rental car makes it in one piece. Otherwise, we would be completely lost here in the darkness, in the middle of nowhere, stuck in a fix with a broken-down car.

Finally, I spy in the distance a pyramid-shaped hill, a good one hundred yards high. That must be Khirbet Qana![1] A Palestinian family owns a cottage here along with a couple of sheds and is in the process of herding their sheep back home. Yuliya locks herself in the car, still traumatized from the experience in Caesarea. I grab my camera and get going. I already strike it rich when I am halfway up the southern slope of the hill. The ground is strewn with clay fragments. Many of these fragments display fine grooves, which are characteristic of Herodian ceramics.

I clearly discern the outlines of a couple dozen homes. A massive stone lid, in which a circular hole has been drilled, covers an ancient cistern. I stumble upon a tomb carved from the rock along the southwestern slope. Judging by its form, it is typical of the first century A.D. Having finally arrived at the knoll, I drink in a marvelous view of the Bet Netofa plain. In the east, I see the distant coast of the Sea of Galilee. To the south, I see the ridges behind which Nazareth lies and whose foothills are gradually being taken over by the town. In the distance, the high-rise buildings of the Jewish settlement of Nazaret Illit tower into the sky. In front of them lies Kafr Kenna with its wedding churches. An olive tree plantation nestles in the hills near my left. Old terraces testify that this plantation was once the "garden" of a wealthy village, some two thousand years ago.

Khirbet Qana's strategically advantageous position on the slope of a hill, a position that allows an overview of miles of Galilean highland, reminds me of the autobiography of Flavius Josephus. When he was commander of Galilee at the beginning of the Jewish uprising, this was probably the very reason why he set up his headquarters in "a Galilean village called Cana". From there, he marched "the whole night through" at the head of a small contingent of some two hundred men in order to reach and to protect the city of Tiberias on the Sea of Galilee. This fact, too, fits better with Khirbet Qana than with Kafr Kenna, since Khirbet Qana is approximately seventeen miles distant from Tiberias, while Kafr Kenna is just over twelve miles west of Tiberias.

---

[1] Only on a second visit did we discover a less adventurous route, which is therefore urgently advisable: via Araba, then south to the canal, and from there on the field path heading west ...

Excavations undertaken in Khirbet Qana between 1998 and 2000 by Professor Douglas Edwards of the University of Puget Sound and by his colleague Jack Olive, in collaboration with the Israeli Antiquities Authority, unambiguously proved the presence of a settlement at the time of Jesus by means of ancient coins (Hasmonean and Herodian) that were found. One ceramic fragment proved to be an *ostrakon*—it bore an inscription in Aramaic, the language of Jesus.

Archaeologists have determined that the oldest part of Qana was located upon a mountain pass on the north side of the hill. Situated there were the larger houses, most often equipped with inner courtyards. Terraces were constructed as the settlement on the south side of the hill expanded. These hillside homes were fitted to the features of the natural landscape. The wider streets ran concentrically around the hill's summit, while the narrower roads, themselves often outfitted with steps, crisscrossed the terraces and led down the slope. The people clearly made their living by agriculture, olive oil production, and pigeon breeding (two columbaria were excavated), but also by handicrafts. In addition, workshops for dying fabrics and tanning leather were also discovered as well as a small glass factory. A network of over sixty cisterns ensured the water supply, and of course there was a public *mikveh*. A public building crowned the village hill. This building was later surrounded by a trapezoid-shaped wall. The building's orientation toward Jerusalem and the meticulous manner of its construction suggest that it was a synagogue that could very likely date back to the first century. The main room had a 492-square-foot surface area and was furnished with three columns and evidently adorned with frescoes, of which the archaeologists found a fragment. A limestone capital to the columns resembled the capital from the synagogue of Gamla, a village in Golan that was destroyed during the Jewish War and afterward abandoned. Three of this synagogue's four walls were lined with a continuous sitting bench. A small room directly adjacent to the main room, itself furnished with a sitting bench, could have been a synagogue school. The entire village was surrounded by numerous tombs, all of which were placed at least 220 yards away from the houses.

On the basis of the number and size of these tombs, but also on the basis of the precise density of the placement of the homes themselves, we can surmise that the population of Khirbet Qana was approximately 1,500. With this population, Khirbet Qana was considerably larger than Nazareth, which fact explains Nathanael's somewhat presumptuous reaction when he realized from what backwater town the Messiah hailed: "Can anything good come out of Nazareth?" (Jn 1:46). Finally, the remains of a large Byzantine church at the foot of the northern slope bear witness to the fact that Khirbet Qana was an important pilgrimage site during the Christian era.

Did Jesus perform his first miracle here, in Khirbet Qana? The archaeologists' strange discovery might answer this question. On the southwestern slope of the hill, they stumbled upon a complex of at least five caves hewn from stone, which was clearly an important pilgrimage site in the sixth century. Its walls were completely covered with graffiti that had been scratched into several layers of chalk plaster. An adjacent building could certainly have been a church with an attached cloister. What was venerated here is unmistakable. In the biggest cave of this compound, right at the entrance, a former sarcophagus lid was furnished with a cross and remodeled as a sort of altar frontal. Originally, six large stone jars were built into the altar, two of which were uncovered by the archaeologists still *in situ*. Marble fragments testify that this cave sanctuary was once lavishly decorated. Clearly, the early Byzantine Christians were convinced that Jesus' first miracle took place in this cave, perhaps once the cellar of a *triclinium*. A structure founded on the caves certainly could have been a church with an attendant monastery. A capital from the pre-Byzantine period and a rectangular basin with seven steps leading down into it—obviously a Jewish-Christian baptismal pool—suggest that this place was used early on for worship. I climb through a door hewn from the rock, then down a staircase into a natural cave, which at first glance appears not at all spectacular. Nevertheless I find still more marble fragments, which testify to how richly adorned this shrine once was.

Was Khirbet Qana, then, the place of the wedding? I cannot get this out of my head while we, in the warm light of the evening sun, attempt to find the next point of entry to a country road. Unfortunately, the earliest reports by pilgrims are too inexact to allow for a sure identification. In 386, Saint Paula mentions merely that Qana is "not far from Nazareth". Saint Jerome adds that she traversed "Nazareth ... Cana and Capernaum ... in a rapid journey". One of the earliest and most precise descriptions comes from a pilgrim from Piacenza, who wrote around the year 570: "[From Diocaesarea = Sepphoris] Three miles further on we came to Cana, where the Lord attended the wedding, and we actually reclined on the couch. On it (undeserving though I am) I wrote the names of my parents.... Of the water-pots two are still there, and I filled one of them up with wine and lifted it up full onto my shoulders. I offered it at the altar, and we washed in the spring to gain a blessing."[2]

Now Sepphoris is located at a distance of about 3.5 miles from Kafr Kenna and 4.8 miles from Khirbet Qana, so that any definite identification is impossible. Forty years earlier, Theodosius had written: "From Diocaesarea [Sepphoris] it is five miles to Cana of Galilee",[3] which would be more or less correct for Khirbet Qana. More problematic is the reference to a spring; there is none in Khirbet Qana, where people were required to use cisterns, but indeed there was one in Kafr Kenna. Willibald (724/726) mentions in *Chana* "a great church, and upon the altar in this church stands one of the six water jugs which the Lord ordered to be filled with water, which was transformed into wine. And they serve out from this wine." Epiphanius (750–800) reports, moreover, a cloister, of which later descriptions also speak.

Not until the time of the Crusades do the testimonies become more concrete. Saewulf, who in 1102 composed the first pilgrim's account since the conquest of Jerusalem in 1099, writes: "Six miles to the north-east of Nazareth, on a hill, is Cana of Galilee, where our Lord converted water into wine at the marriage feast. There nothing is left standing except the monastery called that of *Architriclinius* [home of the master of ceremonies]."[4] As a matter of fact, Khirbet Qana is eight miles (13 km) north of Nazareth, while, on the other hand, Kafr Kenna is just over 3.5 miles (6 km) to the northeast. In 1187, the anonymous author of *La citez de Jherusalem* reports: "The place where the wedding was held is still visible.... It is a good bowshot to the well from which the water was drawn." Yet Thetmar (1217)

[2] The Piacenza Pilgrim, *Travels from Piacenza*, in John Wilkinson, *Jerusalem Pilgrims Before the Crusades* (Jerusalem: Ariel, 1977), p. 79.

[3] Theodosius, *The Topography of the Holy Land*, in Wilkinson, *Jerusalem Pilgrims*, p. 65.

[4] "The Travels of Saewulf", in *Early Travels in Palestine*, ed. Thomas Wright (London: Henry G. Bohn, 1848), p. 47.

clearly identifies the well as a "cistern". Burchard (1238) is the most informative. He finds that "to the north Cana of Galilee has a round mountain, on whose slope it stands. At its foot, on the south side, it has a very fair plain ... it reaches as far as Sepphoris." He also writes: "The place is shown at this day where the six water-pots stood, and the dining-room wherein the tables were. Now these places, like almost all the other places wherein the Lord wrought any work, are underground, and one goes down to them by many steps into a crypt."[5] This is definitely a description of the compound on the southwestern slope of Khirbet Qana. Again in 1422, Poloner asserts: "The place of the wedding is a cave hewn out of the rock, which holds a few men."[6] And in 1636, Neitzschitz adds: "In this way, they still point out the location and the place where the wedding house is said to have stood, which one must believe all the more surely because it goes deep into the ground, so that one must descend several steps."[7] This, too, points to the cave sanctuary in Khirbet Qana. Between the sixth century (as the archaeological discovery shows) and the seventeenth century, it was plainly revered as the site of the wedding. But was it really? And if so, how did the tradition get relocated to Kafr Kenna?

The modern history of Kafr Kenna as a pilgrimage place began in 1566, when the Greek Orthodox purchased property near the local mosque in order to build a church there. They were convinced that the mosque stood atop a Christian sanctuary, a church that had been constructed by Saint Helena over the site of the wine miracle. Yet the Catholics were of a different opinion. In 1621, King Louis XIII sent his ambassador Des Hayes de Courmenin to the Holy Land in order to protect the rights of the Franciscans. Due to his diplomatic skill, ownership of the land surrounding the Grotto of the Annunciation in Nazareth was transferred to the Order in 1620. With regard to Cana, the Frenchman visited "Caffar Cana ... of which the oriental Christians maintain that here is the place where our Lord turned water

---

[5] *Burchard of Mount Sion*, trans. Aubrey Stewart, The Library of the Palestine Pilgrims' Text Society, vol. 12 (London: Committee of the Palestine Exploration Fund, 1897), pp. 38–39.

[6] *John Poloner's Description of the Holy Land*, trans. Aubrey Stewart (London: Palestine Pilgrims' Text Society, 1894), p. 36.

[7] George Christoph von Neitzschitz, *Sieben-Jährige und gefährliche Welt Beschauung durch die vornehmsten Drey Theil der Welt Europa/Asia und Africa* (Bautzen: Baumann, 1666).

into wine, but through the diligence of Father Thomas of Navaria we have discovered that this is a village that is simply called Cana."[8] Instead, the priest led him to Khirbet Qana, of which he reports: "One sees here the ruins of a church that, as is believed, was built in the same place where the miracle was performed." Neitzschitz also led the Franciscans in 1636 to both places and to the conviction that Khirbet Qana is the real Cana. But in the next three years, the tables turned. In his comprehensive work of 1639 on the topography of the Holy Land, Quaresmius, the guardian of the Franciscans in Jerusalem, arrived, more through intuition than through compelling reasons, at the conclusion that Kafr Kenna had been the Cana of the wedding miracle. Khirbet Qana seemed to him to be too far removed. Besides, it bothered him that Khirbet Qana had no spring, as Antoninus described it. *Hierosolyma locuta, causa finita* (Jerusalem has spoken, the case is closed)! But the German priest Clemens Kopp, one of the finest experts on the Holy Land and its traditions, suspected that there were of course practical reasons, instead, behind the "relocation": "The true reason was the utter degeneration of the genuine Cana which, as Roger (1631) says, had become a 'den of murderers where pilgrims had to pay tribute of a zechine, the equivalent of about ten gold pieces. This certainly helped the transference of tradition to the more hospitable kafr kenna, which was also commended by a certain similarity in the sound of the name."[9]

In any case, the Order had committed itself. Only two years later, the Franciscans purchased a plot of land directly adjacent to the mosque. In 1870, they succeeded in acquiring the mosque itself and tearing it down in order to build a church on the lot. The director of the Franciscan mission in Kafr Kenna at that time, the Austrian Friar Father Egidius Geissler, proved to be especially enterprising. Not only did he model the façade of the church consecrated in 1906 on the Salzburg Cathedral, but he also let archaeological excavations take place in advance of the construction work.

During these excavations, the remains of an ancient basilica were uncovered. Geissler assumed that it had once had three *apsides*, like

---

[8] Julián Herrojo, *Cana de Galilea y su localizacion* (Paris: Gabalda, 1999).
[9] Clemens Kopp, *Holy Places of the Gospels*, trans. Ronald Walls (New York: Herder and Herder, 1963), pp. 153–54.

the pilgrim churches of Nazareth and on Mount Tabor. The remains of an ancient grain silo were located somewhat deeper underground. There he found three huge stone mortars, "shaped like giant flower pots", that were put on display from then on. A rectangular building, oriented toward Jerusalem, had already been built earlier at this site. This building contained Geissler's spectacular find, a mosaic floor with an Aramaic inscription: "Blessed be the memory of Joseh, son of Tanhum, the son of Boda, and of his sons, who made this mosaic. May it be a blessing for them. Amen." Following paleographical criteria, it was possible to date this inscription to the fourth century. Everything indicated that this mosaic had once decorated the floor of a synagogue.

Now one could object that Jews would never have constructed a synagogue on the site of a Christian miracle. But the matter is not that simple. For the synagogue over which the Crusaders built the Church of Saint Anne in Sepphoris was also furnished with a mosaic floor that clearly traces back to the same benefactor: "Blessed be the memory of Rabbi Yudan, son of Tanhum, son of...." According to Epiphanius, Sepphoris was where Count Joseph of Tiberias, the Jew who converted to Christianity, endowed a Jewish-Christian synagogue. Even though the bishop does not mention Kafr Kenna, it is quite possible that the count had a house of prayer for Jewish Christians built there, too. This in turn presupposes a Jewish-Christian community, but not necessarily an identification with the place of the wine miracle. At the very least, it proves a Christian presence as early as the fourth century.

In the year 1969, exploratory digs by Father Loffreda and more extensive excavations in the second half of the year 1997 by Father Alliata, both of them Franciscans, provided at least further information concerning the history of their church.

The fact is that the church stands on the remains of buildings from the first century. Among these remains are a corridor paved with stone slabs and a round stone basin that was connected with a cistern. Shards of Herodian oil lamps and fragments from stone jugs made a precise dating possible. On top of these buildings, the (Jewish-Christian?) synagogue arose in the fourth century, with an atrium, surrounded by a colonnade, set up in front of it. The ancient cistern was located in the center of this synagogue. Next to the synagogue, a

Christian sepulcher was constructed in the fifth or sixth century, with the apse pointing north, probably in order to the have room next to the synagogue that was oriented toward the south (Jerusalem). Not until the fourteenth century, and thus after the Crusades, was a mosque built on top of the two sanctuaries, which by then had been abandoned. But as interesting as the finds are, Father Alliata nonetheless has to concede that "nothing came to light that would confirm that Kefr Kenna is the Cana in Galilee that is mentioned many times in the Gospel of John."

The excavations by the Israeli Antiquities Authority in Karem el-Ras, a western extension of the village, brought to light more about Kafr Kenna in Jesus' time. Between 1999 and 2006, the archaeologist Yardenna Alexandre came across a whole row of houses from the Herodian and early Roman times, situated between five-hundred-year-old olive trees. Many of them were equipped with private *mikvehs*, which allows us to conclude that there were devout Jews there, who otherwise led a rather humble life; glass vessels and other luxury objects were completely absent. Instead of these, she dug up multiple fragments of large stone jars, the diameter of which must have been around 24 inches. These fragments were reason enough for the archaeologist to inform the press. So the British native asserted, "All evidence that was brought to light during this excavation indicates that the place we are examining is the Cana of the wedding." This is of course a rather daring conclusion, for such stone jars were found in every Jewish village of that time.

Where, then, was the Cana of the wedding located? It is certain that our two "candidates", Khirbet Qana as well as Kafr Kenna, were inhabited at the time of Jesus. Both villages already had the same names then that they have today; at least there is no evidence to the contrary. But Khirbet (the ruins) Qana is the place that we are looking for. Provided that John did not mix up the confusingly similar place names, then Jesus' first miracle in fact took place on the slope of the hill on the northern edge of the Beit Netofa Valley. Unrelated to this, Joseph of Tiberias had donated a synagogue to the Jewish Christians of Kafr Kenna. Its existence may have very early on led to a confusion of the locations. But as long as there is no definite connection, nothing compels us to suppose a link between the synagogue and the wedding miracle.

In any case, Kana remained an important place of Jesus' activity even after this sign. After the wedding, Jesus did indeed move "down to Capernaum, with his mother and his brethren and his disciples" (Jn 2:12). But when he returned to Galilee from Jerusalem two and a half months later, he first made a stop at Cana (Jn 4:46). On the way there, Jesus must have come through Nazareth, for John notes the brusque rejection of Jesus in the synagogue of his hometown with the words, "Jesus himself testified that a prophet has no honor in his own country" (Jn 4:44). In the Gospels of Mark and Matthew, this rejection took place only after the execution of John the Baptist, but that is rather unlikely. Luke situates it at the beginning of Jesus' ministry in Galilee and before his return to Capernaum (Lk 4:16–30). This circumstance, too, speaks rather in favor of Khirbet Qana, for it is unlikely that Jesus, right after the Nazarenes wanted to stone him, would have taken up residence in the neighboring village. The aforementioned strategically valuable position on a hill could have led him, like Josephus later, to set up his headquarters here. In Cana, he was safe from Antipas' henchmen, whose approach would already be noticed early.

He clearly remained there for a few weeks, perhaps even for the whole summer. In any case, long enough for the news about his new center of activity to spread through all of Galilee. So a royal official from Capernaum, whose son was on his deathbed, did not wait for Jesus to return first, but set off on his way to him. He urgently implored Jesus: "Sir, come down before my child dies" (Jn 4:49). What he means is from the highland down to the sea, thus a geographically accurate formulation. But Jesus wanted to remain in Cana. "Go; your son will live", he assured the official. He believed and set off on his way. Arriving home late in the evening after a march of about twenty-two miles, he discovered that the boy, indeed, was healed—and, in fact, precisely at the seventh hour, at 1:00 in the afternoon, when he had encountered Jesus.

VIII

The Pool of Bethesda

Why John Was an Eyewitness

Now at long last, it is time to inquire about the reliability of our sources. After all, for years we have been indoctrinated with the mantra that the Gospels were in fact not biographies of Jesus but "merely" early Christian testimonies of faith. As such, they told us less about the "historical Jesus" than about the image of Christ in the community where they originated—of course, as late as possible, in any event, all of them toward the end of the first century, undoubtedly after the destruction of the Temple that Jesus (in contrast to the Old Testament Psalms) could never possibly have foretold, even in the most abstract terms. We are urged to distinguish carefully between the semi-fictitious Jesus of the Kerygma, i.e., the post-Easter proclamation of the faith, and the historical Jesus, who must first of all be subjected to a thorough demythologization. What remains as the result of this alleged decluttering, to which everything supernatural must obviously fall victim, is on display in Hollywood director Paul Verhoeven's irreverent yet at least consistent book *Jesus of Nazareth*. In it the Son of God does, in fact, appear as nothing but a failure, as an admittedly gifted and shrewd wandering preacher and exorcist, who soon fell victim to an enormous self-delusion and finally believed that only through an armed insurrection would he be able to bring about the Kingdom of God by force. That this attempt, too, was doomed to failure he experienced in the most painful way on the Cross, before his body was thrown to the dogs or hastily buried at the place of execution and seemed to have "disappeared" only to his disciples, who had long since fled.

But this all-too-human Jesus would have already been forgotten after one generation, regardless of whatever marvelous things his followers might have said about him. Apollonius of Tyana, for instance, a late-first-century "guru", according to his biographer, Philostratus, apparently worked even greater miracles than Jesus, and nevertheless his name was soon remembered only by historians. However, even non-Christian sources leave no doubt that Jesus was in fact much more than a failed dreamer. Accordingly, in his *Antiquities of the Jews* composed around A.D. 94, Flavius Josephus writes:

> Now there was about this time Jesus, a wise man, if it be lawful to call him a man; for he was a doer of wonderful works, a teacher of such men as receive the truth with pleasure. He drew over to him both many of the Jews and many of the Gentiles. He was [the] Christ. And when Pilate, at the suggestion of the principal men among us, had condemned him to the cross, those that loved him at the first did not forsake him; for he appeared to them alive again the third day, as the divine prophets had foretold these and ten thousand other wonderful things concerning him. And the tribe of Christians, so named from him, are not extinct at this day.[1]

Admittedly, the quote is controversial. However, we do already find it in this wording in *The Church History* of Eusebius of Caesarea, which was written around 330. In Roman times, Flavius Josephus was a popular author; his books were considered ancient *best sellers* and were practically required reading for any educated Roman. For this reason alone, Eusebius would never have dared to misquote him. After all, he wrote in a time when most Romans were still heathen; the last persecution of Christians in the Eastern Empire (by Licinius) dated back less than a decade. A falsification, especially one so easily detectable, could have backfired quickly. On the other hand, Josephus' messianic testimony, the so-called *Testimonium Flavianum*, does sound suspicious. Had this Jew, when he was taken prisoner by the Romans, not saved his life by declaring the Roman Emperor Vespasian the true messiah? Quite possibly, he, like many Jews, believed in two messianic figures, the priestly and the kingly messiah. Yet, a minimal edit by Eusebius or other Christian writers, for instance, by omitting the words "it was said" before "he was the Christ", is also

---

[1] Flavius Josephus, *Jewish Antiquities*, bk. 18, chap. 3, no. 3, in *The New Complete Works of Josephus*, trans. William Whiston (Grand Rapids, Mich.: Kregel, 1999), p. 590.

possible. There is no doubt that in the original text Josephus indeed spoke about Jesus, for in a later passage he speaks about James, "the brother of Jesus, the so-called Christ" (he was, in fact, his cousin).

Therefore, the "incredible deeds" as well as the "impossible" resurrection from the dead, which was confirmed by eyewitnesses, also belonged to what a Jew had heard among Jews about Jesus.

I think we will never be able to understand Jesus of Nazareth if we are not ready at least to consider the possibility of God's working in history. That healings can be the result of autosuggestion (and hence, as Jesus himself taught, of the individual's faith) is a different matter, just like the fact that everything in the life of Jesus also had a meta-level and, thus, likewise an allegorical meaning. Modern theology helps us understand the symbolic language. But this should not mislead us to take the events themselves a priori as pious fables or Christian didactic stories. One need only study the history of Church-approved miracles, such as the Marian apparitions in Lourdes and Fatima, or the lives of the saints, to develop a sense of humility in the presence of the working of God. To this day, there are thousands in Italy who claim to have experienced first-hand a miracle through the intercession of the Capuchin priest Padre Pio of Pietrelcina, a stigmatist who died in 1968 and was canonized by Pope John Paul II in 2002. Even an acquaintance of the Polish pope, the psychiatrist Dr. Wanda Poltawska, was suddenly and inexplicably healed of her end-stage cancer when Karol Wojtyła, then-archbishop of Krakow, asked the miracle worker to pray for her. Two miraculous healings that cannot be explained by medical science are required for the canonization of a "Servant of God", a single one sufficient for beatification. God's intervention in our time is therefore a scientifically documented fact. Why, for heaven's sake, should we refuse to admit that Jesus, the incarnate face of God, had this power?

A wonderful example for how modern exegesis, with all due respect, can trip over its own inquisitive feet is John's account of the healing of a crippled man on the Sabbath in Jerusalem. After his summer in Cana, the Evangelist writes, Jesus went back to Jerusalem. The occasion was a "feast of the Jews", likely the Festival of Tabernacles (*Sukkot*), which in A.D. 28 took place from September 23 to 29.

"Now there is in Jerusalem by the Sheep Gate a pool, in Hebrew called Bethzatha [also Bethesda], which has five porticoes. In these lay a multitude of invalids, blind, lame, paralyzed", John maintains (Jn 5:2–3).

In his essay "Fictitious Places of the Baptism of John", published in 1954, the theologian Norbert Krieger claims that Bethesda was an invention by the Evangelist, his description full of hidden symbolism. Others followed suit and declared the "five porticoes" a symbol for the Torah, the pool a baptismal font, and the Sheep Gate a synonym for Jesus, who, after all, had described himself as the "Gate of the sheep" (Jn 10:7, although the Revised Standard Edition renders it as "door of the sheep"). According to them, the name Bethesda alone, "House of Mercy", showed the intention of the symbolic narrative. The Torah could not help this man, paralyzed by the many prescripts, to walk again, but only Jesus could, who deliberately broke the Sabbath and thus liberated the man from the constraints of the Mosaic Law. So far, so good, for this may indeed be the deeper message, the meta-level of this "sign". Yet, this altogether successful decoding led to hasty conclusions—in fact, to a rather un-Christian arrogance toward the source. Indeed, many modern theologians reacted to any attempt to locate the Pool of Bethesda with the same dangerous mix of arrogance and ignorance as that of the American Edgar J. Goodspeed:

> But it must be remembered that topography and chronology were among the least of the author's [John's] concerns. His head was among the stars. He was seeking to determine the place of Jesus in the spiritual universe and his relations to eternal realities. These were the matters that interested and absorbed him, not itineraries and timetables, so that practical mundane considerations that might apply to Mark, Matthew, or Luke have little significance for his work.[2]

The German religious educator Gert Laudert-Ruhm also, as late as 1996, claimed that the Fourth Gospel "for various reasons, holds a special position and is therefore the least suitable as a historical source". As if theology and Christology automatically contradicted topography and historicity! At the same time, the proponents of a

---

[2] Edgar J. Goodspeed, *An Introduction to the New Testament* (Chicago: University of Chicago Press, 1937), p. 310.

purely symbolic interpretation could at least refer to the fact that
Flavius Josephus makes absolutely no mention of the pool (although
he calls the northeastern part of Jerusalem Bezetha). This alone was
sufficient to declare it an invention by the Evangelist. Only there
was no need to discuss the existence of the Sheep Gate; this name for
the northeastern gate of Jerusalem is already attested in the Book of
Nehemiah (3:1), for the Old Testament era.

But inconveniently the pool existed, too. If Krieger and his disciples had gone to the trouble of studying pilgrims' accounts from
late antiquity, they would have realized this, even without consult-
ing archaeology. Eusebius, who calls it Bezatha, already confirms the
existence of "a pool in Jerusalem which is called probatike and interpreted by us 'sheep.' Once it had five porticoes."[3] According to him,
it is a twin pool whose one basin filled up with rain water while the
other appeared reddish, allegedly from the blood of the sacrificial
animals that had been slaughtered here earlier. The latter claim is
impossible, since the traditional slaughtering site was at the altar of
burnt offering in front of the Temple. The pilgrim from Bordeaux,
who came to Jerusalem in 333, likewise saw "two twin pools with
five porticoes, which are called Bethsaida",[4] which of course refers to
Bethesda. Bishop Cyril of Jerusalem calls it Sheep Pool and mentions
the five porticoes, "four surrounding the pool, the fifth in the middle, where there lay a great crowd of the sick."[5] In that very place, a
church was built in 450, which was first called Church of the Paralytic
but then was dedicated to Holy Mary of the Sheep Pool (Probatike).
It was destroyed during the Persian invasion in 614, then rebuilt,
then torn down by the Muslim Caliph Hakim, and finally rebuilt
by the Crusaders on a smaller scale. From then on what was considered to be the Bethesda Pool was actually a small cistern, which of
course does not make the tradition seem more credible.

In 1856, after the Crimean War, the sultan transferred the whole
tract of land to Emperor Napoleon III, and since then it has been

---

[3] As quoted in Marilyn Sams, *The Jerusalem Temple Mount Myth* (Charleston, S.C.: Create
Space, 2014), p. 80.

[4] *The Bordeaux Pilgrim (c. 333 C.E.)*, trans. Andrew S. Jacobs, at http://andrewjacobs.org
/translations/bordeaux.html.

[5] Cyril of Jerusalem, "Homily on the Paralytic by the Pool", trans. Edward Yarnold, S.J.,
in *Cyril of Jerusalem* (London and New York: Routledge, 2000), p. 71.

managed by French Dominicans. But during initial excavations in 1873, only the cistern was unearthed. This quickly led to the impression that the Byzantines had declared a random cistern the Pool of Bethesda, since they thought the compound described by John never existed. During further excavations, French archaeologists soon came upon a second cistern, but this one was not very impressive, either. Furthermore, it became clear that it was from a later period. The Evangelist seemed utterly disgraced.

Not until 1914 did the tide begin to turn. South of the two cisterns and the church, the archaeologists discovered a trapezoid-shaped pool, 197 by 164 feet in size. But for the time being, the First World War interrupted the excavations. When they were resumed in 1931, it became apparent that the cisterns and the church stood on top of a dam that separated the four-sided pool from a second, approximately square, artificial pool on its northern side. After these promising initial attempts, the Dominicans decided to conduct systematic excavations after World War II. The results of this five-year excavation campaign (1957–1962) under the direction of the Dominican archaeologists J.-M. Rousé and Father Roland de Vaux of the École Biblique were truly sensational. The northern pool, as it turned out, was the older part of the compound. Perhaps it dated back to the time of the First Temple; it could be the "upper pool" that is mentioned in the Second Book of Kings (18:17). Originally, the rainwater was probably collected only by a simple dam and then formed a natural pool. Later on, this pool was expanded into an artificial pool, 131 feet long and 174 feet wide. The water flowed from here to the Temple through an uncovered channel.

Toward the end of the third century B.C., a second pool, 197 feet long and 171 feet wide, was built here by High Priest Simon (cf. Sirach 50:3). It was located south of the dam, which was now twenty feet wide. The water channel was turned into a water tunnel.

During the construction of the Herodian Temple, this compound was converted into a gigantic *mikveh*. In the process, the pools were surrounded by four porticoes; a fifth ran across the dam that separated the two pools. Research conducted from 1995 on by the Israeli archaeologist Shimon Gibson, on behalf of the Israel Antiquities Authority, revealed an entire system of subterranean ducts that ensured that the water stayed in motion and could thus, as "living water", serve ritual cleansing purposes. The southern pool was used for the actual cleansing bath, the northern pool, on the other hand, as a water reservoir (*otsar*) from which fresh water was supplied. Only the southern pool is, in fact, on one side equipped with stairs that enabled access. Every three to four steps, there was a wider area, big enough to place a pallet or a bier on it. This is where Jews seeking to purify themselves entered the *mikveh*; this is where a paralytic had to wait to be carried in by others. Thus we read in John's Gospel: "One man was there, who had been ill for thirty-eight years. When Jesus saw him and knew that he had been lying there a long time, he said to him, 'Do you want to be healed?' The sick man answered him, 'Sir, I have no man to put me into the pool when the water is troubled' " (Jn 5:5–7).

The phenomenon of "troubling" also gave rise to all kinds of speculations, including a rather fantastic explanation that an ancient copyist, perhaps rendering a Jewish superstition, interpolated into the text. It says that the paralytics had waited for "the troubling of the water": "For an angel of the Lord went down at certain seasons into the pool and troubled the water; whoever stepped in first was healed of whatever disease he had."

In the twenty-foot-wide wall separating the pools, Gibson, in fact, came upon a vertical shaft, which led to a horizontal tunnel at the end of which a floodgate was installed. Through this floodgate, fresh water could be added and the water in the *mikveh* could be set in motion so that it became "living" water. Rising bubbles, a water swirl, and a gentle wave motion would have indicated to the people waiting that now the right time had come to receive the best possible ritual cleansing. A drain on the south side of the southern pool ensured that the excess water was diverted, perhaps even to the Temple Mount. A layer of red dirt, which Gibson found at the lower end of the separating wall, could have led to the reddish discoloration of the water that was mentioned by Eusebius.

John therefore, merely accurately described the operation of the biggest *mikveh* in Jerusalem, without any angels and other supernatural additions at all. He notes the correct location, and he mentions its five porticoes, a detail that makes sense only if we know about the wide dam between the two pools. Despite the strong symbolic character that the theologians attributed to it, the site actually existed; anyone who comes to Jerusalem can visit the remains. Meanwhile, even the name that John gave to it has been historically attested. In the *Copper Scroll* of Qumran, it is mentioned as the fifty-seventh out of sixty-five stashes for treasures and cultic objects of the brotherhood. The Polish Qumran researcher T. L. Milik translated their specifications as "Nearby, in *Bet Eshdatajin*, in the pool, right by the access to the little sea: vessel with aromatic substances...." "Little sea" probably refers to the northern part of the double-pool that is here called Beteshdatajin (Aramaic: "House of the Twin Pools"), which perhaps the Evangelist, more likely though the Jerusalem folk etymology, reinterpreted as Bethesda = "House of Mercy", in order to signal that people could be ritually cleansed there for the Temple visit.

But it became a place of mercy for the paralyzed man, too. "Jesus said to him, 'Rise, take up your pallet, and walk.' And at once the man was healed, and he took up his pallet and walked" (Jn 5:8–9). Of course he immediately set out for the Temple, the place he had wanted to visit for so long and yet was never able to because the necessary ritual cleansing kept eluding him. The miracle, which probably was more than a symbolic act after all, was nearly fatal for Jesus, because it took place on a Sabbath (perhaps even on September 25 in A.D. 28, the third day of the Feast of Tabernacles?). Thousands of pilgrims, who likewise flocked to the Bethesda-*mikveh*, became witnesses of the miracle, and the paralytic himself also "stood out" because he was carrying his pallet, even though it was the Sabbath. Of course, he justified himself by saying that he had just been healed. When he met Jesus in the court of the Temple, there was no longer any doubt as to who was responsible for that. Thus Jesus was accused of profaning the Sabbath. His defense, "My Father is working still, and I am working" (Jn 5:17), making himself equal with God, did not really solve the problem but added a second count to the first, that of blasphemy: "This was why the Jews sought all the more to kill him" (5:18).

Obviously, the memory of Jesus' miracle lasted a long time. When Emperor Hadrian built the heathen Aelia Capitolina on the ruins of Jerusalem in the second century, the pools were converted into a shrine of the healing god Asclepius. A temple dedicated to him, vaults for therapeutic baths, mosaics, frescoes, votive offerings, and coins attest to this day to the fact that, as the pilgrim from Bordeaux wrote in 333, "those who have been sick for many years have been healed."[6]

One year after the healing of the paralytic, in A.D. 29, Jesus stayed in Jerusalem between the Feast of Tabernacles (*Sukkot*, October 11–19) and the Feast of the Dedication of the Temple (*Chanukah*, December 19–26). At some point during this time, probably in early December, again on a Sabbath, a similar case occurred. This time Jesus met a man who had been blind from birth. His disciples asked him who was to blame for this great misfortune, who had sinned here, the blind man himself or his parents? But Jesus put them off; the reason for this blindness was to reveal the working of God, for he was the light of the world: "As he said this, he spat on the ground and made clay of the spittle and anointed the man's eyes with the clay, saying to him, 'Go, wash in the pool of Siloam' (which means Sent). So he went and washed and came back seeing" (Jn 9:6–7).

John's translation of the name Siloam shows that the Evangelist was well aware that Jesus' miracles are teachings that need to be understood symbolically on a meta-level, while at the same time they are tangible and real. Fortunately, the name of the main spring in Jerusalem is well attested in contemporary sources, from 2 Kings 20:20 to Flavius Josephus. The pool had been constructed by King Hezekiah on account of the impending siege of Jerusalem at the hands of the Assyrian King Sennacherib in 701 B.C. Since the Gihon Spring, the city's only spring, was outside the city walls, the king, in a brilliant feat of engineering, had a 383-yard-long channel hewn straight through the rock to *send* (hence the name) the water into a pool within the walls. In 1881, Arabs discovered an inscription in ancient Hebrew script that tells about the completion of the tunnel and thus confirms the Old Testament account. Later on, this masterpiece was gradually forgotten; even Flavius Josephus only knows the tunnel exit, which he calls *Siloam Spring*. Since it is located at the lowest point of Jerusalem, the tunnel itself exhibits a slight incline that makes the water pour forth from its exit. Today, anyone who has sturdy shoes and is not afraid of getting wet can traverse the tunnel; guided tours start in the Archaeological Park of the City of David in the Arab Silwan district (to which the spring owes its name). They

---

[6] *Bordeaux Pilgrim.*

THE POOL OF BETHESDA

end in a pool that was long presumed to be the Pool of Siloam. Here Ismail Kanan is waiting for us, a personable Arab who time and again proves himself a good guide. He guides us through the most recent excavations, in which he himself took part as a foreman, under the direction of Ronny Reich, an archaeologist with the Israel Antiquities Authority. And again, it was coincidence to which we owe one of the most important discoveries of New Testament archaeology in the last decade.

While Reich and his colleague Eli Shukron were digging in the area of the Gihon Spring, where the tunnel begins, the municipality needed to repair a sewer line that ran straight through Silwan. Heavy equipment was brought in, the ground was opened, and Eli was ordered to make sure that no archaeological remains, of which there is an abundance in the ground around Jerusalem, were damaged in the process. When he arrived at the site, he witnessed two steps being unearthed. He immediately stopped the work and called in Ronny, who speculated: "These must be remains of stairs that led down to the Siloam Pool; they seem to be from the time of the Second Temple." He quickly took a few photos so he could send a report to Jon Seligman, the district archaeologist for Jerusalem, that same day—this was in June 2004. Two days later he had an order by the Israel Antiquities Authority to excavate the "stairs".

But these were not stairs, as the archaeologists soon discovered; the steps seemed endlessly wide. Every three to four steps, there was an extension, just like with the steps in the southern Pool of Bethesda. After a few weeks, they had uncovered enough to get a first impression. The steps, this much was certain, belonged to the large trapezoid-shaped pool, almost 197 feet long and 230 feet wide, which was supplied by the Siloam "Spring" through a channel. Coin finds confirm that it was built toward the end of the Hasmonean period or during the reign of Herod. It was apparently the southern counterpart to the Bethesda complex: a second, gigantic *mikveh*, just without a water reservoir, because it was supplied with "living water", not from a cistern, but through the Siloam duct. A well-paved street led from there directly up to the Temple.

John was therefore more than precise when he mentioned Jesus sending the blind man, not to the Siloam "Spring", but rather to the Siloam Pool. The fact that there were indeed two sites, the basin by the wellspring [*Quellenausgang*] where the citizens of Jerusalem drew their water and the pool for ritual cleansing purposes, was still known to the pilgrim from Bordeaux in 333. He accurately describes "a pool, which is called Siloam; it has four porches; and another big pool outside."[7] When Empress Eudocia (401–460) had a church built at the site of the miracle, the other "big pool" had been long forgotten. The holy site was thus built north of the Siloam "Spring", at the place where today there is a mosque. The actual site of the miracle can now be visited on the way to the spring; whoever is looking for a good guide should ask for Ismail Kanan. But the exploration of the Siloam Pool is far from completed. For one half is on land that belongs to the Greek Orthodox Church. The patriarch has not yet decided whether he will cooperate with the Israelis or commission his own excavations. This would be worthwhile, by all means. For even in Jerusalem, holy sites still waiting to be excavated are becoming increasingly rare.

But John had profound local knowledge outside Jerusalem also, as is shown by his account of Jesus' encounter with the Samaritan woman at Jacob's well. With the precision typical of him, the Evangelist reports:

> [Jesus] left Judea and departed again to Galilee. He had to pass through Samaria. So he came to a city of Samaria, called Sychar, near the field that Jacob gave to his son Joseph. Jacob's well was there, and so Jesus, wearied as he was with his journey, sat down beside the well. It was about the sixth hour. There came a woman of Samaria to draw water. Jesus said to her, "Give me a drink." For his disciples had gone away into the city to buy food. The Samaritan woman said to him, "How is it that you, a Jew, ask a drink of me, a woman of Samaria?" For Jews have no dealings with Samaritans. (Jn 4:3–9)

The history of the conflict between Jews and Samaritans goes back to the time after the death of King Solomon (ca. 930 B.C.). At that time, an opposition formed in Shechem against the Jerusalem monarchy, which eventually led to a division of the empire into Judah (with Jerusalem as capital) and Israel (with Shechem as capital). After the

---

[7] Ibid.

return from the Babylonian Exile, the northern tribes were not ready to contribute to the building of the Jerusalem Temple but instead built their own temple on Mount Garizim, their "holy mountain", which they considered the mountain of Abraham's sacrifice. The fact that Hasmonean King John Hyrcanus had this temple destroyed in 107 B.C. only exacerbated the tensions between the kindred nations. Again and again there were encroachments, as for instance during the Passover festival in A.D. 6 when a group of Samaritans scattered human remains in the Jerusalem Temple in order to defile it, or around A.D. 50, when a Galilean train of pilgrims was attacked by the Samaritans and "many" Galileans were killed, as Flavius Josephus reports. A Samaritan uprising in A.D. 36 was crushed by Pontius Pilate in such a bloody fashion that the emperor recalled him in order to avoid further unrest. Since Jesus also used the pilgrimage route through Samaria to Galilee—he avoided the alternative via the Jewish East-Jordan land of Peraea in order to evade a possible ambush by Herod Antipas—he, too, was confronted with these tensions. But if we believe John, he used them constructively and almost dialectically: "Woman, believe me, the hour is coming when neither on this mountain nor in Jerusalem will you worship the Father.... God is spirit, and those who worship him must worship in spirit and truth" (Jn 4:21, 24). To anticipate an objection: this was no prophecy after the fact, for although Emperor Hadrian had a Jupiter-temple erected on the mountain in 135, there still was a Samaritan cultic site as late as the fourth century. But Jesus was convincing. Word soon traveled that he was teaching at the well and "many Samaritans from that city believed in him". They even "asked him to stay with them; and he stayed there two days." The point of the story is ultimately that the orthodox Jews rejected Jesus while even the Samaritans realized: "this is indeed the Savior of the world" (Jn 4:39–42).

Jacob's well is quickly identified. In the Book of Genesis, we read that Jacob bought land in Shechem (Gen 33:18–20) from Joshua, which he bequeathed to Joseph and his descendants and where he himself was buried (Josh 24:32). To this day the well—the only draw well in the area—is about 262 feet outside the ruins of Sichem, right by the intersection of two roads, one of which was the important north-south connection, the western route for Galilean pilgrims. As early as in Byzantine times, a cruciform church was located here that was destroyed by the Persians in 614. The Crusaders also built here and had to surrender their church, until in 1860 the Greek Orthodox Church bought the land and in 1903 began construction of a basilica that to this day has never been completed for lack of funds.

When John describes this well with two different Greek terms— namely, *pege* (spring) and *phrear* (bored well)—there is no hidden symbolism, much less even linguistic inconsistency, but rather precision in his choice of words. For Jacob's well is both: in the winter, it is supplied from a subterranean spring, but it also reaches as much as 164 feet down to the ground water when the spring dries up in the summer.

Mention of the city of Sychar, however, caused some headaches for the exegetes. Did the Evangelist actually mean Shechem? That would have been a grave mistake, for Shechem was destroyed by John Hyrcanus at the same time as the Garizim temple, namely, in 107 B.C., and existed only as ruins at the time of Jesus. The Evangelist, however, assumes an inhabited city; Jesus' disciples buy bread there, onlookers come to the well, and Jesus stayed two days in Sychar. The nearby Nablus, Greek *Neapolis* (New City), cannot be meant, either, since it was founded by Vespasian as late as A.D. 72. But Eusebius, too, knows a "Sychar before Neapolis", and the pilgrim from Bordeaux explicitly differentiates it from Nablus and Shechem when he writes: "There at the foot of the mountain [Garizim] is a place whose name is *Shechem* (Sichem). There is a tomb where Joseph is buried in a villa, which his father Jacob gave to him ... A mile from there is a place by the name of *Sychar*, where the Samaritan woman went down to that place where Jacob had dug a well."[8]

At that very place, on a small elevation, is the modern village of Askar, which is indeed half a mile from Jacob's well. Did it already exist at the time of Jesus? No excavations have taken place there yet. But the Jewish Talmud also knows of a village named En-Sokher with a neighboring well, and in the *Book of Jubilees*, a Jewish manuscript from the second century B.C., there is mention of a "King of *Sachir*" with whom Jacob's sons had to grapple.

Thus it seems as though John was, in fact, correct here. And yet again, he is the only source that reports so precisely on these almost forgotten sites and events that are not in the Synoptic Gospels. This alone proves that the Fourth Gospel (a) was written as a

[8] Ibid.

supplementary work and (b) is the work of an insider. It is admittedly the Gospel with the most developed theology and Christology, but at the same time it contains the most accurate topographic data, the most detailed descriptions of Jewish customs and practices at the time of Jesus, and the most meaningful chronology. John uses correct Hebrew and Aramaic toponyms and terms and translates them for his obviously Hellenistic audience, just as he explains the meaning of Jewish feasts and religious precepts (especially the purity precept of the Halacha). His date for the first public appearance of Jesus— forty-six years after the beginning of the Temple construction = A.D. 28—is congruent with the data of Luke; his chronology admittedly appears less stringent than the linear outline in the Synoptic Gospels (Baptism at the Jordan—Ministry in Galilee—Ministry in Jerusalem—Death and Resurrection) but for that reason also more credible (why should Jesus, of all people, have shirked his duty to visit the Temple three times a year?). He knows the geography extremely well. He is acquainted with the regions of Judaea and Galilee and knows when it is necessary to "ascend" and where the traveler needs to "descend". He is the only one to name Bethsaida as the birthplace of the apostles Philip, Andrew, and Peter (1:44); only in his Gospel does Cana play a role, not only as the site for the miracle of the wine, but also as the home of Nathanael (21:2) and the base for Jesus' ministry in the summer of 28 (4:46). His numerical data are extremely exact, also and precisely because he acknowledges them as numeric symbols on a meta-level. It seems like he is almost touchingly eager to pass on even the minutest detail, including the days of the week and the exact times. This speaks either for the excellent memory of an eyewitness or the creative imagination of a narrator, but since all data, as far as they are verifiable, are accurate, the former is more likely the case. Thus in 2006 the American theologian Paul Anderson, too, determined that the Gospel of John was "far closer to the historical Jesus than most scholars have claimed or thought for almost a century.... Much of John's tradition appears authentic and even superior to the presentations of Jesus in the Synoptics, and this has extensive implications for Jesus studies."[9] Klaus Berger, the

---

[9] Paul N. Anderson, "Aspects of Historicity in the Gospel of John: Implications for Investigations of Jesus and Archaeology", in *Jesus and Archaeology*, ed. James H. Charlesworth (Grand Rapids, Mich.: Eerdmans, 2006), p. 614.

well-known theologian from Heidelberg, arrived at similar conclusions. In the process, Berger, too, refutes the myth that John's theology was "close to gnosis"—i.e., influenced by an ancient syncretism that interpreted Jesus in the context of Zoroastrian dualism or the initiation rites of ancient mystery religions. On the contrary, says Berger, "the Qumran discoveries and Alexandrian philosophy (Philo) shed plentiful light on the religious-historical milieu of the Gospel. Somewhat more generally, we could also speak about a Jewish type of 'religious philosophy of the Imperial Era'."[10] This means John's theology and Christology are not a novelty that developed late but in fact have their parallels in contemporary Judaism, for instance, in the messianic expectations of the Essenes as they are expressed in the Dead Sea Scrolls. Therefore it may very well have been part of the early Christians' belief system.

This finding is in line with the Christian tradition regarding the origin of the Fourth Gospel. Around 330, the Church historian Eusebius of Caesarea, for instance, writes:

> And when Mark and Luke had already published their Gospels, they say that John, who had employed all his time in proclaiming the Gospel orally, finally proceeded to write for the following reason. The three Gospels already mentioned having come into the hands of all and into his own too, they say that he accepted them and bore witness to their truthfulness; but that there was lacking in them an account of the deeds done by Christ at the beginning of his ministry.[11]

It is therefore indeed a supplemental Gospel, just as we have concluded from clues within the text itself. Eusebius, referring to Irenaeus of Lyon (second century), emphasizes that John lived "until the time of Trajan"[12] (98–117), and thus until about A.D. 100 (which is quite possible if he met Jesus when he was a young man). The oldest fragment of the Fourth Gospel that was discovered in Egypt—experts refer to it as P52, "Papyrus 52"; it contains John 18:31–33

---

[10] Klaus Berger, *Im Anfang was Johannes* (Stuttgart: Quell, 1997).

[11] Eusebius of Caesaria, *Church History*, trans. Arthur Cushman McGiffert, bk. 3, chap. 24, no. 7, *Nicene and Post-Nicene Fathers*, second series, ed. Philip Schaff and Henry Wace (1890; Peabody, Mass.: Hendrickson, 1995), 1:153.

[12] Ibid., bk. 3, chap. 23, 4, p. 150.

and 37–38—is dated between 100 and 125. Thus there is no reason why the text could not have been written down during the apostle's lifetime. Other than that, we know only that it was written after the three Synoptic Gospels, after the death of Peter (A.D. 64 or 67; John references this in John 21:18–19), but apparently before the destruction of the Temple (John still related Jesus' prophecy to the Resurrection, cf. 2:21). A realistic date for the writing of the Gospel, therefore, is around 68, when John was indeed the only one of the Twelve who had not yet been martyred and his witness was more valuable than ever. This is precisely what he expresses in his words toward the end of the Fourth Gospel: "This is the disciple who is bearing witness to these things, and who has written these things; and we know that his testimony is true" (Jn 21:24).

But what about Matthew, Mark, and Luke? Luke's diptych concludes with the Acts of the Apostles, which ends very suddenly with Saint Paul's release from "detention pending trial" in A.D. 62. In his preface, the Evangelist refers to extensive research and conversations with eyewitnesses ("Inasmuch as many have undertaken to compile a narrative of the things which have been accomplished among us, just as they were delivered to us by those who from the beginning were eyewitnesses and ministers of the word, it seemed good to me also, having followed all things closely for some time past, to write an orderly account for you", Lk 1:1–3). Paul's companion could have done this between 57 and 59, when the apostle to the Gentiles was held captive for two years in the prison of Governor Felix in Caesarea and Luke was staying in Jerusalem. Accordingly, his Gospel would have been composed between 60 and 62.

There is a dispute as to the correct order between Matthew and Mark, one based on a misunderstanding. This, in turn, dates back to the earliest source we have on the origin of the Gospels, Bishop Papias of Hierapolis (around 60–140). In the quotes from his writings that Irenaeus of Lyon hands down to us, he describes how early on he was eager to hear stories about Jesus from the lips of still-living eyewitnesses. He traveled, for instance, to the neighboring Ephesus to listen to John. From him he learned that "Matthew first assembled Jesus' speeches in Hebrew." Later, when Peter went to Rome for the first time, Mark worked as his interpreter. After the apostle had left, the Romans asked Mark to write down everything that Peter had told them. Since it was always anecdotes, he wrote them down "carefully, but not in order".

On account of this testimony, for centuries the Gospel of Matthew was held to be the original text, while Mark was considered a shortened version; to this day Matthew comes first in any printed edition of the New Testament. But toward the middle of the nineteenth century, German Protestant theologians made an interesting discovery from which they derived the two-source theory. According to this theory, Matthew was not the model for Mark's "short version", but rather Mark was one of the two main sources for the Gospel of Matthew. The other source was a collection of Jesus' sayings that is commonly called the Q document and was also available to Luke. Yet while Luke skillfully embedded it into his "biography of Jesus", Matthew imported it almost *en bloc*. This rather undifferentiated approach, as well as the dependency on Mark, precludes the possibility that an apostle was the author of the first Gospel as we know it. As an eyewitness and companion of Jesus, there would have been no need for him to copy a collection of anecdotes, published by Peter's interpreter in an almost arbitrary order.

Things look entirely different if we assume that Matthew was the author of Q. This matches the information from Papias that Matthew (merely) "compiled the speeches of Jesus"; the German term *Logien-quelle* = "sayings-source" (or Q document) means precisely that. "Of course, who else?" we are tempted to ask. For if someone, indeed, took down Jesus' speeches "in shorthand", Matthew was the only one of the Twelve with the necessary qualifications.

After all, Levi Matthew, son of Alpheus, publican, was not just a customs official, but, as we know from the Greek original of the first Gospel, a *telones*, a tax collector. He was therefore in charge of the customs station of Capernaum that he had leased from the king—Herod Antipas. Thus, he was not only a wealthy man but also well educated. As *telones*, he had to be able to make records quickly and concisely. He probably used the ancient form of stenography, tachygraphy, a type of shorthand.

Judaism is a book religion. It draws on the written records of the words of the Prophets, just like the Talmud recorded the dialogues and statements of important rabbis. Even before the Easter event, when he left everything in order to follow Jesus, Matthew would have seen in him at least a great prophet and teacher. For this reason alone, it is more than likely that he either recorded Jesus' speeches live or at least wrote them down shortly after. The early Christian community probably had one such sayings-source, largely equivalent to the hypothetical Q construction, at their disposal. The Gnostic *Gospel of Thomas*, which originated in the third century in the area around Edessa, copies its form, which indicates that the sayings-source was still circulating at this time to a limited extent. Only when the Gospel of Mark, which is said to have originated shortly after Peter's stay in Rome in the years 42–44, became known in the Holy Land could the Jewish Christians have felt the desire to create something even better and to combine into one text the information from Mark's book with the sayings-source of Matthew, along with a few local traditions. This is how today's Gospel of Matthew, which was probably completed in its final form sometime between 50 and 60, could have been compiled.

And Mark? Are there serious indications that the Second Gospel could actually have been written in Rome as early as 45, only fifteen years after the Resurrection?

The German papyrologist and archaeologist Carsten Peter Thiede, who unfortunately passed away prematurely in 2004 at the age of fifty-two, was convinced of this. He went so far as to interpret allusions to crucifixions and empty tombs in the ancient romance *Callirrhoe*, which originated in the fifth decade A.D., as well as in the *Satyricon*, the picaresque novel by Petronius Niger (ca. 60), as allusions to the Gospel of Mark. More interesting still are clues from the text itself. For instance, the Evangelist relates one of Jesus' prophecies to his time and quotes him: "But when you see the desolating sacrilege set up where it ought not to be", and immediately inserts "let the reader understand" (Mk 13:14). It is obvious to what Mark is referring. In A.D. 40, as we read in Flavius Josephus, the megalomaniac Emperor Caligula sent his legate "Petronius with an army to Jerusalem, to place his statues in the temple",[13] which led to an insurrection. A statue in itself already violated the Decalogue's ban on images, but one that depicted the emperor as a god would desecrate the Temple. While the emperor threatened them with war unless they condoned the affront, the Jews were ready to go to

---

[13] Flavius Josephus, *The Jewish War*, bk. 2, chap. 10, no. 1, in *New Complete Works of Josephus*, p. 741.

extremes: thousands of them went to head off Petronius and offered
their necks for decapitation—they preferred to die rather than to
tolerate such a sacrilege. Fortunately the emperor died before his
order to attack reached the army. For Peter, who came to Rome
two years later, the incident was still so fresh in his memory that he
naturally quoted it as an example of one of Jesus' prophecies that had
been fulfilled. Since people still remembered it five years later, Mark
knew that his readers would understand the allusion.

Similarly interesting in Mark's Gospel is another comment to his
readers. When he wrote about Simon of Cyrene, the man who carried the Cross of Christ, he added that he was "the father of Alexander and Rufus" (Mk 15:21). This cross-reference, of course, only
makes sense if the two sons were known to the proto-community.
After all, nobody would mention a stranger as the father of two
even less-known sons. Paul, in fact, mentions a Rufus in his Letter
to the Romans, describing him as "eminent in the Lord" (Rom
16:13) and a member of the community in the capital, which Mark,
too, addressed primarily. And Alexander? In 1941, archaeologists
opened a burial chamber in the Kidron Valley between Jerusalem
and the Mount of Olives. In it were eleven ossuaries, stone chests
for the secondary burial of the remains of the dead, all of which bore
inscriptions. They were from the time before the destruction of the
Temple. One of the bone chests bore exactly two inscriptions, in
Greek and Hebrew: "Alexander of Cyrene" and "Alexander, son of
Simon". It can be precarious to connect everyday Jewish names on
ossuaries with Biblical figures, but this case is pretty clear. In Jerusalem, after all, there were not that many Jews from Cyrene, which
is in modern-day Libya. It is rather unlikely that, in addition to this,
another one also had a son named Alexander.

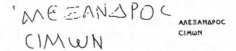

And yet Simon, when he met Jesus, was only a pilgrim who had come to Jerusalem for the Passover. He was "coming in from the country", Mark writes. This does not mean that he was still working on the day before the feast; "the country" referred to the camp of pilgrims' tents west of the city. The fastest way from there to the Temple was through the Ephraim Gate, in front of which Jesus was crucified. He probably had his sons with him; there was no reason to leave them behind in the tent. The encounter with Jesus must have triggered something in Simon and the two boys that changed their lives. Apparently, they remained in Jerusalem and joined the proto-community on Pentecost, at the latest, which would explain why the foreigner's name made it into the Gospels at all.

Rufus and Alexander, therefore, were known, one in Rome, both in Jerusalem. Mark's reference, however, is meaningful only if he wrote his Gospel while both were still alive—in the case of Alexander, this would mean before A.D. 70.

A find from Qumran could deal a mortal blow to the theory of a later date. It was not until 1955 that nineteen fragments of ancient scrolls, along with the shards of the pots in which they had once been stored, were discovered above the Essene monastery, in Cave 7, which actually contained living rooms and workplaces. Two characteristics distinguished them from anything that had been found in Qumran previously. First, they were written on papyrus, not on skins like the scrolls of the Essenes. And secondly, their language was Greek, not Hebrew or Aramaic. It is therefore beyond doubt that they had a special status.

Since most of the fragments were too small to arrange them into a known text, the scientists who worked on the Qumran texts disregarded them at first. It was not until 1972 that the Spanish papyrologist José O'Callaghan—he had Irish ancestors—went public with a spectacular interpretation. In his opinion, the find partially consisted of fragments of Christian texts. He associated four of the papyrus snippets with the Gospel of Mark (7Q5, 6, 7, and 15), one with the First Letter of Timothy, and one with the Letter of James. Twelve years later, Carsten Peter Thiede took up this thesis again and defended it, with his typical passion, until his death. The subsequent debate in the expert community was not always conducted objectively, and to this day there is no satisfactory conclusion. The letters on the papyrus are written in the so-called *decorative style* that is typical of the time until A.D. 50. Unfortunately, only ten of them, in four lines, can be identified with certainty. The core of the debate is whether the letters *enne* belong to the toponym *Gennesaret* or the verb *egennesen* ("begot")—i.e., whether it was passage 6:52–53 in Mark or a Jewish genealogy ("x begot y; y begot z"). Meanwhile, Thiede even troubled the Israeli police forensic laboratory in order to identify traces of ink that would corroborate his interpretation; the results proved him right.

If we follow the debate, one thing becomes apparent: the opponents of the Callaghan-Thiede identification argue ideologically. It cannot be Mark because it must not be Mark. According to them, the Gospel originated later; furthermore, it was unthinkable that the Essenes were interested in Christian writing. They ignore the question of why the Essenes translated a genealogy, of all things, into Greek and then wrote it on imported, and thus expensive, but also less durable papyrus. Time, however, seems to prove Callaghan and Thiede right. As early as 1994, the renowned Italian papyrologist Orsolina Montevecchi wrote: "As to the identification with Mark 6:52–53, there are, it seems, no longer any reasonable doubts. I think it is now time to enter 7Q5 into the official list of New Testament papyri." The well-known Viennese theologian and Bible scholar Karl Jaroš already did this when he included fragment 7Q5 in his catalogue of the *New Testament according to the Oldest Greek Manuscipts*. His verdict: "The hypothesis to identify 7Q5 with Mark 6:52–53 is well-backed by solid arguments.... Whoever does not acknowledge this, insists on preconceived notions."[14] Jaroš, too, dates the fragment to between A.D. 40 and 54.

The most conclusive evidence for this identification, however, is a broken clay pot, right next to which fragment 7Q5 was found. It bears the Hebrew transcription of the name Rome, not only once, but twice. If this should indicate the origin of the Mark papyrus, Christian tradition, and with it the reliability of the Gospels, is corroborated unambiguously. It seems as though Luke was correct when he claimed that they contained nothing but eyewitness accounts. It is time at last to take them seriously again.

[14] Karl Jaroš, *Die ältesten Handschriften des Neuen Testamentes* (Cologne et al.: Böhlau, 2014), p. 63.

IX

The Jesus Boat

The Road by the Sea

The entire country looked anxiously at the lake that threatened to shrink more and more. For three years there had been a drought in Israel. Even the otherwise abundant winter rain, which usually makes the Jordan swell and fills up Lake Gennesaret (the Sea of Galilee), the country's largest reservoir, failed to come. But for Yuval and Moshe Lufan, two young men from the Ginosar Kibbutz on the northwestern shore of Yam Kinneret (as the lake is called in Hebrew), the whole thing was an adventure. Rather by chance, they had found a few Jewish coins from the time of Jesus in the mud that the receding water had left behind. Now the brothers returned almost daily to the spot, hoping that the lake would yield more of its sunken treasures.

But on this evening in January of 1986, it was not a coin that they found on the beach, but an old nail. They were about to ignore it, but then it took hold of their imagination. While Yuval tried to pull it out of the sand, a second nail emerged, which appeared equally immovable. Guessing that they were onto something big, both brothers now dug in the muck until they came upon a wooden plank. With one voice they uttered a shout of joy and then murmured: "This must be ancient. Maybe a ship?"

Dirty and overjoyed they ran to their father to show him the find. They did not have to explain much to him; one look into their eyes revealed how important it was. When he arrived at the shore, he first made sure that no one was watching them. Then he, too, knelt down and dug in the mud. Two hours later, he was convinced that his sons had found the remains of an old fishing boat.

But how old could it be? Two weeks passed, filled with worry that someone could discover their find and claim it for himself, but filled also with fear of a disappointment. Finally the brothers plucked up the courage to tell the directress of the kibbutz about their discovery. She knew at once who would be able to assess the wreck correctly. Mendel Nun from the Ein Gev Kibbutz on the east bank is considered a walking encyclopedia for everything relating to the history, botany, and zoology of Lake Gennesaret. The news that the wreck of a ship had been found on the shores of "his" lake electrified the local historian; only hours later, he was in his car and on his way. Together with their father, almost in silence, the brothers guided him to the spot. Something solemn was in the air when Mendel inspected the old plank, continued to dig, more and more excitedly, faster and faster, until he burst out: "Friends, this is an ancient boat. We must call the Antiquities Authority!" That night—it was a Sabbath—the weekly dance took place in a neighboring kibbutz. Yuval could not help himself. He had to dance. The joy, the excitement, made him feel almost weightless.

It was a drizzly, cold morning in February, and all of Israel hoped that it would bring the end of the drought, when Professor Shelley Wachsmann and Dr. Kurt Raveh from the Israel Antiquities Authority in Jerusalem came to Lake Gennesaret to inspect the boat. "Where do we have to dive?" was their first question when they arrived in Ginosar. When the two underwater archaeologists heard that the lake had already released the wreck, they were relieved. Its water is so muddy that diving here is no fun. "Will you be able to tell us how old the boat is?" was the counterquestion Moshe asked them. The answer was positive. The techniques of boat-building had changed over the centuries, which enabled a rough age determination even upon initial inspection. Typical of ancient times is a mortise and tenon joint between the planks. Finally, Mendel and the brothers led the two archaeologists to the shore. "Now where is the wreck?" Wachsmann wanted to know. "You are standing on it", Yuval replied with a broad grin. The archaeologists then recognized the plank, removed the mud, using the rain water, which had collected here, to aid them, until they came upon a familiar pattern: the outline of a mortise with the broken-off tenon still stuck in it. "The boat is definitely very, very old", they announced to the excited brothers, who sensed that they had just written archaeological history. At that moment, the floodgates of heaven were opened and the land was showered with rain—the heaviest rainfall in three years, the rain for which all of Israel had prayed.

Minutes later, the shower ended as abruptly as it had started. The smell of ozone filled the air, which was now clear and cool. The clouds in the sky parted, the sun broke through. And suddenly a double rainbow appeared that ended somewhere in the middle of the lake.

"Now at least we know to whom the boat belonged", Mendel said jokingly. "And who is that?" Wachsmann wanted to know. "Obviously, it was the lifeboat of Noah's Ark!" Everybody laughed, except Yuval. "I consider this permission to dig up the boat", he said solemnly, "permission from on high." For a moment, Wachsmann felt as if he were part of a movie. But he looked up again—the rainbow was real. What he would have called "exaggerated" and "kitschy" to the face of any movie director was happening right before his eyes. The archaeologist had to pinch himself to make sure that he was not dreaming. Something within him mistrusted his senses. Something else within him asked, "Why not?"

While the news of the discovery of an ancient boat spread like a wildfire and the brothers did all they could to lead astray potential treasure hunters and illegitimate diggers, Wachsmann and Raveh prepared the excavation. The kibbutz provided plenty of volunteers; the police were ready to seal off the area and watch the perimeter. For days on end, they built a dam around the wreck, drained the exposed lake bottom with pumps and pipes. Then the archaeologists came and meticulously worked by hand to clear every plank of the mud and expose it. A wooden scaffold, which they had erected over the site, also enabled them to work on the inside of the boat without having to step on its waterlogged, muddy wood. But how could it be saved from desiccation and disintegration? There were no empirical data—never before had an ancient boat been found in a freshwater lake in Israel. But fortunately there was Orna Cohen. The Antiquities Authority had hired the young conservator a year before. Two years prior, she had still been studying in London—and one morning found herself in a seminar, the topic of which was the conservation of ancient shipwrecks. Without knowing how she would one day use her knowledge, the young woman from Israel felt almost magically attracted by this course. Now, in Ginosar, she was able to show what she had learned. Without her, without her knowledge and know-how, the ancient fishing boat would probably never have been preserved.

For two thousand years, mud, sand, and water had held the wooden planks together. The wood had soaked up the water until it had the consistency of wet cardboard. If the wood were exposed to the sun and the wind now, the moist planks would be in danger of contracting, deforming, or even breaking. The wood was temporarily held together only by means of metal rods for stabilization. In addition, it was regularly sprayed with water to prevent drying out. Cavities were filled with fiberglass.

On the first day after the start of the excavation, the form and size of the boat could already be determined. It was 27 feet long and 7.5 feet wide. An oil lamp, which was still inside it, and a clay cooking pot, which lay right next to it, helped determine its age. It was from the Herodian or early Roman at the latest. In other words: from the time of Jesus. Radiocarbon (C14) dating of the wood later confirmed this estimate. Accordingly, the boat was built between 120 B.C. and A.D. 40. From the beginning, this was not a poor skiff, but rock solid, carefully constructed, and roomy. Its planks consisted of sturdy cedar wood, which probably had been imported from Lebanon, its frame of oak wood. It had a mast from which a large square linen sail was suspended, two impressive stone anchors that weighed forty-two and sixty-eight pounds, two pairs of oars as well as a rudder. Its crew was a minimum of four persons, and it could accommodate as many as sixteen. Later on, a carpenter repaired it, using plenty of nails. It was mended again and again, until altogether twelve sorts of wood had been used. At least three generations of fishermen must have used the Ginosar boat to make a living. A mosaic from the first century, which the Franciscans had discovered in the course of their excavations in Migdal, the ancient Magdala, proved that it was not the only one of its kind. A careful comparison revealed that its construction was practically identical with the wreck of Ginosar.

Although it was easy to determine its former function and its age, it proved difficult to salvage the boat. And time was of the essence. Just as the find was made, the three-year drought in Israel ended, the lake's water level was rising almost daily. With the end of winter and the snow melting on Mount Hermon, it would rise even more. The first plan was to number each plank and take the boat out of the mud piece by piece. Yet, considering how softened the wood was and how quickly it contracted and deformed in the dry air, it would probably be impossible to put the planks back together later. Leaving the boat in one piece was the only chance. Then Moshe had an idea. He had worked on the kibbutz chicken farm, where he used polyurethane foam to build a shelter from the summer heat for the fowl. Polyurethane foam is used for insulation. When it cools, it expands and becomes so light that it even floats on water. It should then be strong enough to hold the boat's fragile skeleton together without a problem.

When Moshe told her about his idea, Orna was skeptical at first, but then she agreed to test the effect of the foam on a piece of wood. The plan worked! After the boat was held together from the top and the bottom by a fiberglass framework, it was sprayed from all sides with polyurethane foam, which created a protective layer around the fragile wood. Until now, the volunteers had pumped the constantly rising lake water out of the excavation site, but now it was flooded and the boat floated. Its final journey on the lake led into the port of the Ginosar Kibbutz. From there a crane lifted it into a specially designed concrete pool, which became its new home for the next fourteen years. During this time, under the supervision of Orna Cohen, the water in the cells of its planks was gradually replaced with a solution of synthetic wax (Polyethylene glycol—PEG). Today the boat stands in a circular concrete bunker and has long since become a tourist attraction. The marketing, which established it as such, was ingenious. It directly appealed to the religious sentiments of potential Israel pilgrims and declared the wreck the Jesus Boat, practically a sort of relic. The circumstances of its discovery, its age, and the proximity to Magdala were sufficient to make this connection plausible. There were even talks about displaying the boat in a special exhibition in the Vatican, on the occasion of the Great Jubilee in 2000, but concerns that it would not withstand the transport prevailed.

Archaeologists, in fact, prefer to connect the find with another historical event, the naval battle of Migdal. It occurred in A.D. 67 when Flavius Josephus was still in command of the insurgent Jews in

Galilee. The inhabitants of Tiberias were unsure whether they should join the revolt or defect to the slowly advancing Romans. In order to intimidate and convince them of the insurgents' strength, Josephus used a ruse. The citizens of Magdala, where he had set up his second quarters after Cana, were willing to help him. He subsequently ordered every fishing boat on the lake to be confiscated, altogether 230 boats, and to appear some distance away from Magdala with a minimum crew of four men. He himself boarded one of the boats with a handful of soldiers, who at least gave the impression of being ready to attack, and steered straight toward the city. Its citizens, who watched the spectacle from the city wall, must have thought that the attack of a tremendous fleet was imminent. In order to avoid unnecessary bloodshed, they surrendered. To keep them from changing their minds, Josephus subsequently had the six-hundred-person city council and two thousand citizens of Tiberias brought to Migdal as hostages on the 230 boats.

Nevertheless, the insurgents were not able to stop the advance of the Romans. Josephus had barely managed to hide in a cistern when someone betrayed him. But again his *chutzpah* saved him. He prophesied to the Roman commander Vespasian that he would become emperor. In him, Josephus said, the prophecy of the Messiah, who accedes to his rule of the world from the land of the Jews, was fulfilled. When the Romans indeed made Vespasian emperor, after Nero's suicide and the failure of Generals Galba, Otho, and Vitellius, the self-proclaimed prophet Josephus was well established.

But first the Jewish revolt needed to be quelled. When the Romans besieged Migdal, its citizens fled onto the 230 boats, which were apparently still in the harbor of the fishing city, and sailed out onto the lake. Without hesitation, Titus, the son of Vespasian, built a fleet of rafts and sent his soldiers in pursuit. After a fierce naval battle, the first and last in the history of the Jewish people, the shore of the Sea of Galilee was littered with wrecks, debris, and corpses.

An arrowhead, which was still stuck in the wood of the Ginosar wreck, reveals that this boat, too, took part in the naval battle. It can no longer be ascertained from where Josephus had fetched it and to whom it belonged before. It is certain, however, that it was already sailing on Lake Gennesaret when Jesus began his ministry on its shores, right after the wedding feast of Cana.

This was in March of the year A.D. 28, and it was a good decision. The highland of Galilee, his home, had a gate to the world in
Sepphoris, but at the same time it remained provincial and remote.
In order to proclaim the Gospel, he needed travel routes, junctions,
and connections. Even Herod Antipas may have been driven by the
desire for more dynamism when he had his residence moved from
Sepphoris to the western shore of Lake Gennesaret in A.D. 20. There
he built a new city and named it Tiberias, after the new emperor. He
equipped it with a stadium by the seashore, a theater, a large synagogue, and a magnificent palace that he inhabited for the next few
years. But, unlike Sepphoris, Tiberias was never accepted by faithful
Jews. During the building of the city, as Flavius Josephus relates, old
tombs came to light, rendering it "unclean", according to Jewish
belief. Still worse was the fact that the tetrarch's palace was adorned
with statues, which contradicted the Jewish ban on images. In order
to realize his vision nevertheless, Antipas settled people who were
poor or owned no land, released prisoners and soldiers in the new
city, but also nouveaux riches parvenus without religious ties. No
wonder, therefore, that Jesus obviously avoided the new capital. It is
only mentioned by John (Jn 6:1), who also refers to Lake Gennesaret
as the "Sea of Tiberias" (the name was used, indeed, between A.D. 20
and 61, as long as Tiberias was the capital of Galilee, but not afterward) and speaks of people seeking Jesus coming in their "boats from
Tiberias" (Jn 6:23).

Instead, Jesus picked Capernaum as his new place of operations,
where he went "with his mother and his brethren and his disciples"
(Jn 2:12) and stayed there "for a few days"—until March 30, to be
precise, but intermittently. The Village of Nahum, named after the
Old Testament prophet, was certainly no metropolis; it was a fishing
village with 1,500 inhabitants at most. But strategically the location
had great advantages. From its port, one was easily able to reach any
other place on the seashore by boat. Only a few miles east, with the
Jordan as the border, was the realm of Philip, the most tolerant and
accommodating of all the sons of Herod. If Antipas were to target Jesus
like John the Baptist, he could quickly leave the realm by sea as well
as by land. On the other side of the lake was the Decapolis—Gentile
territory, which Jesus incorporated into his mission travels as well as
Sidon and Tyre in Phoenicia, which were only a day's march to the

northwest. Furthermore, Capernaum was a toll station on the Via
Maris, the ancient caravan route that connected Egypt with Damascus and from there continued into Mesopotamia, all the way to Babylon. Since Herod had built his port city Caesarea at the place where
it reaches the Mediterranean, this road, too, led to Rome. The ties
with the capital became so close that fish caught in Lake Gennesaret
came to be offered in its markets as a special delicacy. On the Via
Maris, the fish were transported to Caesarea and there loaded onto
ships to make their way by sea to Puteoli and Ostia, the two ports
of Rome. An entire industry developed in Magdala to ensure that
the fish did not spoil on the long journey. The city, which probably
owed its name (from *migdal nunaya*, "fisherman's tower") to a lighthouse by the lake, became famous under its Greek name, Taricheai,
which simply means "fish curing". Cured and smoked fish from Taricheai was so highly regarded among Roman gourmets that even
Strabo in his *Geography* made special mention of the *tilapia Galilaea*,
the tilapia from Lake Gennesaret.

The early Christians considered the fish their distinctive symbol.
This, of course, was due to the fact that the initial letters of the Greek
profession of faith *Iesous Christos Theou 'Yios Soter* (Jesus Christ, Son
of God, Savior) spell the word *ichthys* = fish. But it also recalled the
environment where the Gospel was proclaimed, the disciples, many
of whom were fishermen before they were called to be "fishers of
men", and the fact that Jesus fed the faithful with bread and fish, not
once, but twice. And it was at least significant that the trade with the
commodity of fish indicated the path that the Word of God would
later take, from Lake Gennesaret on the Via Maris to Rome. For his
disciples, however, Jesus' appearance in Capernaum fulfilled above all
a prophecy of Isaiah, from the time when Galilee was still Assyrian
and, thus, heathen: "The land of Zebulun and the land of Naphtali,
toward the sea, across the Jordan, Galilee of the Gentiles—the people
who sat in darkness have seen a great light", as the Evangelist Matthew (4:15–16) quotes it in the opening lines of his account of Jesus'
ministry by Lake Gennesaret. It starts after the arrest of the Baptist,
after the summer in Cana and the Feast of Tabernacles in Jerusalem,
when Jesus returned to Capernaum.

Coming to the Sea of Galilee is a new adventure every time. But
the car ride via Tiberias falls short of revealing the beauty of this

landscape. This is why, just recently, the Israeli tourist bureau has offered a Jesus Trail, a chance to explore the land, so to speak, in the footsteps of the Son of God. The best season for this is spring, when it is not yet too hot and Galilee is covered with flowers. The most beautiful route available to the hiking pilgrim is the ancient path from Nazareth to the lake, through the Nahal Arbel, or Arbel Valley, called Wadi al-Hamam (pigeon valley) in Arabic. Two springs turn the ancient river bed into a green oasis, lined by pastures and green meadows. Before long, bizarre cliffs tower on both sides, riddled with holes like cheese: these are the caves in which rebels hid during the time of the Jewish rebellion. The steep Mount Arbel carries on its back the remains of an old Jewish city, but also a fortress from the time of the Crusades. It guards access to the lake, which looks up to the sky like a gigantic deep-blue eye. Its present Hebrew name, Yam Kinneret, probably stems from the fact that it has the shape of a harp (Hebrew, *kinnor*). Yet its fishermen swear that its splashing sounds like the singing of a harp.

The first city welcoming the hiker is Migdal, the old Magdala, whose most famous daughter was a wealthy widow named Mary. She joined Jesus, after he had driven seven demons out of her, and she seems to have supported him and his disciples financially as well (Lk 8:2–3). Magdala is likely identical with the Magadan that Matthew mentions ("And sending away the crowds, he got into the boat and went to the region of Magadan", Mt 15:39). In several Gospel manuscripts, it actually says "Magdala" in this passage. The letters "l" and "n" were often interchanged when translating from Hebrew into Aramaic (thus, the Hebrew name Nathan is Nethel in Aramaic). When Mark in his parallel account (8:10) uses the place name Dalmanutha instead, he is probably referring to a "small landing" north of Magdala that was likely preferred to the large port of the fishing city.

Archaeological research is still being conducted in Migdal. According to Flavius Josephus, forty thousand people once lived here, a number that is actually rather questionable. Archaeologists estimate that it was at most twelve thousand, at the time still an impressive number. Either way, its inhabitants were considered the beneficiaries of the globalization that the annexation of Judaea to the Roman Empire had brought about. Before the founding of Tiberias, Madgala was the most important and largest city on the western shore of the lake. The trade in cured and smoked fish as well as the cottage industries of weaving and breeding sacrificial pigeons made its inhabitants rich quickly, a wealth that is reflected in the archaeological findings. The excavations conducted by the Franciscans, under the direction of Virgilio Corbo and Stanislao Loffreda, revealed a forum with basalt pavement, lined with porticoes, and a Roman villa whose mosaic floor shows how its owner earned his money—this is where the aforementioned fishing boat can be seen. A surprisingly small synagogue of only twenty by twenty-one feet seemed to call into question the religious zeal of the nouveaux riches inhabitants of Magdala. It consists of massive basalt blocks; three of its walls were lined with columns. In the corners, there were double columns with a heart-shaped cross-section, a shape that is considered typical for Galilean synagogues. On the fourth wall, the excavators found the remains of steps that likely served as benches. Between the columns and the wall was a narrow channel that was supplied with water by an adjacent spring. This circumstance led critics to believe that the building was a spring house rather than a synagogue. They were wrong, it seems, for the synagogue of Gamla in Golan—a Jewish city that was destroyed by the Romans in A.D. 67 and never rebuilt—exhibits the same basic layout. Right next to the synagogue the archaeologists came upon the remains of a *mikveh* that could also be dated to the first century.

Among the Franciscan archaeologists' more recent finds are the remains of the old Magdala harbor and an ancient thermal bath from the time of Jesus. In one pool, the excavators came upon the remains of wooden plates and cups that were probably part of Roman legionnaires' equipment. Another pool seems to have been reserved for women exclusively. Here they found broaches and hair clips, but also small bottles made of terracotta and glass, some of them still sealed, containing ointment that is still precious by today's standard. The ingredients are currently being analyzed in chemical laboratories—a promising development. "We might thus be able to find out which ointment Mary Magdalen used", says Franciscan archaeologist Padre Stefano DeLuca, who directs the current excavations. Although modern exegesis has long since stopped identifying Mary Magdalen with the sinner who anointed Jesus' feet, such an investigation is certainly worthwhile.

That was the status quo of research when the first edition of this book went to press in the summer of 2009. Distribution had just started when the Israel Antiquities Authority (IAA), on September 11, 2009, issued a press release that actually deserved front-page coverage in the world press. But it was ignored by the major newspapers. Only experts and Church-associated media noted that archaeologists had found something on the shore of Lake Gennesaret that revolutionizes our image of Galilee at the time of Jesus. They had, thus the official IAA account, "discovered a synagogue from the first century A.D. in Magdala". Perhaps it was due to the fact that the Israelis said nothing about the implications of the find. For, of course, other synagogues from the first century had been excavated, for instance on the Herodium, the rock fortress of Masada, and in the rebel village of Gamla in Golan—but Jesus never visited those. That he paid attention to the mini-synagogue on the Franciscan grounds remains a possibility, at least. The synagogues in places mentioned in the New Testament, such as Chorazin and Capernaum, are from a later time, even though they were probably built on the foundations of their antecedents. Magdala, on the other hand, had never recovered from the turmoil of the Jewish rebellion. Thus it was preserved in its condition from A.D. 67.

The story of this discovery began when the young religious congregation of the Legionnaires of Christ was commissioned by Pope John Paul II to take over the tradition-steeped papal center of Notre Dame de Jerusalem with its spacious and comfortable guesthouse. It was renovated so thoroughly that it has long since reached the standard of a four-star hotel, with excellent cuisine and a cozy roof-deck bar from which the patrons can enjoy the sunset over the Mount of Olives while sipping choice wines. But for the pilgrim who comes to Galilee following in Jesus' footsteps, Jerusalem is too far. Consequently, the plan was to build a second pilgrimage center on the shore of Lake Gennesaret. In Magdala, of all places, there was an opportunity to purchase land on which to build at a New Testament site. During his visit to the Holy Land, Pope Benedict XVI blessed the cornerstone of the planned Magdala Center, and in July 2009 the Israeli authorities gave permission to build. The condition was, as usual, that the plot be archaeologically examined first. The excavations were directed by Dina Avshalom-Gorni and Arfan Najar of the IAA. They were the ones to announce the find of the century just weeks later.

Three months later, in December 2009, at the invitation of the Legionnaires of Christ, I visit the excavation site and meet Arfan Najar and Father Juan Solana, LC, the director of the Notre Dame de Jerusalem center, who show me the synagogue that by now has been completely exposed. By its outer wall, I recognize a small *mikveh*, behind it the living room of the synagogue leader, a storage room for scrolls (*genisa*), and two stone jugs, which served to store water for ritual cleansing purposes. Its center, however, is the nearly square assembly room of 400 square feet, once lined with columns at the corners, surrounded by stone benches. The floor is paved with pebbles, on top of which there probably used to be mats or carpets. Walls and columns were once adorned with magnificent frescoes, a mosaic decorated parts of the entryway. But the find that most clearly proves the splendor of this Jewish house of prayer is the Torah stone, which the archaeologists found still *in situ*—i.e., in its original position: an oblong block of stone, richly ornamented on all sides, on which the scroll was once placed from which the Scripture was read during synagogue services. Its backside is adorned with a rosette, the Jewish symbol for the six-winged cherubim, flanked by two palm trees. On the front, between two columns, surmounted by arches, are two amphorae; in the center is a menorah, the seven-branched candelabrum, in front of which is the table of showbread from the Temple in Jerusalem. "Generally speaking, this is the oldest known depiction of the Temple-menorah", Arfan Najar explains to me, with a certain sense of discoverer's pride. "Since Magdala was destroyed even before the Temple, we can be sure that the artist, who, like any Jew, must have made the pilgrimage to the Temple feasts in Jerusalem three times a year, still saw the original. The Romans snatched the menorah from the burning Temple of Herod and brought it to Rome, together with the table of showbread. There, both are depicted on the Arch of Titus, as they are paraded through the city during the triumph of the emperor's son. But the stone is older. It must have been made around the turn of the eras." That means it was already there when Jesus taught.

A second Torah stone is located in the area of the synagogue's former storage room, probably the antecedent of this gem. Two depressions held in place the wooden rollers around which the inscribed goatskin had been wound.

No wonder that this find caused a stir in Jewish circles as well. Almost daily, rabbis and archaeologists came to Magdala to visit the excavations. Reason enough for Father Juan to make it the center of a future Jewish-Christian site of prayer and encounter and, thus, the centerpiece of the new Magdala Center. Thus not only are the ruins of the synagogue well protected; they will also be accessible to future pilgrims and visitors. But above all, they are supposed to build "bridges of dialogue between the faithful of the different religions in the Holy Land".

It is certain that many of the last Jews to assemble in this synagogue in A.D. 67 were witnesses to the life and ministry of Jesus. Furthermore, it is likely that Jesus also taught here—after all, the Gospel of Matthew tells us: "And he went about all Galilee, teaching in their synagogues and preaching the gospel of the kingdom and healing every disease and every infirmity among the people" (Mt 4:23). It would be absurd to assume that Jesus could have omitted this synagogue in particular, located so prominently between Nazareth, Cana, and Capernaum, and thus "on his way". But Father Juan believes that one of the greatest miracles of the New Testament took place here as well: the raising of the synagogue leader's daughter.

He was a man named Jairus, whose twelve-year-old daughter was dying. Jesus was just returning from a trip to the other side of the lake and was already being awaited by a large crowd, probably in Tabgha, on the northwestern shore of the Sea of Galilee. When he had at last made his way through the crowd, the synagogue official fell on his knees before the Son of God and asked his help. Jesus went with him at once, but it must have been a rather long way on foot (it is five miles to Magdala). On the way there, mourners already came to meet them: the girl had just died. Accompanied only by Peter, John, and James, Jesus nonetheless entered the house of Jairus, went into the dead girl's room, where she lay on her bed, reached out his hand, and spoke two words in Aramaic: "*Talitha cumi*"—"Little girl, rise!" The girl sat up and was well again.

The Evangelist mentions that Jesus set out "from there" directly for Nazareth, which could indicate that this miracle took place in Magdala. The route from Tabgha to Nazareth does, in fact, lead through Magdala. Moreover, apart from the controversial mini-synagogue on the Franciscan grounds, no other synagogue has yet been discovered on the way from Tabgha to Nazareth. This makes the find in Magdala, at least for the time being, an unrivaled candidate.

In any event, its significance prompted the Legionnaires of Christ to have the entire grounds thoroughly examined. For the next two years, a Mexican archaeologist, Professor Marcela Zapata Meza from Anahuac University, was put in charge of the excavations. She was aided by assistants from all over the world; we, too, were there in the summers of 2011 and 2012, when houses, streets, and the quay wall of ancient Magdala were uncovered in five excavation areas. With each find, the impression of the city's wealth grew stronger. Most homes from that time that were found in Galilee had simple mud floors, but here some of the rooms were floored with slabs, one even with an elaborate mosaic. The fact that it was kept purely ornamental, without figural depiction, shows how strictly the inhabitants adhered to the Jewish ban on images. The villas of Jerusalem's upper class apparently served as models. Fragments of limestone cups, found alongside the usual pottery, but also expensive glass vessels, confirm that devout Jews lived here. Undoubtedly Zapata's most spectacular discoveries, however, were three carefully crafted stone *mikvehs* (or *mikvaoth*), which prove how important ritual purity was to the inhabitants of Magdala. Besides the far less spectacular Franciscan find, these were the only Jewish ritual baths excavated by the lakeshore, which in itself is quite significant. Jews who lived by rivers or lakes actually did not need *mikvehs*; bathing in a natural body of living (i.e., not standing) water was considered the *non plus ultra*;[1] the artificial washbasin was a substitute. Only a considerable, rather Pharisaical snobbery explains why, although only a few yards from the lakeshore, someone would prefer to bathe in a *mikveh* instead of the lake, "like the common people". The three subterraneously connected pools were supplied nevertheless with water from the "Sea of Galilee".

And Mary Magdalen? If she lived here, in this environment of nouveaux-riches fish curers, then she must have indeed been wealthy enough to support Jesus and his disciples financially. A whole series of pilgrims from the Byzantine era and the Early Middle Ages mention "a church which contains the house of Magdalen, in a place called

---

[1] According to the *Mishnah Mikvaot* (1, 7–8; 5, 4), natural sea water has the highest of the six possible degrees of purity and hence is to be preferred unconditionally to rainwater collected in a cistern, for example.

Magdala" (thus the monk Epiphanius around 675). According to the anonymously written *Life of Constantine* (the Great), which was likely composed between the eighth and tenth century, it was the emperor's mother, Helena, who "found the house of Mary Magdalen [in Magdala] and built a church there", as early as A.D. 325. This church has not yet been discovered. But during my visit to Magdala in 2009, Father Juan disclosed to me that in the course of a GPR (Ground Penetrating Radar) examination of the entire shore area, walls had been found amid the ancient houses that could, in fact, belong to the apse of a Byzantine basilica. But for now, the building of the center took priority, and the investigation of it was postponed to a future excavation campaign.

With growing enthusiasm, we continue to drive through a landscape that was already paradisiacal two thousand years ago. Flavius Josephus, too, raved about the area between Migdal and Capernaum, which was already named Ginosar or Genesar then, like the kibbutz with the "boat from the time of Jesus" today:

> The country also that lies near to this lake has the same name of Gennesareth; its nature is wonderful as well as its beauty; its soil is so fruitful that all sorts of trees can grow upon it, and the inhabitants accordingly plant all sorts of trees there; for the temper of the air is so well mixed, that it agrees very well with those several sorts, particularly walnuts, which require the coldest air and flourish there in vast plenty; there are palm trees also, which grow best in hot air; fig trees also and olives grow near them, which yet require an air that is more temperate.... It not only nourishes different sorts of autumnal fruit beyond men's expectation, but preserves them a great while; it supplies men with the principal fruits, with grapes and figs continually, during ten months of the year and the rest of the fruits as they become ripe together through the whole year; for besides the good temperature of the air, it is also watered from a most fertile fountain. The people of the country call it Capharnaum.[2]

Ginosar (or Gennesaret) is also mentioned by the Synoptics as a site where Jesus healed the sick. The Bronze Age metropolis of Chinnereth, known from the books of Moses (Deut 3:17) and Joshua

---

[2] Flavius Josephus, *The Jewish War*, bk. 3, chap. 10, no. 8, in *The New Complete Works of Josephus*, trans. William Whiston (Grand Rapids, Mich.: Kregel, 1999), p. 802.

(11:2; 19:35), after which the lake was originally named, was, in fact, located in the plain of the same name, at a site called Tell el-'Oreimeh. It was, however, destroyed by the Assyrians; in Roman times, only a single house stood here. Consequently, the Evangelists, to be sure, mention only a landing, not a town or village ("And when they had crossed over, they came to land at Gennesaret, and moored to the shore", Mk 6:53). Only the low water level of the lake before January of 1986 enabled Mendel Nun to solve the riddle. Around the lake, the local historian and hobby archaeologist came upon the remains of fourteen ancient ports from the time of Jesus. One of them, halfway between the Ginosar Kibbutz and Tabgha, he was able to identify as the Gennesaret from the Gospels. Again we see how precise the Evangelists' accounts were, how well they knew the lake's harbors, fishing villages, and landings.

As a German, one does not have many privileges in the world, but this is one: halfway between Ginosar and Capernaum, on the northwest shore of the lake, is Tabgha. The Arab place name is a mutilation of the Greek *heptapegon*, which means "seven springs". In the time of Jesus, these seven springs were already used for the irrigation of the plain of Ginosar, which is the place to which Josephus refers. To this day, they turn Tabgha into a garden paradise on the shore of Lake Gennesaret. And in this Garden of Eden, they speak German.

We owe this to Franz Keller, a Swabian master bricklayer, and thus a *tekton*, like Joseph and his foster child, Jesus, once were. Keller came to the Holy Land in 1879 on account of his spiritual longing. He had read the New Testament, but also the accounts of Anne Catharine Emmerich, edited by Clemens Brentano. She was a nun from Coesfeld in Westphalia who had received the stigmata; in her visions, she describes Jesus' ministry and Passion in minute detail. As a hard-working bricklayer, Keller earned his livelihood in the monasteries, while in his free time he hiked through all of Palestine. When Keller reached Tabgha in 1885, it was love at first sight. He knew, he sensed, that this was holy ground. With the tenacity typical of him, he succeeded first in convincing the German Palestine Association headquartered in Aachen, now called the German Association of the Holy Land, to buy this piece of land that was considered malaria-infested. Then the real difficulty began. Three full years passed until the local Bedouins were ready to sell and the Turkish landowners agreed to the purchase. But finally the land acquisition was complete. February 6, 1889, marked the "birth of the German Tabgha". At about the same time, Italian Franciscans had purchased the neighboring parcel of land amid similar difficulties.

Only one year later, the German Palestine Association built a hostel for pilgrims on the premises, at the time the first of its kind by the lake. Under the direction of Pastor Zephirin Biever from Luxembourg, small farms developed in the surrounding area. In addition, Holy Land pilgrims from all over the world were accommodated here, among them in 1900 the German author Karl May, who was traveling through the Middle East. He was so comfortable in Tabgha that he donated a set of his complete works to the house. Despite two world wars, the area remained in German possession, with minor interruptions, although from 1952 to 1993 it had to be rented out to the State of Israel, which operated a youth hostel here. Since it came back under control of the German Association of the Holy Land in 1993, it has been possible to expand the facility on a large scale. Since its reopening in 2002, the former pilgrims' hostel has turned into a grand, modern, and comfortable facility, easily rivaling any four-star establishment. Two-story guesthouses are surrounded by patios, grassy areas, and fountains in a magical garden by the shore of the lake where Christ once ministered.

This time, too, we stay in Tabgha, and we enjoy it. At night, when the last voices on the patios have gone silent, I feel drawn to the lake. The full moon is reflected in the calm waters, a few clouds hover over the land. Crickets chirp, quiet waves slap the stony shore. And for a moment present and past blend together, time stands still. Now it is possible to feel his presence, here, where everything started.

On this shore path, perhaps a hundred yards to the east, Jesus went in November of A.D. 28 to reassemble his disciples. He knew where they worked. At that time it was already cool, and the fish were crowding close to shore, especially near the warm Seven Springs of Tabgha, which was an ideal catch area for the fishermen from the neighboring Capernaum. Above all, it was a winter retreat for tilapia, which prefer tropical temperatures; today they are also known as "Saint Peter's fish" and are indeed delicious. Here, right behind the Franciscan Church of the Primacy, below the Hasil spring, Mendel Nun, the Gennesaret expert from the En Gev Kibbutz, found in

1986 the remains of an ancient fishing port that he fittingly named
Port of Peter. After the catch, the fishermen were washing their nets
in the springs.

> And passing along by the Sea of Galilee, he saw Simon and Andrew
> the brother of Simon casting a net in the sea; for they were fishermen.
> And Jesus said to them, "Follow me and I will make you become
> fishers of men." And immediately they left their nets and followed
> him. And going on a little farther, he saw James the son of Zebedee
> and John his brother, who were in their boat mending the nets. And
> immediately he called them; and they left their father Zebedee in the
> boat with the hired servants, and followed him. And they went into
> Capernaum. (Mk 1:16–21)

From Tabgha it is only 1.6 miles to Capernaum, a half-hour on
foot or five minutes by car. The parking lot is strewn with tour buses,
and their stickers tell us where the groups of pilgrims traveling in
them come from. It used to be predominantly Americans and Italians; today the majority are Russian and Polish. The excavation site is
rightfully the most-visited pilgrim destination on the lake. No other
place in the world, except of course Nazareth, could presume to bear
the title of "City of Jesus". But Capernaum bears this label justly;
Matthew the Evangelist already calls it "his own city" (Mt 9:1).

Capernaum was easy to find. When the American researcher E.
Robinson came to the northern shore of Lake Gennesaret in 1838, he
found the area strewn with rubble. "The whole place is desolate and
mournful", he wrote. "A few Arabs only of the Semekiyeh were here
encamped in tents, and had built up a few hovels among the ruins,
which they used as magazines." A short distance from the lake he
noticed "the dilapidated remains of a building that in terms of labor
and ornamentation surpasses everything we have seen in Palestine so
far". During a second visit, he identified the building as an ancient
synagogue. In 1894, the Franciscans, after tough negotiations, managed to purchase the rubble field from the Bedouins. In order to protect it from further destruction, it was initially fenced in and protected
by stone walls. In 1905, the friars permitted the German archaeologists Kohl and Watzinger to excavate the synagogue; between 1906
and 1915, their work was continued by a Frenchman named Wen-
delin von Menden. Between 1921 and 1926, the young Franciscan

Gaudentius Orfali restored the synagogue and uncovered parts of an octagonal church that was located about thirty-three yards to the south. After his sudden death, it took forty years until the Order continued the excavations. Thus, the major portion of the work was reserved for the two Franciscan archaeologists Virgilio Corbo and Stanislao Loffreda, who between 1968 and 1991 unearthed the entire center of the City of Jesus.

The ancient Capernaum, as it turned out, stretched over an area of 37.28 square miles. Its maybe 1,500 inhabitants lived not only from fishing but also from agriculture, as evidenced by excavated olive presses, grindstones for wheat and grain, stone bowls, and stone funnels. Another mainstay was the manufacturing of glass vessels, of which some particularly beautiful specimens came to light in the course of the excavations. The homes were simple but not poor. There do not appear to have been great social differences. Walls and paving stones were made from local basalt stone in natural condition. Walls were built without real foundations, and the one-story rooms were seldom taller than ten feet, which is evident from several staircases that led to the roofs. These consisted of reeds or wooden slats, covered with dirt or straw. Neither the few somewhat straight streets nor the winding alleys between the insular homes were paved, but all were merely leveled with small stones and dirt. There was no water supply; the nearby lake probably rendered it unnecessary. Thus, there were also no *mikvehs*, since, according to Halacha standards, a bath in the "living water" of the lake was preferable. The private homes mostly consisted of several rooms covered with a roof, which were grouped around a courtyard. They probably served as sleeping and storage rooms for the extended families, while the actual daily life played out in the courtyards. Here the women prepared the meals, the children played, and the craftsmen worked.

But one of these homes in particular stood out. It went through a very special development.

When the Franciscans began their excavations, an octagonal structure caught their eyes whose shape did not at all fit the rectangular pattern of ancient Capernaum. During the 1920s, Father Orfali found that it consisted of three concentric octagonal rings, the widest of which had a diameter of eighty-two feet, while the smallest was only twenty-three feet wide. It was supported by eight pillars and

surmounted by a roof. The entire building was adorned with mosaics, simple floral patterns, but also a peacock, an early Christian symbol for immortality. Everything seemed to indicate that this structure
was a Christian church, a suspicion that was confirmed when the
archaeologists unearthed an apse facing east and a baptismal font. In
Byzantine times, octagonal churches—like the birth church of Constantine or the Kathisma Church in Bethlehem—were almost always
memorials, erected over a holy site. This one seemed to be from the
fifth century.

The first suspicion was confirmed when the Franciscans carefully
removed the mosaics in order to dig below them. In the process, they
came upon an even older sacral building whose walls were covered
all over with Christian graffiti. "Christ, have mercy" or "Lord Jesus
Christ, help your servant" were the pious invocations between which
crosses were carved into the wall. The fact that not only Greek but
also Aramaic and Hebrew graffiti were found indicated that the holy
place attracted Jewish- as well as Gentile-Christian pilgrims. This
building seemed to be from the fourth century and measured thirty
by twenty-six feet. Its roof was held by a two-story-high arch over
the center of the room. Its walls were adorned with colorful frescoes
that showed pomegranates, flowers, figs, and geometrical patterns,
but avoided figural depictions, probably because the artists or their
clients were Jewish Christians. Before the entrance was an atrium
with a well-paved ascent. Apparently for its protection, the entire
complex was surrounded by a wall.

But the origins of this holy place went back still farther. Its central room was directly above the largest room of a private home that
was probably built toward the beginning of the Roman period—
after 63 B.C. This house was made out of black basalt boulders; only
its thresholds were finished; packed dirt served as floor. It had two
courtyards; still standing in the back one was an oven in which the
food for a large family was evidently prepared. In the front and larger
court, fish hooks were found. Initially, this home was no different
from any other in Capernaum, except that its layout was perhaps on a
somewhat larger scale, which suggests the inhabitants' modest wealth.

But as early as the middle of the first century, it changed remark-
ably. Suddenly the walls and the floor of this one room were plastered, which was unique in Capernaum. In the subsequent centuries,

it was renovated and beautified several times. Its furniture and equipment also changed. Cooking pots and jugs were still found in the oldest layer, but now they vanished completely; suddenly only oil lamps and storage containers appear to have been used here. Evidently, the room, in fact the entire house, no longer served as a residence; regular meals were no longer consumed here. Instead, the former living room had become a sacred space.

Why? Two graffiti referred to Peter. When the pilgrim Egeria visited Capernaum in 383, she wrote in her travelogue: "Moreover, in Capernaum, the house of the prince of the apostles has been made into a church, with its original walls still standing. It is where the Lord healed the paralytic."[3] Two hundred years later, long after the octagonal memorial basilica had been built, the pilgrim from Piacenza reports: "We likewise came into Capernaum into the house of blessed Peter, which is now a basilica."[4] The Franciscans had in fact discovered the house of the first pope![5]

It originally belonged to his mother-in-law but was also inhabited by Peter and his wife and his brother Andrew (Mk 1:29–30), as well as by Jesus, temporarily (Mt 17:25). Here he healed Peter's mother-in-law (Mk 1:31; Mt 8:14–15; Lk 4:38–39); here all the sick and possessed were brought to him in the evening, after sunset, so that Mark (whose Gospel is in fact based on the accounts of Saint Peter) is able to report: "And the whole city was gathered together about the door" (Mk 1:33). The wording presupposes that there was a lot of available space in front of the house, which was rather the exception in Capernaum with its frequently winding alleys. But in this case it is accurate. The "House of Peter" was indeed by a main road, the village's north-south axis, and between the broad street and the access to the house's courtyard there was an additional open space. If it was possible for a large crowd to assemble anywhere in Capernaum, then it was here. Mark later writes: "And when he [Jesus] returned to Capernaum after some days, it was reported that he was at home. And many were gathered together, so that there was no longer room for them, not even about the door" (Mk 2:1–2). This wording,

[3] *Egeria's Travels*, trans. John Wilkinson (London: S.P.C.K., 1971), p. 194.

[4] Virgilio Corbo, *The House of St. Peter at Capharnaum* (Jerusalem: Franciscan Printing Press, 1969), p. 53.

[5] See also Michael Hesemann, *Der erste Papst* (The first pope) (Munich, 2003).

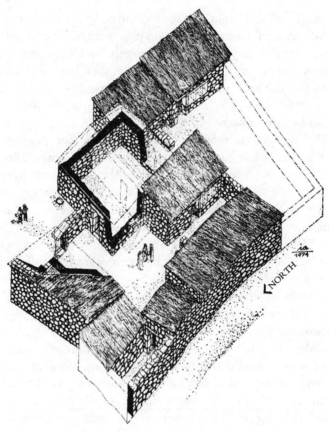

Reconstruction of Peter's House in Capernaum

too, must have referred to the small plaza that the broadened street formed in front of the entrance gate. Jesus "was preaching the word to them" (Mk 2:2), and, doing so, he was probably sitting in the not overly spacious room of 150 square feet that later on was to become a house-church. "And they came, bringing to him a paralytic carried by four men. And when they could not get near him because of the crowd, they removed the roof above him; and when they had made an opening, they let down the pallet on which the paralytic lay" (Mk 2:3–4). The room that later on was venerated did in fact face the street and was located right by the entrance to the courtyard. One could, therefore, without difficulty climb onto the roof from the street; from the courtyard there was even a staircase leading up to it. Since the roof, like all roofs in Capernaum, was only thatched with reed, the men could create an opening without a problem. Only the Evangelist Luke, who was never in Galilee and had to picture the scene in his mind, thought that the men "let him down with his bed through the tiles" (Lk 5:19). No house in Capernaum had a tile roof! If John had made this blunder, we would have to doubt Christian tradition, but in Luke's case, it is excusable.

A third scene in the Gospel of Mark also takes place here:

> And his mother and his brethren came; and standing outside they sent to him and called him. And a crowd was sitting about him; and they said to him, "Your mother and your brethren are outside, asking for you." And he replied, "Who are my mother and my brethren?" And looking around on those who sat about him, he said, "Here are my mother and my brethren! Whoever does the will of God is my brother, and sister, and mother." (Mk 3:31–35)

Again the excavations illustrate the Biblical account. Mary and Jesus' half-brothers or cousins stood outside by the courtyard entrance; Jesus taught around the corner, so to speak, in the large room. The listeners made their way into the courtyard, hoping to catch his words. They blocked the way for visitors—their message reached Jesus only because others passed it on. With his answer, the house of Peter became the first church, and the congregation—the first parish.

How fortunate that the excavators were Franciscans. They did not hesitate long before they returned the site to its original purpose. The futuristic-modern church they built over the ruins in 1990, although reminiscent of a space ship on landing legs, makes it possible to celebrate the Eucharist right over the room that was consecrated by Jesus.

From there, however, our gaze is inevitably drawn to the magnificent synagogue of Capernaum. Fashioned entirely from carefully finished white limestone, supported by sixteen columns with Corinthian capitals, it is now considered the most beautiful ancient synagogue in Israel. Was it already there in the time of Jesus? Father Orfali, who uncovered it, was still convinced of this, while Israeli archaeologists later on dated it to the second or third century. Eventually, the excavations by Fathers Corbo and Loffreda showed that they were all mistaken. A treasure of more than thirty thousand late Roman coins was found in the course of these excavations, which proved beyond

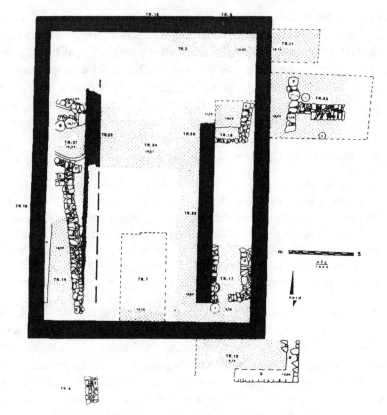

Capernaum: Layout of the first-century synagogue

doubt that the White Synagogue was not built before the end of the fourth century. The local parish can be ruled out as the builder; it was too poor to finance such a magnificent building. The builder was in all likelihood the Roman Emperor Theodosius I (379–395), who intended it to be a symbol of reconciliation between Jews, Jewish Christians, and Gentile Christians, perhaps also a tribute to the Jews, so as to facilitate access to Peter's house for the Gentile Christians. As early as 383, Egeria visited the new construction, which had perhaps just been dedicated, and she emphasized that the synagogue was built "of dressed stones" and that "the way in is up many stairs",[6] which is still true today.

[6] *Egeria's Travels*, p. 196.

But the excavators' initial disappointment at not having found a synagogue from the time of Jesus was soon followed by a surprise. For the White Synagogue stood on an artificial podium, which necessitated the ascent in the first place. Below the synagogue's building blocks were basalt stones; however, in contrast to their use in private homes, these stones were cut and covered with mortar. Instead of simply removing the seemingly inferior foundation, the fourth-century architects quite lovingly strove to preserve it. This went as far as mercilessly cutting to size even the precious limestone blocks, so that nothing was removed from the older layer. Yet another detail stood out: one of the four limestone steps that led to the White Synagogue was specially hollowed out, apparently so that an earlier basalt step protruding into it did not have to be destroyed.

In two places, the archaeologists removed the floor slabs of the White Synagogue to find out what was beneath it. In the process they came upon a completely intact basalt pavement, which in turn was on top of shards and coins from the late Hellenistic era. It could thus be conclusively dated to the years of the turn of the era. A paved floor, not found in any of the private homes in Capernaum, was a strong indication of a public building. Its characteristic layout left no doubt that it must have been a synagogue whose remains were apparently supposed to be preserved below the new construction from the fourth century. Only one thing can explain this diligence: this old synagogue was known to be holy ground, and they wanted to rebuild it as magnificently as possible, but never to replace it. The White Synagogue of Capernaum is nothing but a gigantic reliquary for the inconspicuous house of prayer that was sanctified by the fact that Jesus once taught in it.

We know its builder, the Gentile centurion, who was in command of a group of a hundred soldiers, who were likely stationed east of Capernaum, in the border area. His servant was ill, and so he asked some of the Jewish elders to put in a good word for him with Jesus. "He is worthy to have you do this for him, for he loves our nation, and he built us our synagogue", Luke (7:4–5) quotes them. Jesus went with them into the Roman settlement, which was located approximately where now we see a Greek chapel with not just one, but several strikingly red cupola roofs. This is where in 1985 the archaeologist Vassili Taferis came upon a series of Roman buildings made from cut limestone and, next to them, a Roman bathhouse with *hypocaustum* and *caldarium*, *frigidarium* and *tepidarium* (a room with tepid water). Shard findings allow a dating of at least part of the structure to the first century. When Jesus was getting close to the centurion's home, the latter spoke almost the same words that we now say before receiving the Eucharist: "Lord, I am not worthy to have you come under my roof; but only say the word, and my servant will be healed" (Mt 8:8). The centurion, evidently a God-fearing man, knew that faithful Jews were not permitted to socialize with heathens, that they ritually defiled themselves when they entered the house of a *goi*, a non-Jew. Jesus was impressed with his humility and faith, the likes of which he had not even found in Israel, among the most God-fearing men in Jerusalem. At that moment, the sick servant was healed.

For a Christian, however, the synagogue of Capernaum is first and foremost the place where Jesus revealed the mystery of the Eucharist. Only John relates this for us, presumably because Jesus' words were offensive even then and, in fact, led to a division among the disciples. All this occurred in April of A.D. 29, at the time of the Passover, virtually as the climax of the period of his ministry by Lake Gennesaret, which exegetes call the Galilean Springtime. People had heard of Jesus' first miracle of the loaves, the news had spread all around the lake, and they even came from Tiberias with their boats. When they realized that he had left the site of the multiplication of the loaves, they sailed over to Capernaum, for they were certain to find him there, "in his city". But he had seen through their sensationalism and miracle-seeking. Instead of feeding them again, he explained to them the meaning of this sign. He himself, namely, was "the bread of life; he who comes to me shall not hunger, and he who believes in me shall never thirst." He himself, born in a village called Bethlehem ("house of bread"), would give himself up as the bread of heaven so that those who eat of it might gain eternal life: "He who eats my flesh and drinks my blood abides in me, and I in him" (Jn 6:35; 56).

One year later, in April of A.D. 30, this promise was fulfilled; what he had begun in Galilee was completed.

But so that the place where Jesus made the promise of the Eucharist would never be forgotten, John, the eyewitness, specifically added: "This he said in the synagogue, as he taught at Capernaum" (Jn 6:59).

X

Spring in Galilee

The Sites of His Miracles

The geographical region in which Jesus was active during the Galilean Springtime of the year 29 is easily staked out and can be hiked in one day. The Nestor of German exegesis, Franz Mussner, who died in 2016 at the age of 100, coined the term *evangelical triangle*, whose center is Capernaum and whose corners are Tabgha, Chorazin, and Bethsaida. We know little about Chorazin, except that it, along with Bethsaida and Capernaum, was chastised by Jesus for its unbelief: "Then [Jesus] began to upbraid the cities where most of his mighty works had been done, because they did not repent. 'Woe to you, Chorazin! woe to you, Bethsaida! for if the mighty works done in you had been done in Tyre and Sidon, they would have repented long ago in sackcloth and ashes.... And you, Capernaum, will you be exalted to heaven? You shall be brought down to Hades'" (Mt 11:20–23).

If we are to believe the no-longer-extant *Gospel of the Hebrews*, which Saint Jerome cites, "fifty-three miracles were worked" by Jesus in the cities of Chorazin and Bethsaida. Today Chorazin, located just a little more than two miles north of Capernaum as the crow flies, is a dismal, godforsaken place of black basalt. Of course, the ruins of its synagogue from the second or third century are worth seeing, among them the "Throne of Moses", an inscribed and richly decorated stone chair for reading out the Torah. According to the historian Eusebius, the city was abandoned in the fourth century, although archaeological vestiges testify that people settled here time and again well into the seventh century.

The eastern corner of the triangle, too, Bethsaida, was long considered lost and forgotten. At the same time, this fishing village was still the home of at least three apostles. John (1:44) reports that "Philip was from Bethsaida, the city of Andrew of Peter." According to a later tradition, cited by Theodosius (around 530), it is said to have been the home of the fishing business of Zebedee, the father of James and John. Moreover, it was the place where a blind man was cured (Mk 8:22–26). Finally, it is mentioned by Flavius Josephus as the scene of a battle during the Jewish War. It was even included in the *Natural History* of Pliny the Elder, who describes it as "one of the four lovely cities on the Sea of Galilee" (5.15.71). After that, Bethsaida, which in the meantime was called Julias, vanishes into thin air.

Yet when the English monk Willibald, who was supposed to become the first Bishop of Eichstätt soon, visited the Holy Land in the year 725, he saw "a church where the house of Peter and Andrew once stood". According to the Syrian author Simon of Bassora (Basra), it had been built personally by the apostle James. It was probably destroyed in 1009 by the Fatimid Sultan al-Hakim, like all the Christian churches in his realm, and never rebuilt; in any case, we find no reference to its existence in any pilgrim report from the Crusader era (from 1099 on).

Not until the eighteenth century did Biblical archaeologists start to search for the "lost city". They had little help from the scarce information in the Bible, which merely situates Bethsaida "across the Jordan" "in Galilee" and obviously on the lake (the very name "Beth Saida" = "house of fishing" points to a settlement of fishermen), but some from the much more precise depictions of Flavius Josephus. He describes Bethsaida as "near to the river Jordan"[1] and a swampy area. In 1838 the American Edward Robinson climbed a hillock to the northeast of the mouth of the Jordan River, which the Bedouins unimaginatively named et-Tell ("the hill"), found potsherds from the time of Jesus, and decided that at one time Bethsaida must have been located here. Half a century later, the German Gottlieb Schumacher questioned this identification. Et-Tell, he argued, is too far from the lake to be the Biblical fishing village, whose abundance of fish is praised even in the Jerusalem Talmud (there it is simply called Zajjdan). Instead, he proposed identifying the ruins

---

[1] Flavius Josephus, *The Life of Flavius Josephus*, no. 72, in *The New Complete Works of Josephus*, trans. William Whiston (Grand Rapids, Mich.: Kregel, 1999), p. 40.

of el-Araj (Hebrew: Beit Habeck) 1.25 miles farther south on the lake as Bethsaida. Immediately after the Israeli conquest of the Golan Heights in the Six-Day War of 1967, the industrious Benedictine priest Bargil Pixner set out on a quest for the lost city that at that time was still adventurous. Vestiges of walls on et-Tell convinced him that Robinson had been right.

So the Israeli archaeologist Rami Arav began to dig on et-Tell. He actually came upon the ruins of an extremely ancient city whose origins go back to the fourteenth century B.C. After its destruction by the Assyrians, the hill was settled anew in the Hellenistic period. During Jesus' time, Bethsaida was a flourishing village, and its houses were better built and more spacious than in nearby Capernaum. When the Bethsaida Excavations Project (BEP), in which the University of Munich also participated, continued to dig in 1991–2000, much was brought to light that seemed to confirm the Gospels and the ancient records. Moreover, the archaeologists were able to explain what the Gospel only hinted at. The village in Gaulanitis, Philip's kingdom, was under stronger Hellenistic influence than its neighbors on the western shore. So it was no accident that at least two of Jesus' disciples who came from Bethsaida had Greek names (namely, Andrew and Philip; the name Simon occurred among both Greeks and Jews) and apparently spoke excellent Greek. During the Passover feast in the year 30, when "some Greeks" (that is, Jews from the diaspora) wanted to speak with Jesus, they first approached Philip ("who was from Bethsaida in Galilee", as the Evangelist John emphasizes again in 12:21) and Andrew.

Only a severe earthquake in A.D. 115 forced the inhabitants of Julias to abandon the city cursed by Jesus.

The history of Bethsaida explains why Bethsaida is described as a "village" in Mark and Matthew but as a "city" in Luke and John. Indeed Philip, as we read in Josephus, raised "the village Bethsaida, situated at the lake of Gennesareth, unto the dignity of a city, both by the number of inhabitants it contained, and its other grandeur, and called it by the name of Julias, the same name as Caesar's daughter".[2] Coins found at the site reveal to us the date when it was raised to the

---

[2] Flavius Josephus, *Jewish Antiquities*, bk. 18, chap. 2, no. 1, in *New Complete Works of Josephus*, p. 588.

status of city and correct a mistake by the Jewish historian. For the city was not named after the pleasure-loving daughter of Augustus, who was therefore sent into exile by her father, but rather after the mother of Tiberius, Livia Drusilla, the wife of Augustus, who after his death took the name Julia Augusta and died in A.D. 29. For the first anniversary of her death, on September 22, A.D. 30, Philip had coins minted that bore his portrait on one side and Julia's on the other. On the same day, he granted to Bethsaida town ordinances and privileges and named it Julias. Luke and John were therefore correct, in a purely formal sense, for when they wrote their Gospels Bethsaida-Julias had long been a city. And yet, unlike Mark and Matthew, they both committed an anachronism.

The ruins of a Roman temple dedicated to the divinized Julia, which archaeologists unearthed above the ruins of Bethsaida's city gate from the Iron Age, also bear witness to the founding of the city by Philip. No wonder, then, that faithful Jews observed the transformation of Bethsaida into Julias with dismay and refused to use the new name that was linked to the imperial cult.

Two grand courtyard houses, one of which plainly belonged to a wine merchant and the other to a prosperous fisherman, are among the most important discoveries by the archaeologists in Bethsaida. Here the excavators found net weights, anchors, needles, and fishing hooks. A clay seal shows two men casting nets out from a boat. Some immediately speculated that the seal could have belonged to the father of Peter and Andrew.

When John Paul II visited Israel in March 2000, Father Pixner arranged a meeting with the director of the Bethsaida Excavations Project, Richard Freund. The American told the pope about the discovery and presented to him a copy of a key from the first century that had been discovered in the ruins. "The key of Peter?" asked the Successor of the Prince of the Apostles. After that, there was nothing the American could do but confirm the conjecture. On the evening of that same day, the pope insisted on flying by helicopter over the native city of his great predecessor.

In 1994, archaeologists made an even more spectacular find right next to the house. An equal-sided cross was engraved on a clay fragment from the late first century. Until then, everyone had assumed that the cross became the most important symbol of Christianity only in the fourth century under Constantine the Great. It is quite possible that this discovery will force us to rethink things.

It is no surprise, then, that I, too, was convinced of the identification of Bethsaida with et-Tell when I wrote my books *Der erste Papst* (The first pope) (2003) and *Jesus von Nazareth* (2009) [first edition]—even though the church mentioned by Willibald was never discovered.

Yet now the most recent archaeological discoveries are putting Schumacher's el-Araj back in the spotlight. An Israeli investigation there had brought to light already in 1990 the remains of ancient buildings and fragments from the Herodian and the late Roman period. Nevertheless, not until 2014 did an archaeological team, consisting now of professors and eighty-five students from North Central University (Minneapolis, Minn.), the Institute for the Archaeology of Galilee, and the Center for Holy Land Studies of Kinnaret College tackle the site. They found not only fragments from the Hellenistic, Roman, and Byzantine period, but also sandstone and basalt fragments of a "large public building, probably a synagogue" and fragments of mosaics, which testify to an uninterrupted settlement from the second century B.C. until the seventh century A.D. Thus in 2016 a systematic archaeological excavation was begun under the direction of Professor Mordechai Aviam from the Institute for the Archaeology of Galilee of Kinnaret College and Professor R. Steven Notley from Nyack College in New York.

Right at the beginning of the work in 2016, the team came upon the remains of a Roman bathhouse. Thus it was certain that they were dealing with more than a simple Jewish fishing village, and this brought its elevation to the status of city in the year 30 back into focus. Moreover, it could be demonstrated that the et-Tell excavator Arav was wrong to assume that Lake Gennesaret at the time of Jesus formed a sort of lagoon and extended to the hill and its settlement. It is still possible, however, that the two excavation sites, et-Tell and el-Araj, once formed a single city and that el-Araj was the harbor and the fishermen's suburb, while et-Tell was, so to speak, the acropolis.

By 2018, it was certain that el-Araj in Roman times did not consist of only a few houses but was a large urban settlement extending over several acres. Fragments of frescoes suggested luxurious public or private buildings. Numerous weights for fishnets indicated the strong presence of fishermen. Herodian oil lamps and Jewish stone vessels, the sort used only in the first century, date this flourishing settlement unambiguously to the time of Christ. Geological investigations showed that many houses were buried under the silt from the Jordan River.

The most sensational find, however, was made in the summer of 2018. "In the Byzantine period a building complex was erected which may have included a church", we read in the official report of the excavation. Only in the fourth season of excavations in the summer of 2019 was this proved correct. The buildings proved to be part of a large monastery complex, the premises of which were partly adorned with black-and-white floor mosaics. It bordered on a large church from the Byzantine period that was decorated with golden wall mosaics, as gilded fragments of glass prove. Even the marble fragment of a parclose was discovered. "It must have been a large, splendid church", Aviam, the director of the excavation, told the press. A terracotta fragment shows an early Byzantine cross, as it was drawn in the late fourth century—probably the time when the house of worship was built. Also among the finds is a basalt block weighing 660 pounds with three compartments hewn into it, which Aviam considers to be a reliquary for the apostles Peter, Andrew, and Philip.

Therefore the "church of the apostles" from Willibald's account has been identified with certainty. Now we must wait and see whether it was in fact built over a first-century residence, possibly over the house where Peter was born; the continuation of the excavations in the summer of 2020 will tell. The Bethsaida of the New Testament, in any case, seems to be identified—although not at the same place where we previously thought it was.

The third corner of the evangelical triangle is Tabgha, west of Capernaum. When in 1889 the German land surveyor G. Schumacher arrived at the Seven Springs to inspect the land that Franz Keller had acquired, he wrote on his map: "Area in which excavations should be conducted". Other visitors had already been struck by the wall remains, marble fragments, and mosaic fragments. Yet only in March of 1911 did Professor Paul Karge, on behalf of the Görres Society, begin archaeological excavations near the lake shore. The first thing that he stumbled upon was an ancient mosaic. Today, because it is so fraught with symbolism, it is among the most famous works of early Byzantine mosaic art in general, for it convinces with its simple beauty and expressive power. The mosaic shows two fish on either side of a basket containing four loaves. It was located amid the ruins of an ancient church.

Murky land tenure and the outbreak of World War I hindered further investigations. Thus it was two decades before the Salvatorian priest Andreas Evarist Mader resumed the work in February 1932. In the process, Mader not only laid bare all the foundation walls of the early basilica but also discovered its largest sanctuary. In the middle of its presbytery, he came across the stone on which, according to long-standing tradition, Christ had placed the loaves and fish during the "feeding of the five thousand".

The incident occurred in March, A.D. 29. At the urging of Salome, the then perhaps seventeen-year-old daughter of his new wife, Herodias, Herod Antipas had ordered the execution of John the Baptist at the castle of Machaerus located on the eastern coast of the Dead Sea. When Jesus heard of this, he had himself brought by boat "to a lonely place apart" (Mt 14:13) to be alone with his disciples there and to mourn. It was shortly before the Feast of Passover, and he understood that he could not make a pilgrimage to Jerusalem at this time, since it would have been too risky for him. Before he was ready to sacrifice himself, he had to proclaim the Gospel first. But no rest and no time for mourning his precursors were granted to him. The people apparently knew where he usually stayed, and they set out for the place by land. But where, then, was this "lonely place", in Greek, *Eremos*? Certainly not far from Capernaum, for the crowd was already there waiting just as the boat with Jesus arrived (Mk 6:33). Jesus saw those seekers and had pity on them. They seemed to him "like sheep without a shepherd" (Mk 6:34). And so he taught them until dusk fell.

It was getting late, time for the evening meal. The disciples advised Jesus to send the people away into the surrounding villages and cities, to Capernaum, Ginosar, and Magdala, in order to buy food for themselves there. But Jesus wanted to satisfy the hunger of these people himself. The two fishes and five loaves of bread that the disciples had with them were enough to satisfy five thousand men. When the remnants were collected later, twelve baskets were left over.

The symbolism behind this sign is obvious. The five loaves symbolize the Pentateuch, the five books of Moses. The two fishes perhaps symbolize the Wisdom books and the Prophets, which

Jesus interpreted with crystal clarity to satisfy the spiritual hunger of his audience first. There was enough left over for the twelve apostles to distribute to the twelve tribes of Israel. But we cannot exclude the possibility that a real event lay behind the symbolism. The prophet Elijah and his disciple Elisha are said to have multiplied flour, oil, and bread in a miraculous way. Similar stories are also told of Saint John Bosco (1815–1888): one day when there was no more money, he collected twenty loaves of bread, which he distributed to three hundred young men without the bread diminishing in quantity. For this reason, I advocate here, as with all of Jesus' miracles, a *two-tier model*. There was a real event, however constituted, that on a meta-level became an instrument of proclamation, Jesus' *sign* language.

For to reject a priori everything "miraculous" would be to underestimate the intelligence of ancient readers. Despite all their craving for sensationalism, which has still not been rooted out today, they surely recognized a hoax when they saw one. Thus, even Peter in his Second Letter assured his listeners that he did not "follow cleverly devised myths" but rather had himself become an "eyewitness of his majesty". He wrote this at a time (around 63) when enough other eyewitnesses were still alive, yet thirty-four years had passed since the events he described. Thus, the classicist Ulrich Victor maintains, with compelling logic, that the reports of the Gospels are reliable: "Had they not been, the authors would have made themselves untrustworthy; that incredible things of that sort could have established the Christian Church is, for its part, completely incredible." Such confidence in our sources does not call into question the achievement of modern theology, which has allowed us for the first time to understand the deeper significance of Jesus' signs. Rather, it puts this achievement on a firmer footing. No anonymous communities made up Christ's deeds in order to impart their Easter faith to us, but rather Jesus revealed himself through them!

Obviously the place of the first feeding remained in people's memory. When the pilgrim nun Egeria came to Lake Gennesaret in 383, she also described Tabgha: "[There] is a grassy field with plenty of hay and many palm trees. By them are seven springs.... And this is the field where the Lord fed the people with five loaves and two fishes. In fact the stone on which the Lord placed the bread has now

Interior of the Basilica of
the Annunciation, Nazareth

Nazareth, Basilica of the Annunciation (pillar on left is from the Holy Family's synagogue)

Mary's Well
(Saint Gabriel Church)

Grotto of the Annunciation

Roman bathhouse underneath the Cactus Gallery, Nazareth

First-century house beneath the convent of the Sisters of Nazareth

Herodium, near Bethlehem

Mausoleum of Herod, discovered in 2007

The Magi, detail of a mosaic in Ravenna (fifth century)

The Magi, bas-relief in Nemrut Dagi (first century B.C.)

Horoscope in the form of a lion, Nemrut Dagi

Statues at Nemrut Dagi

Star in the Church of the Nativity, Bethlehem

Grotto of the Nativity, Bethlehem

A large cave-stable in the Shepherds' Field near Bethlehem

Model of the Temple, Jerusalem (Israel Museum)

Sacrifice in the Temple (painting in the Temple Institute)

Stairway to the Hulda Gates, Jerusalem

Herodian street at the foot of the Temple Mount platform

Model of the southeast corner of the Temple

Southeast corner of the Temple, present day

Theater of Antipas, Sepphoris

Site of the Baptism, Bethany, across the Jordan

Khirbet Qana

Cave at Khirbet Qana, revered into the Middle Ages as the site of Jesus' first miracle

Stone jars in Jerusalem

Well of Khirbet Qana

A stone jar in the Greek Church of
St. George in Kafr Kanna

The "Jesus Boat" of Ginosar

View of the house of Peter, Capernaum

Foundations of the White Synagogue, Capernaum
(first century A.D.)

Fisherman House, Bethsaida

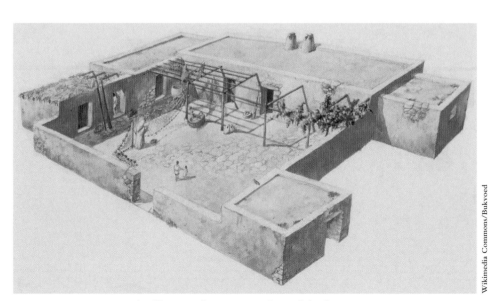

An illustrated reconstruction of the house

Eremos Grotto, Tabgha

View of the Sea of Gennesaret from the Eremos Grotto

Church of the Multiplication, Tabgha

Stone of the multiplication of the loaves
and a Byzantine mosaic, Tabgha

Synagogue of Magdala, aerial view

Torah stone, Magdala

Sanctuary of Pan, Caesarea Philippi

Kursi, where Jesus fed the four thousand

View of the Mount of Olives, Jerusalem

Same view in the first century A.D. (model in the Israel Museum)

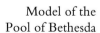

Model of the Pool of Bethesda

Ruins of the Pool of Bethesda

Ruins of the Siloam Pool from the time of Jesus

Byzantine Siloam Pool

Staircase from Mount Zion to the
Siloam Pool from the time of Jesus

Remains of the Jewish-Christian synagogue beneath the Coenaculum, Jerusalem

Essene Gate at the foot of Mount Zion

Saint Peter in Gallicantu,
above the ruins of Caiaphas' Palace

Mikveh of the high priest

Prison of Christ

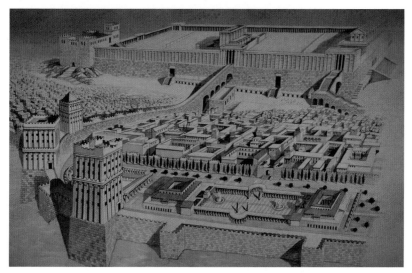

View of Herod's palace, Jerusalem
(reconstruction in the Tower of David Museum)

Wall of Herod's palace

Pilate's *Praetorium*? Model of the Hasmonean palace

Excavations near the Wailing Wall, where the palace once stood

Ecce Homo, a painting by Antonio Ciseri

Titulus Crucis, Church of Santa Croce
in Gerusalemme, Rome

Bilingual inscription from Dan

Pilate Stone of Caesarea

Ruins of the city wall built by Herod, in the Alexander Nevsky Church

Gateway to Golgotha

Herodian threshold to Golgotha

Golgotha rock, Church of the Holy Sepulchre

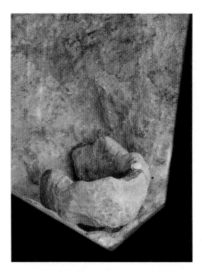

Stone ring that held Jesus' Cross

Ossuary of Caiaphas, Israel Museum, Jerusalem

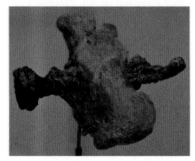

Bone pierced from crucifixion, found in Giv'at ha-Mivtar

Apse mosaic, Basilica of Saint Pudenziana, Rome

Tomb of the Herodians, Jerusalem

Basilica of Emmaus (Nicopolis)

Steps at Tabgha

Mensa Christi, Tabgha

Monument to the Reinstatement of Peter, Tabgha

Pope Benedict XVI praying at the empty tomb of Christ

been made into an altar."[3] The oldest church whose remains Professor Karge and Father Mader discovered came from the first half of the fourth century. It was a simple building in the Syrian style that was built parallel to the old street and was not yet oriented toward the East. An inscription, the original of which has unfortunately gone missing, named one Josepos as the church's architect. It was probably the same Count Joseph of Tiberias who, with the permission of Constantine the Great, also built Jewish-Christian synagogues in Nazareth, Sepphoris, and Cana. In the fifth century, a basilica with three naves and a large-scale atrium decorated with delicate mosaics arose in its place. In the sixth century, the archdeacon Theodosius noted precisely the place of the multiplication of loaves: it was two miles beyond Magdala and two miles short of Capernaum. In fact, it is approximately three miles from Migdal and one and a half miles from Capernaum, but one should not expect ancient indications of distance to be that exact. That the pilgrim Bishop Arculf already saw "ruins" here in 670 suggests that the Byzantine basilica was destroyed during the invasion of the Persians in 614.

In order to protect the mosaics, the Germans first set up a temporary wooden church. Pope Paul VI stayed there during his visit to the Holy Land in 1964. But soon the provisional structure fell into such a ramshackle condition that it had to be remedied. Thus in 1976 the German Association of the Holy Land decided on a new construction, which was almost a reconstruction. The result is more than successful: it is a blessing. For the church not only resembles its predecessor from the fifth century, it also revives the spirit of that flourishing period of Christian pilgrimages. German Benedictine monks from the neighboring monastery celebrate Mass here, in a basilica that seems designed for Gregorian chant and cloistered mysticism. Its altar looms over the stone on which Jesus blessed the bread, right behind the famous mosaic. It is as though his hand still rested over it.

But if the "meadow" where the people listened to Jesus and received bread from him is here, near Tabgha, where then was the *eremos*, the "lonely place apart" to which he used to retreat? Father Bargil Pixner, himself a regular guest in Tabgha, knew an answer. On

<hr>

[3] *Egeria's Travels*, trans. John Wilkinson (London: S.P.C.K., 1971), p. 196.

the slope of the mountain that towers above Tabgha he came across a
natural cave. The pilgrim Egeria had written about it: "Near there [to
the church of the multiplication of loaves] on a mountain is the cave
to which the Savior climbed and spoke the Beatitudes."[4]

I park on the lake shore street, the old Via Maris, and already see
the cave. The ascent is at no point arduous. The cave is surrounded
by grasses and flowers, an olive tree juts out from it. Jesus could have
sought shade here; here he prayed; here he met with his disciples.
Calm and deep peace fill me as I enter. Someone has built a small
bench here, maybe it was Father Bargil himself. I sit down and am
overcome by the beauty of the view. Before me, the palm trees of
Tabgha reach for the sun. Behind them sprawls the lake whose blue
unites with the steel blue of the sky, separated only by the mountain
range with Magdala in front of it and Nazareth behind. I grab my
camera and try to capture this moment, again and again, as though
every picture is a relic that carries in it something from the blessing
of this place. Maybe Father Bargil was right and the word *eremos* in
the Gospels, usually translated as "lonely place", indicates not infre-
quently this very special "hiding place". In that case, Mark was referring to this cave when he wrote that Jesus no longer found peace in
any city: "Jesus could no longer openly enter a town, but was out
in the country; and people came to him from every quarter" (Mk
1:45). Even John knows of such a hiding place. After the multiplication of the loaves, when the people "were about to come and take
him by force to make him king, Jesus withdrew again to the hills by
himself" (Jn 6:15).

This must have been the place, on the slope of the mountain in
the beginning of the year 29, where Jesus went "to pray; and all night
he continued in prayer to God" (Lk 6:12). At daybreak he called his
disciples together and from them chose twelve "to be with him, and
to be sent out to preach and have authority to cast out demons" (Mk
3:14-15). Their names are handed down to us with slight variations
by the Synoptic authors: Simon Peter, Andrew (his brother), James
(son of Zebedee), John (his brother), Philip, Bartholomew, Thomas,
Matthew (in the Gospels of Mark and Luke: Levi, son of Alphaeus),
James (son of Alphaeus—and brother of Matthew?), Jude (in Luke:

---

[4] Ibid., p. 200.

Judas, son of James), Simon the Cananaean (in Luke: Simon the Zealot), and Judas Iscariot.

Not far from here, he delivered his most famous sermon. "Great crowds followed him from Galilee and the Decapolis and Jerusalem and Judea and beyond the Jordan", Matthew reports. "Seeing the crowds, he went up on the mountain, and when he sat down his disciples came to him. And he opened his mouth and taught them" (Mt 4:25—5:1).

Today, on the summit of "Mount Eremos" stands a chapel that was donated by Italian Christians in 1928. Above its windows, the eight beatitudes are depicted in eight panels. In the adjacent hostel for pilgrims, friendly Franciscan Sisters welcome their guests. The view of the lake from here is magnificent, especially in spring, when the mountain slope is covered with flowers that the winter rains have caused to sprout. Red anemones and blue irises extend their calyxes toward the still-gentle sun as they slowly open, just as they did then when they inspired Jesus with his immortal words: "Consider the lilies of the field, how they grow; they neither toil nor spin; yet I tell you, even Solomon in all his glory was not clothed like one of these" (Mt 6:28–29). But no monument, not even the Italian chapel, can make the spirit of the Sermon on the Mount as tangible as Pope John Paul II did when he, on March 24, 2000, celebrated a Mass here out in the open on a hillock near Chorazin. It was supposed to be the climax of his historic pilgrimage to the Holy Land, which took place on the occasion of the Holy Year and the Church's Great Jubilee. I had set out early in the morning and simply parked my rental car at the side of the road and followed the masses of people heading for their destination beyond the gentle hills. The previous night a storm had raged over Israel and had transformed the grassy meadows into a bog. Unperturbed by this, tens of thousands of people waded through the mud until finally they had reached the ground in front of the colossal altar platform with the image of Christ teaching. The lake appeared in the background like an oval mirror, gray as the clouds that hung low over it. But even though a cold wind made me shiver, the joy, prayers, and singing of the hundred thousand mostly young pilgrims were infectious and warmed my heart. So much greater was the jubilation when the white popemobile finally appeared and, with it, the first sunbeams broke through the cloud cover. The pope's sermon sounded like a new edition of the Sermon on the Mount. Here, at the cradle of Christianity, he called for solidarity with the poor, the oppressed, and the losers of society. And finally he dismissed the hundred thousand, who had streamed in from all over the world, with the feeling that they were one big family in Christ.

Yet the Sermon on the Mount, as we know it, is probably a compilation of many of Jesus' instructive talks that were all given here in the area surrounding the Eremos cave, on the slope or at the foot of the mountain, during that Galilean spring of the year 29. One of their locations is rather easy to identify when you follow the trail from the Eremos grotto up to the mountain ridge. There we are greeted by a natural amphitheater with the best acoustics, in whose center the Benedictines have set up a squared stone of white marble as an altar beneath an olive tree. Errant rubble blocks of every size circle around the altar like planets and asteroids around the sun. At least once Jesus used the acoustics of the natural harbor between Tabgha and Capernaum, which harbor is located less than half a mile east of the Eremos cave. His discourse in parables, the so-called lake sermon, could have been delivered here. Mark described it: "Again he began to teach beside the sea. And a very large crowd gathered about him, so that he got into a boat and sat in it on the sea; and the whole crowd was beside the sea on the land. And he taught them many things in parables" (Mk 4:1–2). Actually, American acousticians, under the direction of B. C. Crisler, investigated the natural amphitheater in 1976 with regard to its acoustic properties and judged it to be excellent. Whoever speaks from the center of the bay can still be heard clearly at a distance of fifty-five yards. Father Bargil was himself in a position to test this effect. When he once again led a group of pilgrims to Tabgha, he positioned himself on a boulder in the lake and gave a short sermon; afterward, the participants confirmed the excellent audibility of it.

Jesus spoke, of course, in parables, as the Jewish fishermen by the Sea of Galilee understood them best: "Again, the kingdom of heaven is like a net which was thrown into the sea and gathered fish of every kind; when it was full, men drew it ashore and sat down and sorted the good into vessels but threw away the bad. So it will be at the close of the age" (Mt 13:47–49).

Their most important tool of the trade was the dragnet that can sometimes be up to 328 yards long and is used near the shore. Equipped with weights, the net is spread out parallel to the shoreline and is later pulled in on both sides by up to sixteen men. It then encloses the fish, which can no longer free themselves from its clutches and are dragged with the net onto dry land. A distinction between "good" and "bad" fish was conceivable only among Jews. For them, only fish with scales and fins were considered *kosher*, while eel, turbot, sturgeon, and above all the African catfish that makes its home in the Sea of Galilee were avoided. We can assume with certainty that Jesus' words were not thought up by any urban community anywhere but, rather, came from his mouth, spoken in the milieu of a fishing port by the sea. It is just one of the many examples of fishing lore in the Gospels, which clearly indicates a derivation from eyewitnesses, especially in Mark and John.

In the evening of the same day, as Mark goes on to relate, Jesus wanted to travel across to the other shore. So, "leaving the crowd," his disciples "took him with them, just as he was, in the boat. And other boats were with him. And a great storm of wind arose, and the waves beat into the boat, so that the boat was already filling. But he was in the stern, asleep on the cushion" (Mk 4:36–38).

In his role as Peter's interpreter, Mark once again provides entirely plausible details that lead us to feel that his source was present. There is no reason to cast doubts on the sermon by the sea, since a bay between Tabgha and Capernaum offers the acoustic ambience necessary for it. The suddenly changing weather, too, is typical for the Sea of Galilee in spring. Usually in the evening, the fearsome *sharkiye* storm from the northeast can abruptly sweep across the land and churn up the sea. But just as quickly the weather can calm down again. The find from Ginosar reveals to us how the boat was constructed. It was in any case big enough to accommodate up to sixteen men. But did it also offer a place for sleeping in the stern? The Ginosar boat belonged to fishermen who all worked with large, heavy dragnets. A wide storage shelf, a separate deck in the stern area, was constructed for them. It would be ill-advised to sleep on this deck, on which the helmsman also stood, and during a storm, of all times, it would be a rather damp pleasure. The area beneath the afterdeck, however, was dry and sheltered. And the "cushion"? The definite article in the original Greek text (there he lay on "the cushion", instead of on "a cushion", as in the German ecumenical Unity Translation) indicates that the cushion was part of the equipment on board.

Until the early twentieth century, the fishing boats of the Arabs on the coast of Palestine had one or two sacks of sand as ballast on board. They were called *mechadat zabura*, "ballast cushions". And when one of the sailors was tired, he simply crawled under the afterdeck and lay down on them to sleep, just as Jesus did on that night.

A *sharkiye* also raged during the night after the feeding of the five thousand. The next day, Jesus wanted to go "to the other side, to Bethsaida" (Mk 6:45), which, as was said, lay beyond the mouth of the River Jordan and thus on the northeastern shore of the sea. If Antipas, after executing the Baptist, had ordered his arrest, too, he was safe there, in the kingdom of Philip. He had sent the disciples ahead of him with the boat so that he could take leave of the people calmly. Afterward, "he went up on the mountain to pray"; perhaps he withdrew into his cave in the mountainside. Bethsaida was four miles away from Tabgha by land, a path that Jesus could easily travel by foot in at most one and a half hours. It was "about the fourth watch of the night" (therefore, in the final quarter of the night, which began, according to the Roman way of telling time, around 3:00 A.M.) that he, looking out from the road by the shore, "saw that they [the disciples] were distressed in rowing, for the wind was against them" (Mk 6:48). Here again all of the topographical and meteorological details add up. Since the fishing boat was on a course directly northeast, the *sharkiye* blew head-on against them and did not let them make headway.

Whether Jesus then really walked on the water is a matter not just of faith but also of interpretation. Matthew's dramatic scene, which has Peter running toward his Master and sinking, is conspicuously absent from Mark, Peter's interpreter. John indicates the direction of the course (from Tabgha "to Capernaum", thus in a northeasterly direction) just as precisely as the distance already covered (25–30 stadia, thus 3–4 miles, which means to just short of the mouth of the Jordan), and yet in his account the miracle plays out in somewhat unspectacular fashion near the coast: "They were glad to take him into the boat, and immediately the boat was at the land to which they were going" (Jn 6:21). But its message is all the more important. Just like the first storm miracle, it teaches us that rescue is possible only for someone who trusts completely in Jesus, who does not let himself be led astray from his faith by outward storms.

In both cases, Jesus' destination was located in a region that was no longer purely Jewish. The kingdom of Philip combined Jews and Gentiles. The Decapolis, which extended to the southeastern shore of the sea, was exclusively Hellenistic-Gentile in character. This involved a conflict for Jesus as a devout Jew, as is shown by the example of the Syrophoenician woman. During his farthest trip "to the district of Tyre and Sidon" (Mt 15:21), a woman who was "a Greek, a Syrophoenician by birth" (Mk 7:26) fell begging at his feet. Could he heal her daughter, who was possessed by a demon? Jesus hesitated. Indeed, he answered at first with the arrogance typical of a staunchly orthodox believer: "It is not right to take the children's bread and throw it to the dogs." "Dog" was a Jewish insult for the *goyim*, the unbelievers, and "children" meant the children of Israel. At this moment, Jesus was entirely human. But perhaps then he recalled the words of the aged Simeon, when his Mother presented him in the Temple: "My eyes have seen your salvation, [O God,] which you have prepared in the presence of all peoples, a light for revelation to the Gentiles, and for glory to your people Israel" (Lk 2:30–32). Or he remembered Isaiah's prophecy: "It is too light a thing that you should be my servant to raise up the tribes of Jacob and to restore the preserved of Israel; I will give you as a light to the nations, that my salvation may reach to the end of the earth" (Is 49:6). In any case, he recognized the woman's great faith and freed her daughter from the demon. The incident thus became the turning point in Jesus' life and mission. He appeared for the first time as the Redeemer of all mankind, not just as Israel's Messiah.

Probably by way of the old road that connected Tyre with Dan and Caesarea Philippi, Jesus returned first to the kingdom of Philip and then, along the Jordan, to the sea. Yet this time, his destination was no longer Capernaum but, rather, the region of the Decapolis, the land of the Gentiles. As if he wanted to make a statement that even the Gentiles are invited "to the Lord's table", he repeated here the miraculous feeding of the crowd, but this time with seven loaves, a few small fish, and four thousand hungry listeners.

Only Mark and Matthew report on this sign, although they fail to name the place where it occurred. We learn from Mark only that the place was "near the sea" and was located within the Decapolis, which could have been anywhere along the southeastern shore from Wadi Samak directly north of Kursi to the mouth of the Jordan. Matthew adds that it was a "lonely place" and mentions a mountain on which Jesus sat while the lame, the crippled, the blind, the dumb, and other sick people were brought to him. "The throng wondered, when they saw the mute speaking, the maimed whole, the lame walking, and the blind seeing; and they glorified the God of Israel" (Mt 15:31), who before then had been so foreign to them.

Bargil Pixner situated the second multiplication of loaves in Tel Hadar to the southwest of Bethsaida, where he even had a memorial stone erected. In doing so, he relied on Luke, who in his depiction of the feeding of the five thousand claims that it took place near a "city called Bethsaida" (Lk 9:10). In fact, he makes one miraculous feeding out of two, but he places this one chronologically right after the execution of the Baptist, thus contemporaneous with the first one. But Tel Hadar was not in the Decapolis, nor was the hinterland of Bethsaida a "lonely place". Since Luke was not an eyewitness and did not know Galilee, his statement here has little relevance. It is quite possible that he simply confused Bethsaida and Capernaum or used Bethsaida as a reference point since it was better known. After all, Tabgha was only 4.7 miles away from there.

We can tell how precise Mark is, in contrast, even from his choice of words. During the first miraculous feeding, the leftovers filled twelve *kophinoi*, two-handled straw-lined baskets that were so stereotypically Jewish that they served in the writings of the Roman satirist Juvenal as the distinguishing mark *par excellence* of the Jews. During the second miraculous feeding, in contrast, it was seven *spurides* (or *spyrides*), the one-handled baskets common in the Greek-Hellenistic world. This underlines the fact that it did not take place near Bethsaida, with its Jewish culture, but rather in the purely Hellenistic Decapolis. The fish are different, too; at the first feeding, they are called *ichthuas* or "correct fish", probably tilapia, which were quite common in the headwaters of Tabgha. At the second feeding, the fish are called *ichthudia*, "little fish". The season allows us to conclude that these were not young fish; it was summer. More probably it refers to kinneret sardines, the smallest fish in the sea. Eaten with bread, they belong to the daily fare of the sea-dwellers. The biggest schools hang around the eastern shore near Kursi. In Arabic, *kursi* means "throne". Could the name be a reference to the hill on which Jesus sat and healed the sick?

We travel from Tabgha to Kursi. We want to tour the locality. We are greeted by a wide, flat plain near the seashore with a hill split in two rising above it. Below on the plain are the remnants of a Byzantine basilica and a monastery. Stairs lead up the hillside to a platform where a chapel once stood. Both were first discovered in 1967, when Israel conquered the formerly Syrian northeastern coast of the Sea of Galilee and built connecting roads to the Golan Heights. During this process, excavators first came across the ruins of the basilica and the accompanying monastery, which were completely unearthed and restored in 1979 by the Israeli National Park Service. During the excavations, the archaeologist Vassilios Tzaferis discovered the even older hillside chapel. Its mosaic floor was decorated with crosses, a custom that had been forbidden by Emperor Theodosius II in 427. Therefore, it could have been constructed as early as the fourth century. Its apse, which leans against the rock wall, is surrounded by a semi-circular stone bench with twelve seats. In front of the chapel is a twenty-three-foot-high cliff enclosed by a stone wall.

The basilica on the plain and the attached monastery were built toward the end of the fifth century and were enlarged with a baptistry one century later. A dedication inscription mentions the Byzantine Emperor Mauritius and can therefore be precisely dated to the year 585. Evidently, the sanctuary of Kursi was so well-visited that a pilgrims' guesthouse with its own bathhouse arose next to the monastery. It was only slightly damaged during the Persian invasion in 614, but pilgrims have stayed away since the Arab conquest of Palestine. The facility was apparently abandoned entirely after a massive earthquake in 741.

Unfortunately, there are no reports from pilgrims in antiquity that reveal any additional details to us. We only know that Mar Saba, the great founder of monasteries, visited the locality Korisa in 491 and prayed there. Not until the Byzantine period do sources refer to the so-called "twelve thrones where Christ our God sat and taught and satisfied the four thousand". Evidently, people imagined that Jesus was enthroned on the hillside like a king surrounded by his twelve apostles. As if from a pulpit, he spoke here to the four thousand who had gathered on the plain at his feet. The enclosed cliff face, which was probably revered as the "Throne of Christ", and the twelve seats that were worked into the apse of the chapel could have been the *dodekathronos*, the Sanctuary of the Twelve Thrones, and might have given Kursi its name. The mosaic floor of the lower basilica also speaks in favor of the second multiplication of loaves taking place in Kursi. It shows, alternatively, fish and one-handled baskets with loaves—precisely those Hellenistic *spurides* that are explicitly mentioned in the Gospel.

On the summit of a hill only 1.8 miles southeast of Kursi we find Sussita, the ancient Hippos, one of the cities of the Decapolis, which was recently the scene of a spectacular archaeological discovery. At the time of Jesus, Hippos was a purely Gentile city, which explains why it is not mentioned in the Gospels. In 2013, archaeologists dug up from its ruins a mighty bronze mask of Pan, who was plainly revered here; the Greek god of wild nature, with goat's hooves and horns, later became the model for the Christian image of the devil. Christianity, in contrast, seems to have gained a foothold in Hippos relatively late; not until 359 did it become the see of a bishop. There are no archaeological indications whatsoever that would allow us to infer the presence of Christians before that time.

The Israeli-Polish archaeological team led by Dr. Michael Eisenberg and Dr. Arleta Kowalewska from the Zinman Institute of Archaeology at the University of Haifa, which has been digging in Hippos since 2012, was all the more surprised when in the summer of 2019 the remains of a fifth-century church were unearthed. The place of worship was soon known as the "burned church", because it had plainly been burned down to its foundations during the Persian invasion of 614. Its floor was decorated with a splendid mosaic that was preserved so well by the ash of the fire that its colors still gleamed as they did on the first day. It shows pomegranate-shaped ornaments along with five bread baskets and two fish.

Admittedly, the artist had plainly mixed up the miracles—five baskets of bread and two fishes were used to feed the five thousand Jews in Tabgha, while seven loaves "and a few fish" were used to feed the four thousand Gentiles on the eastern shore of the lake—but the message was nevertheless clear: here too, in pagan territory, there was holy ground where the Lord had worked one of his greatest miracles. From Hippos one can survey the plain of Kursi, and in good weather you can see the ridges of the hills on which the Lord once was enthroned and consoled, taught and cured those who were looking for help. Thus, this new find also confirms the identification of Kursi as the site of Jesus' second miraculous feeding.

It would be indisputable if Kursi had not already long been claimed as the scene for one of Jesus' other miracles, namely, the healing of the possessed man. This, too, can only have occurred in the Decapolis, roughly half a year before the feeding of the four thousand and immediately after Jesus' sermon by the sea and the ensuing first storm.

After the *sharkiye* had subsided, the boat with Jesus and the Twelve arrived in a region that Matthew called "the country of the Gadarenes" (Mt 8:28). No sooner had they landed than a possessed man who dwelt "among the tombs" (Mk 5:5) ran toward them (in Matthew, there are two possessed men). He was considered dangerous, for he often flailed wildly about and could not even be bound by chains. When Jesus saw the man, he ordered the demon to leave him. What we experience next approximates an exorcism exactly as it is performed even today by Catholic priests in many countries. The demon begs permission to remain in his victim, while the exorcist demands his name so that he can have power over him. When Jesus asked what his name was, the "unclean spirit" answered through the mouth of the possessed man: "My name is Legion; for we are many" (Mk 5:9). Finally, the demons asked Jesus to let them go out into a herd of pigs that was grazing nearby. Jesus allowed them to do so; the "unclean spirits" went into the pigs, and, squealing loudly, the herd threw itself over a cliff into the sea.

Only during the rainy season from February to April can pigs graze along the seashore. That fits with the winter storm that preceded this scene. The symbolism is unambiguous. The exorcism clearly occurred in the Gentile Decapolis, since a herd of pigs would be unthinkable in the nation of the Jews; those animals were considered unclean. The Canaanites had sacrificed pigs to their gods, and the Greeks continued this custom. The demons give "Legion" as their name, which makes reference to the military power of the despised Roman occupying force. So they "begged [Jesus] eagerly not to send them out of the country" (Mk 5:10). Moreover, the tenth legion, Fretensis, which was stationed in Syria and had helped put down the rebellions of 4 B.C. and A.D. 6, carried the boar on its standard. The possessed man lived in tombs, a dead world that was, moreover, unclean for the Jews, i.e., the pagan world, whose gods were merely demons for the Jews. But then Jesus came and conquered these "unclean spirits". Furthermore, he let two thousand unclean pigs drown in the sea, thus purifying them ritually. Even this number might have a concrete reference. In A.D. 6, Varus had ordered the crucifixion of two thousand Galilean pilgrims. A crucified man was considered to be cursed and abandoned by God; his soul found no peace. So the belief could have arisen that the souls of the two thousand, instead of returning to their home, had entered into a man here on the border of Galilee who had perhaps been born during this year. Only through Jesus did they find release, whereupon—with a streak of bitter irony—they avenged themselves on the heraldic animal of the Legio Fretensis and drove two thousand pigs to their death. Out of gratitude, the man who was cured of his possession wanted to remain with Jesus. The other people, though, who were witnesses to the event (among them the swineherders who had just lost their livelihood) reacted with anxiety and fear. They asked Jesus to leave their place.

But where did this massive attack on the darkness of paganism occur?

All three Synoptic Gospels give an account of the incident, but information concerning the location varies not only from one Gospel to another, but also from one manuscript to the next. Three spellings are the most common: Gerasa, Gadara, and Gergesa. As a matter of fact, Gerasa and Gadara are cities in the Decapolis. But Gerasa, modern-day Jerash in Jordan, is out of the running; it is thirty-one miles distant from the sea. Nowhere is there any documentation of a place named Gergesa. This variant reading comes from Origen, a third-century Christian scholar, who read in the Old Testament Book of Joshua: "He will without fail drive out from before you the Canaanites, the Hittites, the Hivites, the Perizzites, the Girgashites, the Amorites, and the Jebusites" (Josh 3:10). So he concluded, on whatever basis, that the Girgashites, of course before the land conquests by the Israelites, once occupied a city on the eastern shore of the sea by the name of Gergesa, whose name (from the Hebrew *gerashim*, "the banished") prophetically announced what would come to pass here 1,500 years later through Jesus. The later place name supposedly developed from this. The chapel on the rock ledge would then mark the cliff over which the pigs tumbled into the sea.

If this were the case, then they would have had to bridge a distance of 1640 feet with their headlong dive, since the "cliff" is that far away from the sea. As a matter of fact, there are a few caves in the neighboring crag, though it is unknown whether they once served as tombs. But they are then the only piece of evidence that would allow an identification of Kursi with Gerasa/Gadara/Gergesa. Yet it is difficult to imagine that pigs had grazed on this knoll, when there was a lush meadow at the foot of the hill. Therefore, I consider Kursi to be the site for the "feeding of the four thousand", but not for the "healing of the possessed man" (according to Eutychius of Alexandria, who wrote in 940, during his lifetime Kursi was considered the site of both miracles!). For the sake of completeness, I should mention that not one single mosaic image in Kursi depicts a pig.

The third variant reading remains: Gadara. In Jesus' time, Gadara, too, was a city in the Decapolis, the modern-day Umm Qais in Jordan, only 5.6 miles southeast of the Sea of Galilee. But more important is the fact that Gadara had a sea harbor at its disposal, which was located at modern-day Tel Samra. Coins from Gadara proudly display the prow of a boat; sea battles were reenacted on the lake to entertain the people. In 1985, the regional historian and amateur archaeologist Mendel Nun succeeded in identifying the harbor of Gadara to the south of Tel Samra on the ground of Kibbutz Ha'on. It was the largest harbor on the eastern shore, with a breakwater of 820 feet and a quay 656 feet in length. Its pier was 1640 feet long. No fishing village, but only a metropolis like Gadara could have afforded such a facility. In 1989, archaeologists discovered the remains of a Byzantine church on the Tel Samra next to the harbor. Could it have been in memory of the healing of the possessed man?

In fact, the geography here fits. Directly behind the Kibbutz Ha'on, a foothill of the Golan Heights reaches to the sea. There are caves along its slope. Three sarcophagi were discovered here. Around one mile to the southwest, in the terrain of Kibbutz Ma'agan, a cliff approximately forty-six feet high rises directly over the sea. We were able to view this cliff in person. Did the swine fall from here to their death? A further detail of the story reported by Mark and Matthew seems to fit: "The herdsmen fled, and told it in the city and in the country. And people came to see what it was that had happened", as Mark relates (5:14). And Matthew continues: "And behold, all the city came out to meet Jesus; and when they saw him, they begged him to leave their neighborhood" (8:34). In the case of Kursi, the nearest city would be Hippos, 4.7 miles away. In the event that there were a few fishing huts here, they belonged to the surrounding hinterland, to the *chora* of this city. But the name Hippos is not mentioned in any of the Gospels. The place surrounding Tel Samra was the harbor of Gadara, which agitated swineherders could have reached in one and a half hours. Its "garden suburb" Emmatha (today Hamat Gader), famous for its hot springs, was even just 3.7 miles away. Every one of its inhabitants knew the way. There is no reason not to believe that everything could have occurred here exactly as the Gospels describe it.

Half a year later, in late summer of the year 29, Jesus undertook a final journey to the half-pagan Gaulanitis. First he arrived in Bethsaida, where they brought a blind man to him. Evidently Jesus did not want to make a scene this time. So he took the man by the hand and led him "out of the village" (Mk 8:23), where he healed him. He even expressly asked him not to return to Bethsaida, where the news of the miracle would have spread like wildfire. Henceforth nothing was to hold him up on his journey.

His destination was in the extreme north of the country. These were "the villages of Caesarea Philippi", the capital city of the tetrarch near the headwaters of the Jordan.

The old road from Bethsaida to Caesarea Philippi that Jesus used then can still be made out in the countryside today. It led diagonally through Gaulanitis, which extended as far as Mount Hermon. While many Jews still lived in the south, they were a minority in the north. Here Greek was spoken predominantly. Herodes Philippus, who grew up and was raised in Rome, had his hand in connecting the region to the Greco-Roman world. Since Jews were a minority in his kingdom, he did not need to care much about their religious sensitivities. He minted coins that displayed Augustus, Tiberius, or the emperor's mother, Julia, and himself, without bothering to consider that this contradicted the Jewish prohibition on graven images. And even though he had neither the wealth nor the caliber of his father, he emulated him in all matters regarding the foundation of cities. He built his capital city at the headwaters of the river Jordan, where a temple to the pagan nature-deity Pan had stood since the third century B.C. He named the city Caesarea, in honor of the emperor, just like the most important city that his father had founded. To differentiate it from the Caesarea on the Mediterranean (Caesarea Maritima), the city soon came to be called just Caesarea Philippi, the Caesarea of Philippus. Flavius Josephus describes the tetrarch as an equable, righteous ruler who regularly traveled through his realm to issue decrees and be close to his subjects. He just had a difficult time siring offspring. He was already forty-nine or fifty when, in 29/30, he married his niece Salome (who may have been thirty-two years younger), the daughter of his half-brother Herodes Boethos and his niece Herodias, who at this time was already married to Antipas. This is the same Salome who danced before Antipas in March of 29 to demand the head of John the Baptist. The marriage remained childless up to the time Philippus died three or four years later.

Along the way to Caesarea Philippi, Jesus and his disciples passed by a snow-white temple standing alone on a hill. Herod the Great had it built around 20 B.C. to thank the emperor for handing the former northern territory of Iturea over to him. Josephus describes "a most beautiful temple, of the whitest stone", but notes its location only as being "near the place called Panium".[5] Panium, or Paneion, the Temple of Pan, was the old name of Caesarea Philippi.

As a matter of fact, next to the cave-sanctuary of Pan above the Jordan headwaters, there are ruins of an ancient temple, which generations of archaeologists took to be the Augusteum of Herod. But temples for the emperor were always built separately and on conspicuous sites, never right beside the sanctuaries of other gods. Nevertheless, it took until the summer of 1998 for the error to be cleared up. At that time, the archaeologist Moti Aviam of the Israel Antiquities Authority came across the impressive ruins near Omrit during a trip to inspect the northwestern parts of the country that had been desolated by drought and brush fires. Today, after ten years of excavations on the site, there is no longer any doubt about its identity. The edifice, too, obviously matches the representations of the Augusteum that Philippus had stamped on the reverse of his coins as a sign of fidelity to the emperor. So the temple of Omrit remains a silent witness for the Roman imperial cult that declared Julius Caesar to be God and Augustus to be the "Son of the Divine" (*Filius Divi*, as his official title

---

[5] Flavius Josephus, *Jewish Antiquities*, bk. 15, chap. 10, no. 3, in *New Complete Works of Josephus*, p. 520.

ran), which people in the Greek-speaking East immediately turned into *Huios Theou*, "Son of God". An oath formula from the year 30 B.C., documented by a papyrus discovered in the Egyptian Oxyrhynchus, read: "We swear by Caesar (Augustus), God, descendant of a God." Already during his lifetime, temples were built throughout the empire in honor of this "living God" (*Deus vivus*), and not just by Herod. When Augustus died, he too was officially declared by the Roman Senate to be a God, and the title "Son of the living God" passed on to his successor, Tiberius.

This must have been the place where Jesus asked his disciples: "Who do men say that I am?" (Mk 8:27). They answered that some thought he was a second John the Baptist, while for others he was Elijah brought back, while for still others—one of the major prophets. Jesus followed up with another question: "But who do you say that I am?" Only Matthew delivers Peter's full answer to us, in which the *genius loci* of this place resonates: "You are the Christ, the Son of the living God!" (Mt 16:16). You, not Augustus, not Tiberius, not the ruler in Rome who pretends to be a god, for whom temples are built even though he is quite an ordinary mortal, a sinner, indeed, an oppressor.

Jesus knew how dangerous this answer was, that it represented a frontal attack on the imperial cult and, thus, on worldly power. For this reason, he forbade Peter and the other disciples to speak about it. Otherwise the conflict with Rome would already be preordained.

But before this, he created an *imperium* that has outlasted the rule of the emperors, a spiritual world power, the Church. "You are Peter, and on this rock I will build my Church, and the gates of Hades shall not prevail against it" (Mt 16:18), he promised his disciple, who had just seen Christ's essence with such crystalline clarity that he recognized him as God who had truly become man.

It is certainly no accident that this occurred so close to the headwaters of the Jordan, not far away from a sanctuary of the god Pan. In Greek, *pan* means "all-encompassing". The goat-hooved shepherd god represented unredeemed nature, the powers of the underworld, which made him into a precursor of the Christian devil. Jesus shattered his power right through by founding a Church that was to be not merely "all-encompassing" but "universal" (in Greek: *katholikos*), unconquerable by the power of evil.

The ancient author Plutarch (A.D. 45–125) relates that, during the reign of Tiberius, an Egyptian helmsman off the Greek coast heard a voice ordering him to announce in Palodes that the great Pan had died. When he did this, he heard the wailing of many voices coming from the shore. The emperor, who soon learned about the incident, took the matter so seriously that he ordered investigations. What the explanation of this story might be—it was probably a ritual exclamation within the context of the Adonis/Tammuz Mysteries—is of secondary importance, for its core is true. The great Pan is dead; he was conquered by Jesus Christ during the reign of Tiberius in Caesarea Philippi! Ultimately paganism had to yield to the Gospel.

Of course, scholars like to dispute the authenticity of this scene—especially liberal theologians who are unwilling to believe that Jesus founded a Church. But there is no reason for skepticism. Ultimately, the meta-level that unlocks for us its meaning was not even suggested by the Evangelists. No one who received the Gospels in the Jewish- and Gentile-Christian communities outside of Judaea would have associated the place name Caesarea Philippi immediately with the Sanctuary of Pan, much less the Augusteum. If the Evangelists had invented the scene, which has so much local color, they would have indulged in a hint at least. But there is not even the slightest allusion on their part; instead, twentieth- and twenty-first-century archaeology has provided us with the key to the deeper understanding of Peter's answer.

Jesus certainly did not use the word *church* in its contemporary meaning. In the Greek translation of Matthew's Gospel, the word is *ekklesia*. The same word is used in the Septuagint, the Greek translation of the Old Testament, to mean "congregation" of the Lord (Num 32:2–5), that is, the assembly of the faithful in God's presence. The Aramaic word that Jesus used, then, might have been *qahal*, which similarly means "community" or "assembly". Jesus had already founded and defined one such community in Peter's house in Capernaum (see Mk 3:32–35). When he now spoke about "his Church", it was not an anachronism but, rather, the logical consequence of the recent months since the calling of the disciples.

But even the profession of faith in the Messiah made by the Prince of the Apostles was only a preparation for the next step of Jesus' self-revelation. It was, so to speak, the overture to his Transfiguration.

In this instance, the Gospels are surprisingly vague. They mention only a "high mountain". Jesus led his three closest confidants, Peter, James, John, up the slope; on the summit they saw how he, cloaked in dazzlingly white light, was corroborated by Elijah and Moses and glorified by God. Once again, as before during his baptism in the Jordan, a voice rang out: "This is my beloved Son; listen to him" (Mk 9:7). Three decades later, an eyewitness, Peter, described the scene in his Second Letter:

> For we did not follow cleverly devised myths when we made known to you the power and coming of our Lord Jesus Christ, but we were eyewitnesses of his majesty. For when he received honor and glory from God the Father and the voice was borne to him by the Majestic Glory, "This is my beloved Son, with whom I am well pleased," we heard this voice borne from heaven, for we were with him on the holy mountain. (2 Pet 1:16–18)

Another eyewitness, the apostle John, summed up his impression in a single, all the more suggestive sentence: "We have beheld his glory, glory as of the only-begotten Son from the Father", "full of grace and truth" (Jn 1:14).

Unfortunately, neither Peter nor John nor the Synoptic writers give us the least bit of information as to where the Transfiguration of Jesus took place. An early Christian tradition locates it on Mount Tabor southeast of Nazareth. Actually the idea is appealing. The mountain, which was already sacred to the Canaanites, rises like an inverted Grail goblet from the plain of Jezreel. It was familiar to Jesus from his youth and must have had an almost magical attraction for him. Even today the Arabs call it *et-tor*, the mountain, just as in the Gospels and in the Letter of Peter it is referred to only as "the mountain". It is the same name that they also gave Sinai, the Mount of Olives, and Mount Garizim of the Samaritans. But, nevertheless, two arguments contradict the hypothesis that Jesus had withdrawn there in the company of his three closest friends.

First, there is the chronological aspect. Even if the Transfiguration is dated from "six" (Mt 17:1 and Mk 9:2) to "about eight" (Lk 9:28) days after Jesus' appearance in Caesarea Philippi, Jesus and his disciples appear to have returned first to Galilee afterward (Mk 9:30: "They went on from there and passed through Galilee"), although

this inference is not conclusive. More relevant is the fact that in Jesus'
day there was a fortress on the summit of Mount Tabor. It was built
during the Hellenistic period, then conquered by Hasmoneans under
Alexander Jannaeus, and finally occupied by the Romans under
Pompey in 63 B.C. When Josephus fortified Galilee at the beginning
of the Jewish War, he constructed a wall around the mountain in
forty days. Both ruins have been uncovered by archaeologists. It is at
least possible that this castle was occupied even at the time of Antipas,
since the fortress was located strategically close to the southern border
of his kingdom.

Eusebius of Caesarea, the earliest source concerning the mountain
of the Transfiguration, does not commit himself. Instead, the author of
the first Church history cites Psalm 89: "Tabor and Hermon joyously
praise your name", and continues: "The wonderful transfigurations
[sic!] of our Redeemer took place on these mountains." We are thus
faced with a choice. The 1¾-mile-high, snow-covered Hermon in
the borderlands between Syria and Lebanon was already considered
by the pagans as "the holy mountain" par excellence; this is proved by
the ruins of more than twenty temples and altars that archaeologists
have discovered on its ridge.

The Irish theologian Sean Freyne also argues for Hermon as the
mountain of the Transfiguration because it has a relevance in the es-
chatology of the Essenes and thus in mystical Judaism generally.
According to the Book of Enoch, which was very popular in Jesus'
time, the watchers from heaven came down from Hermon in the
days before the great flood to abandon their holy duties out of earthly
cravings. The Essenes used to compare the Sadducaic priesthood
to these "fallen angels". Only 2.5 miles west of Caesarea Philippi,
"in the land of Dan, that is south of Hermon", the "Writer of Justice", the aboriginal prophet Henoch, experienced a dream vision,
in the course of which he was taken to heaven and saw "the great
glory" of God. Freyne points to Psalm 133, which says that "the dew
from Hermon" waters "Zion", and concludes: "At least the sacred
mountain of the north had been chosen as the most suitable location
for this stinging criticism of Jerusalem and its temple personnel."[6]

---

[6] Sean Freyne, The Jesus Movement and Its Expansion: Meaning and Mission (Grand Rapids,
Mich.: Eerdmans, 2014), pp. 25–26.

Here it is irrelevant whether Jesus actually climbed to the summit of Hermon or merely up a mountain belonging to the Hermon massif. Halfway between Dan and Caesarea Philippi rises a mountain that is not unlike Tabor in form. Perhaps this was the "high mountain" in the land of Dan, in the shadow of Hermon, on which Jesus' mystical Transfiguration occurred.

Assuming that the Transfiguration, in an echo of Enoch, actually announced the imminent judgment against the new watchers, the fallen priesthood of the Temple, then the next step in Jesus' mission, his next goal, was now determined. The fact that Peter quite spontaneously built three tabernacles for Jesus, Moses, and Elijah already contains a hint about the appointed day. And as a matter of fact, John tells us in chapters 7 through 9 of his Gospel about Jesus' appearance and self-revelation during the Feast of Tabernacles in Jerusalem in the year 29, which in that year took place from October 19 to 29.

After they themselves had come to the realization, through his words and deeds, that Jesus is the Messiah, he revealed himself to his disciples in the glory of God. Once again, the Son of Man would be raised up, again on a hillock, which this time has the name Golgotha. Moses and Elijah were not to flank him then, but, rather, two criminals. Yet this happened in plain view of everyone, in the clearest light of history, in a public place in front of the gates of Jerusalem. It was not a divine voice that then declared him the Messiah, the "King of the Jews" but, rather, a wooden plaque inscribed by the Roman governor, the representative of the emperor who took himself to be the "Son of the Living God". On that day, Jesus would descend into the depths of human suffering before conquering death.

XI

The King of the Jews

Showdown in Jerusalem

The foundress of Christian archaeology is Saint Helena, mother of the first Christian emperor of Rome, Constantine the Great. She had come to the Holy Land as a pilgrim, but at the same time she had received from her son the order to build churches on the sites of the birth and Ascension, Passion and Resurrection of Jesus Christ.

The location of these sites was reliably recorded, for there had always been a Christian presence in Jerusalem. Only three years after the destruction of Jerusalem in A.D. 70, a new Jewish-Christian community, led by Jesus' cousin Simon, had already settled again on Mount Zion. When Emperor Hadrian in A.D. 135 prohibited all Jews from entering their holy city, the Gentile Christians officially took over the management of this community, at least temporarily. They witnessed how the pagan emperor, in his endeavor to eradicate Judaism in all its forms, also turned Christian shrines into pagan worship sites. He ordered the terrain where Mount Golgotha rose up, including the rock face into which the empty tomb had been hewn, to be covered with a platform, on top of which the city's new western forum emerged. Over Jesus' tomb, a temple for Aphrodite, the goddess of love, or her Syrian counterpart Astarte, was supposed to be built. On the stump of Mount Golgotha, which still protruded from the platform of the forum, Hadrian placed a statue of the goddess. He was probably thinking of her as the one who descended into the underworld each year in order to awaken her lover Adonis or Tammuz, whose "resurrection" was celebrated at the beginning of spring. Or of the fact that an ancient Aphrodite shrine on her "native island" of Cyprus bore the name Golgoi. In any event, he tried to reinterpret the Resurrection of Christ in the context of the pagan mystery-religions and thus rob it of its singularity, as if the symbolism of the myth could be equated with a historical reality.

He thereby incurred the wrath of Christians for all time, but his misappropriation at least helped ensure that the location of Golgotha was not forgotten. For even then there were already isolated pilgrims, for instance Bishop Melito of Sardis in Asia Minor, who traveled to Palestine around A.D. 160 in order to visit the sites, "where these things were taught and happened". The fact that Golgotha was now located on the West Forum incensed him so much that in his Easter sermon, a shocking document of Christian anti-Judaism, he blamed the Jews, mind you, for crucifying Jesus "in the middle of the city, on the main square". In A.D. 212, Alexander of Cappadocia came to Jerusalem, and Origen, the ecclesiastic writer, even came twice, in A.D. 215 and 230, "so as to learn about the traces of Jesus and his disciples through research". He, too, met other pilgrims and mentions "visitors from all over the world". A scratch-drawing, which was found in the Armenian Vartan Chapel in front of the Grotto of the Holy Cross, below the Church of the Holy Sepulchre, proves that the visitors even came from the western part of the empire. It shows a ship above the Latin (!) inscription: *Domine ivimus*, "Lord, we went", perhaps to fulfill a vow, but in any case alluding to Psalm 122. The graffito is definitely from the time before the fourth century; the Israeli archaeologist Shimon Gibson even dates it as early as "the first or second century", before the erection of Hadrian's West Forum. Either way, it confirms a continuity of the tradition on which the builders of shrines and memorials in the fourth and fifth century could rely.

When Constantine the Great convoked the Council of Nicaea in 325 to resolve the controversy between the bishops and the Arian sect, he came into contact with this tradition. The Palestinian bishops, first and foremost Eusebius of Caesarea and Macarius, then bishop of Jerusalem, were thus able to assure him that the location of the Holy Sepulchre and Mount Golgotha were recorded and known. Their argument must have been so convincing that the emperor immediately issued an order to demolish the forum with the pagan temples, to uncover the holy sites, and to erect a memorial basilica over them, bigger and more magnificent even than the churches over the graves of the apostles in Rome.

He entrusted the supervision of the associated expenses to his mother, who officially acted as co-regent and carried the title *Augusta*. Helena used the opportunity to fulfill her long-cherished wish to make a pilgrimage to the Holy Land, but, more than anything, she was probably curious. The well-preserved old lady, almost eighty years old, wanted to be present when the empty tomb of Christ came to light again, for the first time in almost two hundred years.

If we believe her biographies, which began to be circulated half a century later, she also witnessed an even more spectacular discovery at that time. East of Mount Golgotha, the workers came upon an ancient cistern, long since dried up, which apparently had been used as a secret meeting place and hide-out by the early Christians. Still inside it, the story goes, were the remains of three crosses, or their cross beams, three nails and a wooden tablet, on which the words "Jesus of Nazareth, King of the Jews" were carved in Hebrew, Greek, and Latin. The emperor's mother allegedly divided up the find: one part she sent to her son, who just then was residing in Nicomedia, one part she took with her to Rome, while the bigger part remained in Jerusalem.

What sounds like a pious legend, the story about the finding of the Cross, could quite possibly have a true core. In his biography of Constantine, Eusebius of Caesarea quotes a letter from the emperor to the Bishop of Jerusalem, written in A.D. 325, which explicitly states that "the monument of his most holy Passion, so long buried beneath the ground, ... remained unknown for so long a series of years, until its reappearance".[1] The quote can refer neither to the tomb, which gave testimony to his Resurrection, nor to his Passion, nor to Mount Golgotha, which had protruded from the ground of the West Forum all along. At that time, next to the circular Church of the Holy Sepulchre (or Anastasis, Church of the Resurrection, as it is still called by Orthodox Christians), which is topped by a mighty cupola, the Martyrion was built, an oblong basilica directly over the cistern in which the True Cross had reportedly been found. The stump of Mount Golgotha, however, henceforth arose at the

---

[1] Eusebius of Caesarea, *The Life of Constantine*, III, 30, in *Nicene and Post-Nicene Fathers*, second series, ed. Philip Schaff and Henry Wace, vol. 1 (1890; Peabody, Mass.: Hendrickson, 1995), p. 528.

edge of an atrium between the two churches. Only twenty-three years after its discovery, in A.D. 348, Bishop Cyril of Jerusalem mentions the veneration of the "wood of the Cross" in the Church of the Holy Sepulchre, and says that "the whole world has since been filled with pieces of" it.[2] Three years later, in A.D. 351, he confirmed in a letter to Emperor Constantius II, the son of Constantine the Great, that during his father's reign the "saving wood of the cross was found in Jerusalem".[3] The veneration of the parts of the Cross that stayed in Jerusalem, as well as the inscription, are attested by the pilgrim Egeria in A.D. 383. Church historians Gelasius (388), Rufinus (ca. 400), Theodoret (ca. 440), Socrates Scholasticus (ca. 440), and Sozomen (444) give accounts of the discovery, as do the Church Fathers Ambrose of Milan (395) and John Chrysostom (398). Rufinus, Socrates, and Sozomen confirm that the inscription of the *titulus* of the Cross was trilingual. Sozomen mentions that the wood showed traces of white paint. The pilgrim from Piacenza, who came to Jerusalem in A.D. 570, was still able to venerate the relic and describes it as a panel made from walnut, on which only the words *Rex Iudaeorum*, "King of the Jews", remained written. According to Sozomen, the original inscription, of course, read "Jesus of Nazareth, the King of the Jews", corresponding to the version cited in the Gospel of John (19:19). Apparently, therefore, the inscription was likewise divided. But then the other half, a piece of whitewashed walnut wood, must have borne the name Iesus Nazarenus.

When in 1492 the Basilica di Santa Croce in Gerusalemme in Rome was renovated, the workers came upon a tile inscribed with *Titulus Crucis*, "Titulus of the Cross". When they carefully removed it, a lead box came to light. It bore the seal of Cardinal Gherardo, who was elected pope in 1144 and assumed the name Lucius II. Santa Croce was his titular church; he had it renovated and expanded. When the workers opened the lead box, they found in it an old walnut panel, highly weathered on three sides, covered with the remains of what was once white lime wash. A clean cutting edge on the left

---

[2] Cyril of Jerusalem, *Catechetical Lectures* IV.10, in *Nicene and Post-Nicene Fathers*, second series, vol. 7 (1894; Peabody, Mass.: Hendrickson, 1995), p. 21.

[3] *The Works of Saint Cyril of Jerusalem*, vol. 2, Fathers of the Church, vol. 64 (Washington, D.C.: Catholic Univ. of America Press, 2000), p. 232.

side suggests that it was once cut in two. The words *I Nazarenus* were carved into it in Hebrew, Greek, and Latin, from right to left, for the latter two were in imitation of the Hebrew way of writing. The find was all the more interesting since it fit the history of the basilica. Its oldest part, in which the panel was found, was part of a Roman imperial palace, the Sessorianum. Inscriptions confirm that Empress Helena resided in it. A room, which she had floored with dirt from Mount Calvary in Jerusalem, served as her private chapel. Here she brought her most precious relics and had them immured in the walls, as was customary in late antiquity. After her death, she left the entire palace to the pope, who turned it into a church. Was the wooden panel, then, a part of her collection of relics that she brought from Jerusalem to Rome? Was it perhaps even a fragment of the panel that, according to all four Gospels, Pontius Pilate ordered to be placed on the Cross of the Redeemer stating the reason why he had been sentenced to death on the Cross?

I asked myself this question in the 1990s, when I first visited the Basilica di Santa Croce, where the panel is still exhibited today. If so, this much was clear: it would be an object of world-historical significance, a legal document of the most momentous trial in history. It was at least worth investigating.

I knew that there was a way to determine the age and, above all, the authenticity of the inscription rather precisely. This scientifically recognized and regularly applied method of dating ancient inscriptions is called *comparative paleography*. Each century, the style of writing, the way of writing letters, changes. The age of inscriptions can thus be determined when they are compared with other inscriptions that are dated, for instance, by the name of a ruler. The example of the Dead Sea Scrolls shows how accurate this method is. Decades after their paleographic dating to the second to first century B.C., the scrolls were examined using radiocarbon dating, and the result was the same.

My plan, to have the inscription on the wooden panel paleographically dated, was presented to the Papal Academy of Sciences and then approved by the Vatican Secretariat of State. With a series of detailed photographs, which the Roman photographer Ferdinando Paladini had taken, I flew to Israel in order to present the inscription to seven experts in Hebrew, Greek, and Latin paleography in the Holy Land, namely, Dr. Gabriel Barkay, Professor Hana and Dr. Ester Eshel, Dr. Leah Di Segni (all from the Hebrew University of Jerusalem), Professor Israel Roll, Professor Ben Isaac (Tel Aviv University), as well as the German papyrologist Professor Carsten Peter Thiede, who was teaching at the Beer Sheva campus of Ben-Gurion University of the Negev. Their findings were unanimous. The poorly preserved Hebrew line was dated first to third century, the Greek and Latin line was clearly from the early first century A.D. I prepared a report on this, which I handed over to Pope John Paul II in a personal audience in his library in December 1998, before I presented the results of my research, with permission of the Holy See, during a symposium at the Pontifical Lateran University in May 1999. Half a year later, my book *Die Jesus-Tafel* (The Jesus Tablet) (1999) was published. Since then, Professor Thiede (*Das Jesus-Fragment* [The Quest for the True Cross], 2000) and the Roman Church historian Dr. Maria-Luisa Rigato (*Il Titolo della Croce di Gesù* [The Title of the Cross of Jesus], 2005) have confirmed my findings.

The Vatican then authorized carbon dating to be conducted by physicists of the Roma Tre University, whose findings were published in 2002 in the journal *Radiocarbon*. The result was devastating. Allegedly, the wood was only 1029 (+/- 30) years old; the inscription was therefore from the time between A.D. 950 and 1010; later on, the time of origin was even placed between 980 and 1146.

But it is hard to imagine that the physicists are right about this. For in the Middle Ages, no one had ever thought of paleography, and it would have been impossible to forge the inscription so convincingly in three languages and scripts. One example for this is the infamous document of the *Donation of Constantine*. In the eighth century, Pope Stephen II presented Pepin, King of the Franks, with the alleged document in which Constantine the Great supposedly granted the rule over all of Italy to the pope; it became the legal basis for the creation of the Papal State. Not until the fifteenth century did linguistic mistakes expose the pious fraud, corroborated by paleographic criteria as late as the nineteenth century. But this also means that not even the smartest people in the early medieval papal chancellery were capable of fabricating a convincing forgery. To begin with, dated inscriptions from the Holy Land, which could have been copied, were not even available in the tenth century; all the samples on which the experts whom I consulted based their work were found in recent decades, in the course of archaeological excavations in Israel. This includes a bilingual dedicatory inscription from Dan, in the northernmost part of the country, which is from the Hellenistic era and surfaced only in the last decade during excavations conducted by Hebrew Union College. "To the God who is in Dan", it says in Greek and Aramaic. In Jerusalem, dozens of bilingually inscribed ossuaries were found, i.e., bone urns for secondary burial, which are suitable for comparison. They are almost exclusively from the first century. And finally, there is the most famous inscription from the time of Jesus, the so-called Pilate Stone from Caesarea Maritima, which was discovered by Italian archaeologists in 1961. During the expansion of the Roman Theater in the third century, the stone was simply turned over and reused. The Tiberieum, to which its inscription refers, was probably the port city's lighthouse, which was renovated by Pilate. Most historians read it as

(...)S TIBERIEUM
(Pon)TIUS PILATUS
(Praef)ECTUS IUDA(ea)E
(Fecit, d(E)dicavit)

("This Tiberieum was built and dedicated by Pontius Pilate, Prefect of Judaea"), while it is debated whether the first line refers to the gods (*Dis Augustis*), the inhabitants (*Incolis*), or the sailors (*Nautis*), and whether the last line can also be read as *refecit* ("renovated"). The resemblance between the writing on the Pilate inscription and the Jesus-title is so striking that we have to ask ourselves whether both might not go back to a pattern by the same hand, which Pilate's words in John 19:22 ("What I have written I have written") could suggest. The interesting thing is where the Titulus inscription deviates from John 19:19. The Greek line, unlike the Gospel, which quotes it as *Nazoraios*, is merely a transcription of the Latin NAZARINUS (namely *Nazarenous*), which points to a sentence composed in Latin; the scribe simply did not bother to transfer the designation of Jesus' origin into grammatically correct Greek. In the Latin line it does not say *Nazarenus*, as usual, but instead NAZARINUS, apparently as an early Latinization of the Hebrew *ha-Nazari*, which became the colloquial *ha-Nozri*.

I am no physicist, but I believe the completely unacceptable result of the C14-dating is due to the fact that the panel was hidden inside a lead box for 1,100 years. Lead is the most effective radiation protection. The radiocarbon method, however, measures the radioactive decay of C14 when it is exposed to natural cosmic radiation. A constant shielding must have actually stopped this process and seemingly "rejuvenated" the material.

If the C14 method is wrong and the paleographic dating proves correct, the panel constitutes not only the most important find of the excavations supervised by the emperor's mother, Helena, but one of the most explosive historic documents in general. For it would not only be the sole contemporary evidence of Jesus' life; it also mentions the reason why he was sentenced to crucifixion.

Another sensational find was not made public until December 2018. It is a slender bronze ring that the Israeli archaeologist Gideon Förster from the Hebrew University of Jerusalem discovered in 1968 during excavations in the Herodium. In the first century A.D., Herod's fortress served as an administrative center for the Roman

The Ring of Pilate (Source: Israel Antiquities Authority)

occupying forces. For half a century, the ring was stored unnoticed among other items that had been found; then Israeli experts looked at it again under a magnifying glass. With a special camera they could make out the engraved image of a drinking vessel, surrounded by the Greek inscription πιλατο ("Pilato", Pilate's). The experts are certain that either the governor himself wore this signet ring, or it belonged to one of his officials who sealed documents in his name. "I don't know of any other Pilatus from the period, and the ring shows he was a person of stature and wealth", explains Professor Danny Schwartz of the Hebrew University of Jerusalem.

"Suffered under Pontius Pilate"—these words, already incorporated into the Apostles' Creed by the early Christians, are the third anchoring of salvation history in world history. Jesus' trial is, in fact, an undeniable historical event. This is confirmed not only by Flavius Josephus, but also by the Roman historian Tacitus, who around A.D. 98 in his chronicle of the Roman Imperial period also mentions the Christians and states: "Christus, from whom the name [Christians] had its origin, suffered the extreme penalty during the reign of Tiberius at the hands of one of our procurators, Pontius Pilatus."[4] In the earliest pagan source, a letter written shortly after A.D. 73, the Syrian stoic Mara Bar Serapion mentions the execution of the "wise king" of the Jews, which he considered to be the reason why Jerusalem was destroyed forty years later. As early as the first half of the second century, the Christian apologist Justin Martyr (died A.D. 165) twice refers to a report by Pilate to the emperor about Jesus' trial, which he claims to have examined in the Roman National Archives.

Pontius Pilate is historically attested not only by the Caesarea inscription, but also by the writings of Flavius Josephus and of another educated Jew and contemporary of Jesus, Philo of Alexandria. The impression that they give of the governor and judge of Jesus, however, is rather one-sided, since both pursued a specific agenda with their portrayals. Philo, who wrote during the time of Emperor Caligula, complained about the harsh treatment of his fellow Jewish countrymen, while Josephus tried to justify the Jewish rebellion with the misconduct of inept Roman governors.

---

[4] Tacitus, *Annals*, bk. 15, chap. 44, in *The Complete Works of Tacitus*, trans. Alfred John Church and William Jackson Brodribb (New York: Random House, 1942), p. 380.

Pilate's long term of office—a full ten years—in a province as difficult as Judaea actually speaks for rather remarkable tactical skill. The incidents that Philo and Josephus describe, to prove to us what "a malicious and unforgiving person" (Philo) he was, look in retrospect like trifles instead. The fact that Pilate, when he moved into the Herodian palace in Jerusalem, had standards with the image of the emperor brought in certainly indicates a lack of sensitivity toward the Jewish ban on images, but it would have been a matter of course in any other province. In any event, a public demonstration by the Jews, who preferred to die rather than to accept the sacrilege (Josephus) or an intervention with the emperor (Philo), led him to have the standards brought back to Caesarea. Another time, probably before the Feast of Passover in A.D. 29, Pilate wanted to use Temple funds to build an aqueduct from a source roughly twenty-five miles away (the so-called pools of Solomon) to Jerusalem. Since the largest amounts of water in Jerusalem were used for ritual cleansing, this was actually not a bad idea. Nevertheless, it led to an uprising, which Pilate tried to suppress first with cudgels, then with weapons. Probably during the suppression of these riots it came to what is mentioned in Luke's Gospel: "There were some present at that very time who told him [Jesus] of the Galileans whose blood Pilate had mingled with their sacrifices" (Lk 13:1). Even Josephus conceded that the legionnaires at the time had proceeded with "much greater blows than Pilate had commanded".[5] If it was indeed the same incident, and everything seems to indicate this, it is striking that the protest did not come from the Temple hierarchy, whose money was at stake, after all, but from especially conservative pilgrims from Galilee. The current high priest, Caiaphas, seems instead to have cooperated with the Romans. In any event, the aqueduct was built, and its course can still be traced rather accurately, since the archaeologists discovered remains in several places.

Even the coins, which the governor had minted in the years from A.D. 28 to 31, appear provocative only on secondary inspection. Some of them show a *simpulum*, a ritual vessel for wine offerings; others show a *lituus*, the staff of Roman augurs; pagan symbols, to be

---

[5] Flavius Josephus, *Jewish Antiquities*, bk. 18, chap. 3, no. 2, in *The New Complete Works of Josephus*, trans. William Whiston (Grand Rapids, Mich.: Kregel, 1999), p. 590.

sure, but rather subtle ones, and without any violation of the Mosaic
ban on images. This, too, was nothing new: as early as on the coins
of Governor Valerius Gratus (A.D. 15–26) we find, for instance, the
staff of Hermes and crossed cornucopias. Thus, the renowned historian Alexander Demandt clearly states in his biography of Pilate:
"A religious war with symbols was alien to the Romans. There is no
example of this."

It was not until a third incident in A.D. 36 that Pilate lost his position as governor. At that time, a false prophet was gathering the
Samaritans on Mount Garizim and promised to produce the sacred
vessels that Moses had once buried there. The Roman sent his cavalry
and infantry, dispersed the crowd, and had its leaders arrested and
executed. The Samaritan High Council subsequently complained to
his superior, Vitellius, the procurator of Syria, who ordered Pilate
to Rome in order to answer to the emperor. Certainly, Pilate had
overreacted here, but why? Was it to prevent an uprising, as Josephus
claims, or did he act on behest of Caiaphas, who feared the creation
of a second temple and thus competition in the land of the hated
Samaritans? When Pilate finally reached the capital after a long and
arduous sea voyage, Tiberius was already dead. Hence we will never
find out what he would have alleged in his defense. But it is striking
that the high priest was likewise removed from office by Vitellius
only half a year later. The subsequent fate of Pilate is unknown. Legend has it that he went into exile to Gaul or Helvetia and died there
by suicide.

Perhaps he was sometimes raving in the choice of his means, overly
zealous, and too devoted to the emperor, and, at the same time,
provocative, stubborn, cynical, and arrogant, but definitely not the
unscrupulous man of "insufferable cruelties" that Philo, and to a certain extent Josephus, characterize him as being. The image of Pilate
conveyed in the Gospels is more realistic because it is more nuanced.

The third protagonist in the historical Passion play, Jesus' accuser,
is also attested. The high priest Caiaphas is not only mentioned by
Flavius Josephus as "Joseph who was also called Caiaphas".[6] His
tomb was found, too. In November 1990, during the construction
of the Peace Forest south of Jerusalem, workers came upon a rock

---

[6] Ibid., bk. 18, chap. 4, no. 3, p. 593.

chamber that contained six completely intact ossuaries. The remains of ten additional bone chests, as well as human bones, were strewn in between and gave evidence of partial plundering by grave robbers. The limestone chests were richly decorated; five of them bore inscriptions. One of these read *Qaifa*; another one, on an especially elaborately decorated specimen, read *Jehosaf Bar Qaifa*, "Joseph, son of Caiaphas". In it were, among other bones that had plainly been added later, the skeletal remains of a roughly sixty-year-old man. In another ossuary, inside the skull of a young woman, a coin was found from the sixth year of the reign of Herod Agrippa I, the year A.D. 42/43, after which she obviously lost her life. The tomb was thereby safely dated to the time of Jesus.

As the Evangelist John correctly states, this Caiaphas also held the office of high priest in the year Jesus died, but someone else was really in charge. Caiaphas was the son-in-law of Annas, who held the office of high priest from A.D. 6–15 until governor Valerius Gratus removed him. This removal was not recognized by many Jews, who still considered him the legitimate high priest. From then on, he acted as a kind of "eminence grise", a puppet-master behind the scenes who ensured that the office remained in the family; a total of six out of the eighteen chief priests who came after him until the destruction of the Temple were from his clan. A verse from a song mocking the ruling priest families, preserved in the Babylonian Talmud, reveals that he also made enemies through this and apparently had an entire network of informants at his disposal: "Woe to me on account of the house of Annas, woe to me on account of their informers.... For they were high priests and their sons treasurers and their sons-in-law stewards, and their servants beat the people with clubs."

According to the descriptions of Josephus, the tomb of Annas could also be identified, even though it was plundered and largely destroyed. It is located not far from the "Field of Blood", Hakeldama, on the other side of the Hinnom Valley, opposite the Southern Wall of Jerusalem. It is the only tomb in all of Jerusalem that was richly decorated on the inside, too. Its vestibule was surmounted by a cupola, into which was engraved a rosette flanked by twelve palm branches. Its façade was modeled on the Triple Huldah Gate in the Temple, and towering over it was a structure reminiscent of the profile of the Imperial Hall. It was a tomb that was meant to stand out, and it pointed to the office, the dignity, the rank, and the importance of the clan chief and high priest emeritus long after his death.

Without a doubt, Annas and Caiaphas were the two most powerful men in Jerusalem in A.D. 30 and, at the same time, the biggest employers in the city. The Temple, of which they were in charge, employed about seven thousand priests and ten thousand Levites year round. Through the sacrificial offering, livestock farmers and merchants became rich; the ongoing Temple construction required eighteen thousand workers and craftsmen; weavers, dyers, and tailors produced garments; scribes carefully logged all proceedings. But foremost of all, they presided over a small, intimate clique of wealthy priests and laymen, all of them Sadducees, whom Josephus called "ten ... principal men"[7] and who in their function could be compared with a council of ministers. Among them was also the Temple captain who commanded the Temple police, three to four treasurers, as well as five or six Temple supervisors, who were well versed in ritual and legal matters. Flavius Josephus reports that after the death of Herod and the removal of Archelaus, "the government [of Judaea] became an aristocracy, and the high priests were entrusted with a dominion over the nation".[8] The Roman governors assigned to the high priest the duty of securing peace in the province and maintaining public order. He was expected to cooperate with the occupying power; if he did not do so or proved incapable, he was unceremoniously deprived of his office.

In the innermost circle around the high priest we find the actual masterminds behind Jesus' arrest and conviction. His self-confident manner in the Temple, his popularity, and his claim to work as one sent by God challenged the entire power structure of the "Temple clique". His actions, beginning with the cleansing of the Temple, hit a vital nerve of the big-business Temple and its Sadducee management. "You do not understand that it is expedient for you that one man should die for the people, and that the whole nation should not perish", as the Evangelist John (11:50) quotes the reasoning of Caiaphas. Anything that jeopardized the status quo, and thus the

---

[7] Ibid., bk. 20, chap. 8, no. 11, p. 655.
[8] Ibid., bk. 20, chap. 10, no. 1, p. 660.

well-tuned relation with the Roman occupying power, was to be categorically rejected or eliminated.

The prelude to the tragedy of Jerusalem took place in mid-March of A.D. 30. Jesus knew that this Passover feast would be decisive and that his place was in Jerusalem now. But before that, he once again visited Bethany on the eastern shore of the Jordan, the place where it all had started, to preach there to the pilgrims who were on their way into the city of the Temple like he was. That was where the news of Lazarus' grave illness reached him. Jesus at first hesitated; he did not react immediately. Only two days later did he set out, only to learn that his friend had already been dead for four days. No chance, therefore, that he was simply unconscious or seemingly dead; "by this time there will be an odor" (Jn 11:39), Martha, the sister of the deceased, assured Jesus.

The tomb of Lazarus can still be seen today, assuming one manages to defy the barriers in the landscape, as well as in people's heads, and to venture into Palestinian territory. The place, the *beth anya* or Bethany by the Mount of Olives, even bears his name today, Al-Eizariya, the place of Lazarus. John provides very precise information: "Bethany was near Jerusalem, about fifteen furlongs (*stadia*) off" (Jn 11:18, Douay-Rheims), i.e., two miles, which refers to the walking distance. It is only one mile as the crow flies. Grottoes, cisterns, foundations of houses, a bakery and grain silos, but especially Herodian oil lamps and stone measuring cups, which the Franciscan archaeologist Sylvester J. Saller found here between 1949 and 1953, prove a settlement from the time of Jesus. A burial ground is located toward the east, by the road to Jericho. Burial chambers hewn into stone can easily be dated to the first century. They were not closed with rolling stones, but with smaller stone stoppers. This explains why John in his Gospel does not talk about "rolling away" but "taking away" (literally, "lifting off") the closing stone.

Today, twenty-two narrow rock steps lead into the former tomb of Jesus' friend, but they are from the sixteenth century, when the Muslims blocked the original entrance. Originally, it consisted of an antechamber and the actual burial chamber, which were connected by two steps and a narrow passage. The burial chamber itself measures 7.5 by 8 feet. At first glance, its walls are smooth. But gaps indicate that on three sides there were recesses in the rock that expanded toward the bottom. The deceased once lay on small elevations of the floor by the wall, covered in linen wraps.

This tomb was never forgotten. Eusebius had already mentioned it around A.D. 330, likewise the pilgrim from Bordeaux three years later, and Egeria in 383. Around A.D. 390, Saint Jerome wrote that near the "tomb of Lazarus" a church was built, which the pilgrim from Piacenza visited around 570. But why does only John record Jesus' greatest miracle? Why do the Synoptic Gospels keep the raising of Lazarus a secret? Perhaps in order to protect him. "So the chief priests planned to put Lazarus also to death, because on account of him many of the Jews were going away and believing in Jesus", the Evangelist reports (Jn 12:10–11). According to the tradition of the Eastern Church, the resuscitated man eventually went to Cyprus, where he served as the Bishop of Larnaca, while a French legend claims that he fled to Marseille. When John wrote his Gospel, he must have been dead already, so there was no more reason for considerate silence.

Jesus, too, initially went to a safe place after raising Lazarus. The news of this miracle directly before the gates of Jerusalem must have put the Temple hierarchy on high alert. According to John, Caiaphas even convened the Sanhedrin to discuss the further course of action. "From that day on they took counsel about how to put him to death" (Jn 11:53). When Jesus heard about this, according to John, he went first to Ephraim, into the modern day et-Tayyibe, approximately 12.5 miles northeast of Jerusalem. The place is located on a rise on the eastern slope of a mountain and offers an unobstructed view to the south. Thus his disciples could warn him in case his persecutors were approaching.

On Sunday, April 2, A.D. 30, "six days before the Passover" (Jn 12:1; in the Synoptic Gospels it is "two days"; compare Mt 26:2 and Mk 14:1), Jesus returned to Bethany on the Mount of Olives. There, in the house of Simon the Leper (or of the Pharisee; compare Lk 7:36–44), a meal took place in which Lazarus and his sisters Mary and Martha also participated. This group in the Essene *beth anya* on the outskirts of Jerusalem apparently did not care that the Sadducees were looking for Jesus with a warrant, as it were; on the contrary: through the invitation they assured him of their unconditional loyalty. In the course of the meal, there was a scene that can be understood only at second glance and that was perhaps even the actual purpose of the solemn gathering. Mary, the sister of Lazarus, came "with an alabaster jar of ointment of pure nard, very costly, and she broke the jar and poured it over his head" (Mk 14:3). Then she "anointed the feet of Jesus and wiped his feet with her hair" (Jn 12:3). John specifies the amount as "a pound" and its value as "three hundred denarii", a specification that Mark (14:5) also confirms. This was the equivalent of a year's wages for a day laborer, and it shows how wealthy this family plainly was—probably rich enough to finance the "poor house" of Bethany. Nevertheless, this act drew criticism from Judas Iscariot, but also from other disciples (Mt 26:8; Mk 14:4–5): one could also have given the money to the poor, i.e., used it for charitable purposes within the context of the house. Jesus, who understood the gesture, gave in. With the words "The poor you always have with you, but you do not always have me" (Jn 12:8), he referred to the exceptional situation, but also affirmed the duties of the poor house. Then he emphasized the great importance of this gesture: "And truly, I say to you, wherever the gospel is preached in the whole world, what she has done will be told in memory of her" (Mk 14:9; Mt 26:13). Did he also know that he had practically proclaimed his death sentence when he attested to Mary that she had done this for the day of his burial (Jn 12:7)? The British New Testament scholar Brian J. Capper, whom I have already quoted in chapter 6, believes so and has a plausible explanation for the incident. He says that "Jesus was anointed by Mary as the hoped-for king of Israel and of the world".[9] The anointing of a king was the religious component of the Jewish crowning ceremony. People were certain that the future savior, too, would be a king and therefore called him Meschiach, "the anointed one", in Greek Christos. Mary turned this claim into a fact. She proclaimed to the world that Jesus of Nazareth was indeed the Messiah, the anointed one, whose Evangelion ("good news") would redeem the world. But through her act, which was certainly planned in advance with the approval of her community (comparable to the "spontaneous" crowning of Charlemagne by the

[9] Brian J. Capper, "The New Covenant in Southern Palestine", in The Dead Sea Scrolls as Background to Postbiblical Judaism and Early Christianity: Papers from an International Conference at St. Andrews in 2001, ed. James R. Davila (Leiden and Boston: Brill, 2003), p. 113.

pope during the Christmas Mass of A.D. 800), she provoked both the Sadducee hierarchy and the Roman occupying power. "Mary had sought to make Jesus the Messiah of the poor, as the leader of the highly organised New Covenant network of Judaea",[10] Capper explains. Thereby he automatically became the rival of all those who wanted to maintain the old system at any cost.

On the very next day, on Monday, April 3, A.D. 30, to some extent as a reaction to his anointing, Jesus entered Jerusalem as Messiah-king. We can assume that he and his disciples first subjected themselves to a ritual cleansing in the great Essene *mikveh* of the settlement. The city was full of pilgrims from all parts of the land and the diaspora who had come to the Passover feast as he had, or were presently on the roads and streaming toward the city from all directions—as many as three million, according to the (doubtlessly exaggerated) estimate of Josephus, but definitely as many as 400,000, and thus five times the population of Jerusalem (which, according to recent estimates, was about 80,000).

Those with relatives in the city of the Temple stayed with them in the now overcrowded houses and private properties; the others camped all around the city walls in white tent cities. Jesus had spent the night with his disciples in Bethany. In order to get to Jerusalem that morning, he therefore used the footpath via Bethphage—another Essene colony—and from there the Roman road, which was only 1640 feet away and went around the Mount of Olives to the north. The shorter route past the Dominus Flevit church, which also used to be taken by the traditional Palm Sunday procession until the building of the wall, was likely too steep for the donkey and too narrow for the crowd that followed him. He could have entered Jerusalem through the Sheep Gate by the Pool of Bethesda—appropriate for the Lamb of God. Tradition, however, assures us that he passed through the Golden Gate directly onto the Temple grounds.

Excavations that the Franciscan archaeologist S. Saller conducted here show that Bethphage was continuously settled between the eighth century B.C. and the second century A.D. The discovery of an obviously Christian burial site that was once (like the tomb of Jesus) closed with a rolling stone proved to be absolutely spectacular. The

[10] Ibid., p. 114.

walls were covered all over with Jewish-Christian graffiti, which were examined and interpreted by Father Testa. They refer to salvation, Paradise, the thousand-year kingdom, and the name of Christ and are evidence of an uninterrupted veneration of the site where Jesus of Nazareth first revealed himself publicly as the Messiah.

Apparently, the Son of God placed great value on the staging of this moment. He specifically sent his disciples into the village to fetch a young donkey there (which may have been provided by the local Essene community). On it he rode, in fulfillment of the prophecy of Zechariah (9:9) about the coming King of Peace: "Rejoice greatly, O daughter of Zion! Shout aloud, O daughter of Jerusalem! Behold, your king comes to you; triumphant and victorious is he, humble and riding on a donkey, on a colt the foal of a donkey." Not only his twelve disciples and the other companions who had come with him from Galilee followed him, but apparently also the entire staff of the Essene poor house: "The crowd that had been with him when he called Lazarus out of the tomb and raised him from the dead bore witness", John emphasizes (12:17). Having caught their enthusiasm, the people reacted frantically to the messianic self-staging of the man from Nazareth. Many spread their garments on the road, others tore palm fronds, which have always been a symbol of peace, off the trees and laid them on the path in front of him. "Hosanna to the son of David!" they hailed him, citing Psalm 118, which had always been referred to the coming of the Messiah: "Blessed is he who comes in the name of the Lord!" (Mt 21:9).The Messiah's kingdom of peace had begun; now he entered the city of the Temple to fulfill his true destiny. "The hour has come for the Son of man to be glorified", Jesus declared in his last public speech to a group of Hellenistic Jews, and in his companions' view he seemed to insinuate the imminent triumph: "And I, when I am lifted up from the earth, will draw all men to myself" (Jn 12:23, 32). No one suspected yet that on this Passover he would be the sacrificial lamb.

While his adversaries were alarmed and feared the worst, Jesus eluded the crowd immediately after his arrival in Jerusalem. During the next few days, too, he stayed in Bethany and visited the Temple only in the company of his four most trusted disciples: Peter, James, John, and Andrew (Mk 13:3). On the way back, as evening fell, he spoke with them about the future, prophesied wars and persecutions and eventually his return, and he told them: "And the gospel must first be preached to all nations ... and you will be hated by all for my name's sake. But he who endures to the end will be saved" (Mk 13:10, 13).

When reading the Evangelists' accounts, one is struck by an apparent contradiction. In the Synoptic Gospels, the Passover feast already started on Tuesday evening, as the reference to Sunday being "two days before the feast" already plainly indicates. Accordingly, his disciples asked Jesus "on the first day of Unleavened Bread, when they sacrificed the Passover lamb" (Mk 14:12; compare Mt 26:17 and Lk 22:7), where he wanted to celebrate the feast. This in itself is strange, for the Passover meal, or Seder, as the Jews also call it, usually takes place on the evening before the feast. On the other days of the festival week, they only eat *matzah*, which is the "unleavened bread". It becomes even more confusing when, according to John, on Good Friday the Jews avoid the praetorium of Pilate "so that they might not be defiled, but might eat the Passover" (Jn 18:28), and the Evangelist states the time of Jesus' conviction: "Now it was the day of Preparation of the Passover; it was about the sixth hour" (19:14). In this he is confirmed by Paul, who in A.D. 53, and thus undisputedly at least fifteen years before the Gospel of John, wrote to the Corinthians that "Christ, our Paschal Lamb, has been sacrificed" (1 Cor 5:7). According to this, the festival would have started only on Friday night, not already on Tuesday.

There is, in fact, a very simple explanation for these different and only seemingly contradictory details. Since the discovery of the Dead Sea Scrolls, we know that two different calendars were used in Jerusalem in the time of Jesus. One was a solar calendar, which the Essenes used. According to this calendar, the beginning of each month automatically fell on a Wednesday. The fifteenth of Nisan, the first day of the Feast of Unleavened Bread, was therefore always a Wednesday also and the Seder was always celebrated on Tuesday evening. This prevented the preparation day, when the Passover lambs were slaughtered, from falling on a Sabbath and causing religious complications. Matthew, Mark, and Luke were therefore not wrong, but they exclusively referred to the Essene milieu. The official Jerusalem, i.e., the Temple, followed a lunar calendar, according to which the first of Nisan began with the first new moon of spring, and the fifteenth of Nisan was therefore the first full moon of spring. In A.D. 30, this fell on April 8, a Sabbath. On Friday, the sacrificial lambs were slaughtered and the Seder celebrations were held in the evening. For this reason alone, the disciples' question to Jesus was justified: Master, how should we hold it? When are you planning our Seder?

Jesus, who never wanted to be the Messiah of a sect, decided on a compromise. He celebrated neither the Seder meal of the Essenes nor that of the Pharisees and Sadducees: he went without sacrificing a lamb at all, since he himself would be the sacrificial lamb. Nevertheless, he had a solemn covenantal meal with his disciples. Since this had to occur before the Temple feast, the Essene quarter of Jerusalem was a logical choice. Only here were the rooms and houses already Passover-clean: eager hands had scoured every nook for leftovers of old bread, a ceremony, combined with special prayers, that to this day is the duty of the host. Only here did they still have meat from the lambs slaughtered on Tuesday; only here, in addition to wine, did they have fresh *matzah*, which was not available anywhere else in Jerusalem until Friday. Furthermore, there was another feast day of symbolic importance in the Essene calendar that was worth considering as a date. This was the sixteenth of Nisan, the day on which the *Omer*, the first sheaf of the new grain, was offered in the Temple as a burnt sacrifice. It was therefore a celebration of thanksgiving for the bread (and *Eucharist* means nothing other than "thanksgiving") before the self-sacrifice of Jesus, who, born in the house of bread (Bethlehem), fed Jews and Gentiles with the bread of life and revealed himself in the synagogue of Capernaum as the living bread that came down from heaven. On this Thursday, the sixteenth of Nisan on the Essene calendar, the thirteenth of Nisan in the official Jewish reckoning, for us April 6 of A.D. 30, the Last Supper of Jesus and his disciples was to take place.

Through his contacts with the Essene networks, Jesus could arrange everything. He sent his two most faithful disciples, Peter and John, to Jerusalem to make the last preparations. His instructions were clear: " 'Go into the city, and a man carrying a jar of water will meet you; follow him, and wherever he enters, say to the householder, "The Teacher says, where is my guest room, where I am to eat the Passover with my disciples?" And he will show you a large upper room furnished and ready; there prepare for us' " (Mk 14:13–15). This time the two disciples took the shortest route from Bethany to Jerusalem, the road that is now called Derech Jericho and is blocked off by the wall. It ended by the Water Gate of Jerusalem, which was right next to the well of Siloam. A man carrying water must have indeed caught their attention, since fetching water is and was the women's job in the Orient. The only exception was a celibate community like the Essenes. Also the stairs leading up to the Essene quarter, on which they followed him, are at least partially preserved; their remains are found right next to the church of Sancti Petri in Gallicantu [Saint Peter of the Cock Crow], south of Jerusalem's old city. The path leads straight to Mount Zion, where Christian tradition has always placed the upper room of the Last Supper. In the time of Jesus, the Essene quarter of Jerusalem used to be at that very spot.

At least Flavius Josephus says so in his detailed description of the city of the Temple before its destruction. Herod the Great, whom the sect supported because he disempowered the detested Hasmoneans, had given them an entire district in the city, with its own gate, the so-called Essene Gate. According to the historian, this was at the southwest corner of the city, where the Western Wall met the Southern Wall, i.e., at the foot of Mount Zion. At this spot, at the edge of today's Protestant cemetery, Benedictine Father Bargil Pixner applied the spade in 1977 and got lucky. Not only did he come upon the remains of a city gate from the Herodian period, he was also able to prove that this gate was set into the wall later, since it was obviously necessary for the community to have its own separate access to its quarter.

Only forty-four yards northwest of the gate and outside the ancient city wall, Father Pixner dug up the remains of two mikvehs, both of which had a separate entrance and exit. A cistern, a supply pipe, and a sewer provided "living", i.e., flowing, water. Its location met the demands of the Torah (Dt 23:11ff.) and the Essene Temple Scroll to build ritual baths "outside the camp" (and the Essenes defined their settlements as such). The two-part main mikveh of Qumran was also located outside the actual monastery. A little farther northeast, just as the Temple Scroll prescribed, Pixner located the remains of what Josephus labeled Bethso, the Essene latrines, which likewise served to maintain the ritual cleanliness of the monastery quarter. In 1998, the Israeli archaeologist Boaz Zissu discovered a cluster of tombs in the immediate vicinity, all of which faced north, just like the tombs of Qumran; the Essenes imagined Paradise in that direction. Only 219 yards north of the gate is the room of the Last Supper, which Pope Benedict XVI visited on May 12, 2009. It is the place "where Jesus revealed in the offering of his own body and blood, the new depths of the covenant of love established between God and his people", as the pope worded it in his address there. Here was the first church of Christendom.

We set out again to visit the place of Jesus' Passover celebration. Like no other holy site of Christendom, it shows how deeply Jesus is rooted in Judaism. For the gothic room on the first floor, the *Coenaculum*, that the Crusaders built and where Benedict XVI met the ordinaries of the Holy Land is located over a Jewish synagogue, and that is a good thing. Young Jews with *kippah* and *peot*, sparkling clean white shirts and black pants, come toward us, their books under their arms. We enter, I grab a *kippah* and put it on; Yuliya goes to the left side, which is reserved for the women. Inside the room is a massive stone sarcophagus, covered with an embroidered black cloth, on which there are twenty-two silver Torah-crowns as symbols of the kings of Israel. The Jews who pray here believe that King David, the ancestor of Jesus, is buried in the tomb.

The monumental tomb is, in fact, a work of the Crusaders, and the room did not come into Jewish possession until 1948. But the building in which it is located is much older. I look at its stones in the interior courtyard, and I am certain that they are from the time of Herod. And what is more, they are stones from the destroyed Temple. Archaeologists believe that they were used for a new building immediately after the destruction of Jerusalem, at a time, therefore, when the Jews of the city had just been carried to all corners of the world. When the Israeli archaeologist Jay Pinkerfield examined the Tomb of David in 1951, he discovered an apse, which he at first mistook for a Torah niche, typical of a synagogue. But then he realized that something about it was not right. A Torah-niche must always face the Temple, in this case east. In fact, though, it points north, exactly toward the Christian Church of the Sepulchre. Christian graffiti soon confirmed the suspicion: it must have been a Jewish-Christian synagogue.

The Church historian Eusebius of Caesarea actually reports that the early Christian community returned to Jerusalem in A.D. 73, only

THE KING OF THE JEWS

three years after the catastrophe, under the leadership of their bishop Symeon. There they settled on Mount Zion and built a synagogue-church that was henceforth known as the Church of the Apostles. As Bishop Epiphanius of Salamis learned in Jerusalem in the fourth century, it stood on top of the ruins of the very guesthouse where the Last Supper once took place and "where the disciples went to the upper room on their return from the Mount of Olives after the Ascension of the Redeemer",[11] which then became the seat of the proto-community. This "small church of God" remained undisturbed even when Emperor Hadrian founded the new city of Aelia on the ruins of Jerusalem in A.D. 135. Mount Zion was, as it still is today, outside its walls and became a kind of Christian ghetto with its own walls.

Here, therefore, in the guesthouse of the Essene quarter, according to the Essene calendar, Jesus celebrated the Last Supper. His extremely liberal practice must at first have alienated many conservative follow-ers of the sect, but they knew that everything would be different when the Messiah came and proclaimed a New Covenant with God. After all, the strict rules for ritual cleansing were only in preparation for the coming Kingdom of God, which perhaps had already begun now and which was governed no longer by law and rules but by mercy and forgiveness. As a descendant of David, Jesus was at least a possible candidate for them, and his deeds spoke a clear language: "Go and tell John what you hear and see: the blind receive their sight and the lame walk, lepers are cleansed and the deaf hear, and the dead are raised up, and the poor have good news preached to them", Jesus replied to the Baptist's question of whether he was the Messiah; "Blessed is he who takes no offense at me" (Mt 11:4–6). A fragment of the Essene scriptures found in the fourth cave of Qumran matches his statement almost verbatim. This scripture, entitled *Salvation and Resurrection* and inventoried as 4Q521, foretells about the Messiah: "He will heal the wounded, and revive the dead and bring good news to the poor."[12] He thus made it clear to the Essenes that he was

[11] Epiphanius of Salamis, *De mensuris et ponderibus*, 14 (PG 43:261), quoted in Jerome Murphy O'Connor, O.P., "The Background of Acts 2:44–45", in *Scripture and Other Artifacts: Essays on the Bible and Archaeology in Honor of Philip J. King*, ed. Philip J. King et al. (Louisville, Ky.: Westminster John Knox Press, 1994), p. 298.

[12] James VanderKam, *The Dead Sea Scrolls Today*, rev. ed. (Grand Rapids, Mich.: Eerdman's, 2010), p. 221.

the "Messiah from the house of David" whom they were expecting. He identified John the Baptist as his priestly counterpart and allowed himself to be baptized, i.e., ritually cleansed, by him. Like the Essenes, he, too, retreated into the desert for forty days before he began his public ministry. Then he chose for himself twelve apostles, corresponding to the twelve tribes of Israel, and symbolically sent seventy disciples to the (according to Jewish tradition) seventy nations of the world, in order to proclaim the Gospel of the dawning Kingdom of God to them as well. Finally, following the route of Joshua, he went from Bethany across the Jordan to Jerusalem, via Jericho, and thereby symbolically completed the "new conquest". In the second Essene Bethany, outside the gates of the city, he was anointed the "King of the poor", before he, as Zechariah had prophesied, entered Jerusalem on the back of a donkey. All this happened around Passover, in which the Jews commemorated their liberation from bondage in Egypt. This was an open provocation of those in power, combined with harsh criticism of the Sadducee Temple hierarchy, which must have also met with the approval of the Essenes. For this reason alone, it is certain that he was received by them with open arms.

The fact that the Last Supper took place in the Essenes' guesthouse explains why only the twelve disciples participated in it, but not the women who otherwise constantly accompanied Jesus. According to the rules of the order, women were not allowed to participate in a communal meal. These rules also explain the disciples' dispute about "which of them was to be regarded as the greatest" (Lk 22:24), for they state a specific order at the table: "There shall not lack a Priest among them. And they shall all sit before him according to their rank", it says in the *Community Rule*, one of the Qumran scrolls. Regarding the course of the meal, it goes on to say: "When the table has been prepared for eating, and the new wine for drinking, the Priest shall be the first to stretch out his hand to bless the first fruits of the bread and new wine".[13] The Messiah would celebrate his covenantal meal in the same manner.

The usual ritual cleansing had naturally preceded the entry into the Essene quarter, perhaps even in the Essene *mikveh* that Bargil Pixner excavated. This is probably the kind of ritual bath to which Jesus

---

[13] Ibid., 112.

refers when, before washing his disciples' feet, he explains: "He who has bathed does not need to wash, except for his feet" (Jn 13:10).

The "seating arrangement" of the apostles is also mentioned in the Gospels, at least in its outlines. The custom was not a long table, as Christian art from the Middle Ages and the Renaissance suggests (including the famous *Last Supper* by Leonardo da Vinci), but rather the space-saving *triclinium*, the arrangement of three tables in the form of a horseshoe. The apostles reclined at them on cushions, each leaning on his left arm. Jesus presided and took the "first seat" at the left end of the horseshoe. John and Peter were allowed to sit next to him—on the two seats of honor. With the Essenes, too, the "Covenant of Mercy" (*jahad*) was led by a "central council" consisting of "twelve laymen and three priests". Lack of knowledge about ancient table manners led later on to several rather strange attempts in art to process the little information from the Gospels. In the Gospel of John, for instance, it says that "one of his disciples, whom Jesus loved, was lying close to the breast of Jesus" (Jn 13:23), which painters depicted as if he, like a little boy, had put his head on his master's lap, who, of course, quite anachronistically sat on a chair. In reality, everyone at the table was reclining at his neighbor's side, turning his back to him, and had to first lean back and turn his head in order to tell him something. This was especially true when it was something confidential that not everyone in the room was supposed to catch.

In this case, it was something very confidential, namely, the treason of Judas. The son of Simon Iscariot (Jn 13:26), perhaps because the anointing of Jesus in Bethany was too much for him, perhaps because he wanted to put Jesus to the test, had collaborated with the Temple hierarchy. Since the Temple police did not dare to arrest the man from Nazareth during his public appearances and thereby risk an uprising (see Mk 14:2), Judas' offer to guide them to his night's lodging was more than welcome. Probably because of the great congestion during the feast days, Jesus had left Bethany in the meantime and was camping in a cave, which belonged to a private olive tree plantation and was otherwise used for a *Gat-Schemanim* or "olive press". Jesus had seen through the traitor's plan, but it suited him just fine. Consequently, he announced to his disciples that he was about to be handed over, but he also prompted Judas: "What you are going to do, do quickly" (Jn 13:27). In any event, this is reported by John, who was closest to Jesus at this moment.

There was a reason why the Evangelist in fact took the prominent position at Jesus' side and why he called himself the disciple "whom Jesus loved". His place was traditionally that of the son. But Jesus had no biological children, no matter how often the authors of bad novels claim the contrary. John, the youngest of the disciples, therefore likewise became his master pupil and stepson. Eusebius, Irenaeus, Clement, and other early Christian authors confirm that he died a natural death in Ephesus, during the rule of Emperor Trajan, shortly after A.D. 100. Even though all sources emphasize his old age—the end of John's Gospel, which was added later, spreads the rumor that "this disciple was not to die" (Jn 21:23)—it is quite unlikely that he lived beyond ninety. This would mean that he was maybe sixteen years old when he met Jesus at the Jordan and eighteen at the Last Supper; he was, in a sense, the Benjamin among the other apostles, who were all grown men. So it happened that Jesus, while still on the Cross, entrusted his mother to him ("Behold, your mother!", 19:27), even though John's biological mother, Salome, was still alive and had even accompanied them to Jerusalem. He did, therefore, hold a privileged position, even though Jesus entrusted the governance of the Church to the older and more assertive Peter.

After the betrayer had left, Jesus instituted the most important sacrament of his Church, the Eucharist, the meal of the New Covenant. He symbolically anticipated the sacrifice of his flesh and the shedding of his blood on Good Friday. He had now become the bread of life. In this bread, he would always be present among his people, until the end of time.

Since, however, the Last Supper was likewise a Jewish Passover meal, Jesus also said the traditional "blessing" (Mk 14:22), the *Pesach-Haggadah*, and finished the celebration with the song of praise (Mk 14:26), the *Great Hallel*, during which Psalms 113 through 118 as well as 136 are sung. Only after that did the twelve men go out into the cool night. They left Jerusalem through the Essene Gate and descended into the inhospitable Hinnom Valley, for the Jews the earthly counterpart to hell. In early Biblical times, the pagan Canaanites had sacrificed children here to their idols, "burned their sons and their daughters in the fire", as it says in Jeremiah [7:31]. Below the Water Gate, it ran into the valley of the Kidron stream, which runs only in winter, as John remarks correctly (18:1, literally translated "winter-flowing stream"). Among the Jews the valley was also known as Tal Josaphat, literally "God judges", because this is where the prophet Joel situates the judgment of the world. It stretches from the Temple to the Mount of Olives, whose slope to this day is covered with countless Jewish tombs, whose dead await the coming of the Messiah. By the edge of this path lie three priestly graves, hewn from the stone, from Hasmonean and Herodian times. On the night when Jesus was betrayed, their whitish limestone shone very eerily in the pale light of the full moon. Dogs were barking in the distance. Something ominous was in the air, an anticipation of what was to come. With his descent into the "valley of judgment", Jesus himself had advanced into the deepest darkness of history.

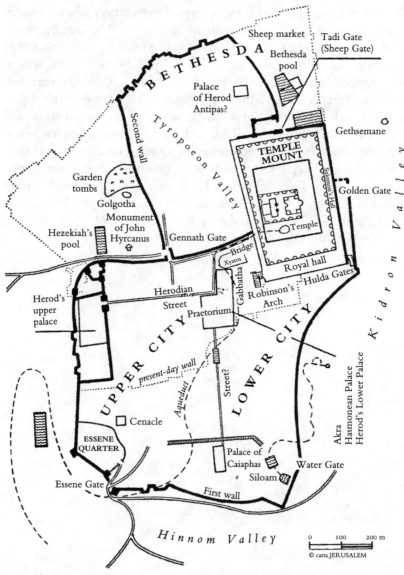

Map of Jerusalem at the Time of Jesus

XII

Ecce Homo, Ecce Deus

Sites of Christ's Death and Resurrection

Soldiers are posted everywhere, hermetically sealing off all access to the Valley of Josaphat. It was recommended that visitors arrive at the checkpoint at least three hours before starting time, but even that was no guarantee. For no one who does not have a personal invitation may pass it. And, of course, only after he is once again thoroughly searched for weapons and explosives. Never before during his whole pontificate was a Mass celebrated by Pope Benedict XVI under such strict security measures as on this May 12, 2009, in the valley between the Temple Mount and the Mount of Olives.

Although the prophet Joel announced in his apocalyptic vision that at the end of all days God would assemble the nations of the earth here to judge them, he obviously had no idea of the tricks of the modern age. More than six thousand tickets have been issued, two-thirds of them to Palestinian Catholics, the rest to the pilgrim groups from all over the world who have come specifically for the papal visit to Israel. Yet only two thousand of the faithful manage to brave the roadblocks and to find their way into the Biblical valley. For most of the Christian Palestinians, in contrast, the pilgrimage to see the pope ends at the passageways through the security wall, which have been barred by Israel as a precaution, officially out of fear of attacks.

We get through, not due to our press credentials (which, as we soon notice, would not have helped us much), but rather because our colleague Paul Badde has quickly procured additional invitations for us. Together with Joan Lewis, the Rome correspondent of the Catholic television network EWTN, we three take our places on the press platform to the left of the papal altar; our colleagues plainly gave up prematurely. The choir, which luckily arrived in full force, is accommodated on a platform farther on. After the obligatory entrance of the bagpipers of the Latin Patriarchate—Palestinians in scouts' uniforms, a relic from the time of the British occupation—and the arrival of Benedict XVI, we experience the most intensive, most concentrated, and thus most solemn papal Mass of this not entirely unproblematic trip to Israel.

This is due not only to the tension, which can still be felt during the Mass, and to the rather small number of faithful, but also to the *genius loci* [spirit of the place] of this site, which is significant in salvation history. On the one side looms the steep Temple Mount, which today is firmly in the hands of the Muslims; on the other side beckons the Garden of Gethsemane, the place of Christ's agony and of his betrayal by Judas Iscariot. Finally, in its form the papal altar is reminiscent of the Church of All Nations, and on it is a picture, painted in the style of old frescoes, of Saint Thomas touching the wounds of the Risen Lord.

The original basilica, consecrated in 1924, whose golden mosaics gleam in the light of the sun setting over Jerusalem, marks the darkest hour in Jesus' life. It rises over the rock on which the Son of God endured his agony.

The most precise information about this place is again in the Gospel of John. Whereas in Luke, Jesus just goes "to the Mount of Olives" (Lk 22:39), and Matthew (26:36) and Mark (14:32) at least mention "a place called Gethsemane", John reveals to us that it was "a garden" located "across the Kidron valley" (Jn 18:1). The Greek word *kepon* that John uses generally stands for a plantation. Gethsemane, as we said, was not a proper name but, rather, the Hebrew word for the oil press that belonged to these grounds. Such oil presses were often situated in caves (an example was found in Ras Abu-Ma'aruf near Tel el-Ful in Israel), and since we should not assume that Jesus and his disciples intended to sleep under the open sky in those cold April nights, we can take it that such a press was meant.

He led the Eleven to this spot. He summoned only Peter, James, and John to come with him when he suddenly began to tremble. "My soul is very sorrowful, even to death; remain here, and watch", he asked the three (Mt 26:38). Then he went "about a stone's throw" farther (Lk 22:41) to pray alone on the aforesaid rock. The place had great symbolic power: the counterpart to the rock over which the Holy of Holies of the Temple (and today the Dome of the Rock) looms, which on that night glowed mysteriously in the light of the sacrificial fire. It is only 490 yards distant, so that Jesus could be close to his Father's house one last time, as he prayed in profound fear and distress: "Abba, Father, all things are possible to you; remove this chalice from me; yet not what I will, but what you will" (Mk 14:36). "Abba", this childlike, familiar way of addressing the Father, comparable to our "Dad" or "Daddy", reveals everything about Jesus' new way of looking at God. God was no longer the stern judge of the Old Testament but, rather, was the loving, forgiving father from the parable of the Prodigal Son, which is so central to his teaching. From now on the Father's love for mankind was to define human coexistence, too, so that love of God becomes love of neighbor, and the rule "as you do to me, so I do to you" becomes "as God does to me, so I do to you", as the [late] Archbishop of Cologne Joachim Cardinal Meisner recently put it so strikingly. Now, though, this love of God for mankind demanded Jesus' self-sacrifice, which was anticipated in this hour of agony. Only Luke, the physician, mentions a medical detail: "And being in an agony he prayed more earnestly; and his sweat became like great drops of blood falling down upon the ground" (Lk 22:44). What was long considered a figurative exaggeration by the Evangelist is in fact a biological phenomenon that is termed *hematohidrosis*, which has been observed in victims of rape or men sentenced to death. The great internal and external tension causes the skin capillaries to burst, and the escaping blood, mixed with the sweat of anxiety, flows out through the pores.

The three who were accompanying him were not yet aware of the significance of this night. Drowsy from the wine of the Paschal meal, they fell asleep. Twice Jesus woke them, but in vain. "The spirit indeed is willing, but the flesh is weak" (Mk 14:38). When he woke them a third time, he heard footsteps. By torchlight, which was reflected in the shiny, polished metal of their helmets, the unit of the Temple guard approached, guided by the betrayer Judas Iscariot, in order to arrest him.

The place of this occurrence must have been held in great esteem by the early Christians. As early as 330, Eusebius mentions the "site of the Agony", and around 390 Jerome adds: "Now a church has been built over it." Egeria, who visited this church in 383, speaks about an *ecclesia elegans*, a "splendid church", that was built on the spot "where the Lord prayed". The church building was probably a gift of the Emperor Theodosius. When the Franciscans purchased the tract, they came upon its remains; apparently it had been destroyed in 614 during the attack of the Persians. Over these ruins the Church of All Nations was built.

Right next to it today there is a garden tended by the Franciscans with ancient olive trees that is revered as Gethsemane. Yet the authentic cave in which oil was pressed is located 109 yards to the north of the Church of All Nations, on the other side of the path that leads up the Mount of Olives. We climb the steps that lead to the church over the Virgin Mary's tomb, a shrine staffed by the Greek Orthodox Church. To the right of it, in an inconspicuous corner, a door leads to the cave, which since 1392 has belonged to the Franciscans. Via a series of steps we reach the stone vault, eleven by twenty-one yards, the ceiling of which is painted with stars. Here the Franciscan archaeologists found in 1955 the remains of an ancient oil press hewn in the rock, which gave the grotto its name. While it is to be assumed that it already served Christians as a shrine in the earliest times, the veneration of the place since the fourth century can be proved archaeologically, too. At that point in time, it was transformed into a place of worship and acquired a new entrance as well as a series of stone benches. Egeria describes in 383 how this cave then had its fixed place in the liturgy that was celebrated in the night from Holy Thursday to Good Friday.

Jesus was not apprehended without resistance. One of the disciples drew a sword and cut off one ear of the high priest's servant. But Jesus ordered him to put the weapon back in its sheath and healed the injured man. While all four Gospels describe the scene, only John gives the names. The disciple was Peter, and the servant's name was Malchus. His name indicates a Nabataean origin. Of course Peter was not trying to fight against the superior might of the Temple guards; the disciples were too poorly armed for that. They owned only two (Lk 22:38) handy short swords—Luke uses the technical term *machaira*—which could be carried conveniently on a belt and if necessary could serve as protection against wild animals and highway robbers. Nevertheless, what he had in mind was a symbolic act directed against the high priest himself. Flavius Josephus reports that the Hasmonean Antigonus, too, in 40 B.C., had the ears of his archrival Hyrcanus II cut off while the latter was in custody in order to prevent him from being appointed high priest again, because "he was maimed, while the law required that this dignity should belong to none but such as had all their members entire."[1] In this connection, he cited an instruction in the Book of Leviticus (21:16–21). It is striking that John alone names as the "perpetrator" Peter, whose volatile temperament we encounter often in the Gospels. This is probably due to the fact that he was writing after Peter's death (64 or 67), while the Synoptic Gospels appeared during his lifetime and did not want to compromise him. Only Mark mentions a young man who, despite the cold, tried to follow Jesus "with nothing but a linen cloth about his body" (Mk 14:51) but was prevented from doing so by the Temple guard and fled naked. Some exegetes think that this was Mark himself, about whom we know at least that he was from a well-to-do family in Jerusalem. Maybe the olive orchard belonged to his parents; maybe he had slept in the cave in order to make sure that it was not seized by other pilgrims.

The men of the Temple guard brought Jesus by the most direct route to the palace of the high priest. To do that, they crossed the Kidron Valley, in which 1,979 years later the papal Mass of Benedict XVI would be celebrated, passed by the old sepulchers from the time of the Hasmoneans and of Herod, until they came to the Water Gate, through which they entered the city. Beyond the Pool of Siloam they took the stairs up to Mount Zion. Halfway to the top, they veered off to the left, at about the height of the present-day church Sancti Petri in Gallicantu (Saint Peter of the Cock Crow). It is one of the places about which ancient pilgrimage tradition and archaeological findings agree.

As early as 333, the pilgrim from Bordeaux described how from the Pool of Siloam "you go up Zion and there is where the house of Caiaphas the hight priest was."[2] Of course the palace had lain in ruins since its destruction in the year 70, and no Christian thought

---

[1] Flavius Josephus, *Jewish Antiquities*, bk. 14, chap. 13, no. 10, in *The New Complete Works of Josephus*, trans. William Whiston (Grand Rapids, Mich.: Kregel, 1999), p. 482.

[2] *The Bordeaux Pilgrim (c. 333 C.E.)*, trans. Andrew S. Jacobs, at http://andrewjacobs.org /translations/bordeaux.html.

yet about building a church here. Fifteen years later, Bishop Cyril of Jerusalem formulated as follows the prevailing opinion of the time: "The house of Caiaphas will arraign thee, shewing by its present desolation the power of Him who was erewhile judged there."[3] The ruin was a memorial and was to remain so for another century. Only in the mid-fifth century did the idea occur to the Empress Eudocia (400–460) to commemorate with a church building the fact that a prophecy of Jesus was fulfilled here, too. He had told Peter to his face that the disciple would deny him three times "before the cock crows twice" (Mk 14:30; Mt 26:34; Lk 22:34; Jn 13:38); a shocking statement that each of the Evangelists considered worth recording. From then on, the new basilica became a popular pilgrimage destination. Around the year 530, Theodosius reported on the "House of Caiaphas which is now the Church of Saint Peter",[4] which was visited then by countless pilgrims. Only after its destruction in 614 did the site sink into oblivion. Now guides showed the pilgrims only a cave "to which Peter went and wept bitterly", while the house of Caiaphas was said to be located on Mount Zion, on a tract that belongs today to the Armenian Church.

In 1888, the French Assumptionist Fathers purchased the land and began archaeological excavations. Not only did they unearth the twenty-two-by-fifteen-yard ruin of the Byzantine church together with its mosaics; they also stumbled on the remains of buildings from Jesus' time. They belonged to a large, palace-like residence that even had its own "domestic wing", including a kitchen, a silo, and a grain mill. Directly under the church, there were caves that, as graffiti prove, were plainly held in great esteem in the Byzantine period. A very deep pit was interpreted as "Jesus' prison", a series of subterranean chambers, likewise hewn in the rock floor, as rooms for the guards. Along their walls, rings were set, which may have served to tie the prisoners during a hearing or a scourging.

In fact, the chambers might have been prison cells. But what was originally taken for the deep dungeon of Jesus and later for Peter's

---

[3] Cyril of Jerusalem, *Catechetical Lectures* XIII.38, in *Nicene and Post-Nicene Fathers*, second series, ed. Philip Schaff and Henry Wace, vol. 7 (1894; Peabody, Mass.: Hendrickson, 1995), p. 92.

[4] Theodosius, *The Topography of the Holy Land*, in John Wilkinson, *Jerusalem Pilgrims before the Crusades* (Jerusalem: Ariel, 1977), p. 66.

cave is something quite different. The two-part entrance and the steps leading down to it indicate that it was a *mikveh* that was fed from a deep cistern. In fact, it is the largest and deepest *mikveh* that has been discovered in all of Israel in an ancient private house. Whereas the twofold division into entrance and exit was usually only suggested, here there were two separate, adjacent entrances. Here someone plainly wanted to demonstrate that in matters of the law he was more than exact. This *mikveh* was in fact worthy of the high priest Caiaphas. The final doubt as to the identity of the palace's owner, however, was removed by a Hebrew inscription that was discovered on the fragment of a lintel. It consisted of only one word: *corban* (sacrifice). That was the official term for Temple donations (see Mk 7:11).

Another detail, too, indicated that the house of Caiaphas stood here. The palace to which the underground rooms belonged was at an absolutely picturesque location on the southern slope of the city. Over its ruins stands today a modern church that was built by the Assumptionists in the years 1924–1931. Not until 1994–1997 was a thorough renovation undertaken thanks to donations from the United States and funding that was made available by the Archdioceses of Cologne and Munich, but also by the German Association of the Holy Land [DVHL].

Whenever I visit this church, I climb up to the platform next to it and enjoy the view across the Hinnom Valley to the Akeldama (field of blood), the location of Annas' tomb, and the Peace Forest in which the family tomb of Caiaphas was discovered. In the distance, one can discern Bethlehem, and in clear weather the knoll of the Herodium looms into the sky at the horizon. For several years now, one can see with particular clarity from here how the ugly Israeli security wall divides the Biblical landscape in two. This location with its wide exposure explains one detail that some exegetes have rejected as a pious invention and a cultural anachronism. And yet it gave to the modern church, too, its name *in Gallicantu*, "of the Cock Crow". No roosters were to be found in all of Jerusalem. The Jewish Mishnah had forbidden keeping chickens in the city of the Temple, because poultry scratched "unclean" worms out of the earth. Of course that did not apply to the villages and farms on the other side of the Hinnom Valley. When cocks crowed there, they could still be heard clearly in the courtyard of Caiaphas' palace on account of its location on the slope. That made it almost the only place in all Jerusalem where Peter could in fact betray his Lord three times "before the cock crows twice" (Mk 14:30).

The Gospels contradict each other in their accounts of what exactly happened in the night from April 6 to 7 of the year 30. The Synoptics right away have "the chief priests, with the elders and scribes, and the whole council" (Mk 15:1) sitting in judgment on Jesus in the house of Caiaphas and formally sentencing him to death. John, in contrast, depicts merely a preliminary hearing by Annas and a hearing by Caiaphas and does not tell us who else participated in the latter. The decisive meeting of the Sanhedrin at which the decision was made to kill Jesus took place according to him in the days between the raising of Lazarus and the anointing in Bethany.

What is certain is that a formal trial with a legally valid sentence by the High Council cannot have taken place in the night after the arrest of Jesus; it would have contradicted Jewish Law and Jewish customs. It should have taken place, not in the house of the high priest, but, rather, in the Hall of the Hewn Stone or, again, in a secluded area of the Royal Portico, both inside the Temple Precinct. At night, however, this was accessible to only a few Levites who were in service; besides, nocturnal court sessions were considered immoral. Most importantly, though, judgments on capital crimes were never handed down on the day of the hearing, but always on the following day. "Therefore one does not judge on Sabbath eve or holiday eve", the *Treatise on the Sanhedrin* in the Mishnah prescribed.[5] This Friday, which according to the Jewish reckoning of time had already begun at dusk of the preceding day, was both: the day before the Sabbath of the solemn Feast of Passover.

The other details, too, that the Synoptics depict are anything but conclusive. According to Jewish Law (Deut 17:6), at least two identical testimonies of witnesses are necessary in order to furnish a proof that would justify a sentence. Yet Mark emphasizes: "And some stood up and bore false witness against him, ... yet not even so did their testimony agree" (Mk 14:57, 59). Therefore, after the taking of evidence turned out to be ineffectual, Caiaphas went over

---

[5] *Tractates Sanhedrin, Makkot, and Horaiot*, ed. Heinrich Guggenheimner, Complete Jerusalem Talmud, vol. 12 (Berlin and New York: Walter de Gruyter, 2010), p. 156.

to the hearing. Only when Jesus revealed himself as the Messiah and prophesied: "And you will see the Son of man sitting at the right hand of Power, and coming with the clouds of heaven" (Mk 14:62) did the high priest stand up in a dramatic gesture of condemnation, tear his garment, declare Jesus guilty of blasphemy, and condemn him to death. The other members of the council, too, spat at him, struck him, and mocked him. But without any further explanation, they then nevertheless refrained from carrying out the sentence and preferred to transfer the man they had just condemned to another authority: the Roman tribunal of the governor.

Luke, who was plainly aware of the discrepancies, shifts the whole proceeding at least to the morning hours and has it end without a judgment. Moreover, he spares the lords of the council; in his account, only the guards ridicule Jesus. That is at least more plausible, but it no longer fits into a realistic chronology, which allows exactly six hours for the Sanhedrin trial, the referral to Pilate, his first hearing, the presentation at Herod's palace, a second proceeding, and the sentence by the governor, scourging, the way of the Cross and the crucifixion. Hence the Jewish historian and Jesus scholar Geza Vermes came to the conclusion that the only credible depiction of the events of that night is to be found in the Fourth Gospel, and John's account "goes back to a more reliable tradition.... His chronology makes sense; that of the Synoptics does not."[6]

Annas and Caiaphas were cunning enough to allow no trial before the Sanhedrin but to hand the case over to Pilate instead. When they were discussing the topic a full week before in council, it had become evident that Jesus also had followers right there in the ranks of the Pharisees—two of them, Nicodemus and Joseph of Arimathea, are even known to us by name. Part of the Essene community seemed to support him, too. After all, he was in fact descended from the house of David, and therefore his claim to be the Messiah was at least dynastically and genealogically legitimate, while their high priesthood was actually illegitimate and therefore could be contested (neither Annas nor Caiaphas was descended from the house of Aaron; they had simply purchased their office). Moreover, his entrance into Jerusalem had shown how beloved he was among the simple folk. Now it was

---

[6] Geza Vermes, *Die Passion* (Darmstadt, 2006), p. 133.

necessary to arrest him by night stealthily in order to avoid an uprising among the pilgrims for the feast day. His critique of the Temple
lobby was not only very widely known; it was also shared by many
believing Jews. No, a condemnation of Jesus by the Sanhedrin was
much too risky. It could have led to disturbances among the people, the weakening of the Sadducean dynastic power, and necessarily
an intervention by the Romans. Annas' own painful experience had
shown how quickly the occupiers were capable of replacing a high
priest if they got the impression that he no longer had the people
under his control.

On the other hand, Jesus' public appearances were becoming more
and more provocative, and they could no longer just leave him alone,
either. In the cleansing of the Temple, he had already shown what
he thought of them. After his entrance into Jerusalem, they could
count on him using the Feast of Passover to gain the people's
endorsement and to proclaim his messianic program. Although it was
unclear to them what he really wanted, one way or another it would
collide with their interests. Hence, there was only one solution. "It
is expedient for you that one man should die for the people, and that
the whole nation should not perish", Caiaphas had declared at the
meeting of the Sanhedrin (Jn 11:50). They had to get the Nazarene
out of the way in the quickest, most efficient way possible—and shift
the responsibility for it onto the Romans. His claim to be the Messiah, which he clearly reasserted in speaking to Annas and Caiaphas,
provided the suitable excuse for doing so.

"Then they led Jesus from the house of Caiaphas to the praetorium. It was early", John's account continues (18:28). The *praetorium*
referred to the governor's official residence. In order to demonstrate
who was now in power, the former royal palace was used regularly for
this purpose. Pilate therefore resided in the opulent palace of Herod
on the western edge of the upper city of Jerusalem, located in what
is today the Armenian Quarter between the citadel and Mount Zion.
Both Flavius Josephus and Philo of Alexandria refer to this palace as
"the governor's house". Right beside it, on the tract of the present-
day citadel, surrounded by three mighty towers, there was a fortress
in which a cohort of Roman legionaries was quartered when the
governor transferred his official residence to Jerusalem for the Jewish feast days. Another cohort of soldiers was permanently stationed

in the Antonia Fortress, which loomed to the north of the Temple area. This strong military presence allowed the governor to intervene quickly and efficiently if troubles arose. The danger of unrest during a Temple feast was never so great as during the Passover, when the Jews commemorated their liberation from slavery in Egypt.

Josephus depicts the magnificent palace for us in Technicolor, but so far only the gate of it has been discovered. It is found immediately in front of the medieval city wall, precisely 361 yards south of the Jaffa Gate. The Israeli archaeologist Magen Broshi unearthed its ruins in the 1970s. Yet it first became well known through his colleague Shimon Gibson, who maintains that this gate is not only the Essene Gate mentioned by Josephus, but also the place where Jesus was sentenced. Unfortunately, Gibson neglects to corroborate either one of his hypotheses conclusively. It cannot have been the Essene Gate, because it does not correspond to Josephus' specifications. The western and the southern walls did not meet here, nor was it a city gate; it led (and Gibson admits this) solely and exclusively into the palace. The Romans sat in judgment on public squares, but not outside the city walls. John names the place where Jesus was sentenced in Greek *lithostrōtos* (stone pavement) and in Aramaic *gabbatha* (height, eminence), in other words, a paved square on high ground, which does not necessarily fit a gate with a staircase flanked by walls leading up to it. Anyway, it was too narrow and secluded to serve as the scene of a trial, and therefore Gibson's suggestion can be quickly filed away again.

Yet the *lithostrōtos* that is shown to pilgrims in the Monastery of the Flagellation on the Via Dolorosa [Way of the Cross] cannot have been the site of Jesus' trial, either. This stone pavement is located to the east of the rock on which the Antonia Fortress once stood, the barracks of the Roman cohort in Jerusalem. There is not the slightest indication that the governor ever resided there, and the tradition claiming that the Via Dolorosa started there is documented only since the thirteenth century, at the end of the Crusader era. Moreover, it is located on a vault that extends over the Struthion Pool. This deep, stone basin, which is still impressive today, not only served as a water reservoir for the Temple; it was also supposed to protect the Antonia Fortress like a moat. Thus Josephus describes how the Roman general Titus in the year 70 had to bridge it first with a causeway in order to be able to storm the Antonia. At that point in time, therefore, it was still outdoors. Not until 135 did Hadrian build on the ruins of the fortress his North Forum, the entrance to which was the Ecce Homo Arch of the Via Dolorosa. In the process, the pool was covered over with the paved vault. It is therefore fully a century too young to be the *lithostrōtos* of John's Gospel. Today's Via Dolorosa is indeed a moving site of religious devotion; nevertheless, it was not the historical way on which Jesus carried his Cross.

Instead, we find important indications for determining the site of Gabbatha in the writings of Josephus when he depicts the disturbances resulting from the decision to finance an aqueduct with funds from the Temple treasury. According to his account, Pilate's tribunal— Josephus uses the same word as the Evangelists: *bema*—stood on a public square on which the demonstrators could be "encompassed" by his soldiers: When "the rebellious exclaimed against Florus, which was the signal given for falling upon them", they started to thrash the infuriated Jews.[7] As they fled, obviously through the narrow streets of Jerusalem, some were trampled to death by their compatriots. In another passage of the Jewish historian's work, we find a scene that recalls the trial of Jesus, except that it played out during the term of a later governor: "Now at this time Florus took up his quarters at the palace; and on the next day he had his tribunal set before it, and sat upon it, when the high priests, and the men of power, and those of the greatest eminence in the city, came all before that tribunal...." A few lines later we read that the Roman had Jews "first chastised with stripes, and then crucified".[8]

Plainly, therefore, in front of Herod's palace in the upper city of Jerusalem there was a square large enough to accommodate a crowd of people, on which formerly the king and now the governor sat in judgment. Here, on an elevated spot, high enough to be seen from every corner, there was a stage (probably covered with a roof) on which the tribunal, the *bema*, stood. Since no excavations of large areas have taken place in the Armenian Quarter of Jerusalem, the exact location of it cannot be determined at this time.

---

[7] Flavius Josephus, *The Jewish War*, bk. 2, chap. 15, no. 5, in *New Complete Works of Josephus*, p. 152.

[8] Ibid., chap. 14, nos. 8–9, p. 750.

There is of course another possibility. Even though it is certain that the governors resided in Herod's palace, we cannot eliminate the hypothesis that they pursued their official business at another location. One suitable for this purpose would be the old royal palace of the Hasmoneans, in which Herod, too, resided during his early years in office. In the writings of Josephus we learn that it was situated on the largest public square in Jerusalem, the Xystos. A "bridge joined the Temple to" it,[9] the ruins of which we know today as Wilson's Arch. We can conclude from this, and from the fact that it was located at the edge of "the upper city"[10] and below the Temple, that it corresponded approximately to the present-day square in front of the Wailing Wall. In fact here, directly at the foot of the rock, archaeologists came upon the remains of a paved square (a photo that I took in May 2009 is found among the illustrations). Since the excavations are ongoing, their findings have unfortunately not been published; in any case, we can await the results with suspense. The palace itself already belonged to the upper city. From one of its towers, according to Josephus, King Agrippa II could observe exactly what was going on in the Temple. If our suspicion about its location is correct, it was connected with the Xystos via a remarkable flight of steps, and that is exactly how it is depicted in the famous model of ancient Jerusalem produced by archaeologists in painstaking miniature and displayed in the Israel Museum opposite the Knesset. Halfway up these steps, there could have been a platform, which was perhaps called Gabbatha, on which the Hasmonean kings already used to sit in judgment. Such a podium in front of "the house of the Asamoneans" is mentioned by Flavius Josephus; there King Agrippa II presented his sister to the people "that she might be seen by them".[11]

In fact, the Byzantine tradition situates the *praetorium* here, opposite the Wailing Wall, and not in front of the citadel. Thus as early as 333, the pilgrim from Bordeaux claims to have seen: "down in the [Tyropoeon] valley, there are walls where the house was, or the *praetorium*, of Pontius Pilate."[12] In the early fifth century, the Church

[9] Flavius Josephus, *The Jewish War*, bk. 2, chap. 16, no. 3, in *New Complete Works of Josephus*, p. 754.
[10] Ibid.
[11] Ibid.
[12] *Bordeaux Pilgrim*.

of Pilate was built over these ruins, which was later consecrated as "Holy Wisdom" (Hagia Sophia). The pilgrim from Piacenza writes that it was located "in front of the Temple of Solomon", by which he means the Wailing Wall. Inside the church "there is also the oblong stone which used to be in the centre of the Praetorium. The accused person whose case was being heard was made to mount this stone so that every one could hear and see him." He goes on to maintain: "The Lord mounted it when he was heard by Pilate, and his footprints are still on it."[13]

Caiaphas' strategy was clear. Jesus, the religious reformer and stumbling block, had to be turned into a political agitator in order for Pilate to be interested in him in the first place. The Romans did not interfere at all in the purely religious affairs of the Jews. Therefore, his purely spiritual claim to be the Messiah was construed as a political claim to the throne. The key to his sentence is provided by the equation of the title "Messiah" with the title "King of the Jews". Luke perhaps records the full wording of the indictment when he quotes the high priest: "We have found this man perverting our nation, and forbidding us to give tribute to Caesar, and saying that he himself is Christ a king" (Lk 23:2).

Pilate hesitated. First he wanted to give the whole proceeding back to the Jews, because he recognized its religious background. Now historians debate whether the Sanhedrin could impose the death penalty for religious offenses during the Roman occupation. The stoning of Stephen three years later, and also the fate of the adulteress whose stoning was prevented by Jesus at the last minute, seem to indicate that they could. Of course, the consul and prefect of the Praetorian Guard Lucius Aelius Sejanus had issued a decree in Rome in A.D. 30, precisely in the year of Jesus' trial, forbidding the Jews to carry out the death penalty. Only in October of the year 31 did the Sanhedrin regain this privilege. Thus, for this limited interval of time, what John quotes the high priest as saying was true: "It is not lawful for us to put any man to death" (Jn 18:31).

The governor had to take seriously the third charge at least. It was reserved to the emperor alone to appoint kings. This prerogative went so far that even legitimate heirs to a throne, like Antipas and

---

[13] The Piacenza Pilgrim, *Travels from Piacenza*, in Wilkinson, *Jerusalem Pilgrims*, p. 84.

Philip, who were confirmed as rulers over a kingdom, were not allowed to use the title "King" unless Rome approved; for the rest of their lives, they simply called themselves "tetrarchs". Someone who on his own authority described himself as a king was automatically a rebel. He incurred the guilt of insurrection and of high treason against the Roman people and the emperor. According to the *Corpus Juris Civilis* of Roman law, the punishment for such a *crimen laesae maiestatis* [crime of injured sovereignty], as the *Lex Iulia maiestatis* calls it, was death on the cross.

As was customary in trials conducted by Roman governors, the accusation was followed by the hearing. It probably took place in Koiné Greek, since the possibility of Jesus speaking Latin or of Pilate speaking Aramaic is ruled out. Here, too, we find in John's Gospel a realistic portrayal. When asked whether he was a king, Jesus replied: "My kingship is not from the world" (Jn 18:36). If he were a political agitator, a danger to Rome, his men would already have put up resistance at his arrest. Pilate was hard pressed. He consulted the opinion of Antipas, who probably lived in the guest wing of the two-part Herodian palace; he listened to the warning of his wife, who had accompanied him to Judaea (which was permitted since the days of Tiberius); he questioned the people; he tried to satisfy the high priests with the scourging and public humiliation of Jesus. Just as his successor, Albinus, did with a certain Jesus Ben Ananus, who in his cries of "Woe!" prophesied the ruin of the Temple. Nevertheless, even the exhibition of the scourged, derided Jesus, wearing a crown of thorns and a soldier's mantle as a mock king, and Pilate's "*Ecce homo*" ("Behold the man!" Jn 19:5; "Here is the man!", in the RSV-2CE) had no effect. In the end, he had no other choice. The threat of the plaintiffs that they would complain about him to the emperor, as the Jews already had done in the case of the standards set up in Jerusalem, worked. At that time he was new in the office, and Tiberius had given him another chance. A second complaint to Rome could cost him the lucrative position as governor. With the words, "If you release this man, you are not Caesar's friend; every one who makes himself a king sets himself against Caesar" (Jn 19:12), they had not only hit his sore spot; they had also made it unmistakably clear to him that he had reached a dead end. In purely formal juridical terms, Jesus' claim to be the Messiah, which he so conspicuously had

demonstrated with his entrance into Jerusalem and had even confirmed in the hearing, was punishable by death. The emperor certainly
would not have understood it at all if his governor had protected a
self-appointed king and thereby further alienated the Jewish Temple hierarchy, on whose collaboration the occupying power relied.
Hence he had no other option but to condemn Jesus. John depicts
the process precisely, like a court reporter: "When Pilate heard these
words, he brought Jesus out and sat down on the judgment seat at a
place called The Pavement, and in Hebrew, Gabbatha. Now it was
the day of Preparation of the Passover; it was about the sixth hour"
(Jn 19:13–14), in other words, around twelve o'clock noon. There
he announced the most terrible sentence of all: "*Ibis in crucem*—You
will go to the cross." He had the reason for the punishment written
on a piece of wood, which was carried in front of the condemned
man and finally nailed at the top of the Cross. It testified both to his
respect for the accused man and to the inevitability of the sentence:
Jesus of Nazareth, King of the Jews.

The Gospels do not have to depict the torments still awaiting Jesus
at that moment. In antiquity the reading public was familiar with
the horrors of crucifixion from firsthand observation, so excessively
was it imposed in the Roman Empire in order to stifle all resistance
at the outset. Only Emperor Constantine the Great finally abolished
"the cruelest and most terrible death penalty", as the Roman orator
Cicero called it; the Turks, in contrast, continued the practice well
into the sixteenth century, and in some Islamic countries (for instance,
in Sudan or in Yemen, where Islamists crucified an alleged American
spy in 2012, or in the former territory of the "Islamic State"), it still
exists today. Flavius Josephus, an eyewitness to countless crucifixions
in the Jewish War, summarizes the course of the execution as follows:
The condemned men "were first whipped, and then tormented with
all sorts of tortures, before they died, and were then crucified before
the wall of the city'.[14]

The scourging alone was often enough to kill a man. The condemned man was stripped naked and tied to a low column. Then
two *lictores* (court attendants) whipped him repeatedly from both sides

---

[14] Flavius Josephus, *Jewish War*, bk. 5, chap. 11, no. 1, in *New Complete Works of Josephus*, p. 873.

with the "terrible scourges" (as Horace called them). These whips consisted of a wooden handle and three leather thongs, which usually ended in little lead dumbbells. Even though in Judaea the number of lashes was limited to thirty-nine in consideration of the Mosaic Law ("forty ... less one", see 2 Cor 11:24 citing Deut 25:3), it led to the most severe injuries, not uncommonly with lethal consequences. Jesus Ben Ananus, too, was "whipped until his bones were laid bare",[15] while other men were "scourged until their entrails were laid bare". Accounts of Christian martyrs cite the order of one particularly sadistic judge: "His back shall be torn open with blows, without intermission; the lead shall hit the back of his head so that it swells until it bursts."[16] The bloody depiction of the scourging in Mel Gibson's cinematic masterpiece *The Passion of Christ* was indeed greatly exaggerated, with regard both to the number of lashes and the choice of scourges, but by no means in the depiction of their consequences.

Nevertheless, as terrible as the scourging was, it served only as a preparation for much greater sufferings. Now Jesus was burdened with the crossbeam (Latin: *patibulum*) of the Cross, his arms outstretched and tied to the wood, and then, like a slave bearing a yoke, was dragged through the streets to the place of execution amid the scorn of the crowd. He carried only the *patibulum*, not the whole Cross, as countless paintings and Hollywood films inaccurately depict it. The weight of the latter would have come to at least 264 pounds; it is impossible that even a sturdy man could have hauled it the many hundreds of yards to the place of execution. Thus all the ancient sources that describe crucifixions, from Dionysius of Halicarnassus to Artemidorus, agree with the Roman Plautus: The condemned men carried only "the *patibulum* through the city".

Nevertheless, even that weighed 77–88 pounds and thus was heavy enough that Jesus, weakened by the brutal scourging, collapsed several times under the load. So the soldiers who accompanied the march of the cross-bearers grabbed a pilgrim from North African Cyrene on the spot and ordered him to haul the Cross for Jesus. Such a compulsory obligation was nothing unusual with the Roman occupying forces. In this case, though, we know not only

---

[15] Ibid., bk. 6, chap. 5, no. 3, p. 899.

[16] Maria Grazia Siliato, *Und das Grabtuch ist doch echt* (Augsburg: Pattloch, 1998), p. 273.

that the man came right "from the field"—so the tent city in the western part of Jerusalem was called—and was evidently on his way to the Temple with his sons. We also know his name, Simon, and the names of his sons, Rufus and Alexander; the men in question here, as the aforementioned ossuary discovery proves, are undeniably historical persons.

Regardless of whether Pilate's praetorium was Herod's palace on the western edge of the upper city or the Hasmonean palace on the eastern edge, the distance to the place of execution came to about 650 yards. Certainly the shortest way was not chosen. "When we crucify criminals," the Roman Quintilian wrote, "the most frequented roads are chosen, where the greatest number of people can look and be seized by this fear."[17] In any case, the genuine way of the Cross of Jesus led through the old Gennath or Garden Gate into the northern part of the city, which was first walled in by Herod, so as to leave the city then through the new Ephraim Gate.

Ruins of the Gennath Gate were found by the Israeli archaeologist Nahman Avigad during excavations in the extreme northwest corner of the Jewish Quarter of the Old City of Jerusalem, between Habad Street and Jewish Quarter Street. From here, Flavius Josephus writes, the second city wall ran directly north, made a wide curve, and eventually met with the Antonia Fortress. The wall had three gates; the new east gate was the Sheep Gate right behind the Pool of Bethesda; the north gate was the precursor of the present-day Damascus Gate; and the west gate, the Ephraim Gate just mentioned, led to the road to Caesarea, past Hezekiah's Pool (Amygdalon or Tower Pool in Josephus' writings) to the left and an old quarry to the right.

The ruins of this gate are found today on the grounds of the Russian Alexander Nevsky Church, which the pilgrim automatically passes by the way from the Via Dolorosa to the Church of the Holy Sepulchre. We ring, and a young Russian man opens the door for us. Past the residence of the last tsars in Jerusalem, the path leads down a stairway to the excavations. The ruins were discovered in 1844 by the Imperial German Consul Ernst-Gustav Schultz, but when Berlin showed no interest, the Russians bought the tract on the spot. In

---

[17] Quintilian, Declamation 274, in *The Lesser Declamations*, vol. 1, ed. and trans. D.R. Shackleton Bailey (Cambridge, Mass. and London: Harvard University Press, 2006), p. 259.

their excavations, which began in 1859 and lasted until 1883, they came not only upon the flight of stairs leading up to Constantine's Martyrion Basilica and a gateway arch that belonged to Hadrian's West Forum, but also upon ruins of walls and a stone pavement from the time of Herod. While it is certain that the stones were reused by Hadrian's architects to construct his Temple platform, they nevertheless seemed to come from the second wall. The street pavement, too, consists of older, often destroyed flagstones from the Herodian period and an addition from the days of Hadrian, which is reminiscent of the alleged *lithostrōtos* of the North Forum. Where the remnants of the wall cross the street, they form a twofold passageway: to the right, a high, wide gate; to the left, a low door through which pedestrians can pass, if necessary, only by bending down. "Eye of the Needle" was the name for the narrow entries through which one could come into the city even at night, when the large gates had long since been shut. "It is easier for a camel to go through the eye of a needle than for a rich man to enter the kingdom of God" (Mk 10:25), Jesus said, meaning: It is not altogether impossible, if one makes himself small and is not loaded with too many possessions. Beneath the larger gate, dividing the ancient street, a stone threshold with clearly recognizable holes for bolts has been set into the ground. No doubt an ancient city gate stood here. The Russians protected it with a glass display case and hung seven perpetual lamps over it. They are certain that Jesus stepped over this threshold as he was being led to Golgotha. The very thought makes me kneel down in front of it. The fact that Jesus suffered "outside the gate"—a tradition found in the Letter to the Hebrews also (13:12)—was in keeping with Roman custom. And, as we heard Quintilian say, "When we crucify criminals the most frequented roads are chosen, where the greatest number of people can look and be seized by this fear."[18] In Rome itself, it was in front of the Esquiline Gate. In Jerusalem, the Romans had no fixed place of execution; nevertheless, the area in front of the West Gate lent itself simply because many Passover pilgrims walked by on their way to the Temple. Thus the Synoptic Gospels, too, mention numerous passersby (Mt 27:39; Mk 15:29; Lk 23:35), and John emphasizes that the inscription over the Cross

[18] Ibid.

was also read by "many of the Jews ... for the place where Jesus was crucified was near the city" (Jn 19:20).

The fact that the gate, which in pre-Herodian times led to this northwest corner of the city, bore the name Garden Gate indicates the manner in which this tract of land was used even down to the time of Jesus. Hezekiah's pool provided good opportunities for irrigation, and so it is not surprising that John reports: "In the place where he [Jesus] was crucified there was a garden" (Jn 19:41). The fact that on the grounds of the Church of the Holy Sepulchre several rock-cut tombs from the first century were discovered leaves no doubt that this area was at that time outside the walls of Jerusalem; according to Jewish precepts, a grave could not be closer than fifty ells or twenty-seven yards from a city. Excavations carried out in 1967 by Lady Kathleen Kenyon on the grounds of the Muristan, in 1970–1971 by Ute Lux in the area of the Protestant Church of the Redeemer, and since 1960 by various Franciscan, British, and Israeli archaeologists in the area of the Church of the Holy Sepulchre clearly confirm that that tract of land was used from the Iron Age until the Hasmonean period as a quarry. Here the precious *meleke* limestone was extracted. Only when the quality of the stone deteriorated more and more was the quarry abandoned. It left behind a rather long, half-moon-shaped stump, about twenty-six feet long, ten feet wide, and sixteen feet high. This stone that even "the builders rejected" was to become the cornerstone of history. Due to its bareness and its rounded-off shape, it acquired its name: Golgotha, literally (from the Hebrew *gulgolet* or the Aramaic *golgota*): top of the skull. On its ridge, Jesus was to be crucified together with two already condemned criminals, in plain view of everyone.

We enter into the mystical light of the Church of the Holy Sepulchre, bear right, and climb a narrow staircase until we have arrived at the first floor, the Golgotha Chapel. A hundred silver perpetual lamps hang over the summit of the holy rock, over the middle of which stands a marble altar. Behind it, in front of a silver-clad icon screen, stands a life-size crucifix, flanked by full-scale icons depicting the Blessed Virgin and the apostle John. To the left and the right of the altar we recognize beneath two glass display cases the ridge of the limestone rock. Only for our generation was it made visible again, after it had been hidden for over eight hundred years under heavy marble slabs.

The first to investigate the foot of the hill were the Italians. In 1977, they unearthed a sacrificial pit right behind Mount Calvary, which proves that the Christian tradition was right. On it really stood the image of a pagan god, before Hadrian's West Forum was cleared away by order of Constantine the Great and in its place a church was built. At least this pagan marking contributed to the fact that the location was never forgotten.

In 1986, the Greeks, who have custody of the upper Golgotha Chapel, removed the precious marble covering in order to get an impression of the condition of the Place of the Skull. They commissioned the architect Dr. Theo Mitropoulos from the Institute for Byzantine Studies at the University of Thessaloniki to carry out the necessary restoration work. After they had removed the rubble of the centuries under his direction, the naked rock lay before them. A deep fissure running across the middle of it still recalls the earthquake that is said to have occurred at Jesus' death (Mt 27:51). Chisel

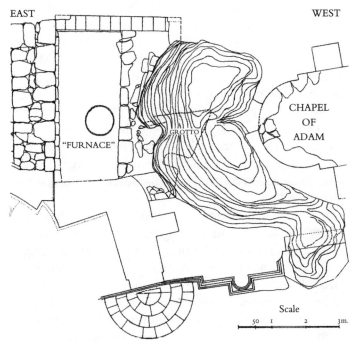

Layout of Golgotha, with pagan sacrificial pit

marks testify that again and again fragments were removed, partly as relics, partly in order to trim the rock for the construction work surrounding it at that particular moment. In the course of his investigation, one particularly soft spot on the rock ridge caught his attention. Upon closer inspection, it proved to be a mass of lime that was supposed to imitate the appearance of the genuine rock. There are some indications that Patriarch Modestus in the sixth century had it applied in order to protect the real rock (which at that time stood outdoors) from the rain and from the clutches of the pilgrims. Mitropoulos wondered what else it might be concealing and began scratching at a particularly deep spot. At some point, he hit upon a round object that was obviously solid. This now aroused the Greek's curiosity. With his bare hands, he kept scraping in the lime until he had unearthed a stone ring. It was extremely crudely wrought, which ruled out the possibility that it had some function in the basilica, in which every detail was lovingly embellished. It took a while, but then Mitropoulos realized exactly what he was holding in his hands. He had discovered a stone mounting in which the upright beam of a cross once stood, probably even the Cross of Jesus.

I kneel on the glass slab over the Golgotha rock and bend over until I can see it well enough, for it still lies right where Mitropoulos found it then. The stone ring has an interior diameter of 4.3 inches. The cross that it held—Greek engineers calculated—could therefore not have been more than 8 feet 3 inches tall. But it did not have to be that large, either. Wood was precious in Judaea, and the rock by itself was tall enough. Or did the ring come after all from the Byzantine period, for instance, from the year 417, when Emperor Theodosius II had a large, golden, bejeweled cross—the so-called *crux gemmata*—set up on Golgotha Hill?

In Rome, in Santa Pudenziana, one of the oldest churches in the Eternal City and also the titular church of the [then-]Archbishop of Cologne Joachim Cardinal Meisner, I find the answer. The mosaic in its apse, dating from the time around A.D. 420, the most beautiful mosaic from late antiquity in Rome, shows the teaching Christ, surrounded by his disciples, in front of the backdrop of early Byzantine Jerusalem. Two women, symbolic figures for the Churches of the Jewish and the Gentile Christians, hold crowns over the heads of Peter and Paul. In the background, the observer can make out the

rotunda of the Church of the Holy Sepulchre, the nave of the Martyrion, and, between them, Mount Golgotha, adorned with the *crux
gemmata* of Theodosius II. Now this removes all doubts. The votive
cross was rectangular, if only so that the jewels could be set into its
surface, and it stood on a four-sided pedestal that was also adorned
with jewels. It would never have fit into the round, rough-hewn
stone ring, which for two thousand years has testified to the position of the Cross, which quite plainly—unlike the usual depictions—
consisted of a round stake and the crossbeam affixed to it.

In fact, many notions about the Cross and the crucifixion of Jesus
that are conveyed to us by paintings and films are historically flat
wrong. The condemned man was not laid on a carefully crafted
wooden cross, fastened to the wood with nails, and then laboriously
lifted up. The Romans, famous for being pragmatic, had a faster and
more efficient method, which an author like Artemidorus sarcastically compares to hoisting a sail on a ship's mast.

The stake of the cross already stood firmly sunk into the rock. The
condemned man, already tied to the crossbeam when he was driven
to the place of execution, now just needed to be lifted up on the
stake (Latin: *stipes*) by the (usually) five-man execution squad—four
legionaries and one centurion. After they had either set the *patibulum*
onto the *stipes* or fastened it with ropes, the feet, too, were nailed to
the wood.

Of course there was an even more painful variant, which, however,
also caused death more quickly. This was used in Jesus' case. Although
his executioners had cut him loose from the crossbeam earlier, now
they used nails to fasten his wrists to the wood, also. The wrists, not
the palms, as the iconography represents it, for they were not capable
of holding the body weight of a grown man. Anatomically speaking, the most stable point that experienced executioners could use for
their brutal handiwork is the so-called space of Destot, also known
as the carpal tunnel, at the base of the hand. Through this space,
however, runs also the median nerve, which has both a sensory and
a motor function. The pain caused by injury to it is almost unbear-
able. In many cases, it must have led to immediate unconsciousness.
Excruciare, "to cause by the cross", became in Latin an established
term describing the most extreme torment of a human being conceivable, the most hellish torture. Yet the pain did not end with the

iron nail being driven through this nerve. Fastened only with nails to the cross, the body was next hoisted up. The Romans spoke about the "dance of the crucified" at the moment, meaning the contorted writhing of their victim, raving in pain, whose torments did not come to an end but rather were intensified when the executioners grabbed his feet, pressed them against the stake and drove nails through them, too. From then on, with every breath he drew, the tortured man had only the choice between supporting himself on his feet, which were burning with pain, and thus relieving his wrists, or else sparing his feet and enduring the now even more lacerating pain of the median nerves and going almost mad from the torment. They spared Jesus only one humiliation. Although men crucified in the Roman Empire were otherwise always naked, the occupiers respected the religious feelings of the Jews in this matter, too, and followed the instruction of the Mishnah: "A man is to be covered in front...."

The Gospels record exactly seven words spoken by Jesus on the Cross, which is still a lot, given the torments that he endured while every muscle of his body became cramped. The treatise "Sanhedrin" of the Jewish Mishnah says: "The court gives one who is being led out to be killed a grain ... of frankincense in a cup of wine in order to confuse his mind ... the prominent women of Jerusalem would donate this drink."[19] To Jesus, too, they offered "wine mingled with myrrh", as Mark (15:23) explicitly notes. But he refused the drink; he wanted to bear his suffering while fully conscious.

Probably he prayed Psalm 22 instead, that deeply moving monument of hope in the most profound abandonment by God, which suited his situation so well. In any case, Mark 15:34 records for us the initial words, "My God, my God, why have you forsaken me?", while in John 19:30 we read the concluding words, "... it is finished" (he has wrought it [his deliverance]). He probably did not force much more than that through his lips, while he struggled to take each breath. In these endless three hours when Jesus hung on the Cross, contorted with pain and praying, the psalm must have seemed like a prophecy. The Evangelists, especially John, were accused of adapting the scene of the crucifixion to the words of the psalm, but we read nothing in them that could not actually have happened

---

[19] *The William Davidson Talmud*, 43a, found online at sefaria.org/Sanhedrin.43a?lang=bi.

at Jesus' execution. "But I am a worm, and no man; scorned by men, and despised by the people" (Ps 22:6) corresponded to the jeering of the people who thought that the one whom they had honored only days before as the Messiah was now a failure. "They divide my clothing among them, and for my clothing they cast lots" (22:18) corresponded to the right of Roman legionaries to divide the executed man's possessions among themselves. "My strength is dried up like a potsherd, and my tongue cleaves to my jaws" (22:15)—his executioners may have understood this verse of the psalm incorrectly, but it was quite certain that the crucified man was totally dehydrated at that point and suffered from terrible thirst. And it can only seem strange to us when John quite correctly observes: "A bowl full of vinegar stood there" (19:29). For it was a rule among the Roman legions that every division that had to carry out an order outside their barracks brought a drink with it in a sort of large common water bottle. This *skeuos*—John uses the Greek counterpart of the correct military term—was filled with *posca*, a mixture of water and vinegar, which was considered both cheap and thirst-quenching. In some rural regions of Italy, they still drink it today, as Vittorio Messori emphasizes in his excellent investigation *Suffered under Pontius Pilate*. Usually a sponge served as a stopper. All four Evangelists say that one of the soldiers put it on a reed and gave Jesus some of the "vinegar", that is, the *posca*, to drink.

Now ancient sources document the fact that a single swallow of water by a crucified man can lead to immediate cardiac arrest. Experienced Roman executioners knew this and employed this expedient when they were bored of their guard duty and intended to cut it short. As late as the nineteenth century, the same phenomenon was observed in the Ottoman Empire when men were impaled. The Gospels, too, record that immediately after he had taken a drink, Jesus "bowed his head and gave up his spirit", as we read in John (19:30).

It was around the ninth hour, about three o'clock in the afternoon, just when the Paschal lambs were being slaughtered in the Temple. It was a ghostly scene, for profound darkness had covered the land for three hours. An eclipse of the sun was not the cause, as is often supposed—that could not possibly have happened, since Passover always fell on a full moon—but rather a meteorological phenomenon that is common in Jerusalem in April, the desert wind *khamsin*, also called the "black southeast wind". It brings so much sand with it that it appears to darken the sun and for hours makes its light ineffectual. But the legionaries, as foreigners unfamiliar with the weather in Jerusalem, only experienced nature unbound, the spectacle in the sky, and did not hesitate to connect it with what was happening on Golgotha. In this respect, it is realistic when Mark has the centurion—who as *exactor mortis* (executor of the death sentence) headed the *quaternio militum*, i.e., the quartet of the execution squad—exclaim: "Truly this man was the Son of God" (Mk 15:39). Yet it is simultaneously a revision of Pilate's statement, "Here is the man." The *ecce homo* has become an *ecce deus* ["Here is God"].

Haste was called for now. Although in the Roman Empire those who had been crucified usually were left hanging for days to terrorize the population and then were buried unceremoniously or else thrown to the dogs to be devoured, in Judaea an exception was made in this regard, too. The Romans respected the religious sentiments of the Jews, for whom the Torah prescribed: "If a man has committed a crime punishable by death and he is put to death, and you hang him on a tree, his body shall not remain all night upon the tree, but you shall bury him the same day" (Deut 21:22–23). Flavius Josephus confirms how scrupulously this precept was observed even in Jesus' time, for he, too, emphasizes that the Jews "took down those that were condemned and crucified, and buried them before the going down of the sun".[20] This task was performed by the aforementioned Pharisee Nicodemus, who learned from a like-minded councilor that he owned a new tomb not far from the place of execution, in one of the gardens that once gave the Garden Gate its name. His name was Joseph of Arimathea.

Yet before Pilate released Jesus' body to be buried, his death had to be verified. That was one of the tasks of the *exactor mortis*, the centurion who saw to it that the execution went smoothly. He "pierced [Jesus'] side with a spear, and at once there came out blood and water", John maintains (19:34). Yet even though he makes this observation expressly under oath ("He who saw it has borne witness—his testimony is true, and he knows that he tells the truth—that you also may believe", 19:35), critical exegetes have suspected theological symbolism here again.

---

[20] Flavius Josephus, *Jewish War*, bk. 4, chap. 5, no. 2, in *New Complete Works of Josephus*, p. 822.

Today any forensic physician can confirm how precisely the Evangelist described the pathological evidence. During hours of traumatic sufferings, which were accompanied by tremendous strain on the circulatory system, blood, fluid, and mucus collected in the lungs, causing traumatic wet lung syndrome. When the legionary thrust the spear, probably through the fifth space between the ribs, he pierced the lung and damaged the pericardium, which was filled with blood. The quick, jerking movement with which he pulled its blade back out of the chest opened a path for the blood and the fluid from the lung to exit.

Another detail that was rashly attributed to John's theology was confirmed, also. To some critics it seemed too obvious that in John's Gospel the soldiers broke the legs of the other crucified men, too suspicious that the Evangelist immediately afterward cited the Scripture verse about the sacrificial lamb: "Not a bone of him shall be broken" (Jn 19:36; see Ex 12:46: "And you shall not break a bone of it"). Nevertheless the *crurifragium*, the "breaking of the legs", which in fact existed nowhere else in the Roman Empire, was not a pious invention of John; it is documented archaeologically.

Construction workers in the northern Jerusalem district of Giv'at ha-Mivtar stumbled on a burial cave from the time of Jesus. As the law in Israel requires, all work was immediately stopped and the governmental antiquities authority was informed. They sent the archaeologist Vassilios Tzaferis to the site to examine the tomb and to recover its contents. Inside the rock-cut tomb, Tzaferis found stone benches on which fresh cadavers were placed to decay, so that the bones could be buried later in ossuaries. In nine of the twelve shafts (*kokhim*), there were skeletons; in three, there were ossuaries with inscriptions. Tzaferis carefully noted their position, then he brought them to the headquarters of the authority, the Rockefeller Museum in Jerusalem.

Only then was it evident how sensational the finding really was. Indeed, in one of the stone chests, which was inscribed with the name Jehohanan (John) Ben Haskul (or Hagakol), they found the bones of a man between twenty-four and twenty-eight years old and also of a child. The heel-bone of the adult was pierced by an iron nail almost five inches long. The end of it was bent, which is obviously why it could not be removed, and was surrounded by remnants of olive wood. Beneath his head, one could still make out the remains of a board of pistachio or acacia wood almost three-fourths of an inch thick, which plainly was supposed to clamp the foot in place. The anthropologist Nicu Haas, who was examining the findings, understood immediately that he was looking at the bones of a crucified man. This proved that crucified men in Roman Jerusalem were not only buried hastily but received a proper burial. But still another discovery confirmed the testimony of the Gospels. The right shin and also the left shin and fibula of the man from Giv'at ha-Mivtar displayed fractures—his legs had been broken before he died in torment.

In fact, the *crurifragium* served not only to keep to a schedule; it was also an act of mercy, since it shortened the suffering of the crucified man. In Jesus' case, the harrowing scourging had already considerably weakened his organism, and the traumatic shock caused by the painful nailing to the Cross had accelerated his physical collapse, so that death occurred relatively quickly. But in the case of the other two condemned men, the agony might have lasted for days, which was forbidden by Jewish Law. Breaking their legs beneath the knee with a club left them unable to support themselves in order to reduce the strain on the chest muscles. The result was either quick suffocation or cardiac arrest. Here again, therefore, John, who according to his own statement was the only disciple to stand beneath the Cross of Jesus, made an accurate report.

Thus, he and the Mother of Jesus were present when the body of the Crucified was carried to the new tomb, less than 130 feet away, and was buried there. It was a makeshift burial, for it was already late in the day. The hundred pounds of aloe and myrrh that Nicodemus had provided would surely have mitigated the smell of decomposition. This was the quantity that was customary at the burial of a king; it indicates that this "teacher of Israel" had recognized Jesus as the Messiah. Dusk was falling; the Sabbath was at the door. So they wrapped him temporarily in a long linen cloth and placed the sudarium, or facecloth, that had covered his dead countenance on the Cross in recent hours[21] in a separate place.

On the morning after the Sabbath, they intended to anoint and wrap his body, as was customary among the Jews.

But that was not to be.

---

[21] See Michael Hesemann, *Das Bluttuch Christi* (Munich: Herbig Verlag, 2010).

XIII

Steps to Heaven

The Road to Emmaus

It is cool this morning, and the grass is wet with dew. We set out
quite early and have come to the garden near the wall in which the
tomb is located. Slowly the city is awakening from its sleep, roused
by the sun, which now bathes everything in its brightest light. Our
shadows are still long as we walk along the beaten track, past nut trees
and rock terraces, which testify that this was once a quarry. Then
finally we recognize it, slacken our pace, and approach with slow,
respectful steps. It is crouched beneath a rock wall made of golden
yellow *meleke* limestone, as if it wanted to escape our notice. Seven
steps hewn into the stone lead down to it, and for a moment the sight
of it causes us to tremble. The tomb is open! The circular stone that
is used to close it, resembling a millstone, has been rolled away. Like
a dark door to the nether world, the rock cave gapes in front of us.

We descend and go inside, look into the first, then into the second
chamber of the stone tomb and determine that they are empty. Gradually we get a sense of how the women must have felt when early
on the morning of April 9, A.D. 30, a Sunday, they discovered Jesus'
tomb empty. This feeling is not unusual for those, like us, who look
for the "tomb of the Herodians" in Jerusalem, located in a somewhat
hidden part of the Mitchell Parks west of Mount Zion, right behind
the famous King David Hotel. The tomb of the Herodians, which
was probably designed in 43 B.C. for Antipater, served as the architectural model for many tombs of wealthy residents of Jerusalem in the
following century, too. Hence it is better suited for sightseeing than
the so-called "garden tomb" north of the Damascus Gate, which only
the most stubborn Anglicans still consider to be the tomb of Jesus; for

it dates back to the Iron Age, probably to the seventh century B.C. If we are to believe the few indications that the Church historian Eusebius from the early fourth century left behind for us, the empty tomb of Jesus must in fact have resembled the tomb of the Herodians. Only one thing distinguished it from all the other tombs that have been discovered in Jerusalem so far: it was a new tomb, plainly designed initially for a single person, without a second bench and, above all, without side shafts for ossuaries.

Unfortunately, not much of it has been preserved. We know only that originally it, too, was located in the rock wall of a former quarry where the tract had been transformed into a garden. Emperor Hadrian built over the area without changing much in its topography, and Constantine the Great uncovered it again. The construction of the Church of the Holy Sepulchre first led to invasive measures. Blame it on the self-willed concept of the court building contractor Zenobius, who may have had creative ideas but certainly no practical knowledge of conservation or capacity for spiritual empathy. Since the rock wall was in the way of his architectural plan, he simply had it chiseled away. But even after that, the Holy Sepulchre seemed to him too large to fit harmoniously into the proportions of the rotunda with a dome that he had planned—emulating the Pantheon in Rome. So he applied the chisel once again, until only the actual tomb chamber and the stump of the rock face encircling it remained. He surrounded it with exquisite columns, connected to one another with silver gratings and golden beams, and then set over it a silver, pyramid-shaped roof that was crowned by a cross. He had probably been inspired to commit this outrage by the so-called Tomb of Absalom that had just been uncovered in the Kidron Valley. The outer chamber with its benches, the niche for the rolling stone, and the steps that led down into the empty tomb had been sacrificed to the reductionist craze of the late-antique avant-garde architect. The outer chamber was reconstructed only when nineteenth-century Greeks built the marble-clad *aedicula* that stands today.

What had not yet fallen victim to imperial monumental architecture was destroyed seven centuries later by the fanatical and probably mentally ill Fatimid Caliph al-Hakim, whose reign of terror started the most brutal persecution of Christians since the end of the Roman Empire. On October 18, 1009, he had the Church of the Holy

Sepulchre destroyed, and a year later he once again attacked the ruins of the Holy Sepulchre. He had his stone masons chisel away the rock of Jesus' burial cave down to the height of one foot, and only the stone bench on which the body of the crucified Lord once lay defied their callow violence. No wonder an outcry of indignation went through Europe, which ultimately led to the First Crusade toward the end of the eleventh century. The Church of the Holy Sepulchre was rebuilt and this time would last a millennium as a monument to the victory of the one by whom death was defeated here.

"Trembling and astonishment", according to the Evangelist Mark (16:8), are the initial reaction of the three women to the empty tomb. He whose body they intend to anoint and then wrap with linen cloths—there was simply no time for that on the day of his death—has vanished without a trace. The large stone closing the burial cave is rolled away; the bench, temporarily covered with a linen cloth on which they laid his dead body, is now empty.

The accounts in the Gospels vary in their details, especially in the sequence of events, yet we must not let that bother us, because the decisive thing is not the chronology but, rather, the event itself. And that is perplexing enough for all who are involved. While two of the women are simply desperate, because they think that someone has stolen the Master's body, the third, Mary Magdalen, takes courage. She runs to the house where Peter and John are and tells them about the empty tomb. Nothing stops the two closest disciples of Jesus from getting their own view of the situation. John knows the location of the tomb and runs ahead; Peter follows him. When they arrive, they see the linen cloths and the facecloth but, above all, the empty bench in the tomb. John describes for us in only four words his own reaction, albeit in the third person: "He saw and believed" (Jn 20:8).

Mary Magdalen goes back to the tomb, also. According to John, only then does she see the angels; according to the Synoptics, all three women had this vision when they discovered the tomb empty. Perhaps it was already revealed to them then that Jesus had risen from the dead. But now he stands in front of her, and at first she does not even notice that it is he. But then it is as if scales fall from her eyes: "Rabboni!", "Master!" she gasps; she tries to cling to him but is not able to do so. For Jesus is risen, not simply reawakened from the sleep of death like Lazarus or the daughter of the synagogue leader. His body is no longer the mangled body of the crucified son of a carpenter from Nazareth with a dislocated arm and a broken nose, the skin shredded by the scourges, the head pricked by the crown of thorns. "Behold, I make all things new!" Jesus' promise is cited in the Book of Revelation by John (21:5); he himself made it come true before her eyes. This is his promise for the time of the coming Kingdom of God, when we all arise from the dead, as it was revealed already to the prophet Ezekiel: "Thus says the Lord GOD to these bones: ... I will lay sinews upon you, and will cause flesh to come upon you, and cover you with skin, and put breath in you, and you shall live; and you shall know that I am the LORD" (Ezek 37:5–6). He appears to Mary Magdalen in such a completely renewed "risen body" and has her proclaim the good news to the disciples, who perhaps are staying in the guesthouse of the Essenes in order to be safe from the high priest's informers. But while they are still discussing her words, unbelieving, he himself appears in their midst, breaks bread with them, eats a piece of grilled fish, and shows them the marks of the nails on his hands and feet, which are now his identifying mark. Their message is unambiguous: the Risen Lord still remains the Crucified; the miracle of Easter morning does not undo Good Friday and its message.

"Christ is risen! Truly he is risen!" This Paschal greeting of the Eastern Churches resounded the first time on the lips of Mary Magdalen, then of Peter and the other ten disciples, and finally of additional witnesses—still alive at the time when Paul wrote his letters and the first Gospels were composed—who gave credible testimony to the greatest and at the same time most incredible event in human history.

"Christ is risen! Truly he is risen!" became the central message of Christianity and echoed down the following two millennia, until on May 12, 2009, it reached the Valley of Josaphat, the Valley of Judgment, where Pope Benedict XVI, right opposite the rock of Jesus' agony, proclaimed his Resurrection. The image over the altar, as we mentioned, showed the still unbelieving Thomas as he touches the wound in the Lord's side and arrives at the most magnificent and blessed insight in Sacred Scripture, sinks to his knees, and exclaims, "My Lord and my God!"

"Blessed are those who have not seen and yet believe" (Jn 20:29), Jesus says to him in reply, in the last words of our Lord in the

original Fourth Gospel, which was later expanded. And yet we are all
Thomas. As people of the twenty-first century, it is difficult for us "to
believe something blindly"; we want to hear witnesses and see proofs.
The pope knows this, too; in his homily in front of this same image
he declared:

> Here in the Holy Land, with the eyes of faith, you, together with
> the pilgrims from throughout the world who throng its churches and
> shrines, are blessed to "see" the places hallowed by Christ's presence,
> his earthly ministry, his passion, death and resurrection, and the gift
> of his Holy Spirit. Here, like the Apostle Saint Thomas, you are
> granted the opportunity to "touch" the historical realities which
> underlie our confession of faith in the Son of God.

This very thing is a key statement from his own book *Jesus of Nazareth*, which, however far into heaven it carries his theology, never
calls into question the fact that it is rooted in history. Thus Benedict emphasizes there, too: "Jesus is no myth. He is a man made of
flesh and blood and he stands as a fully real part of history. We can
go to the very places where he himself went. We can hear his words
through his witnesses. He died and he is risen."[1] He truly rose from
the dead, and that is historically attested. The places where he lived
and ministered have become the Fifth Gospel.

Paul, in his First Letter to the Corinthians, neatly lists like an attor-
ney making a closing argument all the eyewitnesses who with their
reputations and their lives vouched for the truth of the core message
of Christianity: "He was raised on the third day in accordance with
the Scriptures, and ... appeared to Cephas [Peter], then to the Twelve.
Then he appeared to more than five hundred brethren at one time,
most of whom are still alive, though some have fallen asleep. Then
he appeared to James, then to all the apostles" (1 Cor 15:4–7). He
wrote that in A.D. 53, only twenty-three years after the Easter event.
He does not even mention the women, because he knew that the testimony of women unfortunately was not valid before a Jewish court;
to adduce it would have been counterproductive for his preaching.
And he puts everything into one pan of the scales: "If Christ has not

---

[1] Pope Benedict XVI, *Jesus of Nazareth*, vol. 1, *From the Baptism in the Jordan to the Transfiguration*, trans. Adrian J. Walker (New York et al.: Doubleday, 2007), 271–72.

been raised, then our preaching is in vain and your faith is in vain. We are even found to be misrepresenting God, because we testified of God that he raised Christ, whom he did not raise if it is true that the dead are not raised. For if the dead are not raised, then Christ has not been raised. If Christ has not been raised, your faith is futile and you are still in your sins" (1 Cor 15:14–19). Yet Paul knew that the testimony of the aforementioned persons is true; Christ had appeared to Paul himself outside Damascus. Thus, he and all the eyewitnesses were so completely convinced of the Resurrection that they were ready to go to their death, which they no longer needed to fear.

But we let ourselves be fooled by sensational reports that, on closer inspection, have no substance. All it took was an ossuary with the inscription "Jesus, son of Joseph", found in the tomb of a wealthy family in the south of Jerusalem, in the same place where the high priest Caiaphas was buried, and the international press went crazy. Immediately there was talk about "Jesus' family tomb", the pious deception of a staged theft of the body and the proclamation of a false resurrection, while the bones of the crucified were moldering in a bone chest. The fact that Jesus was known as the (adoptive) "son of Joseph" only in Nazareth and that people from other localities, in contrast, were always named after their hometown (cf. Joseph of Arimathea, Simon of Cyrene, Mary of Madgala, etc.) was ignored by the sensationalist television journalists as they cleverly drummed up interest in their alleged "discovery". The question of what a family tomb of the Holy Family from Nazareth, and especially what an ossuary with Joseph's bones, was doing in Jerusalem was left unanswered. Moreover, it is certain that the carpenter died in Nazareth before the beginning of Jesus' public ministry. Nor did they explain how the family, which was certainly not rich, could afford the expensive stone tomb in the first place—even one with a gabled roof over the entrance. Thus, a bit of healthy common sense was enough to debunk the new myth. As an evaluation of Jewish ossuary inscriptions published in 1994 by the archaeologist L. Y. Rahmani shows, Joseph was the second most common name (after Simon) in Jerusalem at the time of Jesus, while Jesus was in sixth place. One out of every four women was named Mary, which is not surprising, since even in the Gospels four Marys appear (the Mother of Jesus, the wife of Cleophas, Mary Magdalen, and Mary of Bethany). In purely statistical terms, therefore, one out of every 240 first-century inhabitants of Jerusalem had a father named Joseph, and one out of 960 also had a mother named Mary, which in a city with around 80,000 inhabitants results in around forty with the same name as Jesus whose parents likewise were named Joseph and Mary. Since we do not even know what family relationship the Mary from this tomb had to this "Jesus, son of Joseph" (it could also have been his daughter, sister, or sister-in-law), the "sensational find" loses all its relevance. If there had been in the year A.D. 30 even a suspicion of a deception, Caiaphas would have done everything possible to clear up the question as quickly as possible. So the finding is good for nothing but a not entirely inaccurate joke among theologians that purportedly takes place at the University of Tübingen. "Did you hear the news?" Professor X asks his colleague, Professor Y from the Theological Faculty. "In Jerusalem they found the tomb of Jesus. His body was still in it!" "What?!" replies Professor Y incredulously. "Then he really existed?"

The attempt to rationalize the Gospels entirely can quickly lead to such doubts. If in fact he was only a Jewish itinerant prophet, if all his alleged miracles were invented and attributed to him "in the light of the Easter faith" along with his self-revelation as "Son of God" and Messiah, then in fact not much is left of the historical Jesus of Nazareth. But why should Jesus' disciples have relativized in its uniqueness the Resurrection that they had just experienced by telling "miracle stories" that can be grasped only with difficulty? Archaeology shows us how precise the Gospels are when it is a matter of documenting the sites of Jesus' ministry. It is practically as if they were inviting us to examine their statements: Come here, make inquiries; it really happened this way! Is it any surprise that, of all people, their "demythologizer", the Protestant theologian Rudolf Bultmann, throughout his life stubbornly refused to visit the Holy Land and to study the Fifth Gospel? Did he suspect that just a few archaeological thrusts with the spade would be enough to topple his whole intellectual construct?

Today the equivalent of Jesus' wounds, which Thomas so urgently wanted to touch then, are the sites at which the Risen Lord appeared. They anchor the Easter event in history, in the tangible reality of people then as today.

One of these is Emmaus. We find the report about this encounter with the Risen Lord only in Luke, although Mark also hints at it, at least in the expanded version of his Gospel (there is no doubt that Mark 16:9–20 was added later). "After this he appeared in another form to two of them, as they were walking into the country" (Mk 16:12), Peter's interpreter informs us. The Third Gospel relates the whole story. It is one of the most moving in the New Testament, yet at the same time it confronts us with many new questions.

First of all, there were the two disciples who set out on the road "into the country". We learn the name of at least one of them: "... named Cleopas" (Lk 24:18). Luke is mentioning him for the first time, but to attentive readers it sounds oddly familiar. Oh, right! In John a woman named "Mary, the wife of Clopas" stands beneath the Cross of Jesus and is even described as "his mother's sister" (Jn 19:25). Jesus' Mother was an only child (and besides, parents would not have given the same name to two daughters), so this can only have been Mary's sister-in-law, who in antiquity was likewise termed her "sister". About this same "other Mary", Jesus' aunt, we learn in Mark and Matthew that she was "the mother of James and Joseph" (Mt 27:56)—Mark 15:40 calls him Joses, a nickname like the Yiddish Josche. Thus James and Joseph/Joses were cousins of Jesus. Once again this rings a bell, and we recall the citizens of Nazareth who, as they rejected Jesus, noted some information about his relatives; they asked: "Is not this the carpenter, the son of Mary and brother of James and Joses and Judas and Simon?" (Mk 6:3). These "brothers of the Lord" were obviously all cousins of Jesus, sons of Clopas and "his" Mary and not identical with the sons of Joseph from a first marriage, who are mentioned in the *Protoevangelium* and who by the year A.D. 30 had long since been fathers of families in their forties or fifties. In fact, both the Greek *adelphos* and the Hebrew *'ach*, which is translated into English as "brother", can designate any male relative.

This is very interesting, because it debunks a modern swindle. In 2002, an ossuary was presented to the public at a conference in Canada; its inscription was described as the "earliest written evidence of Jesus of Nazareth". Actually the Hebrew script on the stone bone chest read: "James, son of Joseph, brother of Jesus". All three names were common, there was no indication of the origins, but the reference to an obviously well-known brother named Jesus (which is altogether uncommon with ossuaries) caused many experts to prick up their ears. Meanwhile, it has become clear that the inscription is a forgery. An Israeli collector, Oded Golan, had obtained an ossuary that was not inscribed on the antiquities market and had someone supply the significant inscription. When the police raided his house, they came upon a well-equipped forger's workshop with a series of objects, several of which had already been inscribed. Since 2003, Golan has been on trial in Jerusalem and maintains his innocence. I do not believe a word he says. An antiquities dealer along the Via Dolorosa, who even now is offering several uninscribed ossuaries, revealed to me that Golan's lawyers offered his father $30,000 to testify that the collector had bought the inscribed ossuary from him. Naturally the immoral offer was turned down. Yet in the end, experts contradicted each other, and Golan was acquitted on March 14, 2012, "for lack of clear evidence".

Nevertheless, they could have known that the inscription could hardly have referred to James, "the brother of the Lord". For his father was not Joseph but, rather, Clopas. If the latter name had been found on an ossuary, it would have been a real sensation. For unlike Joseph, James, and Jesus, Clopas (or, in its Greek form, Cleopas) is an extremely rare name, which compels us to identify the Emmaus disciple with the uncle of Jesus (and, according to Hegesippus, the brother of Saint Joseph). His fellow traveler was, according to the oldest Christian tradition, which Hegesippus (100–180) likewise hands down to us, his son Simon or Simeon, who after the martyrdom of James in A.D. 62 was elected the second Jewish-Christian bishop of Jerusalem. His descent from the House of David led to his crucifixion in 107, as a more than ninety-year-old man, during the reign of Emperor Trajan.

The two men, father and son, were walking along the road "to a village named Emmaus, about seven miles [sixty stadia] from Jerusalem" (Lk 24:13), when they bumped into a traveler. They told him about Jesus, his crucifixion, the women who had come to the empty tomb, the angels, and the disappearance of the body. Then the stranger explained to them how all this had been foretold by Moses and the Prophets, cited Scripture, and declared that Jesus is the Messiah. They may have been amazed at his knowledge, but they did not recognize him. It was late afternoon, evening drew near, and so they invited the traveler to stay with them overnight in the village. Yet when he sat with them at table, pronounced the blessing, and broke the bread, they recognized that it was Jesus. Nothing could stop them now. "And they rose that same hour and returned to Jerusalem; and they found the Eleven gathered together and those who were with them, who said, 'The Lord has risen indeed, and has appeared to Simon!'" (Lk 24:33–34).

Even though Simeon is not named, perhaps because he was still alive, Luke may have heard the story from him when he was staying in Jerusalem in the years 57–59. This guarantees a high degree of authenticity. But can we still figure out today where all this happened?

Actually Emmaus is historically documented. But that very fact poses a problem for us, because the name (from the Hebrew *chammat*, warm spring) was not unique. There were two places named Emmaus in Judaea (and a third was located in Galilee), a city in the western part of the land and a village near Jerusalem. Reason enough for us to visit both localities.

The first Emmaus is right on Highway 1, which connects Tel Aviv with Jerusalem, fifteen miles as the crow flies west of the Holy Sepulchre. You can find it quickly if you use the Latrun Monastery exit but then drive, not to the monastery, but to Canada Park. Ruins are scattered all over the grounds of the park. Particularly impressive are the Roman thermal baths, which were supplied with water from a nearby spring by way of three channels.

The size of the field of ruins testifies to the importance of ancient Emmaus. Judas Maccabeus defeated the army of the Seleucids here in 165 B.C., which made the city the pride of all Israel. It became one of the five Sanhedrin seats and was the capital of a toparchy, that is, a governmental district. Its inhabitants kept the rebellious spirit of their forefathers alive and after the death of Herod revolted against the Romans; to punish them, Varus reduced the city to rubble and ashes. Yet they must have recovered again quickly, for in the Jewish War, too, Emmaus played an important role as a camp for the Roman troops. In the early second century, it became a center of rabbinical learning, until a severe earthquake in 130 destroyed it completely. Only slowly did houses appear again on the ruins, when the Roman Prefect Julius Africanus, a learned and influential Christian, asserted his influence in Rome. In one step, he obtained for the city in 222 from Emperor Elagabalus municipal law, the order to rebuild, and a new name. Nikopolis, "City of Victory", was to be the name of

Emmaus now, commemorating the victory of the Romans in the Jewish War.

Only then, it seems, was it discovered by the Christians, too. Origen was the first to identify it with the Emmaus of Luke's Gospel; Eusebius followed him, and so did Jerome. And since it was really much too far from Jerusalem, the latter immediately "corrected" the note about the distance in his Vulgate version. In the Greek manuscripts, too, a second reading became established from the third century on: Emmaus is no longer supposed to be sixty stadia, or seven miles, from Jerusalem, but, rather, 160 stadia, a full nineteen miles. Admittedly, that was a little much for Emmaus-Nikopolis, but at least it fit better.

Very early a flourishing Christian community developed in the city; it became an episcopal see. In the fifth century, a Byzantine church complex with a baptistery was constructed on the ruins of a second-century Roman villa that was probably thought to be the house of Cl(e)opas. In the seventh century, Muslims destroyed the structure; in the twelfth century, the Knights Templar built a Crusader church on its ruins. Today, friendly Carmelite nuns from Bethlehem tend the shrine. For them, there is no doubt about the authenticity of the site. A mystic of their Order who was beatified in 1983 by Pope John Paul II, Sister Miriam Baouardy, was reassured in a vision by Jesus himself that the Lucan Emmaus was located here.

We inspect the grounds and make an unsettling discovery: the shrine is situated in the middle of a Jewish graveyard. Some stone tombs from the time of Jesus are still preserved in very good condition; others were destroyed during the construction of the Byzantine church. But then the Roman villa that was taken for the house of Cl(e)opas cannot have stood once upon its foundations; no pious Jew would have built his house among tombs. It is much more likely that the Byzantine basilica was originally constructed over the tomb of a martyr.

In fact, the Crusaders already had problems with the identification of Nikopolis with the Lucan Emmaus for two reasons. First, Luke speaks explicitly about a village (*kome*), Mark about the *auros*, which can mean both "countryside" and also a "small, rural settlement". Since the Jews generally described independent communities as "cities"—even Nazareth is a *polis* in the Gospels—by *kome* and *auros*

they must have actually meant a farming settlement in the vicinity—
the *chora*—of a major city, in this case of Jerusalem. Second, the new
reading by Origen simply does not fit Luke's chronology. The
Emmaus disciples could have left Jerusalem at the earliest on Sunday
at midday, and they arrived home late in the afternoon, ate with Jesus,
and then set out on the return trip, only to meet the Eleven as they
were eating their evening meal. The Roman road from Jerusalem to
Emmaus-Nikopolis is seventeen miles long; a round trip is therefore
thirty-four miles, which in one day would be a forced march, to put
it mildly. Therefore, the Crusaders looked for the Lucan village of
Emmaus within sixty stadia, or seven miles, of Jerusalem and determined two alternatives: Abu Gosh and el-Qubeibeh, both situated on
old Roman roads leading west. The latter is managed today by the
Franciscans, who made a thorough archaeological investigation of it
and set up a wonderful garden on its grounds. Whether Jesus really
walked on the Roman street, the remains of which the excavators
uncovered there, quickly becomes a secondary question; his spirit
is present and perceptible here (which is true also of the shrine in
Emmaus-Nikopolis). In fact, the Franciscan archaeologists even discovered ruins from the time of Jesus that were already interpreted by
the Crusaders as the "house of Cl(e)opas" and were incorporated into
their church. But unfortunately the tradition of el-Qubeibeh ("little
dome") goes back only to the year 1280, when the place was known
also as Parva Mahomeria, "little mosque". On the other hand, there
is no documentation that it was called Emmaus; the name would not
have fit, either, since there never was a spring here.

More interesting is Abu Gosh, at least since the archaeological
excavations in very recent times. Since 2017, a French-Israeli team
has been investigating here under the direction of Professor Israel Finkelstein from the University of Tel Aviv. In Kiriath Yearim, only a
few hundred yards distant from the local Benedictine Abbey, where
the Ark of the Covenant stayed for twenty years, until the dancing
King David had it brought into his new capital, Jerusalem, the archaeologists ran into ruins from Old Testament times, and more. In the
summer of 2019, they also unearthed the walls of a Hellenistic fortress
from the second century B.C., which was rebuilt by the Romans in
the first century and was used as a base for a unit of the Tenth Legion.
It seems to have been constructed by the Seleucids in order to protect

Jerusalem from the west from attacks of the Jewish freedom fighters under Judas Maccabeus and his brothers. In fact, the Jewish historian Flavius Josephus, just like the First Book of Maccabees (1 Mac 9:50), lists a series of fortresses that the Seleucid General Bacchides had constructed in a ring around the capital, among them Bethel, Jericho, Gazara, and Beth Horon. Kiriath Yearim is missing from the list, at least under its present name. Instead, Josephus and the Book of Maccabees mention a fortress west of Jerusalem that they call "Emmaus". Since no other Hellenistic fortification has yet been found to the west of the capital, Finkelstein is convinced that the fortress of Kiriath Yearim can only have been the "Emmaus" of Josephus and the Book of Maccabees. The fact that it is located exactly 6.8 miles, or sixty stadia, west of Jerusalem as the crow flies also allows us to identify it with the Emmaus of the Gospel of Luke.

Yet there was still another locality, more precisely a village named Emmaus or Ammaus quite close to Jerusalem, three miles east of Kiriath Yearim as the crow flies. Flavius Josephus reports, in his book about the Jewish War, that Emperor Vespasian settled eight hundred veterans in "a place ... called Emmaus, [which] is distant from Jerusalem threescore furlongs".[2] Since then the place has gone by the name of Colonia among the Romans and Qaloniyeh among the Arabs. Today it has the name ha-Mozah and is located (like Nikopolis) on Highway 1, only 1.4 miles north of the Holocaust Memorial Yad Vashem. It is already mentioned in the Book of Joshua (18:26) and also in the Talmud, which says that there the Jews gathered the willow branches for the Feast of Booths. Today its terraced slopes, on which olive trees and grapevines once grew, are still preserved. Its sparkling stream, flowing abundantly as ever, was already used as a well in the Iron Age. A *mikveh* discovered nearby strikingly resembles the Essene ritual bath in Bethany on the Mount of Olives and could indicate an Essene settlement. Josephus underestimates when he notes the distance. On the old Roman roads, it was not thirty stadia (3.4 miles), but not sixty stadia (seven miles), either, as Luke says, but almost exactly fifty stadia (5.7 miles) to the Essene Gate of Jerusalem. In antiquity, indications of distance are not all that exact.

---

[2] Flavius Josephus, *The Jewish War*, bk. 7, chap. 6, no. 7, in *New Complete Works of Josephus*, trans. William Whiston (Grand Rapids, Mich.: Kregel, 1999), p. 923.

Here now, in Ammaus-Colonia, the German papyrologist and New Testament scholar Carsten Peter Thiede from the Independent Theological College (STH, Staatsunabhängige Theologische Hochschule) in Basel, who unfortunately died much too early in 2004, collaborated on a dig with the Israel Antiquities Authority. In the process, he discovered not only the remains of the Roman veterans' settlement but also the Jewish village that was located 109 yards west of it. *Terra sigillata* [a kind of ceramics] with Hebrew inscriptions but, above all, the artistically embellished fragments of Jewish stone vessels indicate that practicing Jews of quite a high social status lived here. One possible sign of an early Christian veneration of these sites is the ruins of a Byzantine monastery from the fifth century, which Thiede uncovered. Earlier traces were ruled out from the start; we can hardly assume that the early Church maintained a sanctuary directly beside a Roman veterans' settlement. Later, Ammaus was forgotten, since the place was now known only as Colonia, and the tradition concentrated on Emmaus-Nikopolis.

Yet ultimately it is of secondary importance whether Nikopolis, Kiriath Yearim, or Colonia was the Emmaus in Luke. So secondary that even a Christian like Julius Africanus did not even think of protecting the name of his city, but preferred to rename it. Or was his reason for the new name only a pretext and he was really thinking of Jesus' victory over death? That cannot be ruled out, either. Yet one thing is clear to me: The important thing is not the destination, not the place where the Risen Lord manifested himself, but rather the way along which he revealed himself and led his disciples to the knowledge of the faith. It may lead in any geographical direction, toward any church in the world where bread is broken and he is in our midst. The true Emmaus is everywhere!

Moreover, it is worthwhile comparing the concluding sequences of the four Gospels with each other. Mark originally ended with the fear and trembling that first fills the women and us when we are confronted with the incredible, the shocking truth of the Resurrection. Matthew leaves us with Jesus' promise that gives us hope: We are not alone—"I am with you always, to the close of the age" (Mt 28:20). Luke sends us not only on the road to Emmaus, to the warm spring of truth, but also to the Mount of Olives, in his account of the Ascension. Today on the highest point of the mountain stands an octagonal church with a dome, which was temporarily used by the Muslims as a mosque. Here as early as 378 the Roman noblewoman Poimenia, a relative of the emperor, constructed a church, a four-sided building that was open to the sky in the middle of its roof. Today on the floor of the octagon, a stone is displayed on which we are somewhat fancifully supposed to recognize the footprints of Jesus.

I am much more interested, though, in the oldest shrine to the Ascension, which was built earlier in 325 by the Empress Helena. Indeed, the so-called Eleona Church combines Jesus' Ascension with his spiritual testament and stands, moreover, on an authentic locale. As Eusebius of Caesarea wrote: "By the cave that is shown there [the Lord] prayed, and on the hill, his disciples were told the secrets of the end of the world; [from there he also ascended into heaven]."[3] Here, then, Jesus spent the night during his earlier visits to Jerusalem, instructed his disciples, and—so the local tradition maintains—taught them the Our Father. The trail of hope and faith that the Lord's Prayer left behind on its way through the centuries is dearer and more precious to me, if I may say so, than any indistinct impression on rock. It is written in all languages in the interior courtyard of the modern Eleona Church as his present to us, through which his blessing is handed down to all subsequent generations. Thus the Gospel of Luke ends with the admonition to emulate the disciples in prayer, when it says about them: "And [they] were continually in the temple blessing God" (Lk 24:53).

John had originally intended to conclude with an appeal to believe even without visible signs. But then he (or one of his disciples) apparently reconsidered and added to his Gospel the depiction of Jesus' last sign. It takes place in Galilee, sometime between Passover and the Ascension, in late April of the year A.D. 30. The other Evangelists already set up the signpost pointing back to the starting place of his ministry, Matthew, for example ("Then Jesus said to them, '... Go and tell my brethren to go to Galilee, and there they will see me'", 28:10), or Mark ("He is going before you to Galilee", 16:7). Even Luke works in the Galilee motif by having the angel remind

---

[3] Eusebius of Caesarea, *Demonstratio Evangelica*, bk. 4, chap. 18, no. 15 (PG 22:457); quoted in Bargil Pixner, *Paths of the Messiah and Sites of the Early Church from Galilee to Jerusalem: Jesus and Jewish Christianity in Light of Archaeological Discoveries* (San Francisco: Ignatius Press, 1020), p. 234.

them "how he told you, while he was still in Galilee" (24:6). And right there, on the Sea of Galilee, at Peter's harbor in Tabgha, Jesus revealed himself, according to the Gospel of John, one last time.

Once again the disciples went fishing. Maybe they wanted to keep in touch with everyday reality or to have a change of scenery; maybe, too, it was sentimentality: to experience one last time the old routine before the new one begins. Seven of them went along, including Peter, Thomas, and the two sons of Zebedee. They had fished all night, but without success. Maybe the weather was too bad, the water too cold, and the tilapia had hidden too deep and too near the warm springs of Tabgha.

Then the men see on the shore, at their landing place, a man. They do not recognize him. Someone calls to him; the stranger advises them to cast the net on the right side, and suddenly it is full of fish. It is light now; the first rays of the morning sun warm the sea and invite the fish to leave their hiding place and to ascend to the light. Maybe the mysterious stranger observed the school from the shore. In any case, the fishnet was full and too heavy to be drawn up. Now John is the first to understand who the man on the shore is: "It is the Lord!" he exclaims to Peter. The latter is still naked, for he just got out of the water. When a fishnet is full, one of the fishermen dives to the bottom of the sea, grabs the plumb line, carefully pulls the open end of the net together, and lifts it with the catch into his boat. If he is fishing close to the shore or if the catch is particularly large, he can also drag the full net onto shore, just as John (an experienced fisherman) describes it. He even notes precisely the distance to the shore: 200 ells, around 110 yards.

When Peter understands who the stranger is, his temperament carries him away. He quickly girds himself with his outer garment so as not to appear naked before his Master, jumps into the water, dives, grabs the net, and swims toward land. There Jesus has already lit a coal fire and is grilling fish and bread. First, they follow the usual fisherman's routine. Every catch must be carefully counted, if only on account of the tax, which a tax collector at the harbor immediately demands. There are exactly 153 fish. There has been much speculation about this number. Some exegetes say that it is the number of all the nations on earth; according to others, it is an allusion to the Trinity. The latter interpretation goes back to Saint

Augustine and shows in the first place what ingenious arguments the Church Fathers were capable of. If you make a dot on the first line, and two on the second, three on the third, and so on, when you have made 153 dots, the result is an equilateral triangle. This is true, you can try it yourself, and it shows how many encoded messages are hidden in the Gospels, just waiting for clever exegetes to "crack" them. Yet this meta-level does not rule out the fact that there were actually 153 fish and not 152 or 154, and that the disciples, who originally were fisherman and not theologians, simply counted them as part of a routine.

The place where this happened can still be visited today. Personally, it is my favorite place in the Holy Land, and anyone who has ever been there also understands why.

Right on the lake shore near Tabgha stands a chapel that was built by the Franciscans in 1933 on the foundations of a tiny church from the early fifth century. In front of its altar extends a ridge of natural stone, the *Mensa Christi*, the table of the Lord. According to tradition, it is the place on which the coal fire burned to grill fish and bread (which is why in the Middle Ages the little church was also called Place of the Coals). Very early on, the stone table was isolated from the surrounding rock in order to emphasize its importance. Outside, often flooded, stand the stumps of six heart-shaped corner columns, as we recognize from third-century Jewish synagogues, but arranged in a row. They neither testify to a building on this site nor served to moor boats, as people once thought, but are supposed to symbolize the thrones of the twelve apostles. The tiny church, with dimensions of only twenty-one by thirty-nine feet, is nestled against a gray rock in which seven steps were chiseled. "This is Holy Ground", a sign reveals, and a wrought-iron grill prevents access. Comical rock badgers, which can bite sometimes, usually guard it. It is quite possible that the staircase comes from the time of Jesus and that it led from the landing place to the formerly higher lake shore. The water level has receded over the years; before the chapel was built, the site was used as a quarry and thus decreased in elevation. Maybe Jewish Christians performed baptisms here, too. It is certain, however, that this staircase was already there before the shrine was constructed around 420–430. A half-century before that, in 383, the nun Egeria, who on her pilgrimage through the Holy Land came to Tabgha also, reported:

"Not far away from there [Capernaum] are some stone steps where the Lord stood."[4]

Today these seven steps lead straight to heaven.

After Jesus and the disciples had sat here, Jesus left us his greatest present. Three times he asked Peter whether he loved him, and three times the Prince of the Apostles said yes. In the East, a threefold repetition is still considered the ultimate confirmation, an oath. And three times Jesus replied: "Feed my lambs. Feed my sheep." He prophesied that Peter's life would end on the cross; then he commanded him one last time: "Follow me" (Jn 21:15–19).

This scene is recalled today by a movingly unpretentious bronze statue on the lake shore, diagonally opposite from the Place of Coals, which for good reasons is now called the Primacy Chapel. It shows the Risen Lord with hand outstretched in blessing, and Peter kneeling in front of him, shrinking back in deep emotion, his left hand raised to grasp. It is an image that bridges two millennia and leads directly into the present. For the Church that Jesus founded then on the rock of Peter with the command to feed his flock has outlasted time and will continue to exist until the end of days, as he promised. The blessing that he bestowed then on the kneeling disciple has been passed on 266 times since then, most recently on April 24, 2005, to Joseph Ratzinger and, on March 13, 2013, to Jorge Mario Bergoglio.

"Jesus proclaimed the kingdom of God, and what we got was the Church",[5] the modernist French theologian Alfred Loisy (1857–1930) declared, and he meant it sarcastically. Yet it is true: Jesus, who proclaimed the Kingdom of God, gave us the gift of the Church in order to realize his vision with her and through her. Mistakes may have been made in her name by men who were as imperfect as Peter himself, but there is no other church. She guaranteed that Jesus' words would be preserved, spared from all arbitrary interpretations, all misuse for other purposes. She makes it possible for us even today to sense his presence and to follow him, in communion with the Successor of Peter, who leads his flock through time. And that is all that matters.

---

[4] *Egeria's Travels*, trans. John Wilkinson (London: S.P.C.K., 1971), p. 196.

[5] Alfred Loisy, *L'evangile et l'église* (Paris: Picard, 1902), p. 11; quoted in Hans Küng, *The Church* (New York: Sheed and Ward, 1967), p. 43.

We have already arrived back in Germany when the media publish the final photos of the journey of Benedict XVI to the Holy Land. They show Peter on the way to the empty tomb. Not running, as was the case then, but at a leisurely pace, and John is not at his side but, rather, Msgr. Georg Gänswein, his sympathetic secretary. And, nevertheless, a noticeable continuity connects April 9, A.D. 30, with this May 15, 2009, the day on which the pope kneels in front of the tomb bench and kisses its rock, which has long since been covered with marble slabs. For the man who completed here his encounter with history, his entrance into time and space, is truly risen and lives—yesterday, today, and in the future.

This is the real Good News; this remains our hope.

CHRONOLOGY OF THE LIFE OF JESUS

February: Jesus' fast, call of the first disciples

March: Wedding feast in Cana, Passover in Jerusalem, cleansing of the Temple

April: Jesus in Bethany on the Jordan

May: Shavuot in Jerusalem, arrest of John

June–August: Jesus in Cana

September: Sukkoth, visit to the Pool of Bethsaida

November: Jesus again in Capernaum

29 February: Sermon on the Mount, curing of the possessed man of Gadara

March: Execution of the Baptist, feeding of the 5,000 in Tabgha

April: Revelation in Capernaum, journey to Tyre and Sidon

June: Feeding of the 4,000 in Kursi

July: Journey to Caesarea Philippi

August: Transfiguration, return to Galilee

October: Sukkoth in Jerusalem

December: Chanukah in Jerusalem, then return to Galilee

30 January: Sending of the 72 disciples

February: Jesus leaves Capernaum

March: Jesus in Bethany on the Jordan, then in Bethany on the Mount of Olives

April: Passover, Passion, death, and Resurrection

May: Ascension, sending of the Holy Spirit at Shavuot

45–68 Composition of the four Gospels

70 Destruction of Jerusalem and of the Temple by Titus

SOURCES AND BIBLIOGRAPHY

The Holy Bible: Revised Standard Version, second Catholic edition. San Francisco: Ignatius Press, 2006.

Albani, Matthias. *Jesus von Nazareth, zu Bethlehem geboren*. Freiburg: Herder, 2003.

Antonini Placentini. *Itinerarium*. German translation by J. Gildemeister. Berlin: Reuther, 1889.

Arav, Rami, and Richard Freund, eds. *Bethsaida*. Kirksville, Mo.: Truman State University Press, 1995.

Atwill, Joseph. *Caesar's Messiah: The Roman Conspiracy to Invent Jesus*. Berkeley, Calif.: Ulysses, 2005.

Aviam, Mordechai. *Ancient Synagogues in the Land of Israel*. Ramat Gan: Israel National Parks Authority, 1997.

Avigad, Nahman. *The Herodian Quarter in Jerusalem*. Jerusalem: Keter, 1991.

Avni, Gideon, and Zvi Greenhut. *The Akeldama Tombs*. Jerusalem: Israel Antiquities Authority, 1996.

Badde, Paul. *Heiliges Land*. Gütersloh: Gütersloher Verlagshaus, 2008.

———. *Jerusalem, Jerusalem*. Kisslegg: Fe-Medien, 2006.

Bagatti, Bellarmino, O.F.M. *The Church from the Circumcision*. Jerusalem: Franciscan Printing Press, 1984.

———. *Excavations in Nazareth*. Jerusalem: Franciscan Printing Press, 1969.

———. *Il Golgota e la Croce*. Jerusalem: Franciscan Printing Press, 1984.

Bahat, Dan. *The Atlas of Biblical Jerusalem*. Jerusalem: Carta, 1994.

———. *Touching the Stones of Our Heritage*. Jerusalem: Western Wall Heritage Foundation, 2002.

Bar-Am, Aviva. *Beyond the Walls: Churches of Jerusalem*. Jerusalem: Ahva Press, 1998.

Batey, Richard A. *Jesus and the Forgotten City*. Grand Rapids, Mich.: Baker Book House, 1991.

Bauckham, Richard *Jesus and the Eyewitnesses*. Grand Rapids, Mich.: Eerdmans, 2006.

———. *Jude and the Relatives of Jesus in the Early Church*. Edinburgh: T&T Clark, 1990.

Bauer, Thomas Johann. *Who Is Who in der Welt Jesu*. Freiburg: Herder, 2007.

Bauman, Richard A. *Crime and Punishment in Ancient Rome*. London and New York: Routledge, 1996.

Baur, Ferdinand Christian. *Kritische Untersuchungen über die kanonischen Evangelien*. Tübingen, 1847.

Becker-Huberti, Manfred. *Die Heiligen Drei Könige*. Cologne: Greven, 2005.

Benedict XVI/Joseph Ratzinger. *Jesus of Nazareth: From the Baptism in the Jordan to the Transfiguration*. Translated by Adrian J. Walker. New York et al.: Doubleday, 2007.

———. *Jesus of Nazareth*, Part 2: *Holy Week: From the Entrance into Jerusalem to the Resurrection*. Translated by Philip J. Whitmore. San Francisco: Ignatius Press, 2011.

———. *Jesus of Nazareth: The Infancy Narratives*. Translated by Philip J. Whitmore. New York: Image, 2012.

Berger, Klaus. *Im Anfang war Johannes*. Stuttgart: Quell, 1997.

———. *Jesus*. Munich: Pattloch, 2004.

———. and Christiane Nord. *Das Neue Testament und frühchristliche Schriften*. Frankfurt: Insel Verlag, 2005.

Betz, Otto, and Rainer Riesner. *Jesus, Qumran und der Vatikan*. Giessen: Herder, 1993.

Biddle, Martin. *Das Grab Christi*. Giessen: Brunnen-Verlag, 1998.

———. *The Tomb of Christ*. Stroud: Sutton, 1999.

———, Gideon Avni, Jon Seligmann, and Tamar Winter. *Die Grabeskirche in Jerusalem*. Stuttgart: Belser, 2000.

Blomberg, Craig L. *The Historical Reliability of the Gospels*. Downers Grove, Ill.: InterVarsity Press, 1987.

Borgehammar, Stephan. *How the Holy Cross Was Found*. Stockholm: Almquist & Wiksell, 1991.

Bösen, Willibald. *Der letzte Tag des Jesus von Nazaret*. Freiburg: Herder, 1994.

Brandmüller, Walter, ed. *Light and Shadows*. San Francisco: Ignatius Press, 2009.

———. *Qumran und die Evangelien*. Aachen: MM Verlag, 1994.

Bräumer, Hansjörg. *Ort im Leben Jesu*. Holzgerlingen: Hänssler, 2008.

Brown, Raymond. *The Virginal Conception and Bodily Resurrection of Jesus*. New York: Paulist Press, 1973.

Bruce, F. F. *Ausserbiblische Zeugnisse über Jesus und das frühe Christentum*. Giessen: Brunnen-Verlag, 1993.

———. *Basiswissen Neues Testament*. Wuppertal: Brockhaus, 1997.

Butzkamm, Aloys. *Mit der Bibel im Heiligen Land*. Paderborn: Bonifatius, 2008.

Campbell, John K., O.F.M. *The Stations of the Cross in Jerusalem*. Jerusalem: Carta, 1986.

Cano Tello, Celestino A. *La Legalidad del Proceso de Jesus*. Valencia: Comercial Editora de Publicaciones, 2002.

Chancey, Mark A. *Greco-Roman Culture and the Galilee of Jesus*. Cambridge and New York: Cambridge University Press, 2005.

Charlesworth, James H., ed. *Jesus and Archaeology*. Grand Rapids, Mich.: Eerdmans, 2006.

——, ed. *Jesus and the Dead Sea Scrolls*. New York: Doubleday, 1992.

Claussen, Carsten, and Jörg Frey, eds. *Jesus und die Archäologie Galiläas*. Neukirchen-Vluyn: Neukirchener Verlag, 2008.

Connolly, Peter. *Living in the Time of Jesus of Nazareth*. Oxford: Oxford University Press, 1983.

Corsini, Manuela. *Juan el Testigo*. Madrid: Sociedad de Educación Atenas, 1989.

Crossan, John Dominic. *The Historical Jesus*. San Francisco: HarperSanFrancisco, 1991.

——. *Who Killed Jesus?* San Francisco: HarperSanFrancisco, 1995.

——, and Jonathan Reed. *Excavating Jesus*. San Francisco: HarperSanFrancisco, 2001.

Demandt, Alexander. *Hände in Unschuld*. Cologne: Böhlau, 1999.

Drijvers, Jan W. *Helena Augusta*. Leiden and New York: Brill, 1992.

——, and Han Drijvers. *The Finding of the True Cross*. Louvain: Peeters, 1997.

Edersheim, Alfred. *Der Tempel*. Wuppertal: Brockhaus, 1997.

Egeria. *Egeria's Travels*. Translated by John Wilkinson. London: S.P.C.K., 1971.

Eisenman, Robert. *James, the Brother of Jesus*. New York: Viking Penguin, 1998.

Eusebius of Caesarea. *Church History*. Nicene and Post-Nicene Fathers, Second Series, edited by Philip Schaff and Henry Wace, Vol. 1. 1890; Peabody, Mass.: Hendrickson, 1995. Pp. 73–403.

Fassbeck, Gabriele, Sandra Fortner, Andrea Rottloff, and Jürgen Zangenberg, eds. *Leben am See Gennesaret*. Mainz: Verlag Philipp Von Zabaern, 2003.

Ferrari d'Occhieppo, Konradin. *Der Stern von Betlehem in astronomischer Sicht*. Giessen: Brunnen-Verlag, 2003.

Finegan, Jack. *The Archaeology of the New Testament*. Princeton: Princeton University Press, 1992.

Fleckenstein, Karl-Heinz. *Komm und sieh!* Neckenmarkt: Novum-Verlag, 2008.

——, Mikko Louhivuori, and Rainer Riesner. *Emmaus in Judäa*. Giessen: Brunnen-Verlag, 2003.

Flusser, David. *Jesus*. Jerusalem: Hebrew University Magnes Press, 1998.

Foster, Charles. *The Jesus Inquest*. Nashville: Thomas Nelson, 2006.

Freeman-Grenville, G.S.P. *The Basilica of the Annunciation at Nazareth*. Jerusalem: Carta, 1994.

———. *The Basilica of the Holy Sepulchre in Jerusalem*. Jerusalem: Carta, 1994.

———. *The Basilica of the Nativity in Bethlehem*. Jerusalem: Carta, 1993.

———. *The Land of Jesus Then and Now*. Jerusalem: Carta, 1998.

———, Rupert Chapman, and Joan Taylor. *The Onomasticon by Eusebius of Caesarea*. Jerusalem: Carta, 2003.

Freund, Richard A. *Digging through the Bible*. Lanham, Md.: Rowman & Littlefield, 2009.

Fricke, Weddig. *Der Fall Jesus*. Hamburg: Rasch und Röhring Verlag, 1995.

Funk, Robert W. *Honest to Jesus*. San Francisco: HarperSanFrancisco, 1996.

Fürst, Heinrich. *Im Land des Herrn*. Paderborn: Bonifatius, 2015.

Ganzfried, Solomon, *Code of the Jewish Law*. New York: Hebrew Publishing, 1963.

Geva, Hillel. *Ancient Jerusalem Revealed*. Jerusalem: Israel Exploration Society, 1994.

Gibson, Shimon. *The Cave of John the Baptist*. New York: Doubleday, 2004.

———. *The Final Days of Jesus*. New York: HarperOne, 2009.

———, and John E. Taylor. *Beneath the Church of the Holy Sepulchre*. London: Committee of the Palestine Exploration Fund, 1994.

Gilbert, Adrian. *Magi—The Quest for a Secret Tradition*. London: Bloomsbury, 1996.

Gillman, Florence Morgan. *Herodias*. Collegeville, Minn.: Liturgical Press, 2003.

Gnilka, Joachim. *Jesus of Nazareth*. Translated by Siegried S. Schatzmann. Peabody, Mass.: Hendrickson, 1997.

Goergen, Anneliese and Anton. *Tabgha am See Genesareth*. Munich: Schnell & Steiner, 1989.

Gonen, Rivka. *Biblical Holy Places*. New York: Paulist Press, 2000.

Gottschalk, Gisela. *Die grossen Cäsaren*. Herrsching: Pawlak, 1984.

Grant, Michael. *The Twelve Caesars*. New York: Charles Scribner's Sons, 1975.

Gumbert, Ludwig, O.F.M. *Die Basilika in Nazaret*. Munich: Kommisariat d. Heiligen Landes, [1985?].

Gundry, Robert H. *A Survey of the New Testament*. Grand Rapids, Mich.: Zondervan, 2003.

Habermas, Gary. *The Historical Jesus*. Joplin, Mo.: College Press, 1996.

Hanson, K.C., and Douglas Oakman. *Palestine in the Time of Jesus*. Minneapolis, Minn.: Fortress Press, 1998.

Heiligenthal, Roman. *Der Lebensweg Jesu von Nazareth*. Stuttgart: Kohlhammer, 1994.

———. *Der verfälschte Jesus*. Darmstadt: Primus Verlag, 1997.

Herbst, Karl. *Kriminalfall Golgotha*. Düsseldorf: Econ Verlag, 1992.

Hesemann, Michael. *Das Bluttuch Christi*. Munich: Herbig, 2010.

———. *Die Dunkelmänner*. Augsburg: Sankt Ulrich Verlag, 2007.

———. *Die Entdeckung des Heiligen Grals*. Munich: Pattloch, 2003.

———. *Der erste Papst*. Munich: Pattloch, 2003.

———. *Das Fatima-Geheimnis*. Rottenburg: Jochen Kopp, 2002.

———. *Die Jesus-Tafel*. Freiburg: Herder, 1999.

———. *Mary of Nazareth*. Translated by Michael J. Miller. San Francisco: Ignatius Press, 2016.

———. *Paulus von Tarsus*. Augsburg: Sankt Ulrich Verlag, 2008.

———. *Stigmata—Sie tragen die Wundmale Christi*. Güllesheim: Die Silberschnur, 2006.

———. *Die stummen Zeugen von Golgata*. Kreuzlingen: Hugendubel, 2000.

Heyer, Cees J. Den. *Der Mann aus Nazaret*. Düsseldorf: Patmos Verlag, 1998.

Hirschberg, Peter. *Jesus von Nazareth*. Darmstadt: Primus-Verlag, 2004.

Hurtado, Larry W. *The Earliest Christian Artifacts*. Grand Rapids, Mich.: Eerdmans, 2006.

Husemann, Dirk. *Die archäologische Hintertreppe*. Ostfildern: Thorbecke, 2007.

Jacobovici, Simcha, and Charles Pellegrino. *The Jesus Family Tomb*. San Francisco: HarperSanFrancisco, 2007.

Jeffrey, Grant R. *Jesus—The Great Debate*. Toronto: Frontier Research Publications, 1999.

Johnson, Luke Timothy. *The Real Jesus*. San Francisco: HarperSanFrancisco, 1996.

Josephus, Flavius. *The New Complete Works*. Translated by William Whiston. Introduction and commentary by Paul L. Maier. Grand Rapids, Mich.: Kregel, 1999.

Justin Martyr. *Dialogue with Trypho, a Jew*. In Ante-Nicene Fathers, edited by Alexander Roberts and James Donaldson. Vol. 1. 1885; Peabody, Mass.: Hendrickson, 1995. Pp. 194–270.

Kauffmann, Joel. *The Nazareth Jesus Knew*. Nazareth: Nazareth Village, 2005.

Kidger, Mark. *The Star of Bethlehem*. Princeton, N.J.: Princeton University Press, 1999.

Kimball, Glenn. *Hidden Stories of the Childhood of Jesus*. Lawrenceville, Ga.: BF, 1997.

———, and David Stirland. *Hidden Politics of the Crucifixion*. Salt Lake City, Utah: Ancient Manuscripts, 1998.

King, Anthony. *Jerusalem Revealed*. Cambridgeshire: Boxer, 1997.

Kollmann, Bernd. *Die Jesus-Mythen*. Freiburg: Herder, 2009.

Kresser, Gebhard. *Nazareth—Ein Zeuge für Loreto*. Graz: Verlagsbuchhandlung "Styria", 1908.

Kriwaczek, Paul. *In Search of Zarathustra*. New York: Knopf, 2003.

Kroll, Gerhard. *Auf den Spuren Jesu*. Leipzig: St.-Benno-Verlag, 1988.

Krüger, Jürgen. *Die Grabeskirche zu Jerusalem*. Regensburg: Schnell-Steiner, 2000.

Küchler, Max. *Jerusalem*. Göttingen: Vandenhoeck & Ruprecht, 2007.

Läpple, Alfred. *Der andere Jesus*. Augsburg: Pattloch, 1997.

Laudert-Ruhm, Gerd. *Jesus von Nazareth*. Stuttgart: Kreuz, 1996.

Läufer, Erich. *Tabgha—Wo die Brotvermehrung stattfand*. Cologne: Bachem, 2000.

Lewin, Ariel. *Palästina in der Antike*. Darmstadt: Wiss. Buchges., 2004.

Loffreda, Stanislao. *Capharnaum: The Town of Jesus*. Jerusalem: Franciscan Printing Press, 1985.

———. *Die Heiligtümer von Tabgha*. Jerusalem: Franciscan Printing Press, 1981.

Mack, Burton L. *The Lost Gospel*. San Francisco: HarperSanFrancisco, 1993.

Magen, Yitzhak. *The Stone Vessel Industry in the Second Temple Period*. Jerusalem: Israel Exploration Society et al., 2002.

Mancini, Ignazio. *Archaeological Discoveries Relative to the Judeo-Christians*. Jerusalem: Franciscan Printing Press, 1984.

Marxsen, Willi. *The Resurrection of Jesus of Nazareth*. Translated by Margaret Kohl. Philadelphia: Fortress Press, 1970.

Mazar, Eilat. *The Complete Guide to the Temple Mount Excavations*. Jerusalem: Shoham Academic Research and Publication, 2002.

McNamer, Elizabeth, and Bargil Pixner, O.S.B. *Jesus and the First-Century Christianity in Jerusalem*. New York: Paulist Press, 2008.

McRay, John. *Archaeology and the New Testament*. Grand Rapids, Mich.: Baker Book House, 1991.

Meinardus, Otto F. *Auf den Spuren der Heiligen Familie von Bethlehem nach Oberägypten*. Koblenz: Reuffel, 1978.

———. *Die Heilige Woche in Jerusalem*. Würzburg: Catholica Unio, 1988.

Messori, Vittorio. *Gelitten unter Pontius Pilatus?* Cologne: Adamas, 1997.

Millard, Alan. *Die Zeit der ersten Christen*. Giessen: Brunnen-Verlag, 1994.

Molnar, Michael R. *The Star of Bethlehem*. New Brunswick, N.J.: Rutgers University Press, 1999.

Murphy-O'Connor, Jerome. *The Holy Land*. Oxford: Oxford University Press, 2008.

Negev, Avraham, and Shimon Gibson. *Archaeological Encyclopedia of the Holy Land*. New York: Continuum, 2001.

Netzer, Ehud. *Herodium*. Jerusalem: Herodium Expedition, 1999.

——. *The Palaces of the Hasmoneans and Herod the Great.* Jerusalem: Yad Ben-Zvi Press, Israel Exploration Society, 2001.

Nun, Mendel. *The Sea of Galilee and Its Fisherman in the New Testament.* Ein Gev: Kinnereth Sailing Co., 1989.

——. *Der See Genezareth und die Evangelien.* Giessen: Brunnen-Verlag, 2001.

Orthodox Palestine Society, ed. *The Threshold of the Judgement Gate.* Jerusalem: Orthodox Palestine Society, 1972.

Petrozzi, Maria Teresa. *Samaria.* Jerusalem: Franciscan Printing Press, 1981.

Pfannmüller, Gustav. *Jesus im Urteil der Jahrhunderte.* Leipzig: Teubner, 1908.

Pfirrmann, Gustav. *Die Nazareth-Tafel.* Munich: Herbig, 1994.

Piccirillo, Michele. *With Jesus in the Holy Land.* Jerusalem: Franciscan Printing Press, 1994.

Pixner, Bargil. *Mit Jesus durch Galiläa nach dem fünften Evangelium.* Rosh Pina: Corazin, 1992.

——. *Mit Jesus nach Jerusalem.* Rosh Pina: Corazin, 1996.

——. *Paths of the Messiah and Sites of the Early Church from Galilee to Jerusalem.* Edited by Rainer Riesner. Translated by Keith Myrick and Sam and Miriam Randall. San Francisco: Ignatius Press, 2010.

Porter, J. R. *Jesus Christ: The Jesus of History, the Christ of Faith.* New York: Oxford University Press, 1999.

Prause, Gerhard. *Herodes der Grosse.* Hamburg: Hoffmann und Campe, 1977.

——. *Die kleine Welt des Jesus Christus.* Hamburg: Hoffmann und Campe, 1981.

Pritz, Ray A. *Nazarene Jewish Christianity.* Jerusalem: Magnes Press, 1992.

Raanan, Mordecai, ed. *Die Heiligen Stätten: Auf den Spuren des Jesu.* Tel Aviv: Otpaz, 1970.

Rahmani, L. Y. *A Catalogue of Jewish Ossuaries.* Jerusalem: Israel Antiquities Authority, 1994.

Rainey, Anson, and Steven Notley. *Carta's New Century Handbook and Atlas of the Bible.* Jerusalem: Carta, 2007.

Ratzinger, Joseph, ed. *Schriftauslegung im Widerstreit.* Freiburg: Herder, 1989.

Reed, Jonathan. *Archaeology and the Galilean Jesus.* Harrisburg, Pa.: Trinity Press International, 2000.

Reich, Ronny, Gideon Avni, and Tamar Winter. *The Jerusalem Archaeological Park.* Jerusalem: Israel Antiquities Authority, 1999.

Richman, Chaim. *A House of Prayer for All Nations.* Jerusalem: Temple Institute, Carta, 1997.

Riesner, Rainer. *Essener und Urgemeinde in Jerusalem.* Giessen: Brunnen-Verlag, 1998.

Rigato, Maria-Luisa. *Il Titolo della Croce di Gesù.* 2nd ed. Rome: Pontifical Gregorian University, 2005.

Ritmeyer, Leen and Kathleen. *Jerusalem in the Year 30 A.D.* Jerusalem: Carta, 2004.

Roberts, Mark D. *Can We Trust the Gospels?* Wheaton, Ill.: Crossway, 2007.

Sacchi, Maurilio. *Terra Santa sulle orme di Gesù.* Gorle: Velar, 1999.

Saller, Sylvester, O.F.M. *Discoveries at Saint John's Ein Karim.* Jerusalem: Franciscan Printing Press, 1982.

Salm, René. *The Myth of Nazareth.* Cranford, N.J.: American Atheist Press, 2008.

Sandoli, Sabino de, O.F.M. *Emmaus—El Qubeibeh.* Jerusalem: Franciscan Printing Press, 1980.

———. *The Sanctuary of Emmaus.* Jerusalem: Franciscan Printing Press 1990.

Santarelli, Giuseppe. *Loreto.* Bologna: Italcards, [ca. 1980].

Scarre, Chris. *Die römischen Kaiser.* Düsseldorf: Econ Verlag, 1996.

Schinzel-Penth, Gisela. *Was geschah damals wirklich?* Sankt Ottilien: Eos, 2003.

Schonfield, Hugh. *The Passover Plot.* Shaftesbury: Element, 1993.

Schröder, Heinz. *Jesus and Free Enterprise.* Fribourg, Switzerland: Carolikne Press, 1982.

Schulz, Hans-Joachim. *Die apostolische Herkunft der Evangelien.* Freiburg: Herder, 1997.

Schweitzer, Albert. *Geschichte der Leben-Jesu-Forschung.* Tübingen: Mohr, 1906.

Seymour, P. A. H. *The Birth of Christ.* London: Virgin, 1998.

Shanks, Hershel. *Jerusalem.* New York: Random House, 1995.

Sheler, Jeffery. *Is the Bible True?* San Francisco: HarperSanFrancisco; Zondervan, 1999.

Shkolnik, Ya'acov. *Banias and Tel Dan.* Jerusalem: ERETZ Ha-Tzvi, 2000.

Silas, Musholt P., ed. *Nazareth.* Jerusalem: Franciscan Printing Press, 1995.

Silberman, Neil Asher. *Die Messias-Macher.* Bergisch Gladbach: Bastei-Verlag, 1998.

Siliato, Maria Grazia. *Und das Grabtuch ist doch echt.* Munich: Heyne, 2000.

Stanton, Graham. *Gospel Truth.* London: HarperCollins, 1995.

Stegemann, Hartmut. *Die Essener, Qumran, Johannes der Täufer und Jesus.* Freiburg: Herder, 1993.

Stemberger, Günter. *Jewish Contemporaries of Jesus.* Minneapolis, Minn.: Fortress Press, 1995.

Stern, Ephraim, ed. *The New Encyclopedia of Archaeological Excavations in the Holy Land.* vols. 1–5. Jerusalem [IES]/New York: Simon & Schuster, 1993–2009.

Storme, Albert. *Bethany.* Jerusalem: Franciscan Printing Press, 1992.

Strabo. *The Geographica of Strabo.* Translated by Duane W. Roller. Cambridge and New York: Cambridge University Press, 2014.

Strickert, Fred. *Bethsaida, Home of the Apostles*. Collegeville, Minn.: Liturgical Press, 1998.

Tabor, James D. *The Jesus Dynasty*. New York: Simon & Schuster, 2006.

Theissen, Gerd, and Annette Merz. *The Historical Jesus*. Translated by John Bowden. Minneapolis, Minn.: Fortress Press, 1998.

Then, Reinhold. *Unterwegs im Heiligen Land*. Stuttgart: Katholisches Bibelwerk, 2002.

Thiede, Carsten Peter. *The Cosmopolitan World of Jesus*. London: S.P.C.K., 2004.

———. *The Dead Sea Scrolls and the Jewish Origins of Christianity*. London: Palgrave, 2001.

———. *The Emmaus Mystery*. London and New York: Continuum, 2005.

———. *Ein Fisch für den römischen Kaiser*. Munich: Luchterhand, 1998.

———. *Jesus—Der Glaube, die Fakten*. Augsburg: Sankt Ulrich, 2003.

———. *Der unbequeme Messias*. Basel: Brunnen-Verlag, 2006.

———, and Matthew d'Ancona. *The Jesus Papyrus*. London: Weidenfeld & Nicolson, 1996.

———, ———. *The Quest for the True Cross*. London: Weidenfeld & Nicolson, 2000.

Thomas, Gordon. *Trial: The Life and Inevitable Crucifixion of Jesus*. 1988; London: Bantam Press, 1997.

Tsafrir, Yoram, ed. *Ancient Churches Revealed*. Jerusalem: Israel Exploration Society, 1993.

Tully, Mark. *God, Jew, Rebel, the Hidden Jesus*. London: Penguin, 1996.

Vamosh, Miriam Feinberg. *Women at the Time of the Bible*. Herzlia, Israel: Palphot, 2007.

Vermes, Geza. *Die Geburt Jesu*. Darmstadt: Primus Verlag, 2007.

———. *Die Passion*. Darmstadt: Wiss. Buchges., 2006.

Victor, Ulrich, Carsten Peter Thiede, and Urs Stingelin. *Antike Kultur und Neues Testament*. Basel: Brunnen-Verlag, 2003.

Wachsmann, Shelley. *The Sea of Galilee Boat*. College Station, Tex.: Texas A & M University Press, 2009.

Walker, Peter. *In the Steps of Jesus*. Oxford: Lion, 2009.

———. *The Weekend That Changed the World: The Mystery of Jerusalem's Empty Tomb*. London: Marshall Pickering, 1999.

Waugh, Rob. "Bible Proved True as Pontius Pilate's Ring 'Is Found in Israel.'" *Metro*. December 3, 2018. https://metro.co.uk/2018/12/03 /bible-proved-true-as-pontius-pilates-ring-is-found-in-israel-8202472/.

Weidinger, Erich. *Apokryphe Bibel*. Augsburg: Pattloch, 1991.

Wilkinson, John. *Jerusalem Pilgrims before the Crusades*. Guildford: Biddles, 1977.

Wilson, A. N. *Jesus*. London: Flamingo, 1993.

Wilson, Ian. *Jesus, The Evidence*. London: Phoenix Illustrated, 1998.

Winkler, Lea Lofenfeld, and Ramit Frenkel. *The Boat and the Sea of Galilee*. Jerusalem: Gefen, 2007.

Winter, Paul. *On the Trial of Jesus*. New York: De Gruyter, 1974.

Wise, Abegg, Cook, eds. *Die Schriftrollen von Qumran*. Augsburg: Pattloch, 1997.

Worm, Alfred. *Jesus Christus*. Düsseldorf: ECON Verlag, 1993.

Worschech, Udo. *Das Land jenseits des Jordan*. Giessen: Brunnen-Verlag, 2004.

Wrembek, Christoph, S.J. *Die sogenannte Magdalenerin*. Leipzig: Benno, 2007.

Wright, John. *Christ in Myth and Legend*. Cincinnati, Ohio: Cranston & Curtis; New York: Hunt & Eaton, 1894.

Wright, N. T. *Who Was Jesus?* Grand Rapids, Mich.: Eerdmans, 1992.

Yadin, Yigael, ed. *Bar Kockba*. London: Weidenfeld and Nicolson, 1971.

——. *Jerusalem Revealed*. New Haven: Yale University Press, 1976.

Zangenberg, Jürgen K., and Jens Schröter, eds. *Bauern, Fischer und Propheten. Galiläa zur Zeit Jesu*. Darmstadt/Mainz: Philipp Von Zabern, 2012.

Zarley, Kermit. *Das Leben Jesu*. Neuhausen-Stuttgart: Hänssler, 1992.

Zugibe, Frederick T. *The Crucifixion of Jesus*. New York: M. Evans, 2005.